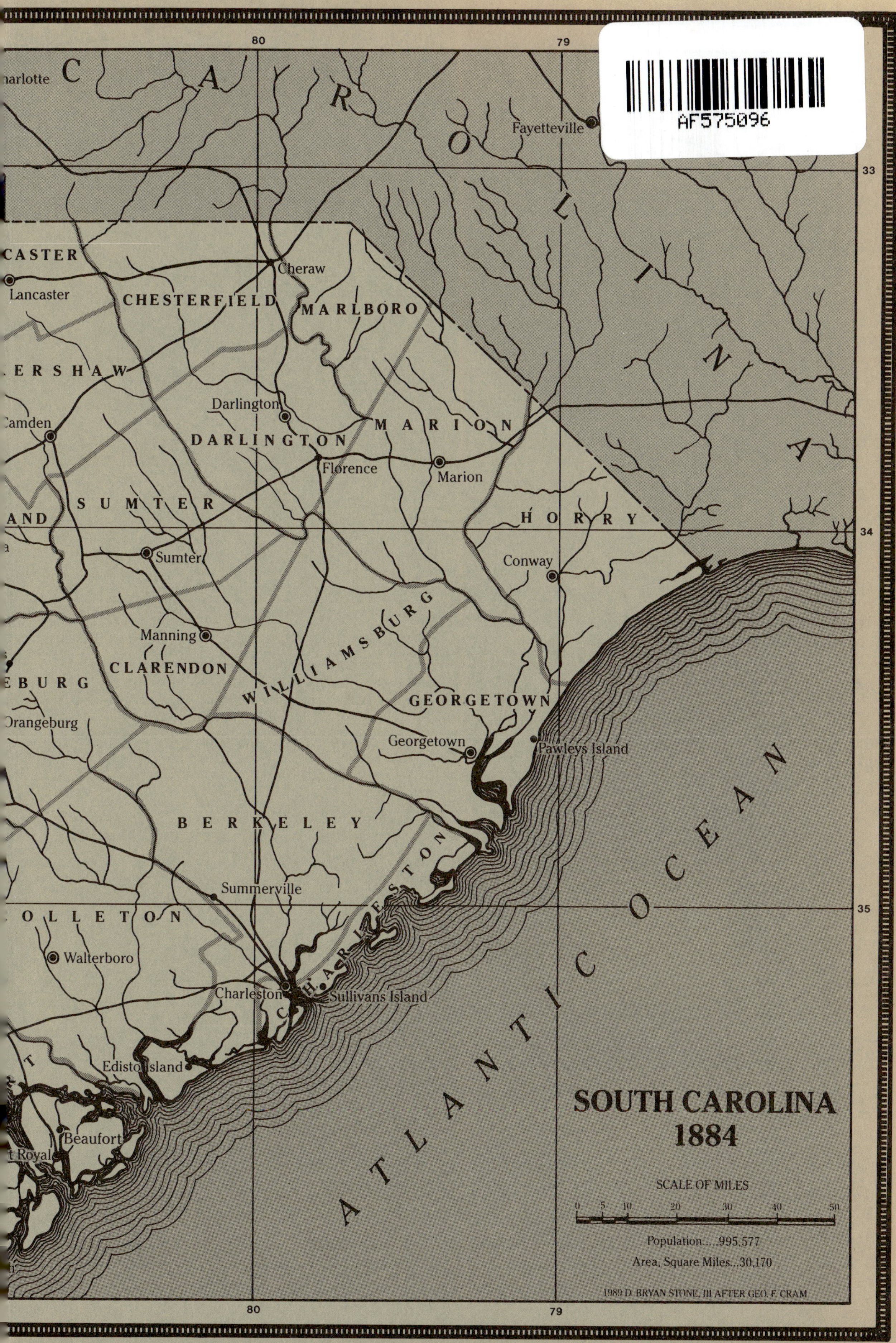
SOUTH CAROLINA
1884
SCALE OF MILES
0 5 10 20 30 40 50
Population.....995,577
Area, Square Miles...30,170
1989 D. BRYAN STONE, III AFTER GEO. F. CRAM
ATLANTIC OCEAN
CAROLINA
Fayetteville
Cheraw
Lancaster
CHESTERFIELD
MARLBORO
Darlington
DARLINGTON
Camden
MARION
Florence
Marion
SUMTER
HORRY
Sumter
Conway
Manning
CLARENDON
WILLIAMSBURG
GEORGETOWN
Georgetown
Pawleys Island
BERKELEY
Summerville
Walterboro
CHARLESTON
Charleston
Sullivans Island
Edisto Island
Beaufort
80
79
33
34
35

South Carolina in the 1880s: A Gazetteer

South Carolina in the 1880s: A Gazetteer

Compiled and
Edited by
John Hammond Moore

Sandlapper Publishing, Inc.
Orangeburg, South Carolina

First Edition
First printing, 1989

Manufactured in the United States of America.

Map on endpapers by D. Bryan Stone III

Book design by Messagemakers
Virginia Ingram and Jane Kelly

A note on illustrations. Period pictures and photographs of structures of the 1880s have been utilized as much as possible throughout this book. All South Caroliniana Library reproductions are the work of Charles Gay. All other credits are noted in captions under photographs.

Library of Congress Cataloging-in-Publication Data

South Carolina in the 1880s.

Includes index.
1. South Carolina—Description and travel. 2. Cities and towns—South Carolina.
I. Moore, John Hammond.
F274.S7 1989 975.7'041 89-6377
ISBN 0-87844-069-0

Contents

Preface

All of the material in this volume, except census data, has been gleaned from the files of the Charleston *News and Courier* between 1880 and 1892. These contemporary sketches of South Carolina communities, compiled by various staff members as they traveled about the state, seem at first to have been secondary to other assignments, but by the close of the decade they had assumed greater significance. At the same time, these descriptive articles became longer, more verbose, crammed with ever greater detail. As a result, those dealing with larger communities such as Charleston and Columbia have been condensed considerably, and extraneous and repetitious material has been deleted from other accounts as well. This has, perforce, resulted in some minor paraphrasing, although every effort has been made to retain the style and flavor of the original material throughout.

Through the eyes of these reporters we see a South Carolina brimming with hope and bustling with activity as it emerges from the wreckage of war and reconstruction. That this is an urban view of conditions in a largely rural society cannot be denied. Also, with the aid of hindsight we know the picture they paint for us is only half true, heavily imbued as it is with the rosy "New South" doctrine of that era. Nevertheless, these sketches provide substantial insight into how people of this state were living a century ago and bring to life a decade often dismissed as colorless and of little consequence.

Introduction

The 1880s were a momentous decade in South Carolina, either because change was occurring or was about to. Seen at close range, these were lively, event-filled, dynamic years, a far cry from the bland, gray decade so often portrayed in history books. The state's population rose at an impressive rate of 15%, up from 995,577 in 1880 to 1,151,149 in 1890. Despite the growth of towns and cities, at the close of that ten-year period the Census Bureau considered only the 78,519 citizens living in Charleston, Columbia, and Greenville (6% of the state's residents) to be true urbanites.

Yet at a time when South Carolina was statistically 94% rural, strange things were happening in the countryside. Cotton mills were altering the Up Country landscape to a marked degree, and new railroad lines were transforming scores of little villages into market towns possessed of regional significance. In addition to the shock waves produced by the whistles of mills and trains, at least two other important forces were at work: increasing uneasiness in the realm of race relations and widespread agricultural discontent.

The black-white question, complex indeed, was complicated still further by the coming to adulthood of the first generation of non-slave blacks, widespread disinterest in their fate on the part of Northerners disgusted with the turmoil of Reconstruction, and realization throughout the South that Yankee-inspired state constitutions created during that era were a heavy burden in a depressed agricultural setting. It was difficult, regardless of one's sentiments, to support new schools and other innovations as tax revenues dwindled. Nevertheless, despite these strains, in the 1880s South Carolina blacks occasionally were serving on school boards and town councils, some were operating stores and business establishments, and virtually every community in the state, large and small, depended upon the assistance of black firemen when disaster struck. Blacks continued to vote and serve on juries and obviously were playing some role in day-to-day affairs. In short, official-style Jim Crow was not yet a reality ... not yet.

The agricultural malaise, really a national and even a worldwide phenomenon, meant low prices for whatever the farmer grew and high interest rates on money he borrowed to finance next year's crop. Between 1875 and 1885 the price of cotton declined by six cents a pound, and the South Carolina farmer began to see the Charleston factor, the state government that continued to demand taxes, the merchant-banker at the county seat, and even the new railroad lines as his enemies. The man who marshaled these sentiments into a most uncharacteristic revolt was, of course, Ben Tillman. Yet in a very real sense, Tillman's homegrown Populism was a "last hurrah," a mere tilting with the windmills of industrialization. That upheaval certainly brought with it elements of overdue democratic reform that farmers and common folk found very appealing—notably new practical learning at Clemson and Winthrop. And Tillman could vow (as he did in January of 1886 as he began his assault on the so-called aristocratic Bourbon ring), "This is a farmer's state and farmers should govern it," but trends inaugurated in the 1880s indicated that the future lay with factories and towns, not in the countryside.

In 1880, some two thousand individuals were working in fourteen cotton mills; ten years later, 8,192 South Carolinians of all ages were employed in thirty-four mills. Capitalization had increased nearly five-fold ($2.7 to $11.1 million), the number of spindles had grown from 82,334 to 332,784, and the value of production had swelled from $2.9 to $9.8 million. In 1890, the average weekly wage for males over sixteen was $11.10; for females over fifteen, $7.33. Yet, as W.E. Woodward tells us in his delightful recollections of a Graniteville boyhood (*The Way Our People Lived*), these sums were a heaven-sent bonanza to farm families who long had battled against great odds and lost.

The only other manufactured goods of much importance were fertilizers, lumber products, flour, tar and turpentine, and cottonseed oil. In all, 2,382 manufacturing establishments of various sizes employed 24,662 workers who turned out goods valued at $31.9 million. The bulk of these factories, foundries, and machine shops were in or near major centers such as Charleston, Columbia, Greenville, and Spartanburg, although smaller communities (Aiken, Anderson, Beaufort, Georgetown, and Rock Hill) also were doing their bit to increase the state's industrial output.

In 1880, slightly more than 60% of all South Carolinians were black, the highest proportion ever recorded by any state since the business of taking censuses began in 1790. Ten years later their numbers had declined to 59.8% (compared to 57.6% in Mississippi, the only other state with a majority of black citizens). This represented, of course, the beginning of a trend that has continued to the present day.

In addition to being predominantly black, in 1890 South Carolina's population was overwhelmingly native-born—99.46%, second only to North Carolina's 99.77%. Those who hailed from other lands congregated largely in Charleston (3,192), most being from Ireland and Germany. Only three other regions (Beaufort, Greenville, and Richland counties) had more than 200 foreign-born residents, most of them again being Irish or German. There were, for example, only seventy-four Italians living in the Charleston area; most counties throughout the state reported none.

Political leaders occasionally talked about the need for immigration and welcomed any band of foreigners that somehow strayed into the state, but they were fearful of importing "troublesome elements" and did little to encourage them. In August of 1881 the State Immigration Bureau issued a twenty-two-page German-English phrase book to help newcomers and their employers understand each other. The little booklet cost a mere ten cents, but the Bureau printed only 100 copies.

In 1880, 134,842 young South Carolinians were enrolled in public schools; ten years later, 203,461, a gain of 50%. Local officials reported that there were

3,264 schoolhouses scattered throughout South Carolina in 1890, but they failed to say how many were serving each race. Total classroom enrollment that year (public and private schools, academies, colleges, etc.) was 225,688—103,132 white, 122,556 black.

Almost every town and city grew somewhat during the 1880s, several spurting ahead in a truly spectacular fashion, sometimes because of real growth and other times as a result of annexation. Although none of the following communities had over 4,000 residents by the end of the decade, towns such as Anderson, Camden, Darlington, Florence, Gaffney, Greenwood, Laurens, Marion, Rock Hill, Sumter, and Walterboro either doubled or tripled in size. The most unusual growth among these small, would-be centers of commerce and trade was recorded by Blacksburg (145 to 1,245), Darlington (940 to 2,389), Gaffney (400 to 1,631), Laurens (752 to 2,245), and Rock Hill (809 to 2,744). Greenville grew from 6,160 to 8,607; Spartanburg, from 3,253 to 5,544; and Charleston, the state's only real metropolis, from 49,984 to 54,955. For an overview of South Carolina's counties, cities, towns, and villages of that era, see the population table in Appendix 1.

Columbia in the 1880s

Yet it was at the state capital—and perhaps appropriately so—that urban growth and change was most apparent. During those years Columbia's population rose from 10,036 to 15,353, and several fundamental innovations altered the way its citizens lived and worked. The telephone arrived in 1881 (Charleston then already had 124 "subscribers"), and within thirty months there were ninety-four of these contraptions in Columbia. On February 1, 1883, a union depot opened on Gervais Street. Constructed by the South Carolina Railroad at a cost of $18,000, the structure also served passengers of the Columbia and Greenville and the Wilmington, Columbia, and Augusta lines. Its ornate salons had eighteen-foot ceilings with frescoes by a Charleston artist. The walls of the ladies' area were painted lilac; those of the gentlemen's, buff. There also were sparkling chandeliers, electric gongs, double-reflecting gas lights, telephone and telegraph connections, spacious washrooms, and a refreshment stand.

Three months later crowds packed the Opera House to watch the annual plume drill. This strange ritual was an elimination contest in precision marching conducted on stage by local militia companies. That year, after six rounds only two men remained. Then, amid loud applause, a private received a red plume; a non-commissioned officer, a white one.

Almost as bizarre, at least by prevailing practices of later decades, was the arrest during these years of those who failed to pay their poll taxes. On February 14, 1884, two Columbia citizens—one white, one black—were told by a judge to pay $10 and costs or spend thirty days in jail for non-payment. The men agreed to pay both the fines and their taxes. This was, the *News and Courier* stressed, a warning to other delinquents.

In November of 1883, Columbia, like the rest of the nation, adjusted its clocks and watches to "standard" time, and on June 1, 1886, the tracks of all major railroads also were standardized, that is, adjusted to a uniform gauge. Before the time change, Columbia actually had *three* different "times"—its own, Charleston time used by the South Carolina Railroad (four minutes faster), and Washington time used by all other railroads (sixteen minutes faster). The adjustment, made at noon on November 19, 1883, set local clocks ahead twenty-four minutes so as to conform to the system adopted by all railroads.

A bentwood chair factory and a Chinese laundry appeared in Columbia in 1885, although the laundry outlasted the ill-fated manufacturing company.[1] In March of that year local merchants tried unsuccessfully to deny a license to the New York Racket Store, an emporium which the *News and Courier* described as consisting of "big 'bargain counters' where old, broken, and miscellaneous stocks are quickly converted into cash at low prices." Within a very short time several Columbia businessmen concluded this "outlet" approach indeed had merit and opened racket stores of their own.

In May of 1885 a diocesan conclave at Trinity Church was split asunder when two black Episcopal priests took communion. For several days church leaders, who defended their colored brethren, wrangled with lay delegates, who did not. The result was a stand-off and the gathering accomplished little. This was, of course, merely a precursor of still greater rigidity in racial attitudes and evidence of an ever-widening white-black gulf, as generations who once had known the mutual association of master and slave passed from the scene, ending a relationship that sometimes had been characterized by mutual respect and even friendship.

In the summer of 1887, Columbia streets were marked with signposts and houses numbered in preparation for free mail delivery, which began on September 1. Four mail carriers, each paid $50 a month, inaugurated this splendid service. A few years later when a Republican postmaster hired a black mail carrier and discharged a white man, howls of protest were both immediate and loud.

During the late 1880s the city fathers developed a street railway system, first drawn by mules and then by horses, and they talked of installing electric lights, at least on major thoroughfares. By the close of the decade several downtown streets were lit by arc lights, although electricity for private consumption was not widespread. And by that date local residents had begun to plan for their first real hospital and were boasting that Columbia had more nickel-operated phonographs in its stores than could be found in all of Charleston. On or about October 1, 1889, Thomas E. Branigan opened a "Ladies Restaurant" over his Main Street eating emporium for gentlemen. Branigan assured would-be patrons that these innovative second-floor quarters were completely separate and could be entered only by a private staircase.

[1]Seven years later the *News and Courier* reported that Sam Lee was returning to China with an $8,000 draft and a liberal supply of cash (September 6, 1892).

Although Columbia still had no public library, citizens of the state capital pointed to various colleges and academies as the basis of their claim as an educational center. Also, envious of Aiken, Camden, and other resort communities, they often portrayed their city as an ideal winter resort—not too cold, served by fine hotels and theaters, a pleasant place to spend a few months each year. The truth is, however, that despite growth and change, Columbia in 1890 still was simply a big country town that had adopted some city ways such as telephones and phonographs, but lacked the invigorating hustle and turmoil of a real metropolis.

Perhaps the most persistent problem of the 1880s was mud. In the summer, city councilmen faced criticism for muddy drinking water; in the winter, for muddy streets. Crack trains could whisk one from Charleston to Columbia in three hours and forty minutes, and one could travel about the capital city in relative ease by streetcar or buggy. But crossing a downtown street on foot often was well nigh impossible. In December of 1886, Narcisco Gener Gonzales, *News and Courier* bureau chief, declared Main Street to be "a disgrace . . . a miry bog." This blast elicited action in the form of granite-block steppingstones at intersections, but only the coming of the auto and the protests of their owners would bring true relief.

In addition to mud, several other topics tended to dominate conversation wherever Columbians gathered. These included projects that seemed to have no end—renovation of the state capitol and completion of the Columbia Canal—and subjects such as cockfighting, baseball, volunteer fire companies, the annual state fair, and politics, all of which might be loosely categorized as "social life."

Few openly approved of cockfights held near South Carolina College, but the mayor and council took the understandable view that, until the state government banned this activity, it was preferable to license the sport each year for $300 and thus retain marginal control over what transpired. In 1887 the legislature finally outlawed cockfighting within three miles of any chartered institution, whereupon Columbia's lone legal cockpit passed into oblivion in a blaze of blood, feathers, and dollars: a three-day marathon pitting North Carolina birds against those from South Carolina. Each side entered twenty-one cocks, with winners getting $50 and the top bird $500.

Meanwhile, baseball struggled to achieve respectability. Each season teams appeared in Columbia and fans came out to watch them, but no group seemed able to develop a coterie of loyal, devoted followers. There were town teams, factory teams, college teams, midget teams, white teams, black teams, lean teams, fat teams, even teams representing various boarding houses. In November of 1884, a female nine appeared, the Blondes and the Brunettes. These young lovelies from New York, Philadelphia, and Baltimore challenged a local group called the Mechanics. The home team prevailed (12-10), but in the evening the victors "devoted themselves to their visitors, who lodged at the Hendrix House."

Three years later the Columbia Baseball Club took the unusual step of ordering official uniforms from Philadelphia. These were gray flannel outfits with cardinal red trim, complete with red socks, gray caps, and "COLUMBIA" in red block letters on a bosom shield. The team's shoes came from Philadelphia, too, but to no avail. The next spring, as always, organizational work had to begin anew. As for football, it was virtually unknown, although a handful of South Carolina College students did play a game in March of 1890.[2]

The true local athlete of the 1880s, the hero of all youngsters and many of their older sisters, was the volunteer fireman. No thrill could quite equal that of watching these daredevils go through their drills or actually do battle with roaring flames ... of which Columbia seems to have had its fair share in those days.

On a Saturday in May of 1887 some six hundred Sunday School excursionists poured into town from various points along the Greenville-Columbia rail line. Eager to entertain this throng, the fire chief decided to hold a mock drill and at 1 P.M. sounded "the alarm." Soon Columbia's four fire companies (two white, two black) connected their hoses to Main Street hydrants and within eight seconds all of them were shooting streams of water high into the air, much to the delight and surprise of the visitors.

A few weeks earlier, black firemen on their own had staged an equally spectacular performance.

> The Vigilant Fire Company had its quarterly parade this afternoon. The company owns the uniforms worn by the members, and the object of the parade is to reveal their condition. By invitation, the other colored fire company, the Enterprise, turned out with the Vigilants. The two companies marched up and down Main Street, making a very creditable appearance. The Vigilants, in their blue coats faced with red, and the Enterprise men in red coats faced with black. The former had 60 odd members out, the latter about fifty. The engines and reels were profusely decorated with flowers. The Wallace Band furnished music for the marchers. At the City Hall the Enterprise was put to work, and sent up a stream higher than the weather vane on the watch tower. Large numbers of colored people were on the street watching the paraders. After the inspection the Vigilants gave a collation at their engine-house.[3]

Other local events attracting the attention of hundreds of citizens each year were commencement exercises at various colleges and academies (including the new Winthrop Training School for Teachers), parades and drills by military units, occasional footraces, political conventions, and statewide meetings of religious and temperance groups, fraternal orders, and black benevolent societies. Blacks usually celebrated Emancipation Day and the Fourth of July with parades and speeches, while whites held special observances on George Washington's birthday and Confederate Memorial Day.

But the high point of each year for most Columbians and for many visitors to

---

[2] On November 14, 1891, Trinity (Duke) beat Furman 96-0 at the state fairgrounds, and on Christmas Eve of 1892, Furman rolled over USC 44-0 in a game played at Charleston's Baseball Park, the first such contest ever seen in that city.

[3] *News and Courier,* April 21, 1887.

their growing city was the state fair, held during the second week in November. The eighteenth such event in this series, which opened on Tuesday, November 9, 1886, might be considered typical. In addition to standard exhibits—livestock, farm machinery, jams and jellies, and homegrown works of art—there was a shooting match, horse racing, a panorama of the Gettysburg battlefield (also shown very successfully in 1885), and many views of the great earthquake that had devastated Charleston on August 31st of that year. Special trains brought hundreds to Columbia, among them several pickpocket artists, and each day some eight thousand people thronged the fairgrounds. Four decorated arches lit with forty gas jets were erected over Main Street, and there were fireworks each night on the State House grounds. But the fair did not have much of a midway, most games of chance having been banned following some unpleasant incidents in 1885. Young ladies from Columbia Female College, who attended in a body escorted by their president, undoubtedly tarried at the WCTU booth, admired scores of cakes and pies, and examined needlework and china painting done by their contemporaries.

This extravaganza ended with a lavish Saturday night ball given by the South Carolina Club and presided over by the governor and his wife. Although the ball was usually held in the House of Representatives (then undergoing repairs), in 1886 the aristocracy of the state gathered in Agricultural Hall, once the notorious Parker's Hall (or "Haul") of Reconstruction days. Music was by the Italian Band of Charlotte, and the following day the *News and Courier* published two columns of minute trivia detailing the "magnificent toilets of the ladies." Here is a sample entry: "Miss Shannon, of Camden, S.C., an elaborate toilette of cream satin en train, draperies of exquisite real thread lace; ornaments, natural flowers and diamonds." Their escorts were listed by name under a simple heading, "The Chivalry."

But while diamonds sparkled and wine flowed, Ben Tillman planned. For, during Fair Week, the farmers of the state held an all-day meeting to plot strategy for the annual legislative session that opened in late November and continued until Christmas. The following year the fair faced temporary rivals in the form of a "Gala Week" in Charleston and a midsummer agricultural "Inter-State Encampment" at Spartanburg. The Charleston fete, a mix of fireworks, horse racing, parades, and balls, was staged early in November, just before the fair. Its original purpose was to demonstrate that city's recovery from the earthquake. The August "encampment," sponsored by the Grange and undoubtedly designed to blunt radical farmer demands, drew ten thousand people from five states: the Carolinas, Georgia, Alabama, and Tennessee. There were speeches, baseball games, glass-ball shooting contests, commercial exhibits, and flag drills by ladies, but not the full-fledged hoopla of a state fair.

A more serious threat to the fair was a rift along racial lines which became apparent in the late 1880s as blacks began to organize their own statewide show. Although the initial effort, also staged at the Columbia fairgrounds, was plagued by discord and bad weather, it is further evidence of changing attitudes in black-white relations.

The Columbia Bureau of the Charleston *News and Courier*

Much of what we know about Columbia and South Carolina during the 1880s comes from the pages of the Charleston *News and Courier.* It was the state's leading newspaper, even outselling Columbia's local dailies. Throughout that decade the proud "Old Lady of Broad Street" constantly increased coverage of events at the state capital, as well as those in scores of little towns and villages throughout the state. In 1880 it was a four-page paper that had just expanded to a Sunday edition (the *Sunday News*); with the aid of new presses it doubled in size in September of 1884 and by 1890 was producing a Sunday special filled with numerous illustrations and columns for women and children. During the 1880s second and third editions and special supplements also became more and more common, as well as weekly and semi-weekly summaries of the news for rural readers.

The key to this success in the Up Country was, of course, the *News and Courier's* Columbia bureau, which handled news, advertising, subscriptions, and other business details. It was, in large measure, a training ground for the *State,* which appeared on February 18, 1891. The man who headed up the bureau in the early eighties was James Calvin Hemphill (1850–1927), son of an Erskine College professor. Hemphill became city editor of the *News and Courier* in 1885 and when Francis W. Dawson was murdered four years later was named editor, a position he had filled from time to time while Dawson was abroad. Hemphill directed the fortunes of the *News and Courier* until 1910, when, unable to acquire stock in the paper, he moved to Richmond and Charlotte, ending his journalistic career in Spartanburg.

In 1882, Narcisco Gonzales (1858–1903), a youthful rival of Hemphill, returned to South Carolina from Washington, D.C., where he had been representing the *News and Courier* for some eighteen months. Gonzales, son of Cuban revolutionary Ambrosio José Gonzales and Harriet Rutledge Elliott, thought he had been promised an editorial slot; but, instead, after covering the 1882 gubernatorial campaign, he became "resident correspondent" in Columbia, beaten out of a Charleston position by Hemphill.

For the next seven years Gonzales ruled the state capital bureau, officially becoming manager in 1885. Yet routine matters often were left to others as he followed political canvasses about the state and covered major events such as presidential inaugurals in Washington and Confederate reunions in Virginia. His assistants included his uncle, Captain Ralph Elliott, in charge of circulation, and William Elliott Gonzales (1866–1937), a younger brother, who joined the bureau as a $5-a-week reporter in 1885. Also, during these years, yet another brother, Ambrose Elliott Gonzales (1857–1926), became a traveling correspondent for the *News and Courier* and, like other family members, helped make the Charleston newspaper indispensable to thousands of South Carolinians.

There was, of course, some risk in the course being pursued by editors Dawson and Hemphill during the late 1880s, for the powerful Columbia bureau might some day strike out on its own, and early in 1891 that was precisely what happened. The precipitating factor was Ben Tillman. Narcisco Gonzales, for one, was scornful of the relatively gentle manner in which Editor Hemphill handled this political upstart. He yearned to lash out, attack, reveal the evil he saw emanating from Edgefield County. In 1890, Gonzales not only reported the gubernatorial campaign of that year, but also helped manage it, working hard for Tillman's opponent, Judge A.C. Haskell.[4]

Ambrose Gonzales, writing in 1922, said that with the Tillman victory all three brothers decided to leave the state, but Haskell and his friends talked them out of it. The most persuasive argument was $20,000 they raised, which in February 1891 launched the first issue of the *State*—eight pages, 3,000 copies. Haskell was president of this new publishing venture; Narcisco Gonzales, editor, aided by various relatives and friends who once had worked for the *News and Courier.* It was rough going at first, but in time the *State* became as much a fixture in South Carolina households as its predecessor had been, eventually even more so.

In retrospect, it seems rather unlikely that the Gonzales boys actually were prepared to pull up stakes and leave South Carolina or that Haskell and Narcisco Gonzales put the *State* together in a matter of a few weeks. Instead, it is quite possible that an independent Columbia daily had been taking shape for several years. The election of Ben Tillman as governor merely turned those dreams into reality.

Town Portraits in the *News and Courier*

Whatever the chain of events, one interesting by-product of the growth of the *News and Courier* and its Columbia bureau remains. To attract readers, from time to time the *News and Courier* produced very revealing word portraits of many South Carolina communities. These accounts, usually two or three columns long, often are crammed with fascinating details—names of businessmen and school teachers, comments on the regional economy, bits of local history, and so on. It is apparent that Hemphill, as resident correspondent in Columbia, was partial to such essays because he produced several of them. Later, as he began to exert more control over editorial affairs, these community sketches increased dramatically, some of them unsigned, others written by Matthew F. Tighe (who became Columbia bureau chief in 1890) and August Kohn (who in turn succeeded Tighe). Still others were composed by traveling correspondents Ambrose Gonzales, Edward P. McKissick, and John I. Green. In all, between July, 1887, and January, 1891, over fifty communities were the subject of these extensive accounts, some of them cities in other states such as Augusta, Georgia, where the *News and Courier* also maintained a bureau.

A key question is, of course, why? What did Hemphill and the Gonzales brothers have in mind? Why the sudden spotlight upon communities such as Clinton, Anderson, Rock Hill, Blackville, Darlington, and Marion? There are at least

---

[4] The *News and Courier,* on the other hand, refused to support Haskell, emphasizing that Tillman was the party nominee. Senator Wade Hampton took a similar view, even though Haskell was his son-in-law.

three possible explanations. As noted, *News and Courier* staffers in both Charleston and Columbia undoubtedly saw this publicity as good business, a means of increasing readership and advertising revenue. They also may have contemplated publishing a collection of these articles, a gazetteer of some sort. After all, the *News and Courier* of those years often reproduced its columns in pamphlet form. Or, a third possibility, the Columbia bureau may have been establishing contacts for the yet unborn *State* while ostensibly working in behalf of the *News and Courier.* Since these sketches cease after 1891, one can conclude that they somehow were related to the internal struggle that culminated in the appearance of a new daily newspaper in Columbia.[5]

In any case, the result is an unusual windfall for generations living a century later. Most of these sketches are unashamedly booster in tone, bragging of the loveliest women, the noblest of men, the handsomest buildings, the purest skies, the most invigorating of climates. Nearly every community attributed its "unique" good health to special factors such as pure spring water, cool breezes, fine drainage, sandy soil, pine trees, ocean air, mountain air, and so on. Orangeburg, some seventy-five miles from the Atlantic Ocean, even boasted of a phenomenal railroad cut that somehow produced "a draught of ocean breeze towards sunset." Only upon reflection does it become apparent that occasionally a town advanced its "healthfulness" claim at the expense of a neighbor.

Folklore undoubtedly takes precedence over fact at times (which is not always such a bad thing), and the reader has to digest occasional doses of flamboyant Victorian phraseology. Nevertheless, in the pages that follow one learns much about how our ancestors lived during the 1880s in communities such as Camden, Barnwell, Cheraw, and Newberry.

It is no surprise that South Carolina's villages, towns, and cities of that era did not differ much from one another. Each was proud of its churches, schools, and stores. Each had its Masons, Knights of Pythias, building and loan association, and bank. And each, regardless of size, much in the same way that communities of today demand suburban shopping malls, had to have a cotton mill. Another essential ingredient of the good life of the 1880s was a railroad; in fact, if a village or town didn't have one already, it was probably too late because just around the corner was the panic of 1893 and a welter of railroad consolidation. But, considering the number of railroad companies operating in South Carolina in the 1880s, almost any community could lay claim to a stretch of track.

---

[5] However, in 1895 a Darlington resident, J.E. Norment, inaugurated yet another collection of community portraits, some highlighting agricultural produce and nearly all lavishly illustrated with excellent drawings of leading citizens and their homes, hotels, churches, factories, and business houses. In most instances, these articles were endorsed by editorials appearing in the same issue of the *News and Courier* and sometimes were accompanied by local advertisements as well. Norment, who joined the *State* in the late 1890s and then became secretary to Gov. Duncan Clinch Heyward in 1903, subsequently returned to Darlington to edit the *News and Press.* See Appendix 2 for a list of his *News and Courier* articles.

Without exception these are upbeat sketches. The tenor of life is improving, we are told, progress is evident on every hand, sales are better than last year. Rarely does the chamber-of-commerce image slip and reveal the hard times being experienced by most South Carolinians of that decade. However, there are hints now and then that everything is not well in paradise. Some towns, as we all know, were run by a snug little band of people who did the banking, bought the cotton, sold seed and supplies, and held the mortgages. Their names appear over and over as the officers of various organizations, both commercial and social. In addition, it is apparent that the Farmers' Alliance, the latest wave of agricultural protest, was demonstrating real strength in some regions. And, on occasions, these reporters refer to glorious new ventures that are taking advantage of facilities abandoned by others that failed.

This is not to say that these sketches are untrue. Not at all. The Gonzales boys and their friends simply believed wholeheartedly in Henry Grady's "New South" and trumpeted its achievements as loudly as they could. And, as always, change is relative. Compared to the chaos of the 1860s and 1870s, their South Carolina of the 1880s was most certainly progressive, self-assured, confident, even a bit cocky. The sketches they wrote describe an inquisitive, dynamic people awestruck by the marvel of the telephone, the magic of electricity, the power of new machines.

Charleston's annual survey of September 1, 1890, boasts that the past is forgotten ... "the present and the future have clasped hands." A bold statement perhaps, but as we now know, the 1880s were a "threshold" age, a time when it seemed to many that the present and future might indeed be one. In short, through the eyes of these *News and Courier* reporters we can watch South Carolinians as they enter a new world, a world that we who live in the twentieth century can understand and appreciate.[6]

[6] In addition to material found in this volume, readers may wish to consult these sketches of out-of-state communities found in the *News and Courier:* Wilmington, N.C. (April 15, 1886), Augusta, Ga. (January 30, 1887, and September 23, 1888), Thomasville, Ga. (August 14, 1888), Shelby, N.C. (January 3, 1889), and Rutherfordton, N.C. (February 6, 1889). During these years this newspaper also published several general surveys that may be of interest: "The Negro in South Carolina," a statewide report compiled by J.C. Hemphill (January 5, 1881), "South Carolina in 1884," also issued as a pamphlet (February 4, 1884), "There's Millions in It," a special supplement on phosphates (March 1, 1884), and "South Carolina in 1886" (January 1, 1886).

Abbeville: Cradle and Grave of the Confederacy

Settled in 1756 by four frontier families who soon were joined by two hundred French Huguenots, Abbeville has a long and glorious history that includes its unique role during the days of Southern nationhood. Ambrose Gonzales, who visited there in May of 1889, recounts the high drama of the 1860s and also describes the Red Shirt Campaign of 1876. In addition, he has some pointed comments concerning Abbeville's rather splendid isolation as a result of poor rail service ("trains of ramshackle cars") and little or no industry.

* * *

This county, which has given to South Carolina so many brilliant statesmen and so many gallant soldiers, in both the Revolutionary and civil wars, dates its first settlement from the year 1756, when Patrick Calhoun, accompanied by four families of his friends, settled on Long Cane Creek. This colonial nucleus was supplemented in 1764 by the arrival of two hundred French emigrants, under the guidance of the Rev. Mr. Gilbert, a Huguenot pastor. Taking up the land on both sides of Long Cane Creek, they named the one side New Bordeaux and the other New Rochelle, after the province whence they had emigrated to seek in the New World a sanctuary from the religious persecution to which they were subjected by reason of their Protestant faith.

The name of Abbeville, a French manufacturing town in the Department of the Somme, was given to the new district, and the French settlers throve in the land of their adoption. The climate was salubrious, the soil fertile, and to the products of the field and the meadow they added the manufacture of silk, which was continued by their descendants in a small way for several generations.

This historic district was, during the Revolutionary War, the theatre of many conflicts with the Tories, as well as with the British. The story of the siege of Ninety-Six by the Continental Army under Gen. Greene is familiar history. Many of the redoubts of the old fort retain to this day their original shape, although they are crowned with great oaks and carpeted with grass and flowers.

Soon after the evacuation of Ninety-Six by the British, the country thereabouts suffered considerably from the inroads of the Cherokee Indians, who violated their pledges of neutrality. Gen. Pickens, with a troop of four hundred horses, penetrated the Cherokee country, destroyed many towns and villages, and killed a number of Indians. The lesson was a wholesome one, and the whites were not further molested.

At the close of the Revolutionary War the people of Abbeville resumed their peaceful avocations, and from year to year increased their wealth and their knowledge. From its earliest settlement this district has been famous for the attention paid to education and for the excellence of its institutions of learning.

Dr. Waddell [Moses Waddel] conducted a famous classical school at Willington, which was regarded as the best in the State outside of Charleston. Here many of Abbeville's noted sons received their earliest education. The influence of this distinguished instructor and his colleagues has extended through succeeding generations.

The present admirable High School at Abbeville Court House, the splendid colleges at Due West, and the excellent graded schools at Greenwood, Ninety-Six, and McCormick are tributes to the wisdom, ambition, liberality, and public spirit of the citizens of this county, which has long been regarded as the leading centre of learning and refinement in the up country.

The town of Abbeville is built on a cluster of hills or slight elevations above the surrounding country, which is gently rolling with fields and forests in attractive diversity. The streets are wide and well shaded with elms and willow oaks. There are many handsome residences, and the shrubberies and rose gardens are particularly extensive and beautiful. Many dwellings are completely embowered in flowers, the twining lamarck and the clinging banksia meeting in fragrant rivalry over porch and lattice, while above them, upreaching to the chimney tops, the lovely purple wisteria droops lazily as if tired by her long climb.

In the northeastern part of the town the historic "Secession Hill" rises to a considerable elevation. No spot in all the Southland is fraught with so much interest to Carolinian and Confederate. Here was the revolution inaugurated, within a few hundred yards lived the author of the Ordinance of Secession, here also lived the first soldier who lost his life in the war. Within a musket shot of this hill Mr. Davis held the last council of war, and the failure of the Confederate arms was formally acknowledged. Here also the Confederate Government collapsed and the officers and men who remained were released from military duty. On this spot, too, the movement was inaugurated which wrestled the State government from the control of the Radical crew in 1876, and here they acknowledged their defeat and abandoned the campaign.

Many of the great white oaks which shaded the amphitheatrical hill during the progress of these stirring events are still standing, and stretch their gnarled and weather-worn arms above the hallowed spot. On the crown of the hill is the modest vine-wreathed cottage of Capt. J.F.C. Dupré, one of Abbeville's most respected citizens. The southeastern slope of the hill has been stripped of its timber and planted with grapes, flowers, and fruit trees. The bees drone among the blossoms, the air is filled with the delightful fragrance of a hundred rose bushes, the tempting fruit swells and ripens under the glowing sun, and all betokens peace.

But let us look back. On November 22, 1860, a great mass meeting was held

Public square, Abbeville, c. 1890. *South Caroliniana Library.*

on Secession Hill. From all parts of the district the crowds came. Companies of minute men rode in from Greenwood, Cokesbury, Ninety-Six, Due West, and other points. The old artillery company and the Southern Rights Dragoons were present. Cannon boomed and banners fluttered everywhere. The excitement and enthusiasm were intense.

The procession was formed at an early hour of the day under Gen. A.M. Smith, marshal of the day, and marched to the hill, where a stand had been erected. Mr. Thomas C. Perrin presided, and after an appropriate prayer by the Rev. Mr. North, the Hon. A.G. Magrath of Charleston opened the meeting with an eloquent and impassioned speech in behalf of States rights and Southern independence.

He was followed by Gen. M.L. Bonham, who brought cheering news from other sections and who thought the sentiment of the State was unanimously in favor of secession. Gen. Bonham was listened to with great attention and at the close of his speech was rapturously applauded.

Speeches followed by Edward Noble, Thomas C. Perrin, John A. Calhoun, Samuel McGowan, A.M. Smith, and others, all favoring immediate secession. The venerable Judge Wardlaw alone lifted his voice in impassioned appeal to the throng to forbear hasty action, and warned them of the disastrous consequences which would inevitably follow the secession of South Carolina from the Union. But to no avail! The secession tide overwhelmed the protestant, and the following resolution, introduced by Mr. Edward Noble, was unanimously adopted:

> Resolved, That in the opinion of the people of Abbeville District the election of Abraham Lincoln as President of the United States and of Hannibal Hamlin as Vice President, upon doctrines destructive of the rights and interests, the equality and safety of the Southern States, by the factions and sectional votes of our Northern confederates, utterly perverts the spirit of the compact formed by the Federal Constitution; that it must be promptly and sternly resisted by the State of South Carolina, and that the secession of the State from the Federal Union is the proper mode of resistance.

A committee of twenty-one, appointed to nominate delegates to a State secession convention, named the following gentlemen, who were unanimously endorsed by the meeting: Edward Noble, T.C. Perrin, John A. Calhoun, Thomas Thomson, John A. Wilson, and D.L. Wardlaw.

The fateful step was thus taken, but few seemed aware of its gravity, and at night the town was illuminated with torches and bonfires and the heavens were bright with fireworks.

The next noteworthy incident in the eventful history of Abbeville was the arrival of President Davis on May 4, 1865, at 10 o'clock A.M. He was accompanied by Gen. Breckenridge, Mr. Benjamin, Mr. Mallory, Mr. Reagan, and Gen. Lawton. Mr. Davis was entertained by Armistead Burt, and the members of the Cabinet by Judge Monroe and Thomas C. Perrin. The party remained twelve or fourteen hours in Abbeville. Before their departure, the last council of war of the stricken Confederacy was held in the house of Mr. Burt. Mr. Davis, who had with him two brigades of cavalry commanded by Gens. Vaughn and Dukes, desired that a stand should be made at this point, that a reorganization of the army might be accomplished, and advantageous terms of surrender at least secured from the enemy before the abandonment of the Confederacy. After consultation, however, he was overruled by his Cabinet. Overcome with emotion the President of the Lost Cause rested his head upon the back of his chair and covered his face with his handkerchief.

At midnight the Presidential party resumed their retreat. During their passage into Georgia the great seal of the Confederacy was committed to the keeping of the tawny waters of the Savannah River.

On the 22nd of August, 1876, notice having been given that Governor Chamberlain and a number of speakers would address a mass meeting of Republicans at Abbeville Court House, the Democrats, under Col. J.S. Cothran, determined to organize and demand a division of the time with the Republican speakers. Couriers on fleet horses were sent in every direction, and in a few hours two thousand mounted "red shirts" had reached the ground, foremost among them the "Dark Corner Club" of Edgefield, commanded by Capt. J.G. Blackwell. Clubs followed from Greenwood, Ninety-Six, Due West, Cokesbury, Millway, Bradley's, Bordeaux, Lebanon, Magnolia, and from every part of the county.

The splendid column of brilliantly attired horsemen marched to the stand which had been erected on Secession Hill, surrounded the immense crowd of Radicals there assembled, and a division of time having been accorded the

Democrats, remained at their posts until the day's proceedings were brought to a close. The brilliant and forcible speeches made by Judge Samuel McGowan, Col. J.S. Cothran, and the Hon. D. Wyatt Aiken, together with the awe inspired by the phalanx of red-shirted horsemen, practically broke the back of the Republican campaign and they acknowledged their defeat from that day.

The Abbeville of today, freighted with historic memories, has neither the population nor the business to which it is justly entitled by reason of the soil and climate. The reason is not hard to find. With a splendid agricultural county, with a healthful climate, and with an industrious population, Abbeville yet lags because of her poor railroad facilities and the absence of manufactures. The trains of ramshackle cars consume nearly an hour in making the trip from Hodges, on the main line of the Columbia and Greenville Railroad, to Abbeville over the "Abbeville Branch." Mails from Charleston and Columbia reach this point at 4 o'clock P.M.

The really charming town is thus shunned by travelling men and others who might visit or settle here because of the difficulty attending the journey. This may be changed, however; the extension of the Carolina, Cumberland Gap, and Chicago Road from Edgefield to Abbeville within two years is practically assured, and Abbeville will then have short and quick connection with Charleston. Hopes are entertained also that the Georgia, Carolina, and Northern Railroad, now completed as far south as Chester, will before very long be extended through Greenwood and Abbeville, giving this point, with the Carolina, Cumberland Gap, and Chicago Road, three competing lines and consequent augmentation of facilities and diminution of freight and passenger rates.

The population of Abbeville is about 1,600. The intendant is R.W. Cannon, and the treasurer is Jones F. Miller.

Abbeville is proud of its churches which are, without exception, handsome and commodious structures. The Methodist congregation was the first organized. Their building is a large and well appointed one, centrally located, and the pastor is the Rev. Leroy F. Beattie. The Baptist Church has a large membership, in charge of the Rev. Mr. Brown. The Catholic Church is a gem, a beautiful and symmetrical edifice, where services are held by Father Hirshmeyer.

The Rev. Wm. Henry Hanckel, a native of Charleston, is rector of the Episcopal Church, an appropriate structure. The organist is Mr. W.C. Benet and the choir of male voices render the music services beautifully.

The Presbyterians are happy in their new church which was completed six months ago. The dedication services will long be remembered by its members. The sermon preached by Dr. W.T. Thompson of Charleston was from the text: "Strength and beauty are in His Sanctuary." The building is of brick painted in brick-color, pencilled in black and trimmed with ornamental stone. The roof is of slate, with ornamental cresting; the cornices of iron, painted granite color. The pews are laid off in a circle. The material used is yellow pine, oiled and beautifully polished. The ceiling, of same material, is in the form of the roof. The church is lighted with large windows of cathedral glass and is splendidly ventilated and heated with registers.

Several Sunday-school classrooms are in the building, which is unquestionably one of the most complete in the State.

The Abbeville High School is an admirable institution, presided over by Mr. J.W. Thomson, a graduate of the University of Virginia and an accomplished educator. Prof. Thomson is assisted by Miss Sarah Thurston and Miss Emma Perrin, both excellent teachers. There are several colored churches in Abbeville and their schools are excellent.

The National Bank of Abbeville was organized three years ago. The president is Mr. J. Allen Smith, and Mr. Benj. S. Barnwell is cashier. The capital is $75,000, the deposits $60,000, and surplus and undivided profits $12,000, besides paying annually a handsome interest.

The new hotel, owned and conducted by T.C. Sexal, is an imposing brick building on the public square and has all the travelling patronage. The Abbeville Hotel is a wooden building on Railroad Avenue and is conducted by Mrs. Miller.

Abbeville's cotton receipts average between 8,000 and 9,000 bales. A great deal of the cotton shipped from here is ginned by Messrs. F.W. McMillan and Frank Henry, whose ginning establishments have an aggregate capacity of seventy bales per day.

Abbeville will at last have a cotton factory and an oil mill. Fifty-five thousand dollars has been subscribed towards the cotton mill, and the oil mill will be in operation by September 1, most of the stock having been taken by farmers, who will be afforded a good market for the sale of their seed, as well as for the purchase of fertilizers at their very door.

The Abbeville Rifles, a crack company, are splendidly equipped and uniformed in the State regulation gray, with the addition of white leggings. The officers are: W.C. McGowan, captain; A.W. Smith, first lieutenant; John A. Harris, second lieutenant; Thos. P. Cothran, first sergeant; and T.L. Douglas, second sergeant. The company parades forty-five men and is regarded as one of the finest military organizations in the South.

The business directory follows. White Brothers occupy three stores and a warehouse with their extensive business in cotton and general merchandise. They have just completed on the southern end of the public square the handsomest grocery store in Upper Carolina, with plate glass show windows, elevators, and every modern appliance for facilitating the transaction of business.

W. Joel Smith & Son occupy two extensive stores and a warehouse, and they do a very large business in general merchandise.

Robert McGowan Hill is a large dealer in general merchandise.

P. Rosenberg & Co. have just erected beautiful stores for the transaction of a large business in general merchandise and clothing.

Dr. W.T. Penney, pharmacist.

B.P. Sneed, druggist.

W.E. Bell, millinery.

H.W. Lawson & Co., tinware, stoves, glass, etc.

John G. Edwards (successor to Wardlaw & Edwards), general merchandise.
R.M. Hadden & Co., millinery.
A.M. Hill & Sons, confectionery and fancy groceries.
R.W. Cannon, general merchandise.
Jones F. Miller, fancy groceries, confectionery, and fruits.
E.A. Templeton, general merchandise.
J.D. Chalmers, furniture and marble.
J.M. McCrary, confectionery.
G.A. Douglas, general merchandise.
Seal & McIlwain, wagons, buggies, etc.
A.W. Smith & Co., dealers in livestock.
A.M. Hill & Sons, livery and sale stables.
Russell & Wallingford, sale and livery stables.
J.S. Hammond, harness shop.
C.E. Bruce, boot and shoemaker.
L.K. Bowie, confectionery.
John C. Douglas, billiard room, etc.
Peter Magliana, baker.
W.G. Chapman, wagon shops.

There are but three practicing physicians in Abbeville, Drs. L.T. Hill, Thomas J. Mabry, and F.E. Harrison, and one dentist, Dr. S.G. Thomson.

The Bar

The law is the true embodiment
Of everything that's excellent.
It has no possible fault nor flaw,
And I, my Lords, embody the law.

The practice of law has always been a leading industry in Abbeville. The people of the county delight in litigation, and when the crops are laid by and business lags they naturally go to law with each other. Whatever effect this litigious spirit may have had upon the county of Abbeville in other respects, it has certainly conduced to the development of the legal mind to a remarkable degree, for the Abbeville Bar has always been a strong one, and some of the brightest lawyers in the State are to be found here today, as the following list will show: W.H. Parker, W.A. Lee, L.W. Perrin, R.R. Hemphill, E.G. Graydon, E.B. Gray, W.O. Bradley, W.P. Calhoun, W.L. Miller, J.C. Klugh, W.C. Benet, W.C. McGowan, Thos. P. Cothran, S.C. Cason, W.N. Graydon, F.B. Gary, M.P. DeBruhl, Thos. P. Thomson, J. Fuller Lyon, and D.L. Mabry.

The Law range is beautifully located at the rear of the Court House. In front of the spacious offices are squares and plots of luxurious blue grass, shaded by pretty elms. The trial justices are: M.P. DeBruhl and Col. Hiram Tilman Wardlaw.

The county officers are: W.D. Mann, sheriff; T.L. Moore, clerk of court; A.W.

Jones, auditor; J.W. Perrin, treasurer; J. Fuller Lyon, probate judge; J.C. Klugh, master; J.W. Lites, J.F.C. Dupré, and John E. Brownlee, county commissioners; B.M. Wilson, coroner.

Abbeville has excellent newspapers. The *Press and Banner,* established in 1853, is owned and edited by Hugh Wilson, who has been connected with the paper for thirty years. His experience and knowledge of the needs of his county enable him to get out a splendid publication of fifty-six columns, with full correspondence from every part of the county, with full locals, strong editorials, and admirably selected matter. An extensive job office is connected with the *Press and Banner,* and the paper is in a flourishing condition.

The *Abbeville Medium,* a handsome, thirty-two column paper, published by Hemphill & Hemphill and edited by Gen. R.R. Hemphill, is a power in Abbeville and is largely circulated throughout the county. Gen. Hemphill, when permitted by his poetic nature to cease temporarily the study of Abbeville's lovely women and roses, writes able editorials, and his local columns are always full and interesting.

Abbeville's editors live together in commendable amity. No cloud of disagreement ever rises between them. Having no quarrels with each other, they are naturally enabled to devote their energies to the regulation of the county and metropolitan press of the State, and withal to control the Legislature and direct the rulings of the Supreme Court.

Only in a refined and cultured community like this could such an institution as the Abbeville Literary Club exist. Established in 1878, its membership includes the brightest minds in the town, and among its honorary members are many prominent Carolinians. At the different meetings hundreds of essays have been read on political literature and a variety of subjects. The club is entertained at the houses of its members, and its sessions are instructive and enjoyable. All of the leading magazines and papers are subscribed for, and the club from year to year enlarges its scope and usefulness.

News and Courier, May 21, 1889. A.E.G.

Aiken, a Mecca for Northerners

Aiken, once a summer resort for Charlestonians and in 1889 a winter retreat for well-to-do Northerners, was the envy of every other town, village, and hamlet in South Carolina, all of whom wanted to emulate that community's economic success. Excellent rail connections, broad avenues, beautiful gardens, and modern hotels created the perfect milieu in which to spend a few weeks away from the ice and cold of less temperate climes. Here is Matthew F. Tighe's report on life there in January of 1889.

* * *

One's impressions of a place are very apt to be made up by the manner of his reception wherever he goes. It was this traveller's rare good luck to have been received by two gentlemen of Aiken, one a lawyer and the other a hotel keeper. The hotel keeper was Mr. B.P. Chatfield, the lawyer, the Hon. D.S. Henderson, both of whom selected Aiken many years ago as the place in which to cast their fortunes.

You alight at Aiken on the platform of one of the neatest and best appointed stations on any line of railway in South Carolina. The depot has been practically rebuilt. It is neat in its architectural design and is built evidently for the convenience of those who sometimes in the nature of things "must wait on the train." If waiting is necessary, then by all means go to the Aiken depot to do the waiting.

There is a handsomely furnished room for the ladies and another for gentlemen who haven't the good fortune to be in attendance upon fair friends. In the centre of the building is the private office of Mrs. North, who presides over the business of the South Carolina Railway at Aiken—a lady of whom both in her business and social relations there are heard golden opinions on all sides. Her assistant is Mr. A.M. Willard, who is polite and attentive, with an eye single to the interests of his company and whose special function is to see that the wrong person does not get the right baggage and *vice versa.*

It was learned from Mr. Henderson that the town and county were called Aiken in honor of one of South Carolina's old-time governors. Mr. Henderson went there in 1872 when the town contained about an even 1,000 inhabitants and when there were only two lawyers at the Bar. The resident population nowadays is estimated at 2,200, and in the height of the winter season there are fully 5,000 people in the town.

The whole town originally belonged to two rich old barons of the realm, who had its site laid out in squares bounded by streets 150 feet wide and of any desired length. They gave every other square to the South Carolina Railway, but this gift has been amply repaid by the things which the railway has done for the town and people. Each of the streets was named after a county in the State, but the baptism must be renewed before long. There must be added a Florence Street and a Craven Street as soon as the Berkeley politicians shall have "created" their new county.

The first look at the streets is obtained when the visitor passes up hill from the depot and enters the main thoroughfare, Park Avenue. There is no finer anywhere, and this is stated without mental reserve. Its beauty begins opposite the depot, near which is the Park Avenue Hotel, with its long and tasteful white front, half-shaded from view by the line of white oaks along the pavement.

Aiken, it might here be mentioned, is a city of hotels, modern hotels and modern boarding houses. At this time the streets, although well kept, indicate nothing of the charming and graceful appearance they present in the spring or summer. There are lines of trees on the grand boulevard, along the pavements, and on either side of two macadamized drives. In the middle of these streets are parks planted in cedar, rose trees, and the usual garden stock. This is a feature which is peculiar to Aiken, for it is about the only one of the summer resorts the streets of which are spacious enough to do duty as streets with room enough to spare for public parks. On this avenue are some of the finest dwelling places imaginable. As a rule they are all recessed from the streets, leaving spaces for gardens unsurpassed anywhere for the luxuriance of what they contain and in the manner in which they are presented to the view of the passerby.

The people, it might be noted, have all the salient characteristics of the four greatest counties in the State—Edgefield, Orangeburg, Lexington, and Barnwell, as out of these four the present county of Aiken was formed. Knowing what the people of these counties are, it is quite easy to imagine what their traits must be when concentrated in the modern son or daughter of the Aikenites.

All progress must have a starting point, and it is conceded that the present evolution of Aiken began when the Highland Park Hotel was built way back in 1869 or thereabouts. The hotel was the pioneer of modern hotels in the South. It made Aiken and it gave the impulse to Northern travel to the South, which is one of the great factors in its present development.

Mr. B.P. Chatfield, its proprietor, came to Aiken, built his hotel at first on a modest scale, but has since added to it so largely that it is now among the first in the Southern States. It is the winter home of the best class of Northern tourists. It contains all that human ease and comfort desire, and especially for that invalid class with whom attention and courtesy count so much in what is left to them of this mortal life. It is situated on a high bluff overlooking the ravine on the west through which the South Carolina Railway runs and crowns a hill which descends, by natural terraces, to the railway embankment.

The grounds about the hotel are kept green both summer and winter. Within everything is indicative of luxury; without the summer season is made to exist the year around. At this time there are more than one hundred permanent guests in the hotel—a larger number than have visited the hotel so early in the season for the past twenty years.

Highland Park Hotel, Aiken, 1894. *South Caroliniana Library.*

One of the newest of the enterprises in which Aiken capital is invested is the Aiken Land and Improvement Company. The lands of the company are the Bauskett and other tracts which lie along the Aiken and Edgefield branch of the Carolina, Cumberland Gap, and Chicago Railroad, about ten miles from Aiken at Lake View Station. It is proposed to restore the old water power on the tract and to establish a new cotton factory and a wood pulp factory. The lands also contain brown sandstone in abundance and fine brick clay. Dr. T.G. Croft and Mr. B.P. Chatfield are largely interested in the company, as are also some Northern capitalists. It was stated yesterday that there was a probability that work would be begun on the lands in a short time. With the reconstruction proposed, a 500-horse power can be had, the supply of water being from one of the most extensive reservoirs in the county.

It is not out of place to mention here that an old Charlestonian, Dr. Charles F. McGahan, is the resident physician at the hotel. He is provided for in one of the handsomest rooms of the building and is enjoying a fair share of that good fortune that follows deserving Charlestonians the world over.

This hotel, and of course the others, are situated in a climate about which whole volumes have already been written and about which it is impossible to say anything new. As to the temperature, there is the best authority for saying that the elevation of the town is 650 feet above the tide level of the Charleston Battery. They also say that it is not particularly hot in Aiken in the high summer and that, if it is, it is only a delusion of sensation—a kind of feeling with which it is the fashion to also delude one's self in Charleston when the mercury stands at 90° to 94° in the coolest kind of shade in this Sunny South.

The climate is just the kind that consumptives have declared to be the kind they need, and ordinarily they are the best authority. When they go away restored in the summer, they are in love with the place, and they very gratefully write about the successful pilgrimage. Hence it is that Mr. Chatfield has a whole library of testimonials as to the wonderful and miraculous cures performed by the climate, to say nothing of the bill of fare, lá Aiken.

The places to stay are either the Highland Park Hotel; the Park Avenue Hotel, by A.R. Taft; the Busch House, by H. Busch; the Ashley House, by J. Ashley; the West View Hotel, by Mrs. D.E. Rockwell; the York Street Hotel, by Mrs. N.E. Senn; the Stevenson House or the Steadman House. If possible the traveller should stay at all these places; but, if he has only time to stay at one, he can put all the names in his beaver, shake them up, take out one, and stay there. He will find that by long odds to be the most charming place east of the Pacific.

Should it be a fine day, and there are usually three hundred and sixty-four fine days in a year in Aiken, a very short walk will take the visitor to the business street of the town. The business street, by the way, has been burned down several times, but the result of the last fire has been the restoration of the street with brick buildings, any of which will vie both in business and appearance with the pretentious piles of the Fountain City [Augusta] just across the river. The merchant princes deal largely with New York, occasionally with Augusta, and more so with Charleston.

Among them are Courtney & Co., wholesale and retail grocers; C.K. Henderson, a large wholesale and retail clothing house; H. Hahn & Co., general merchandise, two large stores; Shroder & Thorp, same business as Hahn & Co.; H.F. Warneke, bakery; C. Klatte, merchandise and liquors (Mr. Klatte is a brother of Capt. Herman Klatte of this city); Robert Powell, wholesale and retail groceries; F. Voght, hardware; and H. Busch & Co., general merchandise. In the druggist line are H.H. Hall (a brother of Jordan Hall of this city), W.J. Platt, and W.H. Harbers.

All these merchants have the option of three large banks: The Bank of Aiken, F.B. Henderson, president, W.W. Muckenfuss (a Charlestonian), cashier; the Aiken County Loan and Savings Bank, W.W. Woolsey, president, J.W. Ashurst, cashier; and the private bank of J.H. Beckman. The impression is that all these presidents and cashiers are millionaires, at least the institutions mentioned are on a sound financial basis.

In matters of education, secular and religious, Aiken stands in the front rank. There are the Aiken Academy, for about one hundred white pupils, taught by Prof. J.R. Mack and a corps of assistants, and the Aiken Institute, with about eighty pupils, taught by Prof. F.H. Curtiss, who is also ably assisted. There is also the Schofield Normal Institute, of which the *News and Courier* gave a very full description not very long ago. There is also another excellent school taught by the Rev. W.R. Coles.

With the schools the churches go hand-in-hand. There are the Episcopal Church, the Rev. E.C. Edgerton; the Presbyterian Church, the Rev. J.C. Ochler; the Baptist Church, the Rev. L. Cuthbert; the Methodist Church, the Rev. R.H. Jones; and the Catholic Church, a mission. There are, of course, colored churches of all known and unknown denominations for the colored people.

There is an Aiken Bar, which ranks high among the legal fraternity. Of these the most prominent are: D.S. and E.P. Henderson, G.W. Croft, W.G. Chaffee, James Aldrich, Walter Ashley, W. Quitman Davis, Col. C.E. Sawyer, O.C. Jordan, M.B. Woodward, F.A. Emanuel, Harland Stevenson, E.S. Hammond, and John Gary Evans.

The faces of a good many of these gentlemen whom the correspondent met yesterday recalled to him very forcibly the famous Deadlock Convention of 1888. The Convention also reminded him of the *Recorder,* edited by Mr. Ford, and the *Journal and Review,* edited by Mr. Ligon, both of which are invaluable institutions in Aiken. Both of these gentlemen have lost that look of weariness and tiredness which was epidemic in the town when the Convention was in session and things were red hot, night and day, at the Tillman, Henderson, and Aldrich headquarters respectively.

In those days and now it was, and is, well that Aiken could boast of such a municipal and peace department as it now possesses. The names of these are all that will be necessary to give their biography: Intendant, F.E. Sommer; Wardens, B.P. Chatfield, H. Hahn, H. Busch, John Phillips, and J.C. Courtney; Clerk, J.R. Jordan.

The county authorities, most of them making Aiken their home, are W.W. Williams, master in equity; B.F. Turner, sheriff; J.H. Hawkinson, clerk of court; D.H. Wise, auditor; J.T. Gaston, probate judge; J.D. Murray, treasurer; D.H. Crossland, school commissioner; and J.A. West, S.A. Hadley, and Eldrige Sumter, county commissioners.

The products of the county come to Aiken, especially cotton, but the receipts must in time be largely diminished by the business done by the Blackville, Alston, and Newberry Railway. There will, however, possibly be a gain along the Edgefield and Aiken branch of the Carolina, Cumberland Gap, and Chicago Railway, which is now in active operation. This, with the South Carolina Railway, has made Aiken a competing point, which has secured a reduction of freight from Aiken to Chester of about 20 per cent. They have by their splendid railway facilities four mails a day, the best thing which they bring in the line of literature being the *News and Courier,* of which Miss L.M. Carson is the active and enterprising agent in Aiken.

The social life of Aiken is not a misnomer. It is social. The composition of the population is necessarily very cosmopolitan. They have the Cosmos Social Club, which will give its annual ball on the 6th of February, and the New Aiken Library and Social Club, which is composed of the most progressive folks in society in town. They have the Lyceum Hall for private and travelling theatricals, and they go to Augusta to attend the theatre there.

The foregoing is only a desultory and necessarily disconnected sketch of one of the most interesting places in the State. The sketch is just the least bit unnecessary because Aiken and its people are so familiar in Charleston. But if any correspondent can visit Aiken even for a few hours, as did this correspondent, and escape the conviction that he ought to write something about it, that individual ought to be put at the head of the black list of Aiken.

News and Courier, January 25, 1889. M.F.T.

Anderson, a Charming Little City

Surrounded by rich farming country, in June of 1888 Anderson seemed to be on the verge of great prosperity. It had a new rail connection to the outside world, was organizing a cotton mill, and was about to build a large hotel on the public square. According to Ambrose E. Gonzales, the Savannah Valley Railroad was the key to this new growth and development, having broken the monopolistic grip in which another line had held the community for many years. For yet another view of Anderson, see a column by Edward P. McKissick that appeared in the *News and Courier* eleven months later on May 14, 1889.

* * *

Situated in the centre of a fertile and flourishing county, one of the brightest gems of the beautiful Piedmont belt of South Carolina, is the city of Anderson. Within sight of the Blue Ridge Mountains, 800 feet above the level of the sea, Anderson is one of the healthiest places in Upper Carolina. While the city has been steadily advancing, her growth so far has not been remarkable, but Anderson is now on the verge of a genuine and well-deserved boom. For some reason her people have been too modest to press the claims of their municipality and have neglected to post the outside world as to the great advantages—social, industrial, and hygenic—which Anderson possesses and which she offers to visitors and settlers.

For years Anderson has been held down almost to stagnation on account of her inability to communicate with the outside world, except by way of a railroad operated by an unprogressive and unsympathetic corporation. But now all this is changed, and the millstone has been taken from her neck by the completion of the Savannah Valley Railroad. Her railroad facilities have been trebled, her shackles are removed, and the city and county of Anderson are infused with new life and hope, and she can now take her place among the booming towns of South Carolina.

The present city administration is broad and progressive. The officers are: Mayor, G.F. Tolley; aldermen, T.F. Hill, J.L. McGee, J.G. Cunningham, Foster Fant, J.M. Payne, and C.F. Jones; clerk of council, J.D. Maxwell. Chief R.F. McKinney and three policemen keep the city in perfect order.

Anderson is justly proud of her fire department, which, under the management of Fire Chief R.F. Divver, has attained a degree of efficiency second to no volunteer force of its size in the country. The department, organized in 1884, bought the old Pioneer steamer from Charleston, which, thoroughly overhauled and remodelled, is now one of the best engines in the State. The hand engine company (colored) is also very efficient. Another colored company will soon be organized.

The hook and ladder company is a crack organization of young white men, who have been first prize winners at Charlotte and elsewhere.

The Anderson Board of Trade, organized fourteen years ago, was reorganized last March under new regulations by the election of the following officers: President, J.M. Sullivan; vice president, J.D. Maxwell; secretary and treasurer, R.S. Ligon; executive committee, S.M. Orr, J.E. Peoples, C.F. Jones, R.S. Hill, and J.J. Fretwell. There are two other standing committees, one on manufacture, in charge of the manufacturing interests of the city, and one on transportation and freight rates.

Over sixty business firms are represented on the board to whose untiring efforts the completion of the Savannah Valley Railroad and the recent organization of the Anderson Cotton Mill are mainly due.

A delegation from the board lately attended the Immigration Convention at Hot Springs. A committee, with Major E.B. Murray chairman, are now engaged in the preparation of an Anderson County exhibit for the Augusta National Exposition. The board is always at the front in any enterprise or movement for the material advancement of Anderson.

The present city tax in Anderson is three mills, the city having been cut off from the handsome revenue previously derived from liquor licenses. The city will, however, be profitably wet after January 1, 1889.

Postmaster C.W. Webb occupies the handsomest post office in the up-country, a new brick building rented by the Government from Mr. J.H. Von Hasseln. The receipts of the office last year were $3,600 and are increasing every month. The money-order business has grown rapidly since the completion of the Savannah Valley Railroad, and the business of the office will require additional clerical force before the coming winter. Five mails are dispatched and five received daily. There are also five Star routes supplying twenty-two offices. Postmaster Webb and his courteous assistant give the Anderson public first-class service, and the office is a model one in every respect.

The Anderson Building and Loan Association was organized in June 1883. President, P.K. McCully; secretary and treasurer, J.D. Maxwell; directors, W.H. Nardin, W.W. Humphreys, G.F. Tolley, D.S. Maxwell, D.S. Taylor, M.P. Tribble, A.B. Towers, and S.M. Orr. Capital stock paid in $61,000, assets $100,000. This association has done more to build up Anderson than any other agency, furnishing money to poor people who could never otherwise have raised the means to build.

The Anderson Bank, organized in January 1873, owns the handsome brick building it occupies. President, Jos. N. Brown; cashier, J.A. Brock; teller, B. Frank Mauldin. Capital $50,000, surplus $135,000, deposits $150,000, loans $280,000. The bank is furnished with a $7,000 fire and burglar proof vault, time locks, and all modern safeguards, and pays a semi-annual dividend of 6 per cent. The last sale of stock was at $300 per share.

The hotels are the Keese House, the Waverly House, and Mrs. Ayer's. A new hotel company has just been organized with capital of $40,000, Mr. F.T. Wilhite, president. Steps are being taken to start the hotel building immediately.*

The Anderson Cotton Mill Company, recently organized, has already raised $100,000 towards the erection of a $300,000 factory. One-half of this amount has been promised by Northern capitalists and ground will be broken within a few days. The president of the new company is Mr. J.A. Brock; secretary, J.J. Baker; directors, J.N. Brown, S. Bleckley, Geo. A. Wagener, A.J. Sitton, W.W. Humphreys, W.G. Watson, A.A. Dean, and S.M. Orr.

The Anderson Oil and Fertilizer Company has been running for three years under the successful management of Superintendent G.H. Townsend, President J.A. Brock, and Treasurer B. Frank Mauldin. The capacity of the mill is 50,000 bushels of cotton seed annually.

Another Anderson enterprise is the new machine shop and boiler factory of Dr. R.F. Divver, a machinist of thirty years' experience. This establishment has been provided with the newest and most approved appliances, planers, drills, forges, &c., for the manufacture and repair of boilers, engines, gins, and machinery of all kinds. Dr. Divver has just signed a contract for the manufacture of the Taylor gin-saw filing machine.

The Sullivan Hardware Company have a factory for the manufacture of combination wire and picket fencing, which they ship all over the State. Messrs. Barton & Townsend run successfully a large planing and turning mill. R.A. Mayfield owns a large planing and grist mill. Mr. James Barton is about to build an extensive wagon factory, employing a number of hands.

The population of Anderson was 1,900 in 1880, 3,000 in 1885, and has increased steadily since.

The cotton shipments, notwithstanding the thousands of bales diverted to the Pelzer and Piedmont mills on the outskirts of the county, are 20,000 bales per annum. The merchants of the town do an annual business of one and one-quarter million dollars.

Anderson claims to be the best stock market in the State above Columbia, the horse and mule sales of one firm alone amounting to $100,000 in six months.

Mr. G.F. Tolley has one of the largest wholesale and retail furniture establishments in the State, shipping furniture to points within a few miles of Atlanta and excelling that city in prices and enterprise.

The merchants of Anderson are liberal and progressive. Among them are the following firms: Bleckley, Brown & Fretwell, general merchandise; McCully, Cathcart & Co., general merchandise; Crayton, Jones & Seybt, dry goods; Sullivan Hardware Company; J.D. Maxwell & Co., insurance and brokerage; Means & McGee, clothing, hats, and merchant tailoring; Brown Bros., general

*The cornerstone of this structure was laid on December 27, 1888. For a description and drawing of the hotel see the *News and Courier,* January 14, 1889.

Cotton market on public square, Anderson, c. 1890. *South Caroliniana Library.*

merchandise; C.F. Jones, dry goods; R.S. Ligon, groceries; Brownlee & Brown, fancy groceries; J.N. Watkins, book store; A.B. Towers, general merchandise; Wilhite & Wilhite, druggists; R.S. Hill, general merchandise; W.A. Chapman, dry goods; W.F. Barr, general merchandise; J.P. Sullivan & Co., general merchandise; Dennis O'Donnell, groceries; Moss & Brown, groceries; D.S. Taylor, general merchandise; Cunningham Bros., general merchandise; A.P. Hubbard, general merchandise; Lewis Sharp, confectionery; J.A. Daniels, jeweller; G.M. Tolley, confectionery; Hill Bros., druggists; C.A. Reed, sewing machines and buggies, also music house; F.M. Butler, cigars; Simpson & Co., drugs; H. Webb, groceries; N.O. Farmer & Bro., general merchandise; L.H. Seel, stoves, tin, and hardware; J.M. Hubbard & Bro., jewellers and silverware; G.W. Fant & Son, books and stationery; Foster Fant, clothing; Clark & Bros., merchant tailors; J.S. Fowler, livery and sale stable; John Cattlet, livery, &c.; J.E. Peoples, livery and sale stable; E.W. Taylor & Co., groceries; Miss Sallie Bowie, millinery and dry goods; S.T. Craig, bakery; J.D. Maxwell, photography gallery; J.E. Peoples, stoves and tinware; A. Lesser, dry goods; Watson & Son, general merchandise; Miss Lizzie Williams, millinery and dry goods; Orr & Sloan, drugs; J.J. Baker & Co., general merchandise; John O'Donnell, groceries; F.P. Mimnaugh, dry goods, hats, &c.; and B.F. Crayton & Sons, groceries and provisions.

The Patrick Military Institute was opened last September by Capt. J.B. Patrick, who for years conducted a military school in Greenville. One hundred and twelve boys are enrolled. The full high school course is exacted and the boys are drilled every day. Capt. Patrick has the able assistance of Prof. W.J. Ligon and John M. Patrick. The cadets are divided into two companies, one commanded by Capt. J.H. Coker of Darlington and the other by Capt. J.D. Lowrance of Columbia. There are three flourishing primary schools in Anderson conducted respectively by Miss L.C. Hubbard, Miss Maggie Evans, and Mrs. J. Scott Murray.

The Methodists have just completed a large and handsome $12,000 church designed by Mr. A.W. Todd, an Anderson architect of much promise. The membership is about 250, and the pastor is the Rev. W.S. Wightman. The Baptist congregation, a very large one, is in charge of the Rev. A.A. Marshall, recently called from Gainesville, Ga. They are about to make a $6,000 improvement to the already fine church building. The Rev. D.E. Frierson, D.D., is the pastor of the Presbyterian Church, which is a handsome building occupied by a large congregation. The Rev. T.F. Gadsden is the rector of Grace Episcopal Church, a pretty little structure.

Anderson is well supplied with newspapers. The *Intelligencer* and the *Journal* are both live and progressive journals, wide-awake to the best interests of the community and Democratic to the core. They carefully reflect the best sentiment of the community on all public questions and have a large number of readers.

The soil and climate of Anderson County are singularly favorable for the raising of fine stock and cultivated grasses. Clover, Timothy, and Lucerne grow to perfection. Blue grass "springs eternal" in every fence corner, and the Bermuda, the bane of so many unprogressive farmers, is a perennial source of profit to the progressive grazier. One farmer-lawyer of Anderson made last season one hundred dollars net from an acre of Lucerne and Bermuda. Messrs. B.F. Crayton & Sons on their farm near the city have a herd of fifty registered Jersey cattle and some fine Hambletonian horses. Their farm of 280 acres is devoted to grass and small grain, and their butter has such a reputation that it is sold by contract the year round at 40 cents a pound at the farm.

Taking it all in all, its soil, its climate, its health, and, above all else, its people, there are few places like the charming little city of Anderson, S.C.

News and Courier, June 13, 1888. A.E.G.

Busy Little Bamberg

In June of 1889, Ambrose E. Gonzales found Bamberg a hubbub of activity. Cotton, although still important, had given way in recent years to other produce, and local farmers were anticipating a return of at least $30,000 from some twelve hundred acres of watermelons. They also were joining the Alliance, the latest vehicle for farmer protest, in record numbers. Yet Gonzales reserves his most lavish praise for the mayor of Bamberg, a dashing gentleman who seems to have been all things to all people: a politico, a civil leader, a nature lover, a baseball umpire, and the most courteous of escorts.*

* * *

This is unquestionably one of the busiest and the best towns in the low country of South Carolina. Not a very old town, perhaps, and not a very large one, but quite old enough to walk alone, and quite big enough to hold her own in a commercial tussle with any of her competitors. Bamberg has no manufactures, but there is no reason why she should not have them, and in a few years the flood of manufacturing enterprise now rising over all of South Carolina will doubtless reach her doors; but, like so many Southern towns, her people have been accustomed to look to agriculture as the source of all their revenues, and manufactures have hardly been thought of until recently.

Like a sensible and progressive people, the farmers of this section of late years ditched and ploughed deeper, manured more heavily, and diversified their crops with watermelons and small grain. Cotton is by no means neglected, as the large shipments from this point show, but fewer acres are cultivated in proportion to the production, and the land saved is devoted to melons and other crops. Throughout this section the melon crop is becoming one of great value. The cultivation is comparatively inexpensive, and the product brings the grower cash at the season of the year when he is generally very far in the pocket of the factor and when ready money commands a high premium. In this neighborhood there are 1,200 acres under cultivation the present season. The crop, which will be marketed in July, will bring at least $30,000 cash, no small addition to the agricultural capital of a small community.

The population of Bamberg is 1,100. The business houses, with but one or two exceptions, are built along the main street, which is a wide and well drained thoroughfare, running at right angles to the South Carolina Railroad track, which

*See the *News and Courier* (December 27, 1892) for another article on Bamberg.

bisects the town. Experience has taught Bamberg's merchants that in the long run it is cheaper to build of brick than of wood, and since the last fires twenty-one of the twenty-five stores have been rebuilt of brick.

The residence portion of the town covers a large area, and some of the houses are very handsome, and most of them are surrounded with flower gardens and shrubbery.

The health of Bamberg is very good. During the past two years the drainage of the town has been greatly improved and cases of malarial fever are only sporadic, while throat and lung troubles are unknown here.

The intendant of Bamberg is D.L. Copeland, who in public spirit and faith in his town is to Bamberg what Mike Brown is to Barnwell. The wardens are J.P. Murphy, John F. Folk, H.F. Spann, and S.W. Johnson. The town marshal is William P. Jones.

The municipal tax is two mills, and the town owns a fine building with two stores on the first floor and a spacious hall above, which is used as an assembly room and for public entertainments.

There are four churches in Bamberg, two white and two colored. The white churches are the Baptist, the Rev. C.P. Ervin, and the Methodist, the Rev. J.L. Stokes. Both churches are in a prosperous condition, with large memberships and fine Sunday-schools.

The Bamberg Graded School is one of the best in the State for the size of the town. The building, designed by Architect Niernsee of Columbia, is very attractive, and the average attendance is upwards of one hundred pupils. The principal is Prof. R.H. Willis, a very competent instructor, and his assistant is Miss Zula Skinner.

There are three private schools, taught by Miss Ida Bamberg, Mrs. M.M. Roach, and B.P. Izlar.

Prof. Klein, an accomplished musician, who has been teaching in Walterboro for some time, has recently removed here and has opened classes for music.

A prosperous institution is the Bamberg Bank. The capital is $25,000, surplus and undivided profits $8,500, and deposits $30,000. The president is F.M. Bamberg and the cashier is H.J. Brabham, both splendid business men. The directors are I.S. Bamberg, F.M. Bamberg, E.R. Hays, J.D. Copeland, C.R. Brabham, and H.J. Brabham.

Two months ago Dr. D.H. Witherspoon, who was for some years the editor of the *Clarendon Enterprise,* moved here and established the *Bamberg Advertiser,* a live and newsy paper, which is certain to prove an important factor in the development of the adopted town of its able and energetic editor. The *Advertiser* is a four-page, seven-column paper, which has already secured a fair circulation and a large advertising patronage.

At a citizens' meeting two months ago a committee was appointed to ascertain the cost of sinking an Artesian well, and the meeting recommended a municipal appropriation of as much as $2,000 for that purpose. When the committee shall have secured the necessary information and make their report there is little doubt that the project will be consummated.

Bamberg ships annually 10,000 bales of cotton, and distributes 2,000 tons of fertilizers. The total business of the town, including merchandise, cotton, and melons, is at least $1,000,000 a year. The merchants are: J.D. Copeland, dealer in general merchandise, cotton, and guano; Cope & Brabham, general merchandise; C.R. Brabham, general merchandise; Thomas Black, general merchandise; H.C. Falk & Co., general merchandise; D.L. Copeland, general merchandise; J.B. Black, general merchandise; J.F. Falk, general merchandise and saloon; J.W. Barr, dry goods and clothing; J.P. Murphy, general merchandise and saloon; J.B. Black, drug store; R.B. Black, general merchandise; Fripp & Rentz, general merchandise; Wanamaker & Simmons, drug store; J.D. Miley, general merchandise; C. Sahlman, general merchandise; J.J. Jones, agent, general merchandise; M.A. Moye, general merchandise; Hornik & Ettinger, general merchandise; G.P. Bamberg, harness and buggies; T.A. Green, dealer in harness, wagons, etc., and wagon factory; Delk & Sandifer, wagons, etc.; Miss Sallie Rice, millinery; Bennett Bros., general merchandise; G.O. Varn, saloon; J.M. Heath, bakery; R.B. Porter, shoe shop; Mrs. S.M. Pearson, millinery; S.M. Pearson, photographer; Martin Breland, shoe shop; T.C. Rouis, jeweller; and R.L. Hopton, barber.

For a number of years Bamberg has been a large distributing point for horses and mules. The dealers are men of large capital and experience in the business and custom has been attracted here from distant points which were really tributary to other towns. The stock dealers are T.J. Counts, E.R. Hays & Son, and G.P. Bamberg.

The Bamberg Hotel is admirably conducted by Mr. S.W. Johnson.

President Harrison has recently appointed A.G. Varn, postmaster, to succeed Mr. D.F. Hooten, who had given thorough satisfaction to the Bamberg public.

Mr. A.V. Eaves is the courteous agent of the South Carolina Railway and the Southern Express Company, and also manager of the Western Union Telegraph office.

The physicians are: Drs. F.J. Wanamaker, J.B. Black, D.W. Barton, and J.F. Baggot, and the dentists are: Drs. H.J. Mouzon and O.D. Faust.

Mr. D.J. Rowe is trial justice here.

In so strong an agricultural community it is natural that the Farmers' Alliance should have a firm foothold. The local branch of the Alliance here is very strong, and its officers are: W.S. Bamberg, president; F.F. Johnson, secretary; P.J. Ziegler, lecturer; and C.B. Free, business manager.

While the writer gladly pays tribute to the social worth and business ability of the people of Bamberg, the town needs no other advertisement so long as Dave Copeland holds the mayor's portfolio. Whether reluctantly drinking water at Glenn Springs, or joyfully imbibing mountain dew under the shadow of great Pisgah; whether with his life in his hand umpiring a game of Hendersonville base ball, or with the breath of the balsam in his nostrils, and the recollection of Lot's

The home of Major William Seaborn Bamberg, built c. 1885.

wife in his heart, handing a party of ladies over the stepping stones of the laughing Swannanoa, he ever wears his faith in Bamberg as a cockade in his hat and as a chip upon his shoulder, and he who would unpin the one or knock off the other must be more adventurous than [A.E.G.].

News and Courier, June 19, 1889. A.E.G.

Barnwell—County and County Seat

Once a cattle-raising empire and a region devoted to horse racing and fine horse flesh, Barnwell County at first shunned railroads, a decision that had profound effect upon the seat of county government. But in the early 1880s the town of Barnwell finally got a rail line, and with it came considerable economic growth and development.

* * *

In the latter part of the eighteenth century Barnwell, called at first Winton County, was formed from a portion of Orangeburg District, and for a hundred years her citizens have been prominent in the social, political, and industrial development of South Carolina. In the early days of the county the people were pastoral, and vast herds of cattle fed through the virgin forests, untracked previously save by the Indians and the game they followed. In fact, until the soft white fingers of the cotton queen throttled other industries, stock raising was very extensively carried on in this section. It is said that on the immense farm of Col. Maham there were 700 brood mares.

Seventy-five years ago horse shows were held here, and about the same time the Sherwood Track was laid out and the first races were run. Stock raising being stimulated by these events, blood horses were brought into the neighborhood, and many noted stallions have left their impress upon the Barnwell horses, which for generations have been famous saddle and draft animals. Col. Cash, Major Bacon, and other racing men brought their stables here frequently, and it is an interesting fact that on the day that the Ordinance of Secession was passed races were run on the Sherwood course, which were really the first, last, and only races run in the "free and independent Commonwealth of South Carolina." All of the horses which participated on that day perished on Virginia battlefields in the Confederate service.

At one time many prominent Charlestonians owned estates in this county, among them, John Rutledge, the "dictator." Upon one of his plantations on the Upper Three Runs near the Savannah River there is an immense mill dam constructed, tradition says, by negroes who carried the earth with rush fanners. By the water power thus developed several saw mills were operated, and the lumber was rafted down the Savannah River and around to Charleston.

The lands of Barnwell County are naturally good, and they are capable of very rapid improvement. The country is almost level, with excellent drainage through the swamps and streams which flow into the Savannah and Salkehatchie rivers. The soil is generally light gray and porous with a red clay subsoil, with here and there a belt of red or "mulatto" land, which is highly valued. Cotton is the great staple here, and Barnwell is near the top of the list of cotton producing counties in the United States.

When the South Carolina Railroad was projected, it was proposed by the engineers to run it through the rich country several miles to the west of its present course through Barnwell County, but there was so much opposition shown by wealthy landowners to its passage through their property that the route was changed and diverted nine miles from the county seat. The short-sightedness of these opponents has been shown in the subsequent creation and development of Blackville, Bamberg, Graham, Williston, Midway, and other towns along the line of the railroad, which traverses what is now the richest portion of the county.

For a short time after the county of Barnwell was formed the assizes were held several miles from the present county seat. A year or two thereafter the Court House was moved to this place, which was then a stopping place on the stage route between New York, Charleston, and New Orleans, known previously as the Old Cherokee Trail.

Having no railroad connection, the village grew slowly. A handful of wealthy planters and graziers and a few lawyers formed about all the population. It was a charming place to visit, truly, but having no business or commercial importance to speak of.

The railroad from Blackville to Barnwell Court House was contemplated about 1845, and the first experimental line was run in 1848. Nothing more was done, however, until just previous to the war when $40,000 or $50,000 was raised and the road graded, trestled, and laid with crossties. Before the iron could be secured the war put a stop to work, and Sherman subsequently burned the crossties. The road was then sold for taxes, bought by Col. W.H. Duncan, and then resold to a Mr. Woodward, who laid it with wooden rails and hauled lumber over it to his saw mill.

Bought by the South Carolina Railroad about eight years ago, the road was ironed and a regular schedule was inaugurated. One year ago Col. Mike Brown secured the property and has spent a great deal of money in the purchase of steel rails, the filling up of trestles, and the general raising and improvement of the road bed.

The town of Barnwell has grown with the railroad. It has now 1,500 inhabitants, and is rapidly increasing its business and its population. The intendant is Mr. G. Duncan Bellinger, and the wardens are Messrs. N.G.W. Walker, M.J. Pate, F.H. Brown, and Alonzo Harriman. The town marshal is Mr. C.B. Swann, and he is one of the best in the State.

The educational facilities of Barnwell are excellent. The graded school is an admirable one and is ably presided over by Prof. B.L. Clark, a graduate of the Citadel Academy. Prof. Clark is assisted by Miss Anna Walker and Miss Hallonquist. The daily attendance is nearly 150 pupils. There are also several private schools where music and modern languages are taught.

There are five churches in Barnwell. The Episcopal, the Rev. Mr. Cornish; the

Church of the Holy Apostles, Barnwell, completed in 1857. *Photograph by Carl Julien, reproduced by permission of the University of South Carolina Press from* Sea Islands to Sand Hills. *South Caroliniana Library.*

Baptist, the Rev. Mr. Bradford; the Methodist, the Rev. Mr. Kistler; the Presbyterian, the Rev. Mr. Dow; and the Catholic, Father Wedenfellow.

There are four hotels in Barnwell and the travelling public are well cared for. In fact, the fare and attention will compare very favorably with that of more pretentious establishments in larger places. The Molair House is owned by Leroy Molair; the Brown House, by Benj. Davies; Pechman's Hotel, by Chas. Pechman; and the Patterson House, by Jno. C. Dowling.

Barnwell has two excellent weekly newspapers, both Democratic, of course, and extensively circulated through the county. The *Sentinel* is one of the landmarks of this section and is edited and managed by Mr. John J. Brunson. The *People* is owned and edited by Major John W. Holmes, a graceful and pungent writer, whose essay read at last summer's meeting of the State Press Association at Greenville will be remembered with pleasure by the readers of the *News and Courier.* Major Holmes is a bachelor and would like to mend his ways.

The municipal authorities of Barnwell have now in course of construction a fine brick building two stories high and measuring 50 by 100 feet. The lower floor will contain two handsome stores, while the upper will be devoted to a hall or theatre, which will be attractively decorated and fitted with a modern stage, opera chairs, scenery, and all that pertains to a first-class place of amusement. The building will also contain a council chamber and lodge rooms.

The public-spirited town council are boring an Artesian well in the public park near the centre of the town. They have already reached a depth of 800 feet, and it is proposed to sink the well 1,200 or 1,300 feet, if necessary, to obtain an ample supply of water for municipal purposes. As soon as sufficient water is secured, a system of pipes and water-works will be established. For the safe-keeping of those visitors who imbibe too freely of the waters of Turkey Creek the council are constructing a strong and commodious guard house of brick and iron.

The Masons of Barnwell are about to erect a handsome temple at a cost of $6,000. The structure will measure 40 by 80 feet and will be built of brick on the lot owned by Harmony Lodge. Two large stores will occupy the first floor, and the hall and several rooms will be above.

Eighteen months ago the Barnwell Bank was established and commenced work in a handsome brick and iron building on the public square. The president is Gen. Johnson Hagood; the vice-president, Col. Mike Brown; and the cashier, Mr. Theo. J. Simons. The bank has been very successful, and at the close of business on January 31, 1889, had assets of over $125,000.

There is every probability that before the next cotton season opens Barnwell will have a large cotton seed oil mill and fertilizer factory. A part of the money required for such an establishment has been guaranteed, and the additional amount needed will be forthcoming in a few months.

A Barnwell enterprise that deserves special notice is the carriage and wagon factory of G.W. Price. This establishment is provided with some of the best modern machinery for planing and woodworking, and in the iron department there are several forges and all necessary appliances for turning out first-class work. Above the shops is an extensive painting and finishing room.

Mr. J.W. Woodward operates a large saw and planing mill near Barnwell and makes very heavy shipments of lumber to northern points. He is now filling an order for 500,000 feet for a Philadelphia firm.

Mr. W.H. Hagood, Jr., also runs a saw mill, grist mill, and cotton gins, and Col. Mike Brown's cotton gins at this place have a capacity of forty bales per day.

Col. Mike Brown is the president and Col. Butler Hagood the secretary and treasurer of the recently organized "Watermelon Alliance" for South Carolina. The melon industry is a large one here, bringing a business to this town alone of perhaps $300,000 per annum.

The cotton receipts of Barnwell are upwards of 6,000 bales, and 2,000 tons of commercial fertilizers are distributed from here annually. The merchants have a rich country to draw upon, and the commercial business of the town is large and steadily increasing. Mike Brown occupies a fine brick store on Main Street and deals extensively in cotton, groceries, dry goods, clothing, hardware, mules, horses, and fertilizers. Other merchants are: McNab, Walker & Co., general merchandise; J.J. Heffernan, dry goods, millinery, and shoes; Charles Pechman, general merchandise; Leroy Molair, general merchandise and saloon; T. Vogel, general merchandise; George K. Ryan, fancy groceries; T.S. Cave, millinery; Mrs. L. Molair, millinery; F.H. Brown, drugs and fancy goods; J.A. Tobin, drugs and notions; A.B. Patterson, drugs and fancy goods; C.F. Nurmberger, general merchandise; S.L. Knopf, general merchandise and optician; John J. Brunson, general store; G.K. Ryan, fancy bakery; Benj. Davies, general merchandise and saloon; C.C. Califf, saloon; Furman Brothers, saloon; J.H. Tobin, saloon; W.R. Christie, saloon; E.W. Vogel, general store; S.L. Heath, beef market; and B.P. Rodgers, blacksmith shop.

Members of the Barnwell Bar include Judge John J. Maher, G. Duncan Bellinger (master), Charles Carroll Simms, B.T. Rice, G.H. Bates, J.M. Skinner, W.H. Duncan, A.H. Patterson, J.J. Brown, Geo. G. Thompson, A.M. Owens, Robert Aldrich, James E. Davis, John C. Davant, R.A. Ellis, J.B. Burckhalter, A.T. Woodward, W.A. Holman, H. Melvin Myers, and J.O. Patterson.

The physicians are J.J. O'Bannon, A.B. Patterson, G.R.C. Tedd, R.C. Kirkland, and W.F. Helmse. Dr. Patterson has recently established an eye, ear, and throat infirmary with rooms at the Brown House, where he will make a specialty of the treatment of these diseases.

The county officers are W. Gilmore Simms, clerk of court; S.W. Trotti, auditor; J.W. Lancaster, sheriff; N.F. Kirkland, Sr., treasurer; and J.O. Patterson, probate judge. The county commissioners are N.M. Walker, W.B. Chitty, and J.A. Chassereau.

With Miss G.L. Tobin as postmaster, the Barnwell post office is in good hands and the public are well served.

The health of Barnwell is excellent. A case of consumption has never been known here, and there has been no diphtheria, typhoid fever, or pneumonia here for a generation. Turkey Creek, a beautiful stream, flows along the base of the elevation upon which the town is built, and the drainage is perfect. Altogether Barnwell is a most enjoyable place to visit, for climate, for business, and for society. The "parting guest" lingers with reluctant feet, and when handsome John Willis, the veteran conductor, gives the signal for departure, the last on board his train is [A.E.G.].

News and Courier, February 25, 1889. A.E.G.

Blacksburg, Where Railroads Meet

In December of 1888, the Charleston, Cincinnati, and Chicago Railroad opened a stretch of track from the capital of York County to Rutherfordton, North Carolina, and reporter Edward P. McKissick was on one of the first trains to travel over this new line. Among the stops made before crossing into North Carolina were Sharon, Hickory Grove, Blacksburg, Earl's, and Patterson's. In addition, a station to be known as Smyrna—a shipping point for iron ore, pyrite, manganese, and other minerals—soon would be opened four miles north of Hickory Grove. "Blacksburg," McKissick noted, "is so prosperous and progressive a place that it is necessary to write of it in a separate letter, which will be published hereafter." That letter, printed with his report of the rail journey, describes a wide-awake community whose population increased dramatically during the 1880s, up from 145 to 1,245.

* * *

It will not be inappropriate, perhaps, in the beginning of this communication to remark that the name of this thriving village was changed from "Black's" to the present name by an act of the last Legislature, and hence the name may not be very familiar to the readers of the *News and Courier.*

Not many years ago a station was built on the Piedmont Air Line Railway, just twenty-nine miles from Spartanburg, at the foot of Whittaker's Mountain. The station was first known as Black's Station. It was not until a short while ago that the name was changed to "Black's," and now it has been metamorphosed into "Blacksburg." The place was named in honor of the well-known family of Blacks which has been established in this section a very long time, and which is famous for the men it has produced who have made themselves known in State affairs and as sterling and worthy citizens.

Blacksburg and its opportunity have met, and its opportunity is the great iron highway which binds Charleston with the Ohio River. And the prevailing impression is that Blacksburg has grasped its opportunity and will make the most of it, which means, in a word, that Blacksburg will in the near future develop into a city of more or less magnitude. The rapid transit of the Charleston, Cincinnati, and Chicago Railroad to Charleston makes Blacksburg in one sense a suburb of the City by the Sea, and by this her chances for development are greatly augmented. The completion of the great Three C's Road to Blacksburg has already been fully described in the *News and Courier,* and the fact of its completion has awakened the deepest interest in Charleston in everything that tends to the advancement and prosperity of the people of Blacksburg.

Train station, Blacksburg. *South Caroliniana Library.*

The situation of Blacksburg is especially advantageous. The town is built on an undulating plateau at the foot of the famous Whittaker's Mountain. The streets are laid out with care and are kept in the best condition. The stores are built in various parts of the town, although a majority are on Main Street. The structures, while not pretentious, are of a substantial character and are all conveniently arranged. There are a number of very handsome private residences in Blacksburg, noticeable among which are those of Major J.F. Jones, Mrs. J.A. Deal, and Dr. J.G. Black. But the most important considerations in the situation of Blacksburg are the fact that it is at the junction of the Atlanta and Charlotte Air Line Railway and the Three C's Railroad and that the county around abounds in minerals.

The municipal government of Blacksburg is in the hands of a mayor and four aldermen. Mr. A.B. Crosby is the mayor and is supported by a sterling set of aldermen. The manner in which the government is controlled and the prosperity of Blacksburg advanced is a sufficient guarantee that the council are trustworthy and valuable men. Heretofore Blacksburg has been a dry town, but by a special enactment licenses will be granted hereafter to sell whiskey within the town.

The health of Blacksburg is excellent, and it is noteworthy that no epidemics have ever occurred here, but in case a stranger should fall ill he would be in no danger of suffering for lack of attention, as there are five physicians resident here whose practice necessarily extends to the surrounding country. The population of Blacksburg is now estimated at 1,300 and is increasing every day.

There are fourteen mercantile establishments here, all of which do a good and lucrative business. There are two blacksmith shops, two livery stables, and two hotels, and it is stated that each of these establishments is very successful. There is also a lime kiln which is successfully operated by Simon Brothers, the well-known lime manufacturers of Limestone Springs near Gaffney.

Blacksburg has good educational advantages, and the indications are that these will be materially increased in the near future. Permission was granted by the last Legislature for the levy of a tax to erect a building for a graded school at a cost of $8,000. The present school at Blacksburg is a high school, of which Prof. J.T. Moore is principal. Prof. Moore, who has two associates, is a former student of the South Carolina College and is well qualified for his position. There are about one hundred and twenty-five pupils in attendance upon this institution, and the attendance is daily increasing under the successful management of Prof. Moore.

There are four white churches and four colored churches in Blacksburg. The Baptist, Methodist, Presbyterian, and Episcopal churches are all substantial and handsome structures, while the churches of the colored people are neat and comfortable buildings.

This section abounds in a great diversity of valuable minerals. The iron ore is taking the lead and its latest developments have been marvellous. The soft ores were the only species that could be worked in the charcoal blast furnaces of the old regime, but now the most valuable ores, the hard ones, which are found in great quantities, can be reduced in the stone coal hot blast furnaces.

A company has been formed of Atlanta and Birmingham capitalists, known as the Magnetic Iron and Steel Ore Company, and are now, with a strong force of hands, exposing immense lodes of iron ore at and around Blacksburg. A Richmond company has also begun operations. Both companies have considerable means and have bought several thousand acres of mineral lands. An average of these ores on analysis shows from 60 to 65 per cent.

The iron ores occur in lodes. The richest yet discovered is the Black-Wilson lode. This lies near the surface and seems to cover a great extent and is made up of the very finest magnetic oxides.

Lying beside the iron ore is limestone and manganese used in the manufacture of steel. Around this locality is found the grey or magnetic oxide, and the red or hermatite ores, limestone, manganese, kaolin, fireproof clay, tin, asbestos, talcose, with a variety of clays and slates. These minerals are found along the King's Mountain range, on which Blacksburg is located, and in Broad River that runs directly across this formation. By dredging these minerals can be taken from the bottom of the river.

In company with Col. J.H. Averill, Mr. W.F. Marshall, and Major J.F. Jones, who kindly drove the party to one of the mines, this correspondent had an opportunity of seeing the vast quantities of valuable ore that have already been extracted from the mines. All the mines in and around Blacksburg will be worked as soon as sufficient machinery can be brought to this place. Prof. Pratt, the State geologist of Georgia, who has visited Blacksburg at different times and made thorough investigations of the ores and their mineralogical situation, says that the ore is of the best and most valuable quality, and from all appearances the deposit is exhaustless. A large quantity of ore has already been shipped from this place to different points.

In this connection it may be well to state that if the water transportation can be had at Charleston, large quantities of ore will be shipped over the Three C's Road to eastern points via Charleston, and thus Charleston will reap a benefit from the mineral deposits of this section.

One of the attractions of Blacksburg is Whittaker's Mountain, upon which a park is now being laid out which will be known as "Overlook Park." In the centre of the park, on the very highest portion of the mountain, is now being built an observatory which will be fifty-two feet in height and will be handsomely furnished with every convenience and a fine glass. The work is being done under the direct supervision of Major J.F. Jones.

The scenery from the top of the mountain is grand and sublime and is said to equal, if not surpass, that which is obtained from the Battery Park Hotel in Asheville. The Blue Ridge range can be easily seen, and as we stood on the celebrated Indian mound and looked toward Charleston the spire of St. Michael's was almost visible (in imagination), while on the other side the cities of Chicago and Cincinnati were some distance beyond the horizon. The scene was a dream, and it would require a poet's pen to describe the profound loveliness and grandeur of the surrounding country.

It is proposed to build a hotel on the mountain, but no decided action has been thus far taken in the matter. On the south side of this mountain the now celebrated cavern and underground river are natural attractions. None of the party who visited the mountain manifested any desire to descend into the well, or cavern, and so we did not visit that place. Dr. John G. Black, Col. R.A. Johnston, Major John F. Jones, and M.R. Reese have formed a joint stock company for the purpose of opening and exploring the cavern, and the work is progressing as rapidly as possible, although no developments of an important nature have yet been made.

It will thus be seen that the resources of Blacksburg are numerous and valuable. The people here are alive to the needs of the hour and are making use of their resources in a manner that insures abundant success.

News and Courier, December 31, 1888. E.P.McK.

Blackville, the Town of the Phoenix

Having survived numerous conflagrations between 1865 and 1888—including one set by General Sherman's men—in the winter of 1889 this Barnwell County community finally seemed to be on the road to success. Although thwarted in efforts to become the seat of county government, it was a regional rail center with an academy, five churches, five saloons, a steam bakery, an undertaking establishment, and four livery stables ... but no bank. Despite lingering wartime memories, the Gordon Volunteers, a local militia unit, recently had adopted the regulation United States uniform.

* * *

About the year 1833, when the South Carolina Railroad reached the present site of Blackville, a little village struggled into existence and at once commenced a certain amount of business. The village became a town by an Act of the Legislature in 1846, and at the beginning of the war the population was about three hundred and fifty.

Sherman, the great cremationist, swept the town with fire on February 7, 1865. The work of rebuilding was immediately begun, however, and the town grew steadily. On December 15, 1876, one or two blocks of wooden buildings were destroyed by fire, giving the plucky town another check. On March 16, 1887, a most disastrous fire swept away almost the entire business portion of Blackville. Every building on the south side of the railroad, covering an area of twelve acres, was burned, and again on May 16, 1888, the northern part of the town was destroyed by fire.

The buildings destroyed were almost without exception constructed of wood, while at present there are but two wooden stores in the town. On both sides of Railroad Avenue, the main thoroughfare, and upon many of the side streets stand handsome brick stores of one, two, and three stories in height, many of them with attractive iron fronts and spacious show windows. Not a few of these stores would compare favorably in size, in appearance, and in convenient arrangement with the best of those in large cities.

Blackville is built on an elevated pine ridge four or five hundred feet above the level of the sea, almost in the centre of the fruit and melon belt, and is surrounded by a fine agricultural district yielding abundant crops of cotton, corn, and small grain. To the north of the town stretch thousands of acres of the finest yellow pine timber, while in the swamps and lowlands there is a quantity of ash, hickory, oak, and cypress, which could be utilized for small manufactures.

The present population of Blackville is 1,600. The net shipments of cotton are upwards of 12,000 bales, and fully 4,000 tons of guano are distributed from this point. Three hundred carloads of melons will be shipped from here during the coming summer, and the commercial business of the town aggregates $1,000,000 —altogether a showing that would do credit to many places of twice her population.

This is the more remarkable because Blackville is not a county seat and cannot command the business which is attracted by the sessions of court and the necessary results of the residence of lawyers and county officials in Court House towns.

The Barnwell Railroad connects this place with Barnwell Court House, the South Carolina Railway with Augusta and Charleston; and the Blackville, Alston, and Newberry Road has already penetrated a region of splendidly timbered land and kaolin beds to a point within thirty miles of Columbia. There is a project on foot for connecting Columbia with Savannah by a route said to be only 136 miles in length, forty miles of which is now covered by the Blackville, Alston, and Newberry and the Barnwell railroads.

The intendant of Blackville is M.W. Felder. The wardens are P.J. Drew, J.W. Martin, O.C. Able, and H.J. Bruce. The chief of police is John Gribbin, also superintendent of streets, who has put a stop to vagabondage in Blackville by employing tramps and loafers to the great benefit of the streets and sidewalks.

Blackville has a good fire department equipped with a hand engine and hook and ladder trucks, reels, &c. It is proposed to secure in the near future a first-class steamer and to bore an Artesian well and construct a system of water-works. The chief of the fire department is J.D. Levy. The assistant chief is Tom Walsh. D.F. Drew is second and R.C. Laughlin third assistant.

The Blackville Academy building is a spacious brick structure erected for the Court House when it was proposed to change the county seat from Blackwell to this place. The lower story contains several classrooms, and the entire upper floor is used as a hall or assembly room. The building is well lighted, heated, and ventilated. The principal is the Rev. Arthur Buist, and Miss Minnie Buist is his assistant. About one hundred pupils are enrolled and the system of instruction is admirable. A private school, taught by Miss O'Beirne, is also very well attended. The colored schools are ample and the attendance is large.

There are five churches here: the Baptist, the Rev. Mr. Jasper, pastor; the Methodist, the Rev. Mr. Ariel, pastor; the Episcopal, the Rev. J.H. Cornish, pastor; the Roman Catholic, Father Wilson, rector; and the Presbyterian, the Rev. Mr. Dow, pastor.

The Molony House, owned by M.F. Molony, Blackville's oldest citizen, is well known to the travelling public and is liberally patronized.

Any notice of Blackville would be incomplete without mention of the Gordon Volunteers, the especial pride of this town and section. Organized in 1877, they have from year to year added to their numbers and improved their military standing until today the organization is one of the best drilled and equipped in the State. They have recently adopted the United States regulation uniform and present a very handsome appearance. The officers of the company are: L.T. Izlar, captain;

Old courthouse, Blackville. *Photograph by Carl Julien, reproduced by permission of the University of South Carolina Press from* Sea Islands to Sand Hills. *South Caroliniana Library.*

J.S. Buist, first lieutenant; J.H. Levy, second lieutenant; P.J. Drew, third lieutenant; and Tom Walsh, color bearer.

The grand ball recently given here by the Volunteers, a full description of which appeared in the *News and Courier,* was a brilliant social event and was attended by guests from Columbia, Augusta, and Charleston.

Several saw mills have recently been established here and large quantities of lumber are shipped to points on the South Carolina Railroad and to Charleston for export. Among those operating saw and planing mills are Messrs. G.B. Lartigue, W.S.H. Brooker, J.E. Hair, and W.T. Walker. There are three firms engaged in the business of manufacturing wagons, buggies, carts, etc.: Messrs. C.C. Rush, Disher & Pickrum, and M.J. Dodds. The industry is an important one, and a large number of vehicles are made and sold not only here but through a large section of the surrounding country. Messrs. Howard Brothers have a well equipped machine shop and do a large amount of repairing of all kinds of machinery.

The merchants are: Simon Brown, wholesale and retail dealer in guano and general merchandise and cotton buyer; P.W. Farrell, extensive dealer in cotton, mules, horses, and general merchandise; W.J. Martin, dealer in cotton, general merchandise, mules, horses, and guano; Briggs, Buist & Co., large dealers in cotton, general merchandise, mules, horses, and guano; J.J. Weissinger, general merchandise and cotton; O.O. Able, dealer in cotton, general merchandise, and guano; J.L. Morrison & Co., general merchandise and cotton; F.P. Groves, dealer in general merchandise and guano; C.E. Gyles, cotton and general merchandise; A.J. Levy, general merchandise and saloon; Still Bros., general merchandise; J.H. Borger, fancy groceries and restaurant; B.J. Hammett, dealer in fancy groceries; Green B. Rich, jeweller and optician; G.D.O. Lange, fancy store and newsdealer; James Kelly, fancy groceries; A. Stone, dealer in drugs and fancy goods; G. Barber, steam bakery; D.K. Briggs & Co., dealers in drugs and fancy goods; D.R. Drew & Co., saloon; J.L. Buist, fancy groceries; W.B. Meyers, saloon; Kitrell & Co., groceries; A.C. Gill, fruiterer; W.H. Devitt, saloon; L. Feldman & Co., saloon; Paul Sanders, dealer in fruit and fish; T.A. Rhoden, watchmaker and jeweller; Baker's London Art Gallery; A. Edwins, saddler and harness maker; Henry Smith, tailor; W.S. Moss, tinware; Mrs. L. Strobel, fruit and fancy groceries; Walter Bennett, tailor; John Newton, butcher; B.R. Carroll, general merchandise; W.S. Moss, butcher; C.C. Rush, general merchandise; A.A. Henderson, restaurant; M.F. Molony & Son, undertakers; Oliver Washington, barber shop; and Martin Keeler, shoe shop.

There are four livery stables owned by Simon Brown, P.W. Farrell, Briggs, Buist & Co., and M.F. Molony. Messrs. William H. Nevils and Morrison & Co. operate cotton gins and grist mills. There is a large ice house in Blackville owned by Messrs. Turner & Henderson. Ice is purchased in the spring in carload lots, stored here, and distributed during the summer to different points on the three lines of railroad which meet at this place.

Miss M.E. Maher is in charge of the Blackville post office. As there is no bank here the money order business is very heavy. Miss Maher and her assistant, Mrs. Felder, manage the business of the office admirably and are attentive to the wants of the public.

There are four physicians here: Drs. G.B. Lartigue, L.C. Stephens, D.K. Briggs, and A. Storne. As their services are very seldom needed in Blackville they are compelled to practice over a large area of the surrounding country. The dentists are Drs. H.A. Ray and J.H.E. Milhous. Dr. Stephens is chairman of the board of health.

One peculiarity of the place is its extraordinary immunity from serious lung infections. Only three or four cases of consumption have ever occurred here, and not one of them was a native of Blackville. Pneumonia and pleurisy are very rare. This freedom from pulmonary complaints is traceable doubtless to Blackville's almost complete environment of dense pine forests, which temper the cutting winds in boisterous weather.

Blackville needs a bank, and as her citizens are willing to subscribe liberally towards the establishment of one here, there should be no trouble about its being organized by the opening of the next cotton season. With the large cotton and commercial business done here, a bank should pay handsomely.

There is also a good opening here for a cotton seed oil mill and fertilizer factory. The admirable railroad facilities would enable Blackville to secure cotton seed at a low price and deliver the manufactured fertilizers cheaper than they could be ordered from a greater distance.

Blackville wants a small cotton factory to be run by steam. There are thousands of cords of fine lightwood rotting in the woods that would be available for fuel. There is abundant brick clay here, and bricks can be made and laid cheaply, and the cotton is at their very doors.

The Blackville people have already all the work they can attend to, but there is a splendid opening here for some active man with command of capital to come here and establish a bank, an oil mill, or a cotton factory. Blackville will subscribe largely to any or all of these enterprises, and when they shall have been secured there is little reason to doubt that, with her fine climate and magnificent agricultural resources, Blackville will take the place in the commercial world to which she is entitled by reason of the splendid pluck and unbounded energy of her citizens.

News and Courier, February 26, 1889 A.E.G.

Camden, the City on the Wateree

After paying homage to Camden's historic past, its role in the Revolutionary War, and the famed visit of Lafayette, reporter John I. Green turned his attention to the community as it appeared to him in December of 1889.* Although still an agricultural-commercial center, the state's oldest inland town was fast becoming something of a health resort. In this instance, we are told, a unique gravel and sand soil produced a remarkably dry climate, and this same sand also filtered the drinking water, making it extremely pure. In any case, inns and hotels were developing to cater to winter tourists from the North, none of them more unusual, it would seem, than Uphton Court.

* * *

Camden stands on a well-drained plateau about two hundred and fifty feet above the sea and seventy-five feet above the Wateree River. It is beautifully laid out. The streets are unusually broad and run north and south. There are several public squares and parks, which are well shaded and well kept. The surrounding country produces a great variety of crops, the forests along the river furnish all sorts of hard woods, and the pinelands are a boundless field to the enterprising lumberman and distiller.

While cotton and rice are the commercial staples, they are by no means the only crops which flourish here. All sorts of grains are cultivated to perfection, and any kind of vegetable which can be grown in the South thrives in the fields of Kershaw. Both the soil and the climate—particularly the latter—are especially adapted to grape culture, and a little enterprise in the matter of vineyards will give proof of the capabilities of the land. It will not be long before canning factories will be erected, for there are exceptional inducements for such enterprises. And soon flourishing vineyards will dot the county, and streams of abundance will pour from their presses.

Camden stands at the head of navigation on the Wateree, and there is no reason why a line of steamboats on this stream would not pay. One would have been built long ago but for the lack of capital. The distance by rail to Charleston is 137 miles, to Augusta 160 miles, to Columbia 60 miles, and to Rock Hill 60 miles. At the latter point connection is made with the Charlotte, Columbia, and Augusta Road for the North, and at Blacksburg, on the main line of the Richmond and Danville system, connection is made with the West. The Charleston, Cincinnati, and Chicago Road will soon connect in Eastern Tennessee with the Western systems, giving the place a direct line to the great Western markets. Several other lines

*See also an article on Camden by Matthew F. Tighe that appeared in the *News and Courier,* April 4, 1888.

are projected. These will shorten the distance to the North and Southwest. New York is now twenty-four hours distant.

Give a place a score of railroads and a soil as fertile as the lands of the Nile, and it is a failure if it is not healthy. The climate of this place is its greatest drawing card. In these days, when every village with a little spring is advertising itself as a wonderful health resort, statistics are of more interest than all-healing claims. Here are a few figures which speak more eloquently than the most gorgeous superlatives:

Camden is in latitude 34 deg 17 min and 80 deg 83 min west longitude. The mean temperature for thirty-two years was as follows—spring 61.90°, summer 79.32°, autumn 62.26°, winter 45.16°; annual 62.16°. The average rainfall for twenty years was 4.2222 inches.* The average death rate was 12½ per thousand. These data were furnished the Smithsonian Institution by Mr. Colin McRae, the observer at this place for the national signal service. In summer pleasant breezes moderate the warmest weather, and the nights are usually cool. A light snow falls about every alternate year.

But read what another has to say. Dr. Willard Parker, Jr., writing in the *Medical Record,* says of Camden:

> Owing to the peculiar nature of the soil, all moisture is almost immediately absorbed, so that the air is remarkably dry. While there are a few cold days, we find none of penetrating cold; nor, on the other hand, do we have any of that enervating heat met with in places farther south. The pine trees and turpentine stills in the vicinity give the air a terebinthine odor, which is very soothing to those harassed by a cough. My two children, neither of whom had ever before passed a winter free from croup, showed not a symptom of it, though exposed in all weathers.

Dr. S. Baruch of 44 East 60th Street, New York, writing to the proprietor of Uphton Court, says: "You may refer to me as regards the climate of Camden for consumption, rheumatism, and kidney troubles."** One of the commissioners of the New York State Board of Health writes: "I know Camden well and can truly testify to its high hygienic character. I cannot conceive an epidemic prospering there."

The following from a descriptive pamphlet on Uphton Court is of interest:

> The healthfulness for which Camden is so justly famed is largely due to the soil, which to a great depth is composed entirely of sand and gravel. This insures the maximum degree of dryness, both of the soil itself and of the lower strata of the air above ground. Water is so rapidly absorbed that in a few moments after a heavy rain ladies may, with impunity, walk upon the ground in the thinnest shoes. The remark-

*This is a typographical error and probably should have been 42.222 inches.

**Simon Baruch (1840-1921), Prussian-born father of financier Bernard Baruch, came to America at the age of fifteen, served the Confederacy as a surgeon, and then settled in Camden where he practiced until 1881. According to his famous son, one reason the Baruch family left for Manhattan was the Cash-Shannon duel.

able purity of the drinking water is largely due to the great depth of sand through which it filters.

So unusual were the climatic advantages of this place that many sought them even when many inconveniences had to be borne before they were reached. Seven years ago the Hobkirk Inn was opened. It stands on the outskirts of the town near the site of the battle of Hobkirk's Hill. Capt. E.H. Eldridge, a Northern gentleman, is the proprietor, and from an old-time Southern mansion he has made one of the most comfortable and home-like hostelries in the South. He succeeded from the beginning, and among his guests were many of the wealthiest people of the North and West, some of whom came in their private cars and spent many weeks. The inn has about forty rooms and is luxurious and cosy throughout. The management caters only to tourists who desire to spend several weeks, at least, of the season here.

The first question which one who has been to Camden asks anyone whom he chances to meet is: "Have you been to Uphton Court?" This is a hotel which is not a hotel. I cannot better explain the paradox than by a bit of sketching. A grand old Southern mansion that seems to be sleeping in the sunshine. On three sides broad piazzas. In front a garden filled with choice shrubs and flowers which seem to woo one to stray among the inviting walks and bowers. A little distance to the southeast a grove of towering pines, with a band stand and a profusion of seats and swings.

And then you meet your hostess. Her manner is grace itself and a warm welcome beams from her eyes. You feel at home in a moment. Yes, those are the words, "at home."

And what a home! Faces from brushes of the old masters smile upon you from the walls. Exquisite bric-a-brac is scattered about in profusion, rare and curious volumes fill the bookcases, and the reading table is covered with periodicals and magazines from both continents. The chairs and lounges are of the past generation and recall the days when there was no hurry and bustle, and everyone took his ease at leisure. In the dining room it is the same picture in a different light. The antique silver, the rare china, are all in keeping with what you have already seen. To complete the effect, the waiters are all negroes, who almost anticipate your every wish.

This is Uphton Court. It is the result of an elegant woman's whim. Mrs. Perkins, the "proprietor," as she styles herself, is a descendant of the old aristrocracy, but is something of a cosmopolitan in taste. She has spent many years at the North and in Europe, and those who visit her charming "hotel" will find every luxury of today amidst surroundings of the past. Her descriptive circular is a little volume from her own graceful pen and is a gem of the bookmakers' art.

There are other hotels here where the traveller of modest means may get the worth of his money. The Latham House, under the management of Mr. S.B. Latham, has enjoyed a good patronage for many years, and the Blanton House does a fair share of business. Both are in the centre of the town.

Reynolds House, Camden, c. 1890, built c. 1834 and burned January 1, 1921. *South Caroliniana Library.*

Now that this place is easily reached from every quarter of the nation, the enterprising hotel men of the country would do well to investigate its claims as an all-the-year-round resort. The tourist can find no better drives in the country, and the hunting and fishing are excellent. Every kind of game found in the South abounds in the fields and forests, from the pheasant and duck to the wild turkey and deer of the river swamps. A mammoth hotel will soon be a necessity.

The population of Camden, including Kirkwood, a suburb which is but a continuation of the town proper, is about 2,500. Despite the many obstacles which existed heretofore, the trade of Camden is thriving, and she makes as good a showing as many of her more fortunately located sisters. About 20,000 bales of cotton are shipped annually, and the rice crop runs up into the tens of thousands. The turpentine business is a large industry in itself and centres here. From the most conservative estimates it is safe to say that over a million and a quarter dollars of business is done annually. The merchants are progressive and conduct their business on modern lines. The old-time stores have been replaced by modern ones, and the till in the counters has given way to the most improved cash registers.

For the information of any who desire to engage in business here, the following directory of the business houses is given, showing how the trade is distributed:

General merchandise—N.T. Purdy & Co., P.T. Villepigue, A.D. Kennedy, Baum

Bros. & Stein, J.C. Man, P. Tobias, S.M. Wilson, John R. Goodale & Son, M.S. Bamberg, D. Wolfe, E.H. Dibble, T.M. Shannon, and Isadore Wolfe.

Wholesale grocers—Springs, Heath & Co. and H.G. Carrison.

Dry goods—W.E. Johnson, Jr., Hirsch Bros., and B. Rich.

Drugs, paints, and oils—A.A. Moore, F.L. Zemp and F.M. Zemp.

Retail grocers—V.E. Deepass, Henry Man, Smyrie & Halsell, W.J. Jones, J.F. Arthur, J.W. Blakeney, J.S. Rhame, J.E. Vaughn, J.J. Watkins, J.T. Nettles, and M. Lollis.

Furniture—Baum Bros. & Stein, D. Wolfe, and M.S. Bamberg.

Buggies, wagons, etc.—Smith & Hall, S.B. Latham, and Baum Bros. & Stein.

Hardware—A.D. Kennedy, H.G. Carrison, and John R. Goodale & Son.

Shoes, hats, and clothing—Zemp Bros.

Shoes—E.B. Capers.

Millinery—Mrs. T.B. Walker, Miss Kate Meredith, and Mrs. S. Tweed.

Books, jewelry, cutlery, sewing machines, and fancy goods—G.G. Young.

Jewelry—J.M. LeGrand.

Liquors, tobacco, etc.—A.M. Rosenberger (also restaurant and billiard parlor), W. Geisenheimer, S.B. Latham, B.F. Hate, and Smyrie & Halsell.

Bakery—Robert Singleton.

Saddlery and harness—W.M. Hinson and Henry Wilson.

Undertakers—R.J. McCreight & Son and Smith & Hale.

Sewing machines—J.C. Reville and T.J. Rodgers.

Gunsmith—A.J. Freitag.

Livery and sale stables—S.R. Latham, W.A. Armstrong, and J.C. Cottrell.

Cotton buyers—Springs, Heath & Co. and J.B. Stedman.

Auctioneer—J.S. Meroney.

Insurance—Williams & Williams (fire) and Coutey & DeSaussure (life).

The Bank of Camden has made a record which, its officers say, surpasses that of any other in the State. This institution began business on August 1, 1888, with a capital of $25,000. For six months it did business on a paid in capital of $6,250. The first year it paid a dividend of 10 per cent and placed 6 per cent to its surplus account. The estimated average deposits are $50,000. The officers are H.G. Carrison, president; S.C. Clyburn, vice president; C.H. Yates, cashier; directors, H.G. Carrison, S.C. Clyburn, P.T. Villepigue, A.D. Kennedy, N.T. Purdy, W.M. Shannon, and John C. Man.

The Building and Loan Association was organized in 1883 with 400 shares. This number has been increased to 700. It has loaned $40,000, and its first series of shares have an accrued value of about 55 per cent. The second series has been running about two-and-half years. The outlook is bright, and the shares are increasing in value. The officers of the Association are: P.T. Villepigue, president; A.D. Kennedy, vice president; directors, P.T. Villepigue, A.D. Kennedy, S.M. Rosenberger, F.M. Zemp, C.J. Shannon, J.C. Man, and G. Geisenheimer. The Association has never lost anything.

The Board of Trade is an organization on which the town must largely depend for its advancement. The officers are: A.D. Kennedy, president; H. Baum, vice president; N.T. Purdy, treasurer; and John W. Corbett, secretary.

A fine opera house was built in 1885. It has a frontage of 60 feet, a depth of 70 feet, and is three stories high. It is one of the handsomest theatres in the State. The scenery is very fine, and the auditorium is fitted with very comfortable folding chairs. The building and fittings cost $21,000, $15,000 of which is the only bonded debt that the town has.

The fire department consists of one steamer, two hand engines, and a hook and ladder company. An abundant water supply is furnished by capacious fire wells.

The total levy of taxes is only three mills, which pays all current expenses and the interest on the town's debt.

The average rate of insurance is 1¾ per cent.

There is a fine graded school which was established about two years ago. The attendance numbers 175. A large and competent corps of teachers are in charge. The following is a list of the faculty: A.L. Moore, superintendent; teachers, Mrs. Mary C. Thomason, Mrs. M.A. Shannon, Mrs. N.S. Withers, Miss Lizzie Stoney, and Miss Anna Davis. There is a negro graded school of which W.W. Carter is principal. There are also several private schools which are well patronized.

Nearly all of the religious denominations have churches. The Presbyterian Church is the oldest house of worship in the town. It has a large membership. The pastor is the Rev. W.W. Wells.

The Methodist Church is a handsome brick building. The pastor is the eloquent E.J. Meynardie.

The Episcopal Church, which has been completed recently, is a beautiful Gothic structure. The rector is the Rev. J.M. Stoney.

The Baptist Church has a very large membership. The pastor is the Rev. Paul V. Bomar.

The Bible Society is doing a good work. The depository is at the store of P.T. Villepigue, who is secretary and treasurer. Judge J.B. Kershaw is the president.

The Camden Bar has produced an unusual amount of talent and has sent forth many men to fill high places. The following is the personnel as it stands today: Gen. John D. Kennedy (late consul general at Shanghai), J. Thornwell Hay, Capt. W.M. Shannon, Col. P.H. Nelson (solicitor for the 5th district), W.D. Trantham, E.D. Blakeney, C.L. Winkler, J.D. Dunlap, T.H. Clarke, B.B. Clarke, T.J. Kirkland, and L.A. Wittkowskey.

The physicians are: A.W. Burnett, A.A. Moore, John W. Corbett, D.L. DeSaussure, and F.L. Zemp; dentist, T.H. Alexander.

If other evidence were wanting, the mere fact that Camden has three newspapers would be a guarantee that there was a large amount of culture in town and country.

The *Wateree Messenger* was founded in 1885 by Mr. C.W. Birchmore, an energetic journalist and active citizen, and has grown steadily in circulation and influence.

The *Camden Journal*, established in 1827, has a rather amusing incident connected with the history of its management. Mr. G.G. Alexander was its proprietor when Harrison was elected and was appointed postmaster to supersede Mr. D.C. Kirkley, the Democratic incumbent. These two gentlemen made a happy exchange of places, reversing the politics of both, and it puzzles the people here to ascertain whether the town has lost or gained by the change, or is "about even."

The *Camden Chronicle* has recently come under the management of Mr. B.B. Clarke, a young lawyer of exceptionable ability. The *Chronicle's* editorials display unusual journalistic talent and are full of promises.

There are two cornet bands in the place, one white and one colored, a flourishing cavalry company, an infantry company, and a flourishing Base Ball Association owning a park where the best amateur games of the State are played.

The town will soon issue $10,000 worth of bonds for internal improvements.

The Knights of Honor, the Ancient Order of United Workmen, the American Legion of Honor, the Knights of the Golden Rule, and the Freemasons have lodges here.

The Kirkwood Reading Club, composed of old and young of both sexes of Camden and Kirkwood, is giving its members valuable literature and literary entertainments.

Efforts are being made to establish a $100,000 cotton factory. If half of this amount is raised by local capitalists the remainder will be furnished by Northerners. All but a few thousand dollars of the requisite amount has been subscribed, and it is to be hoped, for the benefit of the whole town, that some enterprising citizen will not let such an important enterprise collapse for the want of two or three thousand dollars. The slightest retrograde movement at this time would be a great misfortune. The eyes of all are on Camden now, and the manner in which she deals with her opportunities will have much to do in making or destroying confidence in her people.

If one factory is established, others will soon follow, but the first step is always the most difficult. These people should always remember that confidence in the resources of a place must begin at home. It would be awkward to ask others to invest without first taking the initial step.

With the fruits and grapes and vegetables which cover the fields on every hand and the grand treasures of the surrounding forests, factories will surely come—if a beginning is made.

One of the many great natural advantages possessed by Camden is the valuable water-powers almost at her door. The great Wateree Canal, built by the State before the war, is only about seven miles distant and will furnish an unlimited power. About half a mile from town is the site of the old DeKalb Mills, with a most beautiful sheet of water and a horse-power of about 100. Then there is Big Pine Tree Creek, which passes within half a mile south of the town, with six excellent mill sites. This stream affords about 200 horse-power. Little Pine Tree Creek, which enters into Big Pine Tree Creek near the town, also affords good power.

People of Camden, your opportunities are great, and the possibilities of your town are boundless. There is a road to a grand future which you may tread, but the "open sesame" is in your own efforts. Remember the parable of the talents.

News and Courier, December 9, 1889. John I. Green

Charleston, the City by the Sea

No sketches of Charleston similar to those describing life in other South Carolina communities appeared in the *News and Courier* during the 1880s. At first, this may seem a bit strange, but the truth is that newspaper and its staff were reporting events in Charleston on a day-to-day basis and the city was simply too big, too complex to encompass successfully in a few columns. Nevertheless, about the first of September each year the *News and Courier* made an effort to do just that, publishing a comprehensive compendium heavily laced with commercial and industrial data. This "annual report" often covered several pages and presented a mass of statistical information, much of which subsequently was reproduced in the famous *City of Charleston Yearbooks*.

The focus of these surveys varied from year to year, sometimes expanding to regions other than Charleston and to topics such as cotton mills, the condition of crops throughout South Carolina, railroad development, manufacturing, education, and so on. At times, information concerning commercial centers outside the state was also included. Thus the best sources on life in Charleston in the 1880s are these September issues of the *News and Courier* and the *City of Charleston Yearbooks*, although neither provides the reader with the succinct capsulization Matthew Tighe, Ambrose Gonzales, and others achieved during visits to places such as Rock Hill, Greenwood, Aiken, and Marion.

The report of September 1, 1890, covering about five and one-half pages, opens with a summary of exports and imports during the past twelve months, a list of city building permits issued in that period, and an overview of manufacturing. This information is followed by data on wholesale trade, phosphates and fertilizers, regional production of rice, cotton, naval stores, fruits and vegetables, Charleston Harbor tonnage, and the city's rail facilities. The study concludes with a largely social section entitled "The City in General" and a brief survey of economic conditions in Moultrieville, Mount Pleasant, Summerville, Spartanburg, and Greenville. Here are some pertinent excerpts describing life in Charleston as that community entered the "Gay Nineties."

* * *

The manufacturing industries of Charleston have flourished during the year 1889–90, and both in capital invested and value of annual product show a handsome increase over the figures of last year. The total number of manufacturing enterprises has increased from 341 to 360. The number of hands employed has increased from 4,838 to 5,722. The capital invested has increased from $6,946,000 to $8,997,500. The value of the annual product has increased from $11,954,500 to $13,742,879. A large percentage of this increase is due to the very heavy business done in commercial fertilizers and by the addition of new enterprises.

Denomination	Number	Hands Employed	Capital Invested	Estimated Value of Annual Product
Cotton factories	1	700	$ 550,000	$ 1,000,000
Bagging factories	1	325	300,000	450,000
Breweries	1	80	100,000	235,000
Ice factories	1	10	5,000	55,845
Fernolite Chem. Works	1	40	75,000	270,000
Gas companies	1	105	698,000	141,500
Electric light & power companies	1	16	50,000	35,000
Basket & willowware companies	1	8	5,000	9,000
Envelope & box factories	1	20	15,000	40,000
Bag factories	3	65	130,000	375,000
Fertilizer works	12	1,370	3,790,000	4,215,000
Rice mills	3	95	350,000	1,000,000
Saw & lumber mills	5	210	215,000	695,000
Sash & blind factories	5	270	230,000	487,000
Ship & boat yards	2	60	38,000	127,000
Candy factories	9	45	31,500	230,000
Foundries & iron works	3	245	230,000	375,000
Job printing, etc.	5	160	275,000	447,000
Carriage & wagon factories	6	110	45,000	115,000
Flour & grist mills	8	65	165,000	436,000
Bakeries	29	240	72,000	400,000
Plumbers, tin & copper workers	30	80	100,000	200,000
Cigar factories	5	100	50,000	150,000
Saddleries	4	20	40,000	90,000
Shirts & underwear	3	125	70,000	130,000
Marble & granite works	5	60	40,000	75,000
Soda water, etc.	17	115	35,000	450,000
Ice cream factories	6	15	5,000	70,000
Contractors & builders	64	240	200,000	600,000
Men's clothing	11	79	35,000	195,000
Lock & gunsmiths	7	15	15,000	25,000
Watches & clocks	18	40	30,000	50,000
Barrel factories	2	180	140,000	235,000
Cabinet makers & upholsterers	25	123	30,000	100,000
Dyers	2	10	2,500	13,000

Proprietary*	53	162	$ 35,000	$ 95,000
Mattress factories	2	29	12,000	11,034
Cotton ties	2	15	6,000	20,000
Soap & candy factories	2	23	15,000	22,500
Canning factories	1	12	12,500	25,000
Spoke factories	1	15	5,000	11,000
Water-works	1	25	750,000	37,000
Totals	360	5,722	$8,997,500	$13,742,879

Charleston's wholesale trade, despite stiff competition from other metropolitan centers, continued to prosper. The most important commodities were groceries, dry goods, hardware, hats and caps, doors, sashes and blinds, crockery, ice, grain and feed, drugs and medicines, paints and oils, fruit, cigars and tobacco, boots and shoes, paper and stationery, fish and oysters, jewelry and watches, and beer and soda. The following table shows the wholesale and retail trade of Charleston for the year ending August 31, 1890.

	Wholesale	**Retail**	**Totals**
Groceries	$17,500,000	$5,500,000	$23,000,000
Grain and hay	500,000	500,000	1,000,000
Dry goods	3,200,000	1,800,000	5,000,000
Boots and shoes	1,000,000	300,000	1,300,000
Hats and caps	125,000	150,000	275,000
Tobacco	500,000	100,000	600,000
Drugs and medicines	400,000	150,000	550,000
Hardware	2,125,000	250,000	2,375,000
Crockery	200,000	50,000	250,000
Paints and oils	450,000	150,000	600,000
Saddlery	100,000	55,000	155,000
Stationery	300,000	100,000	400,000
Furniture	125,000	40,000	165,000
Doors, sash & blinds	350,000	——	350,000
Beer & soda water	350,000	50,000	400,000
Foreign & domestic fruits	100,000	——	100,000
Ice	10,000	20,000	30,000
Fish & oysters	45,000	25,000	70,000
Jewelry	——	200,000	200,000
Totals	$27,380,000	$9,440,000	$36,820,000

The city government had an income from all sources in 1889 of $596,136.54, about $20,000 less than in 1888. Real and personal property valued at $21.4 million returned $402,790 in taxes. Personal property subject to the 28-mill levy

*A manufacturer of medicines, one who probably holds an exclusive patent.

included 1,477 horses and mules; 284 neat cattle; 1,024 gold and silver watches and plates; 512 pianofortes, melodeons, and cabinet organs; 445 carriages and buggies; 1,036 wagons, drays, etc.; 689 dogs; merchandise (money and credits pertaining to business) valued at $1,643,141; materials, machinery, and fixtures of manufacture valued at $872,180; money, bank bills, and circulating credit worth $492,218; stocks and bonds (exclusive of national, state, and city bonds and receipts of insurance and express agencies, and telephone and telegraph companies) valued at $2,828,877; boats and vessels worth $127,490; and all other property, including household furniture, valued at $414,280. The total value of all personal property was $6,600,087.

Ninety-three new buildings were erected during the year with an estimated value of $150,000. This was considerably less than in 1888–89 when 151 structures valued at $434,000 were erected. Last year's schedule, however, included several public buildings, among them, the Courtenay School ($25,000), the Y.M.C.A. building ($25,000), and the Enston Home ($110,000). In this year's schedule the new Postoffice building is not included. To this $150,000 must be added $65,000 spent in the repairs of old buildings, making the total expenditures for the year about $215,000 in the way of improving the city.

The College of Charleston, one of the oldest and best of the educational institutions of the land, is the crown of the educational system of Charleston. Under the present management it is doing some of the best work ever done within its venerable walls. The College is well supplied with all the facilities for imparting knowledge. Its selected library of several thousand volumes is one of the best in the whole country, and it will be very difficult to find anywhere a better collection of the specimens of natural history than can be found in the Museum of the College of Charleston. Its laboratory and chemical rooms are well supplied with all the apparatus needed in the teaching of the sciences. In all of its work the professors insist upon thoroughness. No effort is made to swell the list of alumni, but a united effort is made by the entire faculty to see that no name is added to that long line of men, many of whom have been leaders of their fellow-men, in religion and literature, in science and in business, in peace and in war, who cannot stand the required test of scholarship.

The College has felt the effects of cyclone and earthquake, but in spite of it all it is still doing good work in the cause of education. The prospects are now brighter than they have ever been. The students are interested in their work and are enthusiastic workers for the College. There is every reason to expect a large number of applicants for admission to the College when its fall session opens on October 1.

The faculty are: H.E. Shepherd, D.D., president and professor of history and English literature and language; Lewis R. Gibbes, M.D., professor of physics, mechanics, and astronomy; A. Sachtleben, professor of Greek and Latin; G.E. Manigault, professor of geology and natural history and curator of the Museum; Beauregard Boaz, M.A., assistant professor of mathematics; and H.F. Wagener, B.A., professor of French and German.

The pride of Charleston, as well as of the whole State, is the Citadel, the South Carolina Military Academy. This noble institution of higher education is now doing its best work. The standard is high and all the work is thorough. The institution is better equipped now than it has ever been. There are now 153 cadets enrolled. They are under the control and direction of the following faculty: Gen. George D. Johnston, superintendent and professor of moral and political science; First Lieut. C.H. Cabaniss, Jr., 18th Infantry, U.S.A., professor of military science and tactics; Major St. James Cummings, professor of English literature and history; Major C.L. Reese, professor of chemistry and physics; Major R.G. Thomas, professor of mathematics and engineering; Capt. P.P. Mazyck, assistant professor in charge of modern languages; Second Lieut. O.J. Bond, assistant professor of mathematics and in charge of drawing and bookkeeping; Second Lieut. J.P. Kinard, assistant professor of English literature and history; Second Lieut. J.T. Coleman, assistant professor of chemistry and physics; F.L. Parker, M.D., surgeon; and First Lieut. W.W. White, quartermaster. Gen. Johnston resigned the superintendency at the close of the last session and his successor has not yet been elected.

In one respect, at least, Charleston leads all other Southern cities and that is in the excellence of her public school system. The schools are the pride of the city. The citizens pay their school tax as cheerfully as they pay their grocer's bill. The public schools have a reputation throughout the United States for thorough work. The system is conducted on modern methods and is constantly kept up with the advancing ideas of this rapidly growing age.

During the past year there were enrolled 5,287 pupils in the six schools of the city, of whom 2,135 were males and 3,152 were females. There were 2,803 white pupils, of whom 1,041 were males and 1,762 were females. There were 2,484 colored pupils, of whom 1,094 were males and 1,390 were females. The total average attendance for the nine and a half months was 4,971, divided as follows: Whites, males 940, females 1,658; colored, males 1,029, females 1,307.

The division of the pupils according to their studies was as follows: Alphabet, 723; spelling, 4,564; reading, 4,564; writing, 3,841; mental arithmetic, 3,563; written arithmetic, 3,563; geography, 2,831; English grammar, 1,429; history of the United States, 1,227; and higher branches, 526.

There are 110 teachers employed in the public schools, of whom 9 are Southern white males, 97 Southern white females, and 4 Southern colored females. The average monthly salary of the male teacher is $135 and of the female $49.75. The city owns 6 school houses, representing a value of $149,334.07.

The High School of Charleston is one of the most thorough training schools for boys in the South. Its course of study is judiciously arranged so that a boy at graduation is prepared to enter college or is fully equipped for work in the business world. The average attendance last year was 150, but that will very probably be exceeded this year, as every indication points to a very large number of new students. The faculty consists of the following well-known educators: Virgil C.

Dibble, principal and teacher of mathematics; Thomas Della Torre, teacher of Latin and Greek; W.M. Whitehead, teacher of English; George G. Leland, teacher of English; William D. Gaillard, teacher of French and German; William H. Schaffer, teacher of preparatory class; and F.P. Valdez, teacher of gymnastics and calisthenics.

The twenty-fourth annual session of the Porter Academy will open on October 1st. This institution of learning has, since its very foundation, done a noble work for the cause of education that extends far beyond the confines of Charleston. The Academy is enjoying a large patronage and every indication points to a future full of good work. The corps of instructors are: The Rev. A. Toomer Porter, D.D., rector; the Rev. Theodore A. Porter, assistant rector; Charles J. Colcock, Jr., head master, mathematics and science; Henry Peagram, Latin and Greek; Horton F. Colcock, grammar, rhetoric, and history; Charles H. Cabaniss, U.S.A., military department and discipline of home; Prof. John Keppler, mechanical drawing, French, German, and gymnasium; F.A. Dillon, manual training department; J. Huguelet, music; and Miss J.DeV. Porcher, primary department.

The Catholic parochial schools are fully equipped for their work and are meeting all the requirements for thorough educational work. The attendance at these schools is as follows:

	Boys	Girls	Total
Cathedral	60	—	60
St. Patrick's	125	—	125
St. Mary's	45	—	45
St. Joseph's	64	—	64
St. Mary's, George Street	—	263	263
St. Peter's	35	40	75
Totals	329	303	632

Charleston is well supplied with schools for the education of young ladies. The select school of Miss I.D. Smith, the Academy of our Lady of Mercy, and the Charleston Female Seminary, of which Miss Etta A. Kelly is principal, are all institutions of high order. They are largely patronized at home and also draw many pupils from abroad. There are also a large number of private schools where the best of training is given. For boys, the University School under Prof. W.D. McKenny, the German School under Prof. C.H. Bergmann, and Mr. Louis Manigault's schools afford excellent private instruction.

Avery Normal Institute and the Wallingford Academy are doing a fine work for the higher education of colored pupils. They are both under excellent management and are largely attended. Both are supported in part by contributions from Northern philanthropists.

It is no news to Charlestonians that the city has been free from epidemic disease for nearly twenty years. The recent improvements at the quarantine station and the establishment of the Holt system of disinfecting ships will promote the health conditions immensely.

In the report of the board of health for 1889 the following statement is made: "We have escaped pestilence and epidemic disease and the list of mortality is not excessive, although there are a greater number of deaths, both in white and colored, than in 1888. The number of deaths among the whites is considerably below the average for the past ten years, 526 being recorded for 1889, and the average for the decade being 547; the population naturally is increasing, so that we may claim some progress in an improved health record.

The population of the city in 1889 was estimated by the health department at 60,145 viz.: Whites 27,605, blacks and colored 32,540. On this basis the proportion of deaths was: Whites, 1 in 52; blacks and colored, 1 in 22. Total population, 1 in 30.

The city is divided for sanitary and medical purposes into four health districts, each district being under the care of a sanitary inspector. These inspectors make a written report every day at 12 o'clock to the health officer, noting all nuisances and reporting all vaults and imperfect drains for cleansing and relief—the early hours being devoted to superintending the removal of garbage.

No new banks have been started during the year. The existing institutions have banking capital of $1,340,000, a surplus account of $1,422,400, and a deposit account of $7,664,000. Of the thirteen banks doing business in Charleston, three are national, two State, and eight savings banks. One of the national banks, the People's, and one of the State banks, the Loan and Trust, have savings banks attached. The banks have all done a prosperous business, all of them paying dividends ranging from 6 to 10 per cent, and some even larger.

Charleston has always been in the foreground in the organization and development of building and loan associations, institutions which contribute largely to the prosperity of the community by enabling the laboring classes to save their earnings and thus become their own landlords. All institutions of this character which have heretofore existed and have wound up their affairs have bourne evidence of successful management, and within one hundred months cancelled mortgages and cleared the homes of all liability. During the commercial year just closed the Co-operative Association has passed out of existence, while three local companies (the Hibernia, the Fidelity, and the Banking System) have been organized, besides numerous other institutions working under local boards of management with charters from other states.

The various active associations with their total stock payments are as follows:

Prudential	$188,000
Mutual	176,000
Paragon	158,000
Artisans' and Traders'	102,000
Assistance	126,000
Safety	106,000
Commercial	51,000

Homestead	46,000
Germania	53,750
Workingman's	48,000
Economy	17,600
Hibernia	6,000
Fidelity	5,600
Banking System	4,800
Southern	2,650
Inter-State	350
Total	$1,091,750*

The Charleston Telephone Exchange is the third largest in the Southern Bell Telephone and Telegraph Company's territory. Atlanta ranking first, Richmond second, and Charleston third. The number of stations in use is five hundred and is increasing daily. The number of connections made daily is about 7,000, all the year around, and during the fall months it is sometimes larger. There are twenty employees connected with the Exchange, eight operators, four inspectors, three in the burglar alarm department, and five linemen.

During the past year the business of the Exchange has been good, and the number of stations larger than in the previous year. There are sixteen long lines connected with the Exchange, notably Mount Pleasant and Sullivan's Island (these two lines are cabled two miles under water), Ashley Phosphate Company, eighteen miles in length, Mead & Co.'s mines, ten miles, and in fact all of the phosphate companies.

The company is now putting in a multiple switch-board at a cost of $3,000, which will add greatly to the efficiency of the Exchange. Its capacity will be eight hundred subscribers; the present board only has room for five hundred. The board will be in three different sections and will be so arranged that each operator will have every subscriber before her.

The company is contemplating the establishment of an Exchange at Mount Pleasant, so that subscribers, instead of having to come to the central office and do their talking with Charleston, can do so from their stations. They also hope to have Summerville connected by telephone with the Exchange in a very short time.

The company is now running, as they call it, a common return wire through the city, attaching the ground wire of every telephone to it in order to avoid the buzzing sound of the electric current, which the subscribers suffer from at night. By attaching each ground wire of a telephone to this wire and relieving the same from the regular water and gas pipe ground, it will give the electric light current some chance to distribute on the common return wire instead of seeking its course through the telephones and then going to the ground through the gas and water

*See the *News and Courier* (September 1, 1890) for additional details concerning both banks and building and loan associations.

ground as heretofore. This will be one great benefit to the Exchange, and the service will be improved more than ever.

The company has in operation the Holmes burglar alarm system. There are ten stores and five banks connected with the system. This system stands first, and the central office is so arranged that should any one of the employers or employees of the places connected enter at any time [during non-working hours] an alarm is heard at the central office and a watchman is dispatched to the place to ascertain who the party is entering. A record is kept of every opening and closing and a statement sent to each subscriber weekly. In this way the employer knows the time his place is opened every morning, the time it is closed, and who enters after closing.

For the past two months the company has had most of its plant reconstructed, which necessitated, of course, the re-running of wires, taking down of poles, and the setting up of new ones in their places. The subscribers during this time suffered more or less on account of their wires being crossed, which could not have been avoided. Now that this work has been completed, the service will in all probability be better than ever, and every effort is being made to make it so.

During the past year two new and powerful steamers have been added to the fire department, which, as is well known, has no superior in any city in the United States. The force now consists of seven steamers in active service, three reserved steamers, a hook and ladder truck, and a salvage wagon supported by the board of underwriters. The seven steamers of the force are concentrated in three improved engine houses, so situated as to give the firemen the quickest access to all parts of the city. So perfect is the discipline and the system that it is impossible that there should be a disastrous conflagration except under the most extraordinary circumstances.

There have been no changes to speak of in the street railroad situation during the year except the extension of the City Railway track through Schutzen Avenue to the gate of the Park. The same company has also in view the building of tracks through Spring Street, connecting the main lines through Rutledge Avenue and King and Meeting streets. This will give the residents of the West End a continuous line to Magnolia Cemetery.

It is probable, however, that the coming year will see important changes for the better in the system. It is understood that the Enterprise Railroad Company has already practically decided upon substituting the electric motor for the present method of locomotion, while the president of the City Railway has been in the North looking over the field with the same object in view. At present the streets of Charleston are traversed by about thirty miles of tracks, over an area of not over seventy-five miles of streets.

The work of the street department during the year has been in keeping with the progress of the past decade. It is the boast of Charleston, and it is by no means a vain boast, that it is the best-paved and best-drained city in the South. The general condition of the streets, especially in regard to drainage, is as perfect as it can be made.

The Government has three enterprises on its hands in Charleston, not counting the work on the Jetties. They are (1) the new Postoffice, (2) the Custom House wharf, and (3) the old Postoffice. The most important of these is, of course, the new Postoffice, with the progress of the work on which the public have been kept pretty well posted. In the Annual Review last year the *News and Courier* said about this work: "There has been a good deal of vexatious delay in the progress of the work owing to the inevitable red tape that hobbles all public work, and also to the failure of the contractors to furnish the piles for the foundation. Most of the piling and the concrete foundations have been completed, and it is hoped that the walls of the new building will be above the ground before the first of January next."

The work during the year just closed may be summed up in a few words. The walls came very nearly up to the surface, but then they had to be taken down again. At present the Government is leisurely engaged in undoing the foundation work that was so loosely and imperfectly done, and at the present rate it is possible that the walls may be seen to rise above the ground some time early in the twentieth century.

It may be stated that most of the granite for the first course of the walls has been cut and is on the ground ready to be put up. Nothing can be done, however, in the way of pushing the work until the concrete foundation has been removed and the seven hundred or more piles upon which the foundation is to rest have been tested.

The work on the Custom House pier is progressing as rapidly as possible and is nearing completion. The north pier is almost completed as far as the granite work is concerned. The contractors are now at work on the iron pier head.

In the old Postoffice the work of repair is going on rapidly and without interference with the business of the office.

In the Annual Review of the *News and Courier* on September 1, 1889, allusion was made to the recent completion of the third and largest Artesian well, constituting our public water supply. The flow from this well has been constant at the rate of 824 gallons per minute. This quantity, together with the yield of the George Street and Marion Square wells, gives a daily supply of more than two millions of gallons, which is considerably in excess of the present consumption.

Immediately upon the completion of the last well the Water Company began to extend its mains so as to cover almost the entire city, and laid, during the past winter, six miles of new water mains, upon which were located seventy-four double fire hydrants and fifty-four water gates. This makes a total of twenty-six miles of water mains.

The following statements, showing the mean monthly temperature and the amount of rainfall at Charleston, S.C., for the year ending July 31, 1890, is furnished by the signal service observatory at this port:

Month		Temperature, degrees		Rainfall, inches
August		78		7.36
September		76		2.17
October		66		0.73
November		60		7.28
December		60		0.03
January		59		1.28
February		61		1.28
March		56		1.72
April		65		2.58
May		73		3.67
June		82		1.32
July		80		12.87
	Mean	68	Total	42.29

It has often been said that the real prosperity of the masses of the people in any city is dependent largely, if not chiefly, upon small industrial enterprises. Regarding this saying as a truth, there is no doubt that the people at large in Charleston are in a better position today than ever before, for the past year shows a record never before equalled in the establishment of small industries. In moderate amounts, placed here and there, thousands of dollars have been invested, and employment has been given to hundreds of people, thereby adding materially to the population and prosperity of the city.

The Emerson Car Company, which promises to be very successful, is the company recently organized to handle an invention of Mr. A.S. Emerson of this city, by which railroad cars will be ventilated. The company has a capital stock of $300,000, most of which has been subscribed. The invention, it is claimed, will secure perfect ventilation and at the same time exclude dust, cinders, etc. from passenger coaches.

The Charleston Trunk Company began business at 260 King Street on the 1st of February, 1890. This thriving establishment is under the management of George W. Rabb & Co. and is one of the first factories of the kind in this part of the State. It manufactures and repairs all kinds of leather travelling goods and makes a specialty of sample work. The wholesale and retail departments of the business are both very large, and much success has been met with in building up a permanent trade in this and adjoining states.

During the past year two new fertilizer companies have been organized in Charleston. The Imperial Fertilizer Company, with a capital of $150,000 and with the following corps of officers, is doing a fine business for a new concern: President, Andrew Simonds; superintendent, Albert Rhett; treasurer, G.W. McIver.

East Battery, the promenade on the southern end of East Bay Street. *Leslie's Illustrated Newspaper,* September 25, 1880. *South Caroliniana Library.*

The Chicora Fertilizer Company was organized a few months ago as follows: A.S.J. Perry, president; B.F. McCabe, vice president; George A. Wagener, secretary and treasurer. The capital stock is $300,000.

The Charleston Mattress and Woodware Company has been in successful operation for nearly a year. The company was chartered in August, 1889, and the factory in King Street was immediately built and operations commenced. The business of the company had not started actively until about the middle of last November, when travelling salesmen were put on the road to sell the wares of the company. A ready and profitable sale was found, and the company is now making money and is on the way to success.

At present the company is engaged in the manufacture of mattresses, cots, pillows, bed springs, and wovenware. In the manufacture of the mattresses the company uses straw, excelsior, corn husk, cotton, moss, and hair. The company now has a large business in this State, as well as Georgia, North Carolina, and Florida. Mr. E.B. Miler is engaged by the company as travelling agent.

The factory employs about twenty hands, of whom two are women. The capacity of the factory is about one hundred mattresses a day. The officers of the company are as follows: President, A. Johnson; secretary, E.B. Miler; solicitor, W.St.J. Jervey; directors, J. Adger Smyth, Jas. F. Redding, A. Johnson, M.D. Maguire, and George A. Wagener.

The McClellanville and Santee Steamship and Transportation Company was organized early in the year with $4,000 capital. They now own one steamer, the *Louise,* which plies regularly between Charleston and McClellanville, doing a splendid business in both passengers and heavy freight. Their freight consists very largely in bringing down turpentine and naval stores and carrying back provisions and plantation supplies. The business is most encouraging, meeting in every way the expectations of the owners. The *Louise* is a compact little steamer, which was built by Mr. Ball of Mount Pleasant. She stands her passage well and gives every promise of a long career of usefulness. The officers of the company are: John L. Weber, president; Leland Moore, secretary and treasurer. Capt. Charlton Leland is in command of the steamer.

Charleston is doing business at the old stand! Its business is growing in every direction. The prospect for the future is brighter than it has been at any time since the close of the war. The opportunities for development are greater, the facilities for handling business are being steadily improved, the railroads are reaching out to new territory, and the ships are coming in from all parts of the world. We are on the threshold of a new commercial era. There is life, and activity, and hope, and courage in the air.

The story which we tell today of what Charleston has done during the past twelve months is enough to encourage the weakest heart and to add new zeal and energy to the stout hearts and strong arms which have in the past stood up for Charleston and Charleston's interests against all competitors—against the world. The time which we have all longed for and hoped for is near at last. The past is forgotten; the present and the future have clasped hands.

The record of the year ending August 30, 1890, is such a record as we all desired to make. It shows that, during the past year, the business of the city, as compared with the preceding year has increased $3,966,293.

The progress has been general and steady. New enterprises and new industries have been added to the city's busy life. The outlook is most encouraging. With improved facilities, with an increasing population, with all Charleston at work, and at work for Charleston, the future contains no height of commercial supremacy which cannot be scaled, and presents no obstacle which cannot be overcome.

In summary, here is "The Year's Work," two subjoined tables exhibiting the trade of Charleston in money value during the fiscal year ending August 30, 1890.

Amount of Trade

	1889–90	**1888–89**
Cotton, upland, bales	342,572	408,701
Cotton, Sea Island, bales	7,256	7,789
Rice, barrels	97,240	72,565
Turpentine, casks	50,548	42,558

Rosin, barrels	219,773	143,188
Phosphate rock (crude), tons	349,762	304,396
Phosphate rock (ground), tons	1,250	7,650
Fertilizers, tons	261,650	172,050
Lumber & crossties	73,397,400	55,532,680
Cotton goods, domestics, bales	63,467	58,194
Total Values		
Cotton, upland	$15,415,740	$18,391,545
Cotton, Sea Island	719,230	739,955
Rice	1,458,600	1,088,475
Turpentine	1,010,960	851,160
Rosin	384,602	259,329
Phosphate rock (crude)	4,000,000	1,826,376
Phosphate rock (ground)	10,000	72,562
Fertilizers	5,494,650	3,613,050
Cotton goods, domestics, etc.	3,490,685	3,200,670
Lumber & crossties	807,371	610,852
Fruits & vegetables	1,480,000	1,578,000
Manufactures, exclusive of fertilizers	9,527,879	8,341,450
Wholesale & retail trade	36,820,000	36,080,000
Grand totals	$80,619,717	$76,653,424

News and Courier, September 1, 1890.

Cheraw: The Old Town on the Hill

After many years of neglect, in 1889 Cheraw was visited twice by members of the *News and Courier* staff and then again in 1891.* The third report, written by J.K. Blackman, deals largely with the undeveloped mineral resources of Chesterfield County. He describes in great detail the Brewer Gold Mine near Jefferson then being operated by Captain Emmanuel Motz. Motz, a Pennsylvania-born veteran of the California rush, had as partners Senator George Hearst (father of William Randolph), Washington's "Boss" Shepherd, and several other well-known capitalists. Gold valued at $20 an ounce was going regularly from the Brewer Mine to the government assay office in Charlotte. According to Blackman, the county also was rich in kaolin, granite, and iron. Here is the second portrait of Cheraw, written by "C.N.D.," a Confederate veteran, who was reminded of a hasty departure he made from this same town in 1865.

* * *

It is almost twenty-five years since the writer, then a young Confederate soldier, made a hurried exit from the town of Cheraw, and, crossing the bridge over the Pee Dee as it was burning, joined his comrades in retreat and took up the line of march through North Carolina.

A quarter of a century! As it passes in mental review what transformations! The opening scene illuminated by the lurid glare of burning homes, which marked the track of "Sherman's bummers," and its most prominent features are battle and bloodshed, disaster and despair. Then follows that pathetic picture of the reconstruction period, exhibiting a people oppressed by the cares of grinding poverty and the added curse of political degradation.

Thank Heaven, the last scene in the panorama is brighter and better, and through the bitter processes of fire and sword, and the painful and often humiliating experience of sectional rehabilitation, we have at last reached a point where he who looks at this part of the South can see, not a region of desolation, but a new land of promise; not an era of gunpowder and battle smoke, but one of wonderful industrial life and prosperity, and the boys of twenty-five years ago, who were known to us as dashing cavalrymen, or smoke-begrimed artillerists, or dust-stained foot soldiers, are now gray-bearded merchants or doctors or lawyers, with scarcely anything about them to indicate their once warlike appearance.

I was forcibly impressed with this last stated fact as I wandered down to the river bank this afternoon to revisit a spot so memorable to me, and found there in

---

*See also the issues of January 7, 1889, and February 26, 1891.

charge of the bridge, which now replaces the one which was burnt on the occasion I refer to, a gallant officer of the 1st regular infantry, Capt. J.G. Powe. No one seeing him sitting so quietly at his present post of duty would imagine for a moment that this man was one of that immortal band of heroes who held the defence of Charleston Harbor against all comers until the word was given them to abandon their post. He is, however, but a type. Go where you may you find them filling some modest position, quietly, contentedly, in peace illustrating the same soldierly quality of fidelity to duty which distinguished them in war.

But all this is a digression; pardon it under the circumstances, and let us turn away from the bridge and note the prominent features of "the old town on the hill" as the grandmothers of the present inhabitants used to call it. Before we leave the bridge, however, let me note this unique inscription placed before its entrance by some rural sign painter. It puzzled me; perhaps it may puzzle others:

> Five Dollars Fine to cross
> this bridge with any Bea
> st
> Faster than a walk.
> Five Dollars Fine
> to cross this Brid
> ge smoking.

On my way back from the river bluff I passed two objects which again brought before me the striking contrasts between the old and the new; the one was an ancient church, the other a new railroad. The church (St. David's) was built in the colonial period, or, to be more exact, its erection was commenced in 1768. In 1782 it was first used for public worship and it was completed in 1784. According to Gregg's *History of the Old Cheraws,* it was once occupied as a British barrack, and for the first half century of its erection was used in common by all of the religious denominations of the neighborhood, and for a brief period the claim was set up that it was so intended to be used by those who erected it. However, the original act for the organization of the parish was discovered in time to settle the controversy and prove its right to the name of an Episcopal church. The building has, from time to time, undergone some repair, but enough of the original structure remains intact to justify the good Bishop when he says in his history:

> Unharmed by the ravages of time, the venerable building still remains, one of the few material relics of that era. It was erected by the sturdy men of that day with the care befitting such a work and upon a sure foundation. There has been wonderful progress since in every department of human labor, but a progress rather in matters of outward adornment than in those durable elements and that thorough finish which are calculated for lasting use.

The location of this venerable edifice is picturesque. It stands on rising ground and is surrounded by a beautiful grove; the little spire of the church barely peeps above the top of the trees and gives to it a pretty rural appearance. The churchyard appears to be kept with some care, and many of the old monuments are well worthy of an antiquary's notice.

There is one tablet supported by four small pillars on which is engraved an inscription which has been quoted far and wide, but which will, I think, bear repetition:

> My name, my country, what are they to thee;
> What—whether high or low my pedigree;
> Perhaps I far surpassed all other men;
> Perhaps I fell below them all.
> What then—suffice it stranger that thou seest a TOMB;
> Thou knowest its use: it hides—no matter whom.

This is all that appears upon the stone, but it is known to be above the remains of W.R. Robbins, the generous friend and patron of Thornwell in his early youth and the promoter of his greatness.* By some the inscription is regarded as original, but many of the readers of the *News and Courier* will recognize in it the production of one of the great English poets, Cowper, I believe.

Crossing the new railroad, of which I made brief mention a moment ago, and leaving the old church with its reminiscences of the past, I took a quiet stroll through the beautiful and well-shaded streets of Cheraw. The town somewhat resembles Columbia, at least it is laid off pretty much in the same way, and like Columbia has very wide streets adorned by magnificent elms on either side and down the centre from beginning to end. The residences are many of them quite pretty; the business houses, nearly all of them built since the war, are not as fine or commodious as in some other towns of like size and importance, but no doubt as occasion demands improvements will go on.

Cheraw is confident of her future. As the head of steamboat navigation on the Pee Dee and a coming railroad centre, she has the right to be confident, for her advantages are almost unrivalled. The Cheraw and Darlington Road gives her daily connection with Charleston; the same road under a different name (Cheraw & Salisbury) gives her connection with Wadesboro and the country tributary thereto. The river gives boat connection with Georgetown and Charleston and, still better, gives the opportunity of reducing railroad rates on account of the competition. In other directions the outlets are abundant; the Palmetto Road is now running from this point to Hamlet on the Carolina Central and places it in direct connection with Charlotte, Wilmington, Raleigh, and Norfolk, and by this route shipments are also made to Charleston via Monroe, N.C., the Three C's, and the South Carolina Railway. The extension of this important railroad link

*James Henley Thornwell (1812–62), Presbyterian clergyman and president of South Carolina College, was the son of a Marlboro County overseer who died when the youth was only eight years old. As indicated, Robbins and others aided in his education.

St. David's Episcopal Church, Cheraw. *Photograph by Carl Julien, reproduced by permission of the University of South Carolina Press from* Beneath So Kind a Sky. *South Caroliniana Library.*

from Cheraw to Sumter is confidently looked forward to by the business men of the place.

The advantages of Cheraw as a shipping point have induced the location here of the Cheraw Iron Works, an important industrial enterprise, which was at one time established at Clio in Marlboro County. These works employ some forty or fifty operatives, who are paid about $30,000 a year, which is, of course, mostly spent among the merchants of the place. The works turn out almost all kinds of agricultural machinery, but make a specialty of iron mills, and in this manufacture have an enviable reputation. Mr. W.A. Hinshaw is the superintendent and is the right man in the right place; foreman, J.A. Fetner; directors, J.L. Laughlin, H.D. Malloy, R.T. Caston, H.W. Finlayson, Edward McIver, and J.W. McCoy. They propose to make an exhibit at the State Fair, which will certainly command attention.

Another of the new business features of this place is the Bank of Cheraw, which has been only two years in operation and has already increased its capital from $25,000 to $50,000, while paying to depositors quarterly interest at the rate of 4 per cent per annum. Mr. H.D. Malloy is the president and Dr. F.A. Wallace the cashier; directors, R.T. Cason, Edward McIver, H.W. Finlayson, H.L. Laughlin, and A.G. Kollock.

Cheraw also has a building and loan association and a land and improvement company. The former will wind up one year hence; its stock is now worth $150 a share, and it has during its business career aided in the construction of some forty or fifty dwellings, besides making advances to farmers. The Land and Improvement Company owns ten or twelve new brick stores in the town, besides other property, and its affairs are in a prospering condition.

There are some thirty-five or forty general stores in the town, one newspaper, the *Cheraw Reporter,* edited by Mr. A.G. Kollock, two hotels, Catholic, Episcopal, Presbyterian, Methodist, and Baptist churches for the white, and Presbyterian, Methodist, and Baptist churches for the colored population.

The officers of the railroads at this point are courteous and efficient and accommodating. The Cheraw and Darlington and Cheraw and Salisbury is represented by Mr. W.R. Godfrey as agent, and Mr. John H. McIver, the treasurer of these two roads, is also a resident of Cheraw. The agent of the Palmetto Road is Mr. S.G. Godfrey. Mr. W.R. Godfrey is president of the Cheraw Bridge Company, and Capt. J.G. Powe, bridge-keeper.

The town council of Cheraw is at present composed of the following gentlemen: Mayor, Dr. W.C. McCreight; aldermen, Dr. C. Kollock, H.M. Tomlinson, T.L. Liles, and W.L. Rhodes. The town officers are: P.H. Brock, clerk and treasurer; John H. McCreight, marshal.

The finances of the town are in a sound and healthy condition. No debts are owing, and everything is run on a cash basis. The levy for town purposes is one-half of 1 per cent and five mills additional for special school tax.

There is a good market and market hall and also a town hall of larger size. The latter building will be well remembered by some of the Charleston boys who were at the evacuation of Cheraw, as one of the places where our hospitals were established, and incidentally it may be remembered that nothing but the yellow hospital flag saved it from destruction. The upper half of this building is under the control of the Masonic Order and is used by the Masons, the Knights of Honor, the Legion of Honor, American Legion, and Chosen Friends as their regular place of meeting.

The fact has already been mentioned that there is but one newspaper in the place, but I neglected to state that it will soon be enlarged and improved and run by a Campbell press. The editor and proprietor, Mr. A.G. Kollock, is an enthusiast, and rightly so, on the subject of railway extension and a free bridge, both of which would be of incalculable benefit to Cheraw.

General stores—J.T. McNair, Coward & McIntosh, H.D. Malloy, C.A. Brock, M.L. Rhodes, W.T. Brantley. Messrs. McNair, Malloy, and Rhodes are also each engaged in making advances to farmers and are large cotton buyers. C.A. Brock and W.T. Brantley are liquor dealers as well as dealers in general merchandise. W.A. Adkinson and Buchannan Bros. deal exclusively in liquors.

The druggist trade is represented by Dr. W.C. McCreight and Dr. J.H. Hardin, the latter being a practicing physician as well as druggist.

Dry goods, clothing, and shoes—H.W. Finlayson, A.L. and W.R. Evans.

Millinery—Miss R. Roddy.

Groceries—A.B. Horton, Finlayson & Whitley, H.M. Tomlinson, J.C. Huntley, E.L. Stubbs, J.F. Grant, Israel Myers, colored.

Furniture and undertaker—J.H. Liles.

Jewelry—R.B. Hanneman, J.B. Stubbs, H.L. Laughlin.

Fruits and newsdealer—J.N. Strickland.

Livery stable—Jackson & Jackson.

Steam cotton gins—E.W. Nell, C.S. Lynch.

Butchers—P.H. Brock, E.J. Bevens, Smith & Burton (col.).

Wheelwrights and blacksmiths—John J. Barber, H.T. Rakestraw, Charles Campbell, (col.) Sharper Lynch.

Photographer and general agent—L.H. Festerman.

Hotels—Cheraw Hotel, H.H. Wilson; Timmons House, the Messrs. Timmons.

Boarding houses—L.H. Festerman.

Barbers—C.F. Moses (col.), Louis Green (col.), Tom Marshall (col.).

The legal and medical professions are represented here by the following gentlemen: Physicians—Dr. C. Kollock, Dr. J.A. James, Dr. J.J. Wilson, Dr. B.B. Thurman, Dr. J.H. Harden; attorneys at law—Gen. W.L.T. Prince, R.T. Caston, A.A. Kollock, J.M. McQueen, S.W.G. Shipp, Col. Edwd. McIver.

The pastors of the respective white churches located here are: the Rev. Hartwell Edwards, Baptist; the Rev. Walter I. Herbert, Methodist; the Rev. T.C. Wheeling, Presbyterian. St. David's (Episcopal) Church has no rector at present, and the Catholic Church has only occasional services conducted by a priest from Charleston.

The rectors of the colored churches are: McDonald, Methodist; Frierson, Presbyterian; T. Drake, Baptist.

Cheraw, long proverbial for her social excellence, has also a most enviable reputation as a literary centre. "The Cheraw Lyceum" is known far and wide, and it still flourishes notwithstanding the wholesale thefts of William Tecumseh Sherman, who deliberately stole some 2,500 of the choicest volumes of the Association. They now have about 2,000 volumes in their library, meet monthly, and are at present making preparations for their thirty-fourth anniversary, on which occasion the orator of the day will be Prof. Woodward of the South Carolina University. The officers of the Lyceum are T.C. Whiting, president; A.G. Kollock, vice president; Dr. C. Kollock, chairman of the executive committee.

The Chautauquan Circle of Cheraw is now in its third year, has some twenty members, and is in a flourishing condition. Its officers are R.T. Caston, president; Col. Edward McIver, vice president; and Mrs. J.T. McNair, secretary and treasurer.

Kollock's Station, two miles the other side of the river, ships some two or three hundred bales of cotton, which is practically a part of the shipments of Cheraw as it is cotton bought by Cheraw merchants. This is the point where the Bennettsville connection would be made, provided the people of that town should decide to come this way. There is only eleven miles to connect at a cost of $11,000, and it is urged by those friendly to the scheme that if such a connection was made both Bennettsville and Cheraw would be mutually benefitted and would be on the line of the shortest and best route to Charleston.

The graded school for whites, under the supervision of Major McLaughlin, has 140 pupils in attendance. The colored free school is also well attended and some three or four private schools are very well patronized. The Y.M.C.A. has about seventy-five active members. So that, taken all in all, Cheraw, with its present population pushing close on to 2,000, possesses, in its social, industrial, educational, and religious features, a combination of attractions that may well invite the attention of the outside world.

The cotton shipments are about 15,000 bales per annum, nearly all of which, I am sorry to say, goes to Norfolk or Wilmington, and notwithstanding the fact that boats make weekly (and railroad trains make daily) trips from here to Charleston. When asked why this is so the merchants of Cheraw reply: "Because of more favorable inducements elsewhere." Will it always be so?

The farming lands of this section are not claimed to be as productive as those of Marlboro, yet they do yield fair crops annually and command good prices, say from $10 to $25 per acre, and higher for choice locations. The average cost of the fertilizer used is from $8 to $10 per acre. The crops of the present season were rather backward, the yield for grain good, for cotton about three-fourths of the usual average.

The Alliance men are holding back their crops, some, as I am informed, on account of low prices; others are waiting for the arrival of the Alliance bagging.

This policy is regarded as injurious to the merchants, especially so when the holder belongs to the debtor class. The Bank of Cheraw is trying to relieve the situation and has offered to advance the farmers on cotton that they do not wish to sell, provided it be stored in a ware house and covered by insurance, and if this offer is generally accepted a better feeling will no doubt prevail.

News and Courier, October 25, 1889. C.N.D.

Chester, William Penn's Scotch-Irish Offspring

Chester, site of a four-county fair each fall, was, according to this glowing, anonymous report, the most fortunate of communities. In 1887 it had a good fire department, excellent schools, and fine rail connections that soon would be even better. It also enjoyed extremely healthy surroundings, and, like most Up Country towns, was looking forward to the not-too-distant day when it could boast of its own cotton factory.

* * *

Chester is a very healthy place. In point of health it will compare favorably with any place in or out of the State. Situated on a hill, as the main portion of the town is, the drainage is excellent. A small stream that runs along the eastern and southern sides quickly carries away the water that falls in our midst. The climate of Chester is pleasant. It is a rare thing for the mercury in winter to fall to zero and in summer to rise to 95°. During the cold months the thermometer generally registers about 25° and during the hot months about 85°. Our town has an efficient board of health consisting of Dr. Sumter Davega, Mr. J.J. Stringfellow, and Mr. E.P. Moore, who report to the municipal authorities any violation of the sanitary regulations.

Chester has greatly increased in population during the last few years. The increase has been two-fold since the close of the war. Our town claims about 2,500 inhabitants, of which the whites are in a majority. It possesses at present an excellent town council, who have done good work in improving and beautifying our streets. They have also accomplished a great deal in restricting the sale of whiskey. Their terms of office do not expire for nearly two years, and with a continuance of the present satisfactory course of action they will be able, at the end of their official existence, to show the benefits accruing from a wise and energetic administration of municipal affairs. The council consists of the following: S.M. Jones, intendant, and H.W. Hafner, F.L. Whitlock, J.B. McFadden, and J.A. Blake, wardens.

Chester has a good fire department. It consists of a steamer, manned by whites, of which Mr. David Hemphill is president, of a hand engine manned by colored citizens with a colored president, Harrison Bailey, and of a colored hook and ladder company under the presidency of Daniel Beattie. The chief of the department is Mr. B.M. Spratt, who has been for many years an efficient and zealous fireman. Our town has been visited with several destructive fires since the close of the war, but they proved to be blessings, for old frame buildings were destroyed and in their place handsome brick structures were erected. With our efficient department and present class of buildings the danger of a general and disastrous conflagration is almost removed. The water for the fire department is obtained from cisterns.

The buildings of the Agricultural, Horticultural, and Mechanical Association of Chester, York, Fairfield, and Lancaster counties are located at this place.* The next exhibit will be the ninth annual fair of the association. Fair week is a great time in Chester, as a large number of people collect here from our own and adjoining counties to meet friends as well as to see the interesting and beautiful articles on exhibition. The fair has accomplished much good in leading to the purchase and breeding of fine varieties of stock and cattle and in securing better varieties of field and garden products. The officers of the association are: Jesse H. Hardin, president; John S. Bratton, Gen. John Bratton, and Gen. John B. Erwin, vice-presidents; R.T. Mockbie, Capt. W.O. Wylie, T.J. Cunningham, S.M. Wylie, and J.S. Withers, directors; E.T. Atkinson, secretary and treasurer; R.E. Ellison, general superintendent.

Our town has excellent school facilities. The Chester Graded School, under the management of Prof. W.H. Witherow, won an enviable reputation as an educational institution. This reputation has been sustained by the learning and experience of Prof. Banks Thompson, the present principal of the institution. He is assisted by an excellent corps of teachers in the persons of Prof. Robert Morrison and Mrs. Bland, Mrs. Webb, Miss Katie Atkinson, and Miss Annie Gott. About two hundred pupils attended the graded school during the last session. At the final exercises they gave satisfactory evidence of the thoroughness of their instruction. Boys and girls are prepared here for the higher institutions of learning. Our town also has a good school for colored pupils. It has been for many years under the control of the Rev. Mr. Loomis, a Northern gentleman, who is assisted by his son, Mr. L. Loomis, and Prof. Green. This institution, in addition to the assistance received from the State, obtains a considerable sum every year from a Northern Presbyterian church. It possesses several good buildings and is prepared to accommodate boys and girls of color from a distance, as well as those at home.

Chester is favored with excellent railroad facilities. It is on the line of the Charlotte, Columbia, and Augusta Railroad, which places it in communication with points north and south; it has two narrow gauge railroads, which connect it with Richburg and Lancaster on the east and with Yorkville, Lincolnton, and Lenoir on the north. Our town has communication with the Air Line at Gastonia, and persons desiring to go to Atlanta from this place have the choice of two routes, by Augusta or over the Air Line. Chester expects in a few months to be blessed with the additional advantages of the Georgia, Carolina, and Northern Railroad. A good portion of the line is already under contract and grading is

---

*This four-county fair existed from 1878 to 1891. See the *News and Courier* (October 3, 1892).

rapidly progressing. This line, when finished, will place us in direct communication with Atlanta, Abbeville, Greenwood, Monroe, Norfolk, and New York. A charter for a railroad from this place to Camden has been obtained, and several townships in this county have decided to subscribe to the capital stock of the company. It is earnestly hoped that definite action looking to the construction of this important line of railroad will soon be taken. This will give us another line to Charleston, which is greatly to be desired.

Chester's sanitary, educational, and railroad facilities, reinforced by the industry and enterprise of its citizens, could not fail to make our town one of the best business points in the State. It hopes to increase its business this season with a happy issue of crops. The amount of business done here during the past commercial year was about $700,000, of which S.M. Jones & Co. and Joseph Wylie & Co. did about $100,000 each. In addition to these two large firms, we have the prominent firms of W. Holmes Hardin & Co., W.T.D. Cousar & Son, Culp & Irwin, Crawford & Blake, R. Brandt & Son, J.J. & T.B. Stringfellow, Gregg & Means, J.S. Calvin, Hafner Bros., J.D. Ratterree, W.H. Rosborough, E.C. Stahn, L. Samuels, Gunhouse & Co., Fishel & Walker, A.H. Davega, S.B. Massey & Son, and several smaller firms.

Our town has a sound financial institution in the name of the Chester Building Loan Association. The officers are W.T.D. Cousar, president; J.L. Agurs, vice-president; and B.M. Spratt, secretary and treasurer. The directors are W.H. Hardin, Joseph Wylie, S.B. Latham, S.M. Jones, R. Brandt, E.C. Stahn, M.H. Carpenter, J.L. Glenn, and J.K. Henry.

The National Bank of Chester is an indispensable agent in the transaction of business at this place. It is well and wisely managed. The officers are John J. McLure, president; Joseph Wylie, vice-president; J.L. Harris, cashier; David Hemphill, assistant cashier. The directors are J.J. McLure, Joseph Wylie, James Hemphill, Matthew White, J.L. Agurs, J.F. Wallace, W.H. Hardin, S.B. Latham, and J.J. Hemphill. The capital of the bank is $150,000, and it pays an annual dividend of 8 per cent. During the past commercial year from September 1, 1886, the bank paid out $605,000 for cotton bought at this place. It paid out an additional amount for cotton bought at Richburg, Blackstock, Lowryville, and other places in the county. Chester is surrounded by fine cotton lands and is one of the best cotton markets in the State.

Our town does not boast of a cotton factory, but some of its citizens have invested considerable capital in two factories in the county. One is the Fishing Creek Cotton Factory of which Capt. F.H. Barber is president; the other, the Cedar Shoals Factory, of which Capt. O. Barber is president. The Fishing Creek Factory is one of the best equipped cotton mills in the State, and at the late meeting of the stockholders declared a handsome dividend. The success of these mills has led to the discussion of the advisability of building a cotton factory at this place. Many of our citizens are of the opinion that an enterprise of this character would pay well and have expressed their willingness to back their judgment with their money. While no definite action has been taken, I believe the day is not far distant when Chester will have a cotton factory.

The machine shop of W.E. Moffett is located here. This is an extensive shop and does a vast amount of work, not only for this but adjoining counties. In addition to making and repairing various articles of machinery, cotton gins and cotton planters are manufactured here, lumber is planed, cotton is ginned and pressed, and different kinds of work done, which show it to be a place abounding with great life and activity.

The lumber yard of D.B. Spratt & Co. is quite extensive. They supply the public not only with lumber but with doors, blinds, sashes, and all articles of building materials.

Chester is proud of the Law Light Infantry, Capt. G.J. Patterson, one of the best companies in the State. It is ever ready to support the State in the enforcement of law.

Our town has two newspapers, the *Chester Reporter,* edited by Mr. John A. Buchanan, and the *Chester Bulletin,* edited by Mr. F.T. Morgan.

The hotels and boarding houses of Chester are very good. The Central House, kept by Mr. Sidney Nail, is located on the hill, and the Railroad Hotel, kept by Mr. W.M. Nicholson, is located at the depot. The latter hotel is said by commercial travellers to be one of the best houses between Atlanta and Richmond. They are fond of making it a stopping place on Sunday.

Chester is blessed with beautiful churches. The Rev. R.W. Sanders is pastor of the Baptist, the Rev. George Summey, pastor of the Presbyterian, the Rev. H.F. Chrietzberg, pastor of the Methodist, the Rev. J.S. Moffett, pastor of the Associate Reformed Presbyterian, and the Rev. Mr. Joiner, pastor of the Episcopal. We have a Catholic Church, but the priest does not visit his flock with much regularity. There are colored churches of the Presbyterian, Methodist, and Baptist persuasions.

Our town is favored with several societies. The Masonic fraternity, Odd Fellows, Knights of Honor, Legion of Honor, and Good Templars are here and prospering greatly.

Our town was settled about the time of the Revolutionary War by the Scotch-Irish from Chester, Pennsylvania, after which it takes its name. Sprung from noble parentage, it is not strange that the sons of Chester have always been worthy and patriotic citizens, whether in peace or war. They manifested their devotion to country by their gallant bearing on the fields of Mexico, and in the late war between the States they did all and suffered all that brave men could do and suffer for the support of the cause they believed to be right and just. At the close of that tremendous conflict the survivors among them returned home and, though ruined in fortune, went to work with undaunted spirits.

With its substantial stores and beautiful private residences, Chester is "a thing of beauty" and will be a "joy forever." It is by no means a completed city, as some are inclined to believe. When it secures additional railroad facilities, it will move

'86 Association Counties '86

FAIR.

CHESTER, S. C.,

OCTOBER, 26, 27, 28, 29.

All Exhibits must be made by 6 o'clock Monday, October the 25th.

A FULL AND COMPLETE PROGRAMME EACH DAY.

-:Special Attractions:-

WEDNESDAY AND THURSDAY.

Orations By

CAPT. B. R. TILLMAN & COL. A. COWARD

ON

THE NEEDS OF FARMERS.

A Most Excellent Band of Music.

FRIDAY

SPORTS & RACES

Excursion Tickets on All the Railroads.

For particulars and Premium List apply to

J. K. HENRY, Sec.

GRAY'S!

Advertisement in the *Chester Bulletin,* October 15, 1886.
South Caroliniana Library.

forward in the path of improvement and progress. These facilities will bring in their wake a cotton compress, a cotton factory, and smaller industries, which will greatly add to the population and wealth of our town. With the completion of the Georgia, Carolina, and Northern Railroad, Chester will increase its business with Atlanta and the West, and with the construction of the Chester and Camden line will increase its business with Charleston.

The happy day will then have dawned when circumstances will enable our merchants to deal more extensively with the metropolis of the State. Instead of adding to the wealth of other places, they will join in the effort to build up our own "City by the Sea." In adding to her riches they will benefit the State and indirectly their own town. Chester rejoices in the rapid and wonderful recuperation of Charleston from the disastrous effects of the great calamity of last year. Our citizens will give evidence of this joy by their presence in the metropolis during Gala Week.

News and Courier, August 29, 1887.

Clinton, a Town That Saw the Light

If this anonymous sketch is to be believed, Clinton indeed had a wild and woolly childhood. In the 1850s land was worthless, malaria and fish ponds abounded, bullies dominated the local scene, and travelers shunned the place. Then, just as the railroad and woman's "refining influence" began to have some impact, the Civil War and its aftermath dealt this struggling little Laurens County community yet another cruel blow. But after 1877 all had changed, we are told. In August of 1887 Clinton was an educational, religious, and commercial center, a law-abiding, wide-awake town (built largely of solid rock and concrete), and ready to contribute to the economic well-being of South Carolina. Its citizens had, however, no ambition to become a city and wanted nothing to do with streetcars and electric lights. Their only goal was to become a "children's paradise."

* * *

The town of Clinton, thirty-three years ago, was in the woods. Every outlook from the highway was dark and sombre. The ground was not thought to be worth more than twenty-five cents an acre for farm purposes. Pools filled with fish were scattered everywhere, and these, partly dry in the summer, spread malaria around. It had the reputation of being a low, unhealthy, uncanny place, and travellers hurried through it. Some living people remember away back in the century when bear and deer were in its tangled woods.

As the years went by the scene shifted. The railroad came to Clinton. That was in 1854. The forests were cut away and the sunlight allowed to come in. One by one the fish ponds were slowly drained, and people began to live about the rough board depot. A barroom or two, with a gang-plank flung across the pools where the rains settled, were the first signs of a coming village. About 1853 the village had a year or two of spasmodic life. It became incorporated. It built a schoolhouse and a couple of churches and more barrooms and a gambling den or two. It aspired to the dignity of having horse races and gander-pullings. It became noted for its chicken fights and chicken fighters. Its glory was that its bullies could whip out all Spartanburg, not to mention the rest of creation. One chap threatened to grease the town whole and swallow it. It was a bad day for him when he reached Clinton. The most prominent citizen of the place greased him, swallowed him whole, and hung his clothes on the outer wall as a trophy. That is a legend of the ancient days.

People still feared to pass through Clinton. The ponds were now drained and the place was getting healthier. But most travellers thought it still the unhealthiest place about, and they kept their eyes skinned when they passed through it. Some passed by it some other way.

But woman's refining influence had come to Clinton, and the churches were doing their level best to save the town. Then came the war, and it looked as if Clinton was dead forevermore. Not a house was built; hardly a nail was struck until 1869. The bad odor that hung over the place, the moral malaria, still continued. People still spoke of Clinton as a plague-spot. But the forces were mustering that were to make the place all that a place ought to be. The people had discovered before this that the village was built in a little cup on a lofty ridge. They had felled the forest and caught sight of the distant blue mountains. They had swept their ponds into the Enoree on the one side and the Saluda on the other. The mountain breezes had swept away the malaria. Sweet water only twenty feet under ground bubbled up almost at the touch of the spade. They had suddenly awaked to the consciousness that theirs was a lovely spot. They had opened their forest glades to the blue heavens, and they determined to win the smiles of Heaven's King.

It was in 1878 that the Waterloo for the barrooms came. It was only three years afterward that Governor Simpson signed the bill to prohibit the sale of liquor in the town of Clinton. He remarked, "Twenty years ago I would have had to send a regiment of militia to enforce this bill on that town." Every man in the town but two signed the petition for its passage. This is the town that on Tuesday, August 10, gave an overwhelming majority for prohibition and came very near saving the county for the cause of sobriety. Twenty years had wrought a wonderful moral revolution. Ten years has worked up an equally surprising change in the matter of its temporal prosperity. Let it be premised that everything was against the place. It was overshadowed by Laurensville, its county seat. It was on a little branch railroad with railroad discrimination always against it. Its people were entirely without capital, and no foreign capital has ever come in to build up the place.

In these ten years past there has been a new town built on the site of the old. The population has increased from about three hundred to eight hundred. New streets have been opened up, and these have been lined with new residences, many of them very neat and stylish. Fifty or sixty have been built in the past eight years. All the streets have been set with shade trees and have excellent hard-packed sidewalks. A simple but complete system of drainage makes the town thoroughly healthy, and there has not been, for ten years past, a greater annual death rate than 11.9 per thousand. At one time there was not a death among the whites for sixteen months.

The entire business quarter of the village has been rebuilt. A dozen handsome brick stores have been built and filled with large and varied stocks of goods. Messrs. M.S. Bailey & Sons, Bailey Bros., Owens Bros., R.R. Blakely, R.Z. Wright & Co., Summerel Bros., R.N.S. Young, M.B. Vance, J.W. Young, J.M. Blakely, D.M. Fulton, and Little Bros. & Co. are among the principal merchants. Mrs.

Albright and the Misses Copeland have fine millinery establishments. We have an excellent hotel in Dr. Irby's, known as "The Drummers' Retreat," and a fine boarding-house called the "Toni-Dora." Only a year ago a handsome bank building was erected, and a large banking business with $75,000 capital is conducted by Messrs. M.S. Bailey & Sons.

The manufacturing interests of the place are not neglected. There is a shingle mill, a planing mill, two flour and grist mills, several steam ginning establishments, a tin manufacturing establishment, a brick factory, carriage and wagon building and repair shops, a photograph gallery, &c.

The press is represented by the *Clinton Enterprise,* which was established this year by a joint stock company, and is conducted by T.B. Crews & Co. *Our Monthly,* now in its twenty-fourth volume, is also published here and is a literary and religious publication of a local character that has done a great deal for the place. It has recently completed a very handsome little two-story office of concrete that is an ornament of the village.

And that reminds us to say that it was this town of Clinton that has most extensively used the common quartz or flint rock for building purposes. There are more concrete structures in this town than in any other town in South Carolina. The buildings are all handsome, durable structures, and the untractable material is used in various ways. One of the buildings is, perhaps, the only one in the State in which the quartz boulders are used as rough ashlars, the stones all showing like brick.

But it is her school system that Clinton is most proud of and justly so. Her citizens have devoted their untiring energies to the purpose of making the town a school centre of the county. The ornament and pride of the town is the Thornwell Orphanage, which is presided over by the Rev. W.P. Jacobs, the pastor of the Presbyterian Church. This institution was begun in faith twelve years ago with half a dollar. Today it has a beautiful seminary building of concrete, one of the best-appointed school buildings in the up-country. There are three very handsome stone cottages erected at an average cost of $5,000, a couple of industrial buildings, all concrete, besides several wooden buildings. A farm, a printing office, and other industrial work is carried on in connection with the institution and others are soon to be added. There are now sixty inmates in this Orphanage, and a happier set of children are not to be found. As they are kept till a regular course of studies are completed, they become greatly attached to their home, to the town, and to each other. They often come back to the old home on visits and look upon its president as their father. The children are from ten different states and seven different denominations. The institution is supported mainly by the charitable gifts of Presbyterians throughout the South, the "City by the Sea" being among its principal benefactors.*

*Eighteen months later, on January 31, 1889, the *News and Courier* published yet another profile of Clinton in which Ambrose E. Gonzales described the work of the Thornwell Orphanage in still greater detail.

Thornwell Orphanage, Clinton. *South Caroliniana Library.*

A jewel in the crown of Clinton is its college. This educational establishment has been of long growth, being the outcome of the school set up in Clinton in the days when it was not decided whether it would live or die. What a change since those days! A handsome, three-story structure of stone and Clinton-made brick, located in a lovely grove, commands the head of one of its finest streets. It has ample accommodations for the first-class college it intends to be. The building is now finished at a cost of $7,000, the generous contributions of Clinton's citizens. Its president, Robert P. Smith, was called from Reidville College to this place. Prof. Barnes is a young man of remarkable insight into the dead languages. Prof. Lee, of the Lees of Edisto, has had thirty-five years experience as a teacher. There are other instructors of experience, and the students are gathered from all parts of the State. This also is a Presbyterian college and expects to be the Princeton of South Carolina in the years to come.

Clinton Academy, under the guiding hand of Prof. Parrott, the editor of the *Enterprise,* is rapidly winning its way into favor, not only in Clinton but throughout the State. It had a large number of boarders last year and will open with a full house in September. The Academy is of high grade, preparing for the junior class in the State colleges. Miss Gilmer of North Carolina is in charge of an excellent school for the infants, which is a gem in its way.

Clinton is energetic and enterprising, but she has no intention of being a city. It is her ambition to be a village of homes, happy Christian homes. She wants no street cars nor electric lights. She isn't aspiring after a daily newspaper. The *News and Courier* is good enough for her. But it is her ambition to be a "Children's Paradise."

A notice of Clinton that would leave out the churches would simply be an account of the city without mention of that which made it. There are three churches for the white people and three for the colored—Presbyterian, Methodist, and Baptist. All have excellent properties, all are well attended and well equipped, and all stand high up on the roll of their respective churches. The Presbyterian Sabbath School is excelled by but few outside of the cities. Its regular recurring anniversaries are the best known events in the county.

Clinton has a brass band that has achieved an enviable notoriety. There is an organized building and loan association with all shares subscribed and only waiting for a charter. There is talk of an association for the purpose of putting building lots on the market at prices and terms within reach of the humblest. The Georgia, Carolina, and Northern Railway was early encouraged by citizens of the town. Three of them were on its original board of directors, and one, Dr. Wm. A. Shands, is a director in the consolidated company. Clinton is on the chartered route.

The J.W. Copeland Company is a new departure in the way of merchandising, shares being held at $25, and farmers around subscribing freely.

The town has an active, energetic, wide-awake town council, with Wm. A. Shands, intendant. This council is adorning and beautifying the town. There is money in the treasury. The guardhouse is a luxury only, for there are none who avail themselves of its solitary pleasure. At present it is stored full of old plunder. This town is a prohibition town, out and out, fair and square. The law is strictly enforced. It is needless to add that taxes are lower than in the old whiskey days, and there is no need for a town marshal or even for locks on the front doors.

News and Courier, August 26, 1887.

Columbia, the Capital City

Columbia, like Charleston, defied simple analysis of the sort appropriate for smaller communities throughout the state. However, on September 4, 1888, and again on October 2, 1889, the Gonzales brothers published comprehensive summaries of life in that city, each of these reports covering about one and one-half pages. Here in somewhat condensed form is the 1888 survey compiled by Narcisco and William E. Gonzales.

* * *

According to the census of 1880, Columbia had a population then of 10,036, an increase of less than 800 over 1870. In this year of 1888, it has, according to a careful and scrupulous enumeration just made by Mr. C.M. Douglas in the dullest month of the year, 12,765 inhabitants, an increase of 2,729 or over 27 per cent. Mr. Douglas made his canvass while securing materials for his city directory, soon to be published, and his figures can be relied on.

The growth and actual importance of Columbia are not fully shown even by this census, for within three-quarters of a mile of the city limits—they extend only one mile in each direction from the centre of business—are suburbs containing an aggregate population of fully 2,500 people, who spend their days and work in Columbia. Among these suburbs may be mentioned Waverly, Liberty Hill, Wheeler's Hill, Kellytown, Barhamville, Cottontown on the Winnsboro Road, north of Elmwood Avenue, and New Brookland at the Lexington terminus of the Congaree Bridge, a mushroom town, with half a dozen stores and an increasing population. The colleges and schools bring fully 300 additional population to the city to reside from September to June; and, even excepting the members and attaches of the General Assembly, the floating population is very large, indeed greater than any city in the State. So with the most moderate estimates, Columbia, as an aggregation of people, and not as a municipality, must be credited with a population of 15,000.

Mr. Douglas indicates that Columbia has a majority of 967 white people and 457 more white than colored males. It was not always thus.

His classification of business and professional firms reveals that Columbia is a much bigger and busier place than most people believe it is: agricultural implement dealers, 3; agricultural implement manufacturers, 3; architects, 3; attorneys at law, 30; auctioneers, 2; bakers, 5; banks, 4; barbers, 10; beer bottlers, 3; billiard parlors, 5; blacksmiths, 4; boarding houses, 12; book and job printers, 5; books and stationery, 5; boot and shoe dealers, 9; boot and shoe makers, 14; boot and shoe manufacturers, 1; builders materials, 3; building and loan associations, 3; butchers, 13; candy manufacturers, 2; carpet dealers, 2; carriage dealers, 3; carriage and wagon manufacturers, 5; china and glassware dealers, 4; clothing dealers, 13; coal and wood dealers, 2; colleges and schools, 12; commission merchants, 7; confectionery dealers, 11; contractors and builders, 10; cotton brokers and buyers, 6; cotton compress, 1; cotton factory, 1; cooper, 1; dentists, 5; druggists, 10; dry goods dealers, 6; engine manufacturer, 1; express company, 1; fertilizer company, 1; fish and oyster dealer, 1; foundries, 3; furniture dealers, 4; grocers and provision dealers, 62; gunsmiths, 2; hardware dealers, 6; hay and grain dealers, 4; hosiery manufacturer, 1; hotels, 8; house, sign, and ornamental painters, 6; ice dealers, 3; ice manufacturer, 1; insurance and real estate brokers, 14; livery and sale stables, 4; lumber dealers, 2; marble yards, 2; machinery dealers, 4; merchandise brokers, 4; milliners, 6; music dealers, 3 ; news depots, 4; newspapers, 4; oil manufactories, 3; paint and oil dealers, 4; photographers, 3; physicians, 12; planing mills, 2; plumbers and gas-fitters, 4; junk shops, 2; railroads, 5; restaurants, 7; saddlery and harness dealers, 2; saloons, 35; sash, blind, and door dealers, 3; sewing machine dealers, 2; soda water manufacturers, 2; stock and bond brokers, 5; tailors, 12; undertakers, 3; watchmakers and jewellers, 6; ware house (commercial), 1; stove and hardware dealers, 2; telegraph company, 1; tannery, 1; steam laundries, 2. It is quite a city after all!

Since the surrender by the State of the Columbia Canal to the city, a wise act consummated last December, real estate values in and around Columbia have advanced from 25 to 35 per cent. In certain sections of the city values have more than doubled. Actual sales prove this assertion. There is a demand for dwellings to rent at rates ranging from $12 to $18 a month. Lands near the city—say within five miles of it—rent from $3 to $5 an acre and sell from $25 to $60 an acre, according, of course, to location and quality.

Columbia's financial condition is better now than it has been in twenty years. The receipts of the city government for the year ending August 1, 1888, were $77,395.66, and the expenditures during the same period amounted to $75,253.24. Some of the extra expenses during the year were for the new reservoir, water pipe, hose for the fire department, interest on Canal bonds, cancellation of old city bonds, special appropriations for city schools, and street improvements.

The premium receipts by insurance agents in Columbia for the year ending August 15, 1888, amounted to $41,340.68. The amount of fire losses paid during the same time, including those on the big cotton fire of Jones and Robertson, which occurred June 6, 1888, and consumed or injured 1,300 bales, was $36,172.35. The fire referred to was the first disastrous one which Columbia has experienced for several years and the losses by it were, of course, exceptional.

All of the Columbia banks have done a prosperous business during the year and are stronger than ever. The Carolina National Bank is the senior institution, having been established over twenty years ago. Its capital stock is $100,000. A

Looking north from the capitol, Columbia, c. 1890. *South Caroliniana Library.*

savings department is attached to the institution, its deposits at this time being $107,000. Its officers are: W.A. Clark, president; R.S. Desportes, vice president; and Willie Jones, cashier.

The Central National Bank was established in 1871 and has been uniformly successful. Its capital stock is $100,000. Capt. W.B. Stanley, the president of the bank, died a few days ago. Dr. James Woodrow is vice president and J.B. Sawyer, cashier.

The Commercial Bank, a private institution, organized by Levi Metz and Capt. C.J. Iredell, opened its doors September 1, 1883. Its capital is $25,000, and it has individual wealth to the amount of $100,000 to back it. The bank has done an excellent business and is prospering well. Capt. C.J. Iredell is manager and Mr. James Iredell, cashier.

The Loan and Exchange Bank was organized under State laws less than two years ago and began business October 1, 1886, with a paid up capital of $50,000, since gradually increased to $112,000, the amount subscribed to being $127,000. The officers are: A.C. Haskell, president; W.C. Fisher, vice president; and Julius H. Walker, cashier.

Much of the remarkable progress made in building up this Sherman-burnt city is attributable to the good work of the Building and Loan associations. A number have completed their mission and closed their books with handsome results to their stockholders, but three are now in successful operation.

1. The Workingmen's—President, Dr. W.T. Moore; vice president, Capt. John S. Wiley; secretary and treasurer, T. Hasel Gibbes. Began business five years ago

with 1,500 shares, which have been reduced by surrender and purchase to 774. The profits up to June 1, 1888, amounted to $16.36 per share.

2. The Mutual Beneficial—President, D. Gambrill; vice president, Dr. Jas. Woodrow; secretary and treasurer, G.M. Walker. Began business four and a half years ago with 2,452 shares, since reduced to 1,635. The profits have been about $14 per share.

3. The Richland—President, Col. John T. Sloan, Jr.; vice president, Col. Geo. K. Wright; secretary and treasurer, Wm. Barnwell. Began business in January last with 1,000 shares. Interest charge limited to 8 per cent, which has resulted in such a demand for its loans that enough have been made to absorb the receipts for five months in advance.

The other associations have their funds invested now, but are required to charge 10 per cent.

The last year has been an important one in the history of the old South Carolina College, for it witnessed its development into a State university as broad in foundation and as liberal in equipment as any in the South. The octogenarian college, with its glorious memories of the past, is now the young state university, strong, alert, and progressive, stimulated by its new powers and elevated by the noble record of former years.

The University, as now constituted, has six departments: a graduate department, a college of agriculture and the mechanic arts; a college of liberal arts and sciences, a college of pharmacy, a normal school, and a law school. There are 27 teachers, 41 graduate and 20 undergraduate courses: general, special, or professional for degrees and certificates. Instruction is given in bookkeeping and phonography [a system of shorthand]. There are thoroughly equipped chemical, mineralogical, biological, physiological, physical, and pharmaceutical laboratories. The mechanical department is equipped with an engine and all necessary machinery and tools and there are shops for iron and wood work.

An experimental farm is attached to the University and is under the able direction of President McBryde. A draughting room, model classes connected with the normal school for practice teaching, and other advantages are offered. The tuition fee is only $40 a session and will be remitted to all students certifying their inability to pay. With so complete an equipment for the instruction of the youth of the State, the University should double even the large attendance which the College sessions enjoyed. It is a great institution.

The Columbia Female College is one of the famous institutions of the city and one of the most popular educational agencies in the State. It graduated its first class in 1860, and except during the interruption of its work in the years of chaos immediately following the war has steadily advanced in efficiency and influence. The College is under the auspices of the Methodist Church. The course of study is divided into ten schools, embracing every department of accepted study for young ladies. The Rev. O.A. Darby, D.D., is the president, and the corps of officers and teachers numbers fifteen. During the last scholastic year there were in attendance ninety boarding pupils and forty-three day scholars, making a total enrollment of 133.

The Columbia Theological Seminary, which is under the care of the four Presbyterian Synods of South Carolina, Georgia, Alabama, and South Georgia and Florida, will begin its next session on Monday, September 17. The institution has passed through serious difficulties and changes during recent years, but although grave obstacles to its success still continue, its prospects for usefulness appear to be brightening. Profs. Tadlock and Girardeau expect to occupy their old chairs, and two new professors have been chosen by the board of directors. Most of the students who attended last year expressed their intention to return, and a respectable junior class of new students is looked for. The discussions in regard to the administration of the Seminary are not over, but there is ground for hope that an institution founded in faith and prayer is destined to a future of usefulness not inferior to the past.

The Columbia Graded Schools, during the five years of their existence, have achieved a reputation for excellence and good management which has not only extended throughout South Carolina but far beyond the borders of the State. The success of the schools has been brilliant from the first, and Superintendent D.B. Johnson has been the chief factor in it. But the schools have been loyally supported by the people, and their board of control has been liberal and efficient.

The excellence of the school facilities here has attracted many families to Columbia and has contributed as much as any other thing to the rapid growth of the city. The State school fund is supplemented by a local tax of two mills, which, with careful and economic management, is sufficient to maintain them at a high point of efficiency.

There are three schools, one for white girls, one for white boys, and one for colored children of both sexes. The corps of instructors comprises a superintendent and twenty-seven teachers. The following table shows the enrollment for the session of 1887–88, closing June 15:

	Boys	**Girls**	**Total**
White	421	462	883
Colored	365	508	873
Grand Total	786	970	1,756

The increase in attendance over the last preceding year was 120. The cost of each pupil per month was only 78 cents, a very low rate in comparison with other first-class schools. The schools have a library of over 800 volumes.

From the high school grades there were graduated in June three young men and four young women. The schools will be able to accommodate next session a larger number of pupils than ever before, and thus meet the increasing demand for education which the augmenting population of the city creates.

The Winthrop Training School, a purely professional institution for the training of young women as teachers for the common schools of the State, was established two years ago by Superintendent D.B. Johnson, who induced the Peabody Board to contribute to its maintenance. Prof. Johnson has been its superintendent, and from a small beginning it has developed into a State institution of value and importance.

At the commencement in June eight young women thoroughly and practically trained for teaching were graduated. The faculty now consists of a superintendent and four assistant teachers and is controlled by eight trustees, of which the State superintendent of education is ex-officio a member. The student teachers are required to do practice teaching in a school room with a class of forty children. The State, according to an Act of the last General Assembly, proposes to support one young woman 18 years of age from each county while she is being prepared to teach in the common schools of her county. This is done for the improvement of the common schools and will result in much good.

So far from destroying the private schools of the city, the Graded School system appears to have stimulated them. There are over 200 pupils in excellent schools conducted by the following ladies and gentlemen: Miss I.D. Martin, Miss Elmore, the Misses Reynolds, Miss Janney, for girls; Mr. C.H. Barnwell, Mr. R.B. Clarkson, for boys; the Catholic School, for girls and boys.

The Benedict Institute, supported by Northern philanthropists, and Allen University, an establishment of the A.M.E. Church, give instruction to a large number of colored youth.

Among the most important of Columbia's industrial enterprises are two cotton seed oil mills, which do an immense business. Several years ago the Oliver Bros. of Charlotte established a big oil mill in the southwestern part of the city and operated it successfully. Then the Cotton Oil Trust secured control of it, and the Olivers, with other moneyed men, originated the Southern Oil Company and built mills at a number of points in the South, including Columbia. This was last year, and the new mill began work in September, 1887. The first mill, still known as the "Oliver," had a capacity of manipulating from 80 to 90 tons of cotton seed a day. The Southern Mill was built to have a capacity of 100 tons.

The plant of the Oliver Mill has been enlarged this summer, so that it begins this season with a capacity of 125 tons a day, and the two mills combined, employing some 120 hands, will use 225 tons every twenty-four hours, for the mills work all night by electric light. Mr. Geo. L. Baker is secretary and treasurer of the Oliver Oil Company and manager of the mill. Mr. Thompson is the new manager of the Southern Mill.

The Columbia Oil Mill, a minor but a pioneer enterprise, should not be ignored. It is conveniently located near the railway junction and was established about six years ago by H.M. Gibson & Co. of this city. The initial capacity was six tons a day, and it was satisfactorily operated until a year ago when the fight between the Oil Trust and the Southern giants threatened to make it unprofitable and it was closed.

Mr. Gibson has been greatly enlarging it this summer with the purpose of re-entering the field, and soon a joint stock company with a capital of $25,000 will be in operation. Put Columbia's oil mills down for a consumption during the season of 1888–89 of 250 tons a day, making it the greatest centre of such manufactures east of the Mississippi.

A branch of the monopoly, the Standard Oil Company, is established here in Columbia and does a big business buying turpentine locally and selling oil over the greater portion of the State. The purchases of turpentine are about 250,000 gallons and the sales of kerosene 150,000 gallons annually.

The South Carolina Penitentiary Boot and Shoe Factory was established in May, 1881, by Mr. A.C. Dilbert and has been successful. It is located in the Penitentiary yard and is operated by a force of 100 convicts, superintended by free labor. The factory is run to its full capacity and turns out about 300 pair a day. There is a separate department for hand-made shoes, and the goods range in quality from the commonest to the finest "solid goods" for both sexes and all ages.

M.A. Markley & Co., proprietors of the Congaree Hosiery Mills, occupy a large factory building within the Penitentiary yard where convict labor is superintended by Northern experts. The manufactory was established about five years ago by Messrs. Moulton of Laconia, N.H., and conducted by them until June 1, 1887, when Mr. Markley purchased the plant and enlarged it. The products are cotton, wool, merino, and silk hosiery, plain and fancy, from the coarsest cotton at 40 cents a dozen to fine silk goods at $12 a dozen. The annual product is worth about $72,000.

The machine shops of the South Carolina branches of the Richmond and Danville system are very important to Columbia. These shops, under the competent management of Master Mechanic Green, do a great volume of work in building and repairing engines and cars. During the summer months about 155 employees are engaged in work in these shops, and in the winter their number is increased to 200. The annual pay roll reaches $110,000. The value of the products of these shops during the past year was $234,000.

The Tozer Engine Works, formerly the Tozer & Dial Works, has a wide reputation for excellence of product. The buildings are of brick, are located on West Gervais opposite the Union Depot, and are connected with all the roads by a branch track. Mr. Thornwell McMaster is manager and Mr. W.P. Lester foreman of the shop. The capital invested is $20,000, and at present 23 hands are employed.

The works construct agricultural and new mill engines from 6 to 40 horse power (using the pattern of the famous Tozer engine) and boilers from 6 to 100 horse power. The shop has a capacity of three engines a week and is well equipped in the foundry line. Over 500 Tozer engines are in use in South Carolina, Georgia, Florida, and Alabama.

Mr. C.C. Habernicht's Ice Factory is the largest and most successful in the State. It began business six years ago with a plant having a capacity of ten tons a day, but since that time has twice been burnt out and rebuilt each time on a larger scale. The present factory has a daily capacity of twenty-five tons and is complete in all of its appointments. It is operated by a 60-horse power engine. Ice from this establishment finds purchasers all over the State, and beyond its borders. It is shipped as far away as Charlotte, Anderson, and Barnwell, and has in time of famine even supplied Charleston and Augusta.

In the spring of 1887 Mr. J.E. Turner opened a canning factory at the northwest corner of Main and Greene streets. He had had no previous experience in the canning business, but said that Columbia offered a fine opening for such an industry. The season last summer was so unfavorable that his crop of vegetables was almost destroyed. This year the crops of vegetables are good and Mr. Turner is in the middle of his packing season. He cans tomatoes, green corn, and okra combined. His farm, about two miles from the city, has about 30 acres in tomatoes and the same number in corn. His okra he buys from other farmers.

The factory is a very interesting place to visit. Mr. Turner employs five or six regular hands and during the season has frequently as many as fifteen extra hands at work. He has the patent machines and appliances for making his own cans. This he does in the winter or before the packing season commences. The outturn of the factory this year will be about 60,000 cans of the vegetables already named. Of these, 35,000 are large and wholesale at about $1.10 a dozen, and 25,000 of lesser size sell at 80 cents a dozen. The sales made and assured this season will reach about $4,874.

H.M. Gibson & Co. have been manufacturing fertilizers at their oil mill during the last year. The outturn of their works was about 1,000 tons, which sold at an average of $23 a ton. The demand could not be supplied, and the works will increase their capacity and product during the season now opening.

This review does not attempt to give in detail the outturn of such minor manufactures as carpentering, tin, copper, and sheet iron ware, grist mills, and others reported in the census. It would necessitate a minute canvass of the city, which is not practicable. Yet there are, indeed, various manufactures deserving of full mention which can only be referred to briefly.

Mr. F.A. Burroughs manufactures brick machines of his own invention, which are declared to be the most satisfactory on the market.

F.W. Wing has a large steam grist mill with the latest improvements.

Mr. James Hunter is a manufacturer of grist mills, who keeps his own counsel about his business, but is said to supply a large trade.

The Stanley Manufacturing Company at Eastover near Columbia manufactures large quantities of pine oil.

The minor manufactures not classified in this review turned out in 1880, according to the census of that year, over $150,000 worth of products. No one who compares the Columbia of today with the Columbia of 1880 will doubt that these manufactures have doubled at least, and their total product is, therefore, placed at $300,000.

Everybody ought to know the history of the Columbia Canal. At any rate it has been a political "issue" for so long a period that everybody ought to know it, and no attempt will be made here to outline its distant past. It is enough to say that after the State, its owner and developer, had abandoned it for twelve months, the Legislature, at its session last December, surrendered the property to the city on condition of its completion from Gervais Street to the upper terminus within a specified time—two years according to the bill, but seven years by the terms of a final amendment.*

Cotton manufacturing by water power must wait on the completion of the Columbia Canal, but steam will be the motive power of Columbia's first cotton mill. The Congaree Manufacturing Company was organized last spring, mainly through the efforts of Judge A.C. Haskell, for the purpose of inaugurating the business in this city. The capital stock was placed at $100,000, which amount was subscribed in Columbia and Philadelphia, but most of it here. Opportunity was offered for securing at reasonable figures the Bentwood Furniture Factory, unused since the collapse of that enterprise, and at a great bargain the outfit of a Northern yarn mill but little used.

The mill is located in the southwestern part of the city near the Union Depot, within a stone's throw of all the railroads, is connected with all by branch tracks, and has, altogether, an ideal position for such an enterprise. About 125 hands will be employed and the weekly consumption of cotton will average forty bales. Ten neat, double six-roomed houses have been erected to the south of the mill for the operatives. By the middle of September the 8,000 spindles will be hard at work increasing the already handsome total of Columbia's business.

Columbia has long longed for illumination by electricity. The Congaree Gas and Electric Company, with $20,000 capital subscribed in Columbia and Charleston, was recently organized and at once began the work of preparation. The officers are Col. John T. Sloan, Jr., president; Major W.H. Gibbes, vice president; and Mr. John P. Thomas, Jr., secretary and treasurer. Major George B. Edwards of Charleston, who is interested in the enterprise, will exercise general supervision over the works.

The system adopted is the Thomson-Houston, and a 60-arc plant will be put in at once, to be followed soon by an incandescent system. The station and offices of the company are now being erected on Gates Street between Lady and Washington, and the materials are being purchased. The company has a contract with the city for lighting Main and West Gervais streets with fifteen arc lights, and the remainder of the lights will be promptly taken by private parties. It is expected that the system will be in full operation by October 1.

The Columbia Compress Company operates a first-class steam compress in the southwestern portion of the city convenient to all the railroads. Memphis

*See the *News and Courier* (September 4, 1888) for an extensive discussion of the canal's potential, as well as hopes for steamer transportation on the Congaree and for completion of the Columbia, Newberry, and Laurens Railroad. At that time, a South Carolina Railroad bridge at Kingville blocked traffic up the Congaree. The new rail line, however, was erecting a fine granite bridge over the Broad River and soon would open up a new trading area to Columbia merchants.

capital originated the enterprise, but an agreement has been made by which the local cotton firms of Jones & Robertson, Ford, Talley & Co., and Miller Bros. will control the capital stock of $100,000. Dr. J.S. Dunn, who has been in successful charge of the enterprise under the old ownership, remains as manager. The charge for compressing is 50 cents a bale. Most of the Columbia cotton and some from other points is compressed here. During the season just ended, 40,000 bales passed through the compress.

There has been a great deal of complaint, and justifiable complaint, as to the quality of the water furnished by the city water-works to the public. There are in the city park several bold springs which yield a supply of delightful water, but the trouble is that while they turn 300,000 gallons a day into the reservoir the city requires about 600,000 gallons. Accordingly, the practice has been to pump from the river a sufficient quantity of the strong solution of red clay, for which it is so famous, into the reservoir at the crest of Taylor's hill, thus supplementing the natural and pure supply. The mixture has been exasperating, and the city last spring undertook to secure a purer supply.

A new reservoir has been constructed in the northwestern section of Columbia with a capacity of 4,300,000 gallons. It is simply a huge pit with shelving banks, dug deep into a bed of hard red clay. There has been dissatisfaction on account of its freedom from concrete, but the water-works committee are assured that the plan on which it is constructed is practicable. The cost is about $8,000 for the reservoir and new piping. The experiment of the new reservoir will be watched with great interest.

During the year a fine Gamewell fire alarm system has been completed, and the rates of insurance have been lowered in consequence. There are fifteen stations, and this equipment, added to the excellence of the fire department, give great assurance against fires.

The Columbia Postoffice shows in its receipts the effect of the increasing business in the city. Exclusive of money order business, the receipts for the last three years ending June 30 have been as follows: 1885–86 $16,038.62, 1886–87 $16,672.00, 1887–88 $17,839.96.

The carrier service was inaugurated here nearly a year ago and has been very satisfactory. There are four carriers who make three general deliveries and one special in the business section. The same number of collections are made.

The telegraph business of Columbia is rapidly increasing. The Western Union office here employs six operators, and its receipts during the year exceeded those of the previous year by 30 per cent.

The telephone exchange showed no material increase, the public being dissatisfied with the charge of rent of instruments, but there will be a decided increase this year on account of the inauguration of new industries and increased general business.

The railroad facilities of Columbia are exceptionally good. The South Carolina Railway connects the city with Charleston, Augusta, Camden, and (by way of the

3 C's) Lancaster and Rock Hill; the Wilmington, Columbia, and Augusta with Charleston, Georgetown, Wilmington, Wadesboro, and the North; the Charlotte, Columbia, and Augusta ("South Carolina Division, Richmond and Danville") with Augusta, Charlotte, Lancaster, and Lenoir; and the Columbia and Greenville ("Columbia and Greenville Division, Richmond and Danville") with Greenville, Spartanburg, Laurens, Asheville, and the West.

When the Columbia, Newberry, and Laurens Railroad is completed next spring, trains from Columbia will run into Newberry, and later they will pass Glenn Springs into Spartanburg and Rutherfordton, N.C.

Efforts have been made to ascertain the local receipts of the several roads entering the city so as to indicate by this test the increase in Columbia business during the year, but only partial success has been attained.

The Columbia Street Railway Company was organized in 1886 and opened for business in September of the same year. The lines run from the Union Depot across the city to three points: the Charlotte, Columbia, and Augusta Railroad Depot, the Asylum, and Elmwood Cemetery. The equipment consists of six cars and thirty horses. Mr. E.M. Cole of New York is president of the company.

During the year 1887 the city railway, according to the annual report of Superintendent W.D. Starling, took in an average of $40 a day, or $14,600 for the year. Its expenses were $25 a day, or $9,125, leaving a profit of $5,475. It is understood that so far this year its receipts have increased. As fares are five cents each it is easy to estimate that last year over 200,000 persons patronized the line, or an average of 800 a day.

The recent history of the cotton trade in Columbia can be told with a very few words and figures. Here are the figures in bales per year: 1876 12,257, 1882 24,660, 1887 31,000, 1888 51,731. The words are almost as brief. Columbia, on account of its location and its freight rates and facilities, is, of necessity, a fine cotton market; and we have a sufficient number of enterprising buyers in the field to ensure the purchase in this market of the crop in a dozen counties. While the local receipts have been 51,000 bales, Columbia buyers have bought fully 13,000 bales at other points, which were shipped without being brought to this city. The profit on 60,000 bales remains, therefore, in the State Capital.

There are tributory [sic] to Columbia about twenty-five turpentine distilleries with an average annual yield of about 23,000 barrels of rosin and 8,000 casks of spirits of turpentine. Prices of rosin have ruled low throughout the season and are very much depressed at present. Spirits of turpentine, however, have yielded very satisfactory returns. Rosin will average this season for all grades $160 per barrel net to producer, while spirits is worth $14 net, making a total net valuation of $40,000 for rosin and $112,000 for spirits of turpentine. The navigation of the Congaree, incomplete as it is, has greatly facilitated the movements of rosin, giving a savings of 40 to 50 cents per barrel to the producer.

During the past year produce brokers in Columbia have done a business which aggregates nearly $1,225,000. The value of the several products sold is as follows: meal $154,330; flour $88,350; corn $226,960; oats $89,050; hay $28,000; bran $10,250; bacon $588,000; and sundries $20,000.

Publishing, bookbinding, and printing are increasing in Columbia. The establishments of Mr. C.A. Calvo, Jr., and Dr. James Woodrow have large capacities and do excellent work, while the job printing of Wm. Sloane is recognized for its efficiency. There are several minor printing offices. The value of the work in these lines was $90,924.73.

Summary: The Trade of the City

Groceries	$1,501,000
Produce brokers	1,184,940
Naval stores	152,000
Coal and wood	74,000
Hardware, oil & paints	195,000
Machinery	126,838
Jewelry, watches & clocks	26,000
Dry goods	442,000
Millinery	65,000
Clothing, hats, &c.	259,000
Wines, liquors, cigars & tobacco	265,000
Boots & shoes	220,605
Drugs & medicines	88,500
Crockery, glassware, &c.	43,200
Saddles, harness, &c.	30,000
Books & stationery	55,878
Furniture & undertaking	42,000
Lumber & building materials	85,000
Fruits & vegetables	63,000
Beer & soda water	85,000
Ice (less amount manufactured)	10,900
Buggies & wagons	72,000
Stoves, tinware, &c.	18,000
Contractors' work	123,000
Butchers' meats	126,000
Livery stables	24,000
Musical merchandise	18,000
Fertilizers (not manufactured here)	30,039
Sewing machines	85,000
Carpets	32,000
Guns & ammunition	7,000
Car grease	50,000
Kerosene	18,000
Cotton compress	20,000
Bakery & confectionery products	15,000
Miscellaneous	75,000
Total	$5,727,900

Manufactures

Oil mills	$ 680,000
Shoe factory	150,000
Hosiery mill	72,000
Canning factory	4,874
Ice factory	15,000
Fertilizer works	23,000
Marble & granite works	20,000
Iron foundries	65,000
Confectionery & bakery	49,000
Photographers	7,500
Publishing, bookbinding & printing	90,924
Machine shops	234,000
Blacksmith & wheelwright	35,000
Miscellaneous manufactures	300,000
Total	1,746,298
General trade	5,727,900
Cotton	2,224,476
Grand total	$9,698,674

Conclusion

There is nothing now to arrest Columbia's progress. No city in the South is less "shaky" financially. Money is made here by legitimate business, not by speculation. Commercial failures are almost unknown, and every new and old enterprise of which the Bureau has knowledge is on a safe and satisfactory basis. Trade is widening yearly and the establishment of a few jobbing factorage and wholesale houses here is all that is necessary to make Columbia a really great centre of business, because no place in the South has superior advantages for buying and selling goods.

The winter climate attracts an increasing number of Northern visitors, and we only need a big, well-located hotel to draw thousands here from January to June. The development of the Canal, the river improvements, and the new manufacturing enterprises are full of the promise of wealth. The State fair is being aided by a local association which will double the attractions the city has heretofore offered to visitors on the occasion of the annual festival.

Unity and liberality and a progressive spirit can make Columbia in a very short time what her position entitles her to be, and even the achievements of today will be cast into shadow by those of 1889 and 1890.

News and Courier, September 4, 1888. N.G.G.-W.E.G.

Conway, Capital of the Hermit County

In the winter of 1884, J.C. Hemphill called Horry the "Hermit County," noting that Conway seemed "as near out of this world as any place my wandering feet have ever found."* To get there from Marion, only thirty-seven miles away, he rode for eight hours through swamps with water sometimes up to the buggy cushions. It was largely, he wrote, "an exceedingly dreary and desolate reach of country" with crude houses and few crops ... a land that traditionally produced only lumber, shingles, naval stores, hides, and wool. Nevertheless, despite the absence of railroads, Hemphill wrote that "the much derided 'Independent Republic of Horry' is beginning to break down the walls which so long shut it out from the world." John I. Green, who visited there six years later, was certain that change had come and still more was on the way. Green, dreamer that he was, even suggested that the ocean beaches of Horry—now South Carolina's famed "Grand Strand"—might someday welcome Northern tourists.

* * *

Conway, the site of Horry County, stands on a high bluff on the west side of Waccamaw River, about fifty miles above Georgetown, at the mouth of Lake Kingston. There is not elsewhere in the lower part of the State a more beautiful site for a town. The Waccamaw is one of the prettiest and more important streams in the low country, and the waters are so pure that vessels going to sea ascend it to fill their water casks. The cause of this purity is found in the river's source, which is in the highlands of North Carolina.

Standing at the wharves here, where the trains run down to the water's edge, one enjoys several lovely views. To the south and west is the river, a broad and placid stream. On one side rises the bluff, covered with trees and plants of the temperate zone, while on the other the eye loses itself in a swamp, where the vegetation flourishes in a tropical vigor and luxuriance. In the spring there is a wealth of radiance and color. The air is vibrant with the songs of birds, and redolent with the exquisite perfume of flowers innumerable. Here one may revel in all that goes to make Southern life so delicious. Nature has been prodigal with her rarest charms. There is on every hand an infinitude of variety and deep draughts of enjoyment intoxicate every sense.

North of the wharves the lake stretches for several hundred yards before it bends. At its mouth there is a draw bridge almost Venetian in delicacy of construction. A little further up, a grove of giant liveoaks crown the bank, and at the bend

---

**News and Courier,* February 12, 1884.

there is a pretty residence and a mill. Viewed from the wharves, all this forms a charming tout ensemble.

The country around here was originally an unbroken pine forest, and only a small portion has yet been cleared. The soil is light and is especially suitable for truck farming and grape culture. The scuppernong grows wild here in many places. As several residents have remarked to me, it is so easy to live here that the people have grown lazy. But this is only according to the general law—that where nature does much man does very little. This, however, only applies to a primitive state, where the population is sparse and the people have a very limited knowledge of the artificial wants of civilization. Now that this section has been opened to the world every resource has a value, and every advantage will find appreciation. But, before considering in detail the advantages and resources of this section it is necessary to look upon the place in its isolation, and its gradual emergence therefrom, for in this will be found the causes of the lack of development which surprise the stranger.

Where in the whole country will you find another county seat which is not incorporated? Public opinion is the only direction of municipal affairs in this town, if it is not too much to say that there are any municipal affairs. While this speaks well for the fraternal spirit of the inhabitants and the influence of the Gospel, it does not indicate much advancement on worldly lines. Thus it is throughout the county—the Golden Rule is more potent than the laws of the land. Some years ago a correspondent of the *News and Courier* called Horry "The Hermit County." It was a very appropriate sobriquet. If the county was hermit-like in its isolation, it was equally so in the rectitude of conduct which prevailed among its population. Today one may find throughout the county many houses whose welcoming doors are never barred by locks and many barns without any doors at all. Is not this as worthy a source of pride as costly structures and the veneer of social refinement?

Until the fall of 1887 there was no railway connection with this place. Immediately after the war a small steamer began to come here occasionally. Irregular communication continued until 1870, when all boats ceased to visit this place. Two vessels came as far as Pott's Bluff, ten miles below here. Freight had to be carried to and from that place on lighters, which were poled. It sometimes took a week to make this trip of ten miles. This deplorable state of affairs continued until 1875, when a small tug began trading by lighters with this place. These lighters were vessels, wharves, ware houses, and shops combined. They were roofed with canvas, counters and shelves were improvised, and when they came up to the wharves the clerks were in their places ready to serve customers.

In 1880 the trade had grown to such an extent that three vessels were trading between Pott's Bluff and New York regularly, and extra vessels were put on in the turpentine season. In 1878 Messrs. Burroughs & Collins had laid the foundation for the present line of steamers by purchasing the *Juniper.* About this time Capt. T.W. Daggett, the present Government contractor for river improvements in this section, put on the *J.M. Cook*. Four or five years later the *Maggie* was built, and a short while afterwards the *Ruth* and *Driver* were put on. The *Maggie, Driver,* and *Ruth* form the present line of steamers between this place and Georgetown. Vessels come as far as Bucksport where there is the largest lumber mill in the State, and a mail steamer makes a trip there three times a week.

It will be seen from the above that the trade of this section has grown steadily and rapidly since the war. In 1874 there was not a steam gin in the county—only two horse-power gins and two water gins. The whole county produced only 75 bales of cotton.

A report of trade for the year ending July 1, 1889, indicates that 7,000 bales of cotton, 98,400 barrels of rosin and tar, 16,400 barrels of turpentine, 8,200,000 feet of lumber, 200,000 shingles, 11,500 barrels of clean rice, 131,500 bushels of rough rice, and some hides, honey, poultry, and fruit were shipped down the Waccamaw. Ninety per cent of this produce, it is said, originated in this county.

This is only what has been done. There is practically no limit to what may be accomplished. Doubtless for many years to come the naval stores trade and the lumber business will be the principal industry. Heretofore the lumbermen have confined themselves almost exclusively to the making of yellow pine lumber and cypress shingles. While there is great room yet for development in the latter industry, the field that offers the greatest advantages to the enterprising capitalist is the manufacture of hard woods. He would have the option of a rail or water route to the North. There is an abundance of white labor here, which can be employed at half the price paid for labor at the North.

This is unquestionably "a white man's country." At the last election the voting was as follows: whites, 2,502; negroes, 866. A third of the negro vote was cast with the whites. In other words, one-third of the people who, according to certain Republican Senators, live in a constant fear of being butchered, vote to maintain Democratic rule. I lay particular stress on the fact of the supremacy of the whites in this section, because it is a well-known fact that the negroes have been an obstacle in the way of immigration. In 1880 the total white population of the county was 10,639; negroes, 4,935. Since then the negro population has decreased about 25 per cent by emigration to Georgia and Western States. During the same period the white population has increased about 25 per cent from natural causes and influx of immigrants from Marion, Marlboro, and Williamsburg counties, where the "no fence" law proved onerous to many of the people engaged in stock raising.

While upon this subject it may be as well to quote a few figures to show the condition of the county. The only debt of the county is that of $37,000, which was voted by four townships to the Wilmington, Chadbourne, and Conway Railroad. The current expense account of the county is smaller than that of any other county in the State. The total expenses for the year amount to about $5,500. The criminal docket is lighter than that of any other county, the General Sessions lasting but two days, and the jail is frequently empty. When it is remembered that there are no municipal ordinances to violate, and that the sheriff has charge of all criminals, one perceives the full significance of the facts which have just been stated.

There are no statistics as to the health of any portion of the State, save the larger cities, which have their own laws on the matter, but, if one may offer the evidence of competent and credible physicians, it can be easily proven that the rate of mortality for this county is as low as that of any section of the South. There are not, probably, half a dozen consumptives in the whole county. The mild climate and the terebinthine odors from the pine forests are the causes of this.

Now that it has been shown that there is nothing in the population or climate which is unfavorable to the investment of large amounts of capital, we will examine further the county's resources.

There are thousands of acres of land, worth $2 or $3 an acre, which would grow numerous varieties of vegetables or grapes. On every hand there is an abundance of small woods of every variety. For thirty or forty miles along the river above here there are beds of the finest marl, and along the lake there is any quantity of lime rock. Under the marl beds there are phosphate deposits which have been declared valuable by competent experts. A few miles down the river there are old salt works, which were very profitable before the war. By solar evaporation salt can be made for 15 cents a bushel, in large quantities. At Little River and Murrell's Inlet, near the coast, there are beds of fine oysters, where canning works would doubtless pay well. Coral reefs run parallel with the coast at a distance of three miles. Between the reefs and the coast there is deep water, where fish abound. There are already in operation several extensive fisheries.

A movement is on foot for the establishment of a cotton factory. This project is supported by some of the most influential men in the county and will doubtless succeed. The establishment of this factory means a great deal to both the town and county—probably more to the county. It is very necessary to turn the attention of the people to new enterprises, and to show them that a greater prosperity may be had from new pursuits than from the old ones. Now there is nothing to keep money in the county. All manufactured goods are purchased at the North. The question arises: "What is to be done when the naval store supply is exhausted, when the pine forests are destroyed?" These are being sent away each year, and nothing is derived from their sale but the necessaries of life. A stimulus to agriculture is necessary. Money should be kept in the country as far as possible, and the rising generation should find employment at home. Further, it goes without saying that if this factory is satisfactorily established, other manufacturing industries will follow, and soon some of all the various kinds of raw material at hand will be utilized by local factories.

But, much as this factory is needed, I think a fine hotel is needed more. In attractions for the Northern tourists this section easily surpasses every other in the State. Shooting of every kind, boating, and fishing would be right at the door of a hotel here. Every kind of game from partridges to deer abounds. The lake and river teem with all sorts of fish, and in winter good ducking can always be had. A turnpike road of twelve miles length would give access to the ocean, where there is as fine a beach as there is in the country. What is lacking? People go in thousands every year to Florida to get what abounds here. This section has one advantage—that of climate. While the air is balmy here it is not enervating. You will ask, perhaps, "If there is such a bonanza in a fine hotel, why don't these people build one?" I must give you the musty answer: "Because they haven't the capital." But wait a moment. There are two capitalists who are willing to put their money into a hotel, but their other interests are so large that they cannot give the matter their undivided attention. They are Mr. B.G. Collins and Mr. J.H. Chadbourne, Jr., the genial and enterprising superintendent of the Wilmington, Chadbourne, and Conway Railroad. Mr. Collins has large mercantile and shipping interests, which require all of his time, and Mr. Chadbourne is largely interested in cotton factories and the lumber trade. But both of these gentlemen are anxious to subscribe for the stock of a company that will build a first-class hotel and are willing to take a majority of the stock. This looks like business, doesn't it? This is certainly a golden opportunity for an enterprising hotel man. The table can be supplied for a mere song, so to speak, from the fields and dairies about here, while the great stock ranges of the lower part of the country would furnish superb beef. If seeing is believing, the best thing that these people can do to advertise their many resources is to bring people to look at them.

There is not a more kindly or hospitable people than the citizens of this town. They are ready to welcome all who wish to join in the development of the place. Old fogyism is dying out rapidly before modern ideas and modern methods.

In educational and religious advantages Conway is the equal of many of her more fortunate sisters. About fifteen years ago the Burroughs High School was founded by Mr. F.G. Burroughs of Burroughs & Collins. Today it will compare favorably with any high school in the State. It is a two-story building, with a large recitation room, music rooms, and sleeping apartments for students. In mathematics the course extends through plane geometry, and in Latin through Caesar and Virgil. Mr. J.H. Dysinger is the principal, and Miss Effie Burroughs is his assistant. Miss Mary E. Pearce has charge of the music department.

In the school building is the Burroughs Library, which was founded for the use of the town. It contains five hundred volumes of choice literature. "Trash" finds no place in its bookcases.

The professions are represented as follows: Lawyers—Johnson & Quattlebaum, Thos. F. Gillespie, and R.F. Scarborough; Physicians—C. Norton, A.H.J. Galbreith, and P.K. Bethea. The business houses are Burroughs & Collins, F.P. Cammack, J.A. Mayo, M.B. Beaty, W.K. Lewis, and ——— Dusenbury.

The Railroad Hotel, Mr. H. Hardee, proprietor, is one of the best kept little houses in the State. If you ever come here, give it a trial, and [take] my word for it, you will not regret it.

Kingston Presbyterian Church, Conway, built c. 1858. *Photograph by Carl Julien, reproduced by permission of the University of South Carolina Press from* Pee Dee Panorama. *South Caroliniana Library.*

The *Horry Herald* is under the management of Dr. E. Norton. It is not only one of the most progressive little sheets in the State editorially, but its "make-up," if you will pardon a technicality, displays considerable enterprise.

The Masons and Knights of Honor have flourishing lodges, and the former own a handsome little hall.

I cannot better summarize than by reproducing from the *Horry Herald* the following:

> Only a few years ago we were completely isolated from the world, comparatively unknown beyond our borders and ignorant of the ways and manners of living of our nearest neighbors, with nothing ahead of us to encourage or impell [sic] us to greater efforts. We were content to live as our fathers before us had lived, struggling along in darkness and eking out an existence of a precarious and uncertain kind. Then came the revolution in the shape of the railroad, and with its advent new life seemed to be infused into us.

Verily, there is no time like the present for investment here. The people are thoroughly aroused to the necessity of new enterprises, and anyone who will assist them in the development of their great resources will find a welcome with every opportunity and gratitude mingled with profit.

News and Courier, February 20, 1890. John I. Green.

Darlington, Pride of the Pee Dee

Ambrose E. Gonzales, who visited Darlington in April of 1889, found it a community rich in history, commerce, and agricultural produce. Interestingly, Darlington had a paid fire department, and a black man was on its board of school trustees, evidence of relatively progressive attitudes. Gonzales also notes that Darlington was a weather station, one of many villages and towns throughout the state, which, in the wake of the Charleston earthquake of 1886, displayed colored flags in an effort to indicate and predict weather conditions.*

* * *

The *News and Courier,* ever alive to the interests of the people of South Carolina, has, from time to time, noted the material progress of various cities and towns in the State. While most of this development has been in the upper or Piedmont section, there is at least one town in the great Pee Dee country whose people are fully abreast of the leaders in the great industrial race, for under the shade of the lovely oaks whose branches stretch over the streets of the beautiful little city of Darlington, two thousand of the best people in this or any other State live their busy lives and from day to day add to their business and their prosperity.

The county of Darlington was created in 1785 by an Act of the General Assembly which divided the famous old district of the Cheraws into the counties of Chesterfield, Darlington, and Marlboro. This section was settled in 1737 by a colony of Welsh from Pennsylvania, supplemented soon after by a number of English, Scotch, and Irish families, some from Virginia and some from directly across the sea.

In the early days hemp and flax were cultivated in the Pee Dee Valley, but the native grasses and the splendid ranges along the river swamps soon diverted the attention of the settlers to stock raising and for many years cattle, horses, and swine were most profitably reared, and immense herds were driven south to Charleston and north as far as Philadelphia. Subsequently the discovery was made that indigo grew almost spontaneously in the greater portion of South Carolina, and all other industries were more or less subordinated to the cultivation of this great product.

About this time, according to Dr. [David] Ramsay, "wealth poured in upon the colonists from a thousand channels. The fertility of the soil generously repaid the labor of the husbandman, making the poor to sing, and the industry to smile

*For an earlier report on the Pee Dee region, see James C. Hemphill, "Prosperity on the Pee Dee: Resources and Development of Marlboro County," *News and Courier,* July 20, 1880.

through every corner of the land. None were indigent but the idle and the unfortunate. Personal independence was fully within the reach of every man who was healthy and industrious."

In the beginning of the present century indigo yielded to the sovereign sway of cotton, which, in turn, became the chief source of wealth, and about the commencement of the war between the States Darlington was among the very wealthiest of the purely agricultural counties of the United States.

The devastation of war followed, homes were wrecked, barns and fences destroyed, cattle swept away, and labor demoralized. Nothing daunted, however, these people braced themselves up, saddle and carriage horses were put to the plough, and soft but firm fingers grasped the handles, and once again under the new order of things the land blossomed. With so fertile a soil, so genial and salubrious a climate, and withal so industrious a people, the achievement of material success, even without capital and slaves, could not long be deferred.

In this fine region the yellow pine and other valuable woods abound, and broad cotton fields, as level as a prairie, stretch from river to river, along whose banks the fertile bottoms lie, where, in favorable seasons, the bourgeoning corn uplifts a thousand bristling blades—the bayonets of peace. Here, nestling beneath the embowering oaks, the little city of Darlington, like a coy beauty, hides her modest head. But no dreamer she! The drummers, those hustling "harbingers of trade" who periodically visit Darlington, play no Prince Charming role, but find her very wide awake and alive to business. A very pretty little city it is, too, with wide, deeply shaded streets and many beautiful and extensive flower gardens and shrubberies. Swift Creek, a clear stream, flows along the base of the slight elevation upon which the town is built and affords a channel for the drainage, which is excellent.

From a population of 950 in 1880 Darlington has, as shown by a recent census, increased the number of her inhabitants to 2,000.

For three years past the municipality has been fortunate in having as mayor Dr. J.C. Willcox, a bright and energetic young man, under whose progressive and business-like adminstration Darlington has been greatly improved and her revenues considerably augmented. The aldermen are J.J. Ward, S.A. Woods, J. Lewenthal, and P.C. Beck. The clerk of the council is Mr. S.S. Burch.

For a long time Darlington has felt the need of an adequate supply of pure water. This want has recently been supplied by an Artesian well 420 feet deep. An immense tank will be built on the public square and kept constantly filled for the use of the fire department, and a system of pipes and plugs will convey the water to various points within the corporation.

Darlington has a paid fire department, equipped with a splendid steamer. Under Fire Chief C. Alexander, the men are well drilled and the department is very efficient.

The school district of which Darlington is the centre has been extended, a special tax of three mills has been voted, and bonds will be issued for the purpose of enlarging the white school building and erecting school houses for the colored children. The entire work is in the hands of Mr. R.W. Boyd, chairman of the board of trustees, a gentleman who has made education a life study and whose management assures success. The schools will be opened on the 1st of October next. Mr. Patterson Wardlaw of Abbeville, who is now teaching in the Columbia graded schools, has just been elected principal of the white academy. For a young man Mr. Wardlaw's reputation as an educator is unusually fine, and the trustees have made a fortunate selection.

The board of trustees are Messrs. R.W. Boyd, J.J. Ward, George W. Dargan, E. Keith Dargan, B.W. Edwards, C.S. Nettles, G.B. Moore, C.B. Edwards, and Jeremiah McLeod, colored.

There are three private schools in Darlington taught by the Misses Dickinson, Mrs. Spain, and Miss Player.

There are four churches in Darlington, the Baptist, Rev. G.B. Moore; the Methodist, Rev. J.A. Rice; the Presbyterian, Rev. John G. Law; and the Episcopal, Rev. W.A. Guerry. There are several colored churches, all in a prosperous condition.

Four years ago the Enterprise Hotel Company was formed and speedily erected at the southwestern corner of the public square one of the handsomest and best arranged hotel buildings in the State. The edifice is of brick, three stories high, with a Mansard roof. The establishment is elegantly furnished, is lighted throughout with gas, and under the management of Mr. T.C. Stewart affords excellent accommodations to the public. The officers of the hotel company are J.J. Ward, president, and J.C. Willcox, J.M. James, E. Keith Dargan, C.S. McCullough, and J.J. Ward, directors. The Darlington Hotel, kept by Mrs. C.E. Hymes, is pleasantly located on the city square and is an excellent hostelry. Boarding houses are kept by J. Walter Parrott and Mrs. Rowena L. Warley.

The Darlington Building and Loan Association was organized nine months ago with six hundred shares subscribed for. The large number of buildings recently erected or in the process of construction in the southern portion of the city has created an unusually active demand for money for building purposes, and the short life of the association has been very successful with every indication of future prosperity. The president and solicitor is E. Keith Dargan, the vice president is J.J. Ward, with Charles K. Rogers secretary and treasurer, and J.J. Ward, E. Keith Dargan, John Siskron, J. Frank Early, and J. Lewenthal, directors.

The Knights Building Association of the Knights of Honor owns a fine two-story building on the public square, the upper portion of which is fitted up as an Opera House and answers the purpose very acceptably. The association is in a flourishing condition, and Mr. J.J. Ward is president.

The banking facilities of Darlington are admirable and both of her banks are prosperous. The Bank of Darlington, one of the most flourishing institutions in South Carolina, commenced work in 1881 as the Darlington National Bank, with a paid up capital of $50,000, which was subsequently increased to $100,000. From the commencement of business the bank paid handsome dividends and the stock rapidly rose to $140. Two years ago the stockholders, finding it to their interest to discontinue operations under the National Banking Act, changed the title of the bank and commenced work under a state charter. The officers are J.L. Coker, president; R.W. Boyd, vice president; Bright Williamson, cashier; L.E. Williamson, teller; and George H. Edwards, clerk. The directors are Messrs. R.W. Boyd, W.C. Coker, J.J. Ward, C.B. Edwards, E.R. McIver, and Bright Williamson.

Last summer, while the matter of a building and loan association was under discussion, a number of the building and loan projectors, having money to invest, decided to organize another bank, the People's Bank of Darlington. The president is Mr. E. Keith Dargan, a keen business man, who is largely interested in financial institutions here. The vice president is W.A. Carrigan, with H.L. Charles cashier, Geo. Onslow teller, and E.C. Lide clerk. The bank occupies handsome rooms in the Enterprise Building. According to the last quarterly statement it had $89,550 in capital stock and deposits of $54,172.25.

Another successful corporation is the Enterprise Grocery Company, owning handsome and spacious stores near the city square. Mr. A.S. White is manager, and Messrs. J.J. Ward, A.S. White, C.S. McCullough, J.C. Willcox, J.A. Boyd, and J.C. Blackwell, directors.

Nothing perhaps has so largely contributed to the building up of Darlington as the erection, three years ago, of the fine cotton mills of the Darlington Manufacturing Company. The buildings are of brick and are located on the line of the Cheraw and Darlington Railroad within the city limits. The capital employed is $222,500; and, the plant having recently been enlarged, 11,000 spindles and 320 looms are now in use with a capacity for manufacturing 4,500 bales of cotton per annum into the heavy brown standard drills and sheetings for which the mills have already become famous. The motive power is supplied by a splendid Harris-Corliss engine of 350 horse power and two pair of Babcock & Wilcox boilers capable of generating steam to the extent of 500 horse power. The fuel used is pine wood, of which there is an abundant supply at hand. Two hundred and fifty hands find employment in the mills and live in comfortable cottages built by the company.

The enterprise has paid from the start, as was to be expected, under the wise and conservative management of President and Treasurer W.C. Coker. Mr. J.T. Bristow is secretary of the company and F.T. Biggs is superintendent of the mills.

Another successful organization is the Darlington Ginning, Milling, Fertilizer, and Warehouse Company, with mills at the Cheraw and Darlington Railroad depot. The company owns a fine brick warehouse, 80 by 140 feet, and two spacious wooden warehouses. They are now engaged in manufacturing fertilizers and find a ready sale for them at remunerative prices. The cotton gins have a capacity of sixty bales per day, and the company, having all the steam power required for a small cotton seed oil mill, have ordered a $15,000 plant, which will be put up before the opening of the next cotton season. The president and treasurer of the company is C.S. McCullough, and the secretary is Bright Williamson.

The extensive wagon, carriage, and blacksmith shops of John Siskron are largely patronized throughout this section, and the quality of the work turned out is said to be first class. The shops are fitted with the most approved modern machinery for wood and iron working, and large paint shops are attached. Fifteen or twenty hands are constantly employed.

Just beyond the limits of the incorporation are the brick yards of Messrs. A.C. Spain & Co. Within a few feet of the yards clay of very fine quality abounds; and, with the improved machinery just ordered, the works can manufacture annually two million bricks, which will supply the local demand and leave a surplus for shipment.

Within two years the southern portion of Darlington has been built up with surprising rapidity. What was then a cotton field is now dotted with handsome residences with wide streets and good sidewalks. Encouraged in this growth, the Darlington Land and Improvement Company has just been formed with a capital of $25,000. A suburban tract of 1,500 acres has been secured and is now being cleared and ditched. The capital of the company will be increased, and there is every indication that in a year or two, what is now a forest will be a handsome suburb.

The Darlington Agricultural and Mechanical Fair Association owns beautiful grounds, thirty acres extent, and handsome buildings just without the incorporation limits. Two fairs are held each year, bringing the farmers of the Pee Dee section together for pleasure and profit, and these reunions have done much to stimulate the improvement of livestock and agricultural methods hereabout. The company has been paying good dividends. The following are the officers: F.R. McIver, president; W.F. James, secretary and treasurer; and E.R. McIver, K.W. Cannon, S.A. Gregg, J.W. Ferguson, Lucas McIntosh, H.E.P. Sanders, E.M. Ervin, W.E. Dargan, C.S. McCullough, and W.L. Galloway, directors.

The visitor is well repaid by an inspection of the agricultural station located here. Mr. J.D. McCall, the superintendent, has the farm in capital order; the drainage is being improved and everything is ready for the experiments which will cover 230 plots of cotton, 140 of corn, 52 of oats, 78 of various grasses, with lots of tobacco, peas, and sugar cane. The barns are spacious and well arranged, and a fine silo contains a quantity of well-cured ensilage. The superintendent's cottage is a tasteful building, and the grounds in front are being planted with hundreds of varieties of flowers and shrubs.

W.E. Dargan, the most extensive planter in the county and who grows annually nine hundred bales of cotton, has on his farm here a large herd of Jersey and graded cattle, which are well housed and cared for. The dairy products are sold in Darlington and yield a handsome interest on the investment.

Real estate is rising rapidly here. A prominent local capitalist just paid $5,000 for a lot on the public square, upon which he will erect three large, two-storied brick stores, which have already been rented in advance of laying the first brick.

Under the management of H.T. Thompson, editor and proprietor, the *Darlington News* has become a political and industrial power in this section. The paper is handsomely printed and ably edited; and, giving as it does full local news and excellent selected matter, it is not surprising that its circulation is large and steadily increasing.

Mrs. B.C. Law, the postmaster here, attends admirably to the duties of the office, and the people of Darlington are afforded excellent facilities for the transaction of their postal business. Miss Mary Ormond is the manager of the Western Union Telegraph office, and the Darlington public are under frequent obligation to her for the courtesy and efficiency with which she performs the duties which devolve upon her. The office of the Southern Express Company is in charge of Mr. C.D. Evans, a war-scarred veteran.

The Darlington Guards are fully armed and equipped with the State regulation uniform. The officers are: Captain Jno. R. McIver, First Lieutenant J.D. Birch, and Second Lieutenant Bright Williamson.

The various secret societies are well represented in Darlington. St. David's Lodge, A.F.M., is one of the oldest in the State and is in a very flourishing condition, as is also the Darlington Lodge No. 7, Knights of Pythias. There are also lodges of Knights of Honor, the American Legion of Honor, and the Royal Society of Good Fellows. There is, too, the Rogers Division No. 3, Uniform Rank K. of P., officered by Sir Knight Captain W.E. James, Sir Knight Lieut. C. Alexander, and Sir Knight Herald L.J. Parrott. Thirty men are in rank and are regularly and thoroughly drilled and expect to be heard from at some coming prize contests.

Dr. J.C. Willcox is president of the Darlington Society for the Prevention of Cruelty to Animals, and C.S. Nettles is solicitor.

The cotton receipts of Darlington aggregate 18,000 bales per annum, and the commercial business of the city is very large in proportion to the population. The men who do the business are: J. Frank Early, general merchandise; Woods & Woods, general merchandise; Edwards & Norment, general merchandise; Marco & Lewenthal, general merchandise; M.C. Alexander, general merchandise and saloon; M. Manne, general merchandise and saloon; Blackwell Brothers, general merchandise; G.J. McCown & Bro., general merchandise; A. Nachman, general merchandise and saloon; A. Weinberg, general merchandise and saloon; the Misses Fountain, millinery; J. Rosenberg, general merchandise and saloon; A.J. Brown, general merchandise; P.C. Black & Bro., saloon; Mrs. W.C. Byrd, millinery; J.A. Boyd, druggist; Willcox & Co., druggists; W.J. Garner, druggist; J.H. Mason, watches and jewelry; R.B. Strozer, jeweller; J.M. James, saloon; Martin Hanley, restaurant; Welling & Bennoitt, hardware; J.J. Sheppard, racket store; Geo. Webb, restaurant; McCullough & Blackwell, livery and sale stables, dealers in grain, buggies, harness and wagons, and owners of the standard-bred trotter Highland Red; C.W. Hewitt, livestock, furniture, and buggies; H.T. Thompson, books and stationery; Houston & Iseman, livestock dealers; Geo. O. Mertz, fruiterer and flower dealer; J.H. Shmid, baker and confectioner;

In Darlington, the south side of the public square in front of O.B. Davis Drug Store, c. 1905. The hardware store of Welling and Bonnoitt, on the right, is still the site of a hardware business. *Courtesy of Horace Fraser Rudisill,* Darlington County: A Pictorial History, *(Norfolk/Virginia Beach: Donning Publishing Company, 1986).*

J. Gregg McCall, men's furnishing goods, boots, and shoes; S. Lewenthal, general merchandise and saloon; C. Mooney, furniture and lumber; J.J. Ward, dealer in real estate; and F.E. Norment, fire and life insurance. The cotton buyers are W.H. Talley, C.R. Woods, G.K. King, J.C. Keys, J.W. Buchanan, and J.W. Waters.

While the health of Darlington is excellent, eight doctors manage to make a more or less comfortable living by practicing over a large section of the surrounding country. They are J.C. Willcox, W.A. Player, B.C. Norment, A.H. Hayden, J.M. Earle, A.M. Hill, W.J. Garner, and John Lunney. The dentists are A.C. Spain and J.B. Garner.

The lawyers are R.W. Boyd, George W. Dargan, E. Keith Dargan, W.F. Dargan, C.P. Dargan, J.J. Ward, George W. Brown, J.E. Nettles, C.S. Nettles, H.T. Thompson, E.O. Woods, and T.H. Spain. The trial justices are Messrs. C.P. Dargan and H.E.P. Sanders.

With all that has been said of Darlington's health, her wealth, her resources and prospects, it can readily be seen that she needs very little to complete a perfect whole. One of her wants, however, is a better railroad building. The present old and contracted structure does not afford adequate accommodation either to passengers or freight traffic, and it is to be hoped that the Atlantic Coast Line, a corporation that has always been liberal and accommodating to the people of this section, will supply the deficiency at the earliest practical moment.

Darlington needs, too, a street railway from the depot to the public square. Capitalists are interesting themselves in the matter and are figuring upon the cost of construction. When the road shall have been built, the weather flags, which Signal Officer Thompson flies from the tallest pole in South Carolina, will float over assuredly one of the thriftiest, the busiest, and the happiest communities in the commonwealth.

News and Courier, April 24, 1889. A.E.G.

Edisto Island: Happy Blacks, Pearl Grits, and Lonely Women

In an effort to assess conditions on the Sea Islands, in the spring of 1880 the *News and Courier* sent reporter J.K. Blackman on an extensive tour of Edisto, Wadmalaw, Johns, and James islands. His eight-column report, covering an entire page, provides a detailed picture of life in that little-known region fifteen years or so after the demise of slavery. Here, in somewhat condensed form, is what Blackman had to say about Edisto.*

* * *

Indented by a variety of creeks, Edisto is extremely irregular in form; and, in fact, what is known as Edisto Island is really two islands separated by a small creek, and to the residents these portions of land are known as Little and Big Edisto islands. To the northwest, separated by a very narrow stream, lies the little island of Jehossee, which in the early history of the State appears to have been classed as a portion of Edisto. Edisto Island is twelve miles long and in the widest part between four and five miles broad. It contains 28,811 acres. It is so generally level as to exhibit few inequalities of surface, the high lands, strange to say, in every instance being situated directly along the banks of the rivers and creeks. The more elevated parts consist of a light, sandy soil. The low grounds or bottoms are of a stiff, clayey quality. It contains a smaller proportion of barren land and is more generally fertile than any of the adjacent islands. Timber in some localities is scarce and with difficulty procured.

The Edisto lands being ill adapted to the growth of rice, the islanders turned their attention at an early period to the culture of cotton and the indigo plant. But in time the demand for indigo decreased, and the whole attention of the planters was given to the cultivation of long cotton, the consumption of which increased from year to year until now this peculiarly fine and fleecy staple enters largely into the manufacture of silks and all the finer classes of cloth. In 1808 the population of the island was 238 whites and 2,609 blacks.

As to the relations existing between the races today, I think I can safely say that in no section of the State are the white planters on better terms with their colored laborers than they are on Edisto Island. This may seem a sweeping assertion, especially as the colored population—owing to their preponderance over the whites and the evil teachings of selfish politicians during the earliest stages

*See also a six-part essay, "A Peculiar People: The Ex-Slaves of the South Carolina Coast," by "Strobart," which appeared in the *News and Courier,* May 24 and 31 and June 7, 1885.

of Reconstruction, and even up to 1876—were, at times, very truculent and ungovernable. From this fact they have acquired a bad name throughout the rest of the State which it will take years to dissipate. Since the inauguration of the Democratic government in 1876, however, the colored people have improved their conditions so materially as to become very conservative, and in every portion of the island I found them orderly, civil, good-natured, and obliging. The planters are unanimous in saying that an era of good feelings exists between all classes. The colored man, if left to himself, is invariably orderly and good-natured, and of course he becomes more conservative as he acquires property. Political harangues have lost much of their charms, and while they are to a considerable extent under the influence of the Republican leaders of the county, they are rapidly beginning to see that their political friends have use for them only at election time, and they are consequently paying more attention to their own interests and less to the interests of the office hunters.

The progress of the colored people in improving their material condition has been more rapid than in any other portion of the State. In 1866, many colored people, becoming dissatisfied with their old homes, sought labor in the up-country, but in a few years those who still lived had found their way back to the island and are today owners of little farms making comfortable livings. The population has not increased to any considerable extent since 1866. The present population is 300 whites and about 3,800 blacks. The colored people today own 4,000 acres of land, and it is estimated that they raise two-thirds of the cotton produced on the island. Their holdings range from 10 to 25 acres, and in some instances they own as much as fifty or sixty acres. Nearly every head of a family owns a neat little house, with a cow and horse or mule, and the majority of them have acquired buggies and carts and improved agricultural equipment. During the past year the colored people alone purchased over 500 horses and mules, 300 carts, and 100 buggies. Many of them have so managed their affairs as to be almost independent of aid from capitalists, and there are some few instances where they advance heavily to their own race. It is a fact that cannot be disputed that the leading colored planters on Edisto Island today carry to a higher degree of perfection the cultivation of their lands than their masters did before the war. The average yield of lint cotton per acre made by the colored planters is about 75 pounds. There are, of course, some instances where the yield has been considerably greater, and in one instance the yield has been as high as 225 pounds to the acre.

The most prominent colored planter on the island is John Thorne, and the success which he has met with will give an idea of what a steady, industrious, and thrifty colored man can accomplish in this section. I had a long conversation with Thorne and found him a very intelligent man. He went down to the island in 1872 as the agent of a company of colored men for the purpose of purchasing for them a tract of 750 acres, formerly known as the Baynard Seaside Tract. There were thirty-five men in the company, and the place was purchased for $5,000. Each member of the company held so many shares, and the land was apportioned out among them according to the shares they held. The holdings ranged in size from 10 to 25 acres. Thorne himself secured 160 acres of this tract and owns altogether on the island 250 acres of land. He is the proprietor of an extensive store and storehouse and owns a comfortable residence. He also runs a gin house with six gins and last year ginned out upwards of 400 bags of cotton of 300 pounds each, for which work he received four cents per pound. He advances largely to several colored planters and is worth from $15,000 to $20,000. In speaking of the material condition of the colored people, Thorne said: "In 1866 very few of the colored people owned any personal property, and at present there is hardly a colored man who does not own a horse or mule, a cart, and a cow, as well as household goods and agricultural implements. The colored planters average a bag of cotton to three acres and make from $500 to $800 a year, upon which they can live comfortably and save money."

The colored planters, I found, raise about the same quantity of corn as cotton. They also raise hogs and a few cattle for their own use. The success which they have achieved during the last few years enables them to secure, without the slightest difficulty, all the capital they need for the proper cultivation of their lands. They obtain their advances almost exclusively from the planters and storekeepers on the island and deal only, in a few instances, with factors in the city. Of late years the colored planters, and the whites also for that matter, have sold to a great advantage the bulk of their crops to a Northern buyer, who takes the cotton in the seed or lint and pays prices which are higher than those that could be obtained in Charleston, after deducting the cost of transportation and commissions.

The poorer colored people, who do not own lands of their own, comprise the bulk of the labor by means of which the white planters cultivate their lands, and so great has been the improvement of their condition that the most serious problem which the whites have to deal with is the securing of sufficient labor at any price. Thorne thinks, however, there is really no cause for serious apprehension as many of the colored people who are land owners themselves have shown a willingness to add to their incomes by working for daily wages.

I think the facts I have related bear out the assertion that colored people on Edisto Island have improved their material condition greatly. I cannot express the truth of this fact more forcibly than by quoting the language of a colored planter. After asking several questions, I made general inquiry as to how the colored people were getting along. Without a moment's hesitation, he replied, in his own peculiar way, "We de eat de pearl grits dis year, sah." This tells the whole story. During the trying years from '60 to '70, everybody was compelled to live on short commons. The negroes ground their own corn in small hand mills—a process which is tedious and laborious. To be able to live on pearl grits, therefore, to the average Edisto negro, is the acme of happiness and exhibits a degree of improvement which cannot be appreciated by those of their race who live in cities and subsist in many instances on the same fare as their employers.

The colored population of the island remains very much the same as in 1866, if anything it is less. The cause of this is not so much from mortality among the adults as it is from the want of proper care of their children. While in slavery the negroes had every attention paid to their wants and in sickness received the same medical aid as their owners did. As freedmen this has changed. Dr. Pope, the leading physician on the island, attributes this increased death rate solely to the failure of the negroes to secure prompt and proper medical attendance. The mortality among the children is very large and is due partly to the same cause and partly, it is thought, to infanticide, a crime which is said to be very common among the poorer classes. It is hard to reconcile the fact that a class of people who deem it sinful to kill the cotton worm should be prone to murder their own children.*

The colored people have made decided and gratifying progress in education since 1866. The school session is from four and a half to six months in length each year. There are on Edisto and Jehossee islands four colored schools with an attendance of 657 pupils, although the average attendance is much less since the children are required to assist their parents in the fields. The schools are admirably conducted by four white and three colored teachers, and the rising generation, from 12 to 20 years of age, can all read and write and are acquainted with the elements of arithmetic. The schoolhouse on Jehossee is the private property of ex-Governor Aiken and is furnished by him for the use of the colored children.

There are on Edisto five colored churches. The denominations are Methodist, Baptist, Presbyterian, and Reformed Episcopal. All of the churches are in good order, some of them having been recently erected. The attendance can hardly be estimated as every man, woman, and child who can walk flock to their respective houses of worship on Sunday, and the majority of them spend three or four evenings out of every week at prayer meetings and revivals.

The white population of Edisto is about 300, and, with the exception of about 4,000 acres owned by the negroes, they own the entire island. The majority of the planters own handsome residences and live as comfortably as they could desire. They all have horses and buggies for riding purposes, besides their ploughing stock, and have of late years supplied their plantations with improved agricultural equipment.

The area planted in cotton this year by whites and blacks is about 6,000 acres, which is estimated to be just about the same as was planted last year. Commercial fertilizers were first used on the island in 1868, and each successive year the manuring has increased. Now about 800 to 1,000 pounds are used to the acre, representing in money an average of $20 to $25 an acre in fertilizers alone. The additional yield per acre, under the new system of cultivation, is almost incredible. When formerly 80 to 100 pounds of lint cotton was considered a fair yield, 200 to 250 pounds per acre is now looked upon as nothing extraordinary. I heard one

*According to Blackman, Edisto Island blacks refused to kill these worms because they thought them to be a visitation sent by God.

gentleman remark that a man who could not raise an average of 200 pounds to the acre had better go to Charleston and sell tape.

The labor question is a problem which the planters of Edisto are giving their most earnest attention. The main cause of the scarcity of labor is the improvement in the condition of the laborers. Colored men who ten years ago worked as field hands for 50 cents a day now own their own farms and earn a comfortable support without doing day labor. The means adopted to remedy this difficulty are varied, but the most popular mode seems to be what is called the "two day" system. The planter furnishes from five to seven acres of land and a house (with the privilege of using the wood on his place). In return for this the head of the family agrees to give the planter two days' labor in every week. The days are generally Monday and Tuesday, and the rest of the week the laborer has to himself to work on his own crop. An able-bodied hand is expected to work two "tasks" or half an acre a day, so that for the land, &c., furnished by the planter he cultivates one acre in the week. The additional labor required is supplied by other "two day" hands or by day labor, for which wages of fifty cents a day are paid. Both the planters and the negroes seem to like this "two day" system better than any other. I should think the negroes would be very well satisfied, as I have seen them returning from the fields having accomplished their day's work by 9 o'clock in the morning. The head of the family puts his wife and children to work and accomplishes in three hours what it would take him all day to do.

The planters, in addition to furnishing land, &c., have of late years made advances to their hands. Almost every planter on the island has a commissary store attached to his dwelling, and during certain seasons of the year it is no small day's work to attend to the wants of the hands who are coming and going from early in the morning until late at night. In short, each planter tries to offer as many inducements to the negroes to settle on his place as possible, and success in this branch of the business is now considered a most important factor in the cultivation of Sea Island cotton.

There is one white school on the island conducted by a highly cultivated gentleman, whose long experience and scholarly attainments render him a valuable adjunct to the school system. There are on the island forty-two white children within the school age. Twenty-four of them attend school, the others being unable to reach the school house, owing to the great distance at which they live and the inability of their parents to afford vehicles. The island needs another white school and will probably have one within the next year.

There are two religious congregations for the whites—the Presbyterian and Episcopal. The former have a very neat church building. The pastor, the Rev. J.E. Fogartle, is given a salary of $1,000 a year, thirty acres of land, and a summer residence. The church is comparatively well off, having about $12,000 to its credit. The Episcopal congregation lost their fine church building in 1875 by fire and are now worshipping in the portion of the building used formerly as a parsonage. The Rev. Messrs. Prentiss and Bellinger preach alternately.

Edisto Presbyterian Church. *Photograph by Carl Julien, reproduced by permission of the University of South Carolina Press from* Beneath So Kind a Sky. *South Caroliniana Library.*

The roads and bridges on the island are in first-class order and bear a striking contrast to their condition under Radical rule. The island is bisected by a road which was built years ago and was well constructed with ditches and dams on each side. Charleston would be well off if she had such a drive. The facilities for transportation are ample. The steamers *Pilot Boy* and *St. Helena* both make several trips to the island each week, and the rates of freight have recently been reduced. The *Pilot Boy* is owned and commanded by Capt. Frank Phillips. She is a comfortable and remarkably swift little boat, and her officers enjoy an enviable reputation. The *St. Helena* is partly owned by the islanders and is commanded by Capt. Togilo, an old and efficient captain.

The price of land can hardly be correctly estimated as very little land has been sold of late years, and such as has been sold is of inferior quality. Such sales as have taken place within a year or two show the prevailing price to be from $10 to $25 an acre. There is at present no good land for sale, and in some of the most favorable localities the lands are valued at from $50 to $75 an acre.

The general outlook for the future of Edisto Island is brighter than it has been since the close of the war. Last year the total yield of the island was 2,000 bags of cotton. With the exception of a very small proportion all this cotton was ginned on the island. There are thirteen gins in operation, and they are found to pay almost as well as raising the cotton. The toll charged is four cents a pound, which includes the furnishing of bagging.

Of the hospitality of the people of Edisto I need not say one word. Yet there is one great social drawback. This is the want of social intercourse among the ladies. This is due to the breaking up of Edingville, the beautiful seaside summer resort of many years ago. The encroachment of the sea has driven family after family away, until now only a half dozen houses remain. This, of course, has tended to break up the summer gatherings, and many of the families have sought houses in the city. By careful calculations it is estimated that 180 souls have left the island since 1865. The ladies who remain are situated at great distances from each other, owing to the intersection of the island by creeks which cannot be bridged and must be circumvented, and it is very seldom they meet.

There seems to be little or no amusement among the young people, and most of their time is spent in attending to home duties. The churches, of course, afford a certain amount of social intercourse, but this is hardly sufficient to produce a healthy state of society. Several of the ladies informed me that they had been compelled to take up sewing as an amusement. And by sewing they did not mean fancy work—they meant heavy work for the plantation hands, such work as I was informed by one lady had netted her a profit of $400 last year. Such is the condition of Edisto Island today socially and industrially, and it is doubtful if any section of the state can show a similar improvement during the same time.*

---

*Edisto Island residents were not pleased with these comments concerning their social life. They not only engaged in debate with Blackman in the columns of the *News and Courier,* they also supplied the paper with news of any and all social happenings in their midst during the next few months.

News and Courier, April 22, 1880. J.K. Blackman

Florence—New County, New County Seat

In some ways, this salute to the city of Florence was a bit premature. The county was a reality, having been created a few weeks earlier, but as "J.A.M." was writing in January of 1889, the city of Florence was neither city nor county seat, although the writer assures us that it soon would become both. For a picture of Florence at other times, see "Flourishing Florence" by "Carolina" (August 1, 1882) and an article by John I. Green (June 23, 1890).

* * *

The "Baby County" of South Carolina was born in December last and is already out of its swaddling clothes. Before the 1st of February it will have cut all its hardest teeth and will be strong enough to toddle around without holding on to the apron strings of any one of its four parents—Darlington, Marion, Williamsburg, and Clarendon. On the 15th inst. a county convention will meet at the proposed county seat, Florence, for the purpose of nominating county officers who will be appointed to serve until the first Monday in November next, when the "Baby County," having been by that time weaned, will be left to take care of itself.

The principal towns in the new county are Florence, Timmonsville, Cartersville, and Effingham. Florence has already put in a handsome bid and therefore may be regarded as the Court House of the new county. Florence has, for the past decade, impressed the visitor with a sense of a peculiar fitness for this honor. Ever since the "deepo" was moved from the old Gamble Hotel some twelve or fifteen years ago, a move which the town almost immediately followed, the place seems to have "picked up." Today there is no mistaking the signs of the times. The Florentines have realized their dream and are determined to make their progressive little town what nature intended it to be—the Gate City of the South Atlantic coast.

The new county has a population of about 22,000, which, by the next census, will be found to have increased to nearly 30,000. Its area is about 650 square miles.

As part of the history of Florence County it would be well to put on record the names of the committee under whose management the campaign for the formation of the county was conducted. It was composed as follows: Chairman, Dr. James Evans; Secretary, Belton O'Neale Townsend; West Marion—R.G. Howard, Walter Gregg, Geo. J. Myers, Dr. J.F. Pearce, John S. Scott, B.B. McWhite, A.A. Myers, J.B. McCall, W.F. Claussen, R.F. Coleman, A.J. Frier, T.C. Crawford, Dr. W.R. Johnson, W.E. Finkles, J.M. Timmons, John Cain, P.M. Timmons, J.B. Lewellen, J.G. James, J.H. Bostick, P.I. Bostick, J.I. Finkles, Brunson Munn, and R.S. Leggett; Darlington—S.A. Gregg, Sr., F.M. Rogers, Sr., J.E. Pettigrew, John

Florence Graded School, c. 1897. *Courtesy of Darlington County Historical Commission.*

McSween, R. Peel, W.E. McKnight, J.W. King, J.A. Rowe, G.G. Lynch, T.W. Williamson, Jerome P. Chase, W.A. Brunson, Z.T. Kershaw, W.H. Day, Dr. E. Miller, D. Sternberger, James Allen, C.M. Covington, and L. Sulzbacher.

The new county is especially rich in railroads. It has within its borders over forty miles of railroads already in operation. Florence is but 102 miles from Charleston, 108 miles from Wilmington, 87 miles from Columbia, and 80 miles from Charlotte.

The governing power in the new county seat is vested in an intendant and four wardens, the town being divided into four wards. The present administration, intelligent and progressive, is composed as follows: Intendant, W.H. Day; wardens, G.G. Lynch, Wm. Hoffmeyer, E.R. Roberts, and F.H. Hudson. The council has in it several representatives of the railroad interest; but, as the future of Florence is largely dependent upon its railroads and as the railroads pay a considerable tax both to the municipality and the new county, there can be no objection to this.

The town is circular in shape, its limits being extended for one mile in every direction from a given centre. There are eleven streets running north and south and nine running east and west. Its population is between 3,500 and 4,000. The taxable property is valued at from $800,000 to $1,000,000. The municipal tax is five mills for municipal purposes, and two mills for special purposes. The town has been pledged to furnish a site and build a Court House and jail, provided it is selected as the county seat—of which there is now no doubt—at a cost of not less than $20,000.

It has an efficient fire department consisting of one Silsby steam engine, the Hope Fire Company, of which Mr. Boston Mims is president, and a hand engine, the Florence, manned by colored men, of which W.J. Bradford is president. The steamer is drawn by horses. The police department consists of four men who are under the immediate command of the intendant.

The following is a list of the places of worship and the pastors: Presbyterian Church, the Rev. J.H. Dixon; Episcopal Church, the Rev. E.F. Guerry; Methodist Church, the Rev. J.T. Pate; Baptist Church, the Rev. B.G. Covington; and Roman Catholic Church, Father Wright. The colored people have three churches: M.E. Church, the Rev. F.W. Sasportas; A.M.E. Church, the Rev. Alston; and Baptist Church, the Rev. E.R. Roberts.

There are at present six lawyers located here, two of whom, Messrs. Harllee & Youmans, are immigrants, so to speak. The new firm is composed of Gen. Harllee, the veteran lawyer and statesman of Marion, and Mr. Rhett Youmans, a son of United States District Attorney Leroy F. Youmans, the renowned orator of South Carolina. The other four lawyers are W.A. Brunson, J.P. McNeill, Belton O'Neale Townsend, and J. De Joghn.*

Mr. Jacobi, resident correspondent of the *News and Courier,* kindly provided the following list of the leading professional and business men in town. Trial justices—J.P. McNeill and E.W. McLoyd; physicians—J.W. King, E. Miller, F.P. Covington, James Evans, J.B. Jarratt, and T.S. Hinnant; dentists—R. Rutledge and R.M. Galloway; real estate—Jerome P. Chase & Sons; insurance agents—Jerome P. Chase & Sons, J.P. McNeill, and W.M. Brown; general merchandise—D. Sternberger, H. McSween, W.J. Brown, G.O. Bethea, J.L. Barringer, S.A. Gregg, Sr., S.J. Morgan, W.E. Herring, Harris Joseph, G.W. Kirby, Jas. Allen & Son, E.S. Buckheit, C.A. Robbins, ——— Willoughby, C.D. Hoffmeyer, A.W. Lyons, W.L. Hutchel, and F.J. Fuller; clothing—S. Elias; groceries—Sidney Jacobi, A.A. Cohen, R.L. Whiteheart, Geo. Stackley, Husbands & Taylor, J.F. Stackley, and A.L. McRae; dry goods, clothing, &c.—Loeb Bros.; boots and shoes—C. Bultman; millinery and fancy goods—N.W. Trump, Miss S.J. Stackley, E.S. Buckheit, and Loeb Bros.; furniture—W.B. LaFar, W.D. Heape, and George Stackley; fruits and confectionery—C.D. Bristow; drugs—King & Lake, James Evans, Covington & Gregg, and J.B. Jarratt; musical instruments—J.B. Killough; tinware and stoves—L.L. Lambkin and the Florence Tinware Manufacturing Company, S.B. Fant, manager; butchers —L.R. Ives & Co. and D.H. Howell; livery and sale stable—Covington Bros.; buggy and wagon warehouse—Covington Bros.; bottling works—Florence Bottling

*This account includes thumbnail sketches of these four men, all said to be upstanding, energetic citizens. The reporter notes, however, that De Joghn "has been a little bit off on politics at times, having been a candidate once on the Greenback ticket for adjutant general."

Works, Cramer & Kersten (proprietors), C.L. Stickney, manager; planing mills—Florence Planing Mills, Hodges and Newton, proprietors; cotton gins and compresses—Z.T. Kershaw and D.H. Hamby; provision broker and commission—W.M. Brown; hardware—F.H. Hudson; liquors—R.L. Whiteheart, J.L. Barringer, George Stackley, A.A. Cohen, and A.W. Lyons; restaurants—Duncan Stewart, G.C. Cole, C.A. Buckheit, and the News Depot, Atlantic Coast Line, Paul Capel (manager); racket store—R.D. Oglesby; and jeweler—Isaac Sulzbacher. In the business catalogue should, of course, be included the extensive railroad shops of the Wilmington, Columbia, and Augusta Railroad, of which Mr. W.M. Day is the superintendent and Mr. John Bissett the master mechanic.

Most of the interior towns of the State owe a good deal of their present prosperity to the establishment of banks. Florence Court House will start out with a bank. The Bank of Florence was established on the 12th of October last. Its capital stock is $25,000, and its officers are: President, W.A. Brunson; vice president, S.A. Gregg; cashier, S.A. Gregg, Jr.; directors, James Allan, Dr. E. Miller, D. Sternberger, C.M. Covington, J.L. Barringer, T.W. Williams, and B. Mantoue.

Florence is a great stopover place for the ambassadors of trade, and wherever these gentlemen gather one may always be sure of finding abundant and excellent hotel accommodations. The Eden of Florence, like that of Charleston, is yet to be built, but in the meantime there is plenty of accommodation at these hotels: Jacobi Hotel, M. Jacobi, manager; Central Hotel, J.L. Barringer, proprietor; Commercial Hotel, Mrs. H.D. Hulbert, proprietress; and Clifton House, Mrs. Clifton, proprietress.

The new county starts with two "maps of busy life." The *Florence Times*, of which Mr. C.H. Prince is the editor and proprietor, has been in the field for some time. Always a lively and sprightly journal, it will keep abreast of the times and will in all things represent the interests of the new county.

The *Farmers' Friend*, lately published in Timmonsville, has been removed to the new county seat and will probably change its name. It is edited and published by Mr. J.W. Hammond, who, like Mr. Prince, has had considerable experience in the rather difficult feat of running a newspaper, having published newspapers in Darlington and Charleston. The new county will doubtless support two newspapers and both are bound to prosper.

The various local organizations include Masonic Hampton Lodge No. 206; Knights of Pythias, Harmony Lodge No. 8; American Legion of Honor; Knights of Honor, Florence Council No. 915; Brotherhood of Locomotive Engineers; the Order of Chosen Friends; and the Florence Rifles.

The new Court House is certainly starting out in the right direction. At present its illumination is in the nature of oil. But the town and its inhabitants will not have to go through the gradations from oil to gas and thence to electricity. They hope to escape the tribulations of gigantic gas bills and street lamps run on almanac schedules and to jump from oil to electricity direct. Mr. Geo. B. Edwards has been skirmishing around the town for a day or two, and as a result of his visit an electric light plant will be established at once. Major Edwards says that he will establish this plant on his own account and that its establishment will doubtless lead to the organization of the Florence Electric Light and Power Company, which will furnish the new Court House with the light of the future.

It may be mentioned, as a matter of history, that Mr. M. Jacobi is the veritable and "onliest" oldest inhabitant of the town of Florence. The site occupied by his hotel was virgin forest and the Northeastern Railroad had not been built when Mr. Jacobi settled here, and yet one would by no means take him for a centenarian.

A great deal more might be written about this fair city, which, after a brilliant and brief semi-municipal career, promises to become one of the most thriving and populous cities of the State, but time and space forbid. The facts I have presented are doubtless crude and certainly not as elaborate as they can be made, but I have made no attempt to color them.

Florence is on a boom and a considerable boom, too; five years hence its own people will scarcely be able to realize it. Within one month the value of real estate has advanced over 50 per cent, and by the dawn of the next year it will have more than doubled in value. There is plenty of land available for building purposes, but this will speedily be taken up. There is a brilliant and prosperous future in store for the new city, and the *News and Courier* only voices the sentiment of Charleston when it utters a hearty God-speed to the Gate City of the South Atlantic coast.

News and Courier, January 8, 1889. J.A.M.

Gaffney, Athens of the Piedmont

Gaffney, which increased its population from 400 to 1,631 in the 1880s, largely by annexing surrounding territory, could not long escape the attention of the roving reporters of the *News and Courier,* and in April of 1890, Edward P. McKissick visited this thriving, Up Country community. He found there numerous schools, a wide-awake business establishment composed of energetic young men, and H.G. Gaffney, son of the town's founder, known to everyone as "the Squire." Yet Gaffney lacked the prime essential of the good life of that era—a cotton factory. And, according to McKissick, it also could make good use of additional rail connections.

* * *

Perhaps never in the history of the steady and conservative State of South Carolina was an old field turned so suddenly into a thriving and busy town. Scarcely twenty years ago the site that now marks the place where health, wealth, and intelligence prevail was then known as Gaffney's old field. At that time the only vestige of a building was at the forks of the road leading from Limestone Springs to Shelby, N.C., and the principal industry of the settlement was horse racing, a sport which gathered to the old race course there many of the wealthy people who summered at the Springs.

Antedating this, in the year 1803 Michael Gaffney, a native of County Longford, Ireland, settled here after living briefly in New York City and Charleston. Shortly after his arrival, the "Father of Gaffney City" married a Miss Smith at Smith's Ford on Broad River in Union County. Here he planted for many years, at the same time carrying on the regular country merchandise business.

One of the most interesting characters of this section is Mr. H.G. Gaffney, known to everybody as the "Squire." He is a son of the original Gaffney. For forty years he has been a magistrate and now occupies the position of trial justice. Speaking of the history and traditions of this section, Squire Gaffney related many interesting reminiscences.

> The first man who settled at Limestone Springs was Vardy McBee, who owned the Springs for many years. He was a surveyor and a leading citizen. McBee was, I think, the grandfather of Col. V.E. McBee, who now has control of so many railroads belonging to the Richmond and Danville system. He lived near the Springs in a large log cabin, but a peach tree and an old chimney are all that remains to mark the spot.
>
> My first recollections of Limestone go away back into the thirties. It was then a watering place, and some of the richest families spent their summers here. In 1844 Dr. William Curtis came here and bought the hotel, which had been built by a joint stock company. It was changed to a school and has remained one ever since. In those

days John Belton O'Neall, than whom no better man ever lived, the Mileses, and the Hamptons, and the Prestons, all were wont to come here and enjoy our grand, health-giving atmosphere, and drink the best water that flows from the bowels of mother earth. In those days Gaffney's old field was the regular rendevouz for the brigade encampments. The reviews generally took place about where the male and female seminary now stands. Another amusement was found in the races that used to take place at the old race course, which was in the immediate vicinity of the drilling grounds. The down country horses belonging to the first families who came here during the summer tried their speed with the fine animals of the few farmers who were rich enough in those days to own blooded stock.

The battle of the Cowpens was fought just ten miles northwest of this place, while the battle of King's Mountain was waged only fifteen miles east of here. In 1812, when war was declared between England and the United States, Father Michael Gaffney raised two companies from this section: one was from Limestone Springs and the other from Grassy Pond. He was captain of one, while the two companies were under the command of Major Elijah Dawkins. The two companies met at Lipsey's old field, where the rest of the battalion rendezvoused for a while and then marched away to Charleston. This battalion was stationed at Haddrell's Point.

It is a somewhat peculiar fact, which perhaps has never appeared in print, that the Air Line Road, which passes through here, is built along the old Cherokee Trail from the Southwest to Washington. In my earlier days I remember seeing the Cherokee Indians, or at least a few head men of their tribe, pass here on their way from their reservation to Washington. That was long ago before railroads were ever thought of.

Perhaps the best indication of Gaffney City's advancement and excellent position as a business centre is found in the financial standing and commercial character of her merchants. They are live, enterprising, pushing business men, and are principally young men. There is not a business enterprise in Gaffney City which is not controlled in whole or in part by young men. In reality the place might well be called the young men's town. It is estimated that the business annually transacted here amounts to $1,000,000. Fully 6,000 bales of cotton are shipped from here each year, and this too in face of the strongest competition, inasmuch as the Clifton and Glendale factories are within easy reach of the farmers in this immediate territory.

Here is a list of the solid, substantial merchants of Gaffney City: Carroll & Stacy, bankers and cotton merchants; Carroll & Carpenter, general merchandise, cotton, fertilizers, and almost everything imaginable, with an excellent mantua-making and millinery department; R.S. Lipscomb, general merchandise, cotton, and groceries; Mabry, Cook & Co., general merchandise and groceries; J.O. & J.N. Lipscomb, general merchandise; Lipscomb & Tolleson, general merchandise, dry goods, etc.; J.I. Sarratt, general merchandise; J.W. Tolleson, dry goods, boots and shoes, and almost everything you want, besides a first-class millinery department; J.B. Mocca, confectionery and soda water; Jones & Holmes, confectioneries; R.C. Bishop, pool and billiard rooms; J.D. Goudelock, general merchandise and

Gaffney street scene in the 1880s. *Courtesy of the B.G. Moss Collection.*

furniture; Sarratt, Sims & Co., general merchandise; William B. DuPre & Co., drugs, medicines, cigars, tobacco, and oils, with a full line of druggist supplies; O.S. Kendrick, confectionery and canned goods; Simon Bros., drugs and medicines; A.N. Wood, wagons, buggies, and fertilizers; Robert A. Jones & Co., general merchandise and groceries; R.F. Spencer, confectioneries; J.G. Galloway, tin shop and general dealer in stoves; R.S. Lipscomb, fire and life insurance, furniture, and carriages for children; J.R. Tolleson, dry goods, boots, and shoes; James Cook, notions and bric-a-brac; H. Gaggstetter, jeweller; M.R. Sams, books, stationery, newspapers, and school supplies; C.C. Harris, general merchandise; John Geddes, confectioneries; T. Davenport, general merchandise; W.T. Teague, shoes and boots; W.W. Hayes, shoes and boots; and J.T. Rodgers, jeweller and watchmaker. Besides these there are several other smaller firms, which do a very good business, which are here too numerous to mention in detail.

Another great factor in the prosperity of Gaffney City is the banking house of A.N. Wood. A general banking business is done and collections are made a specialty. The bank has been in operation over ten years and Mr. Wood has been very successful in all his dealings.

The famous firm of Carroll & Stacy, both of the members of which are young men, also do a very large banking business. It has been estimated that this firm does annually a business in cotton that aggregates at least three million of dollars. This is not confined to Gaffney City, but extends to nearly all the counties in upper South Carolina and a number of counties in North Carolina.

The wagon and buggy factory of Capt. A.M. Gilmer is one of the best and most substantial business establishments in the country. All sorts of wagons, buggies, carriages, and the like are manufactured here, and the trade which Capt. Gilmer commands is very extensive.

Mr. T.G. McGraw runs very successfully a saw mill, grist and flour mill, and cotton gin within a few rods of the depot. Mr. J. Franklin Gaffney is the proprietor of a very flourishing cotton gin and saw mill establishment within the corporate limits of this place.

A first-class livery and sale stable is run here with great success by Capt. A. Smith Corry. His establishment has been built on the latest pattern and will be connected with the various hotels by telephones, and every convenience has been adopted by Capt. Corry. He keeps a large stock of first-class horses and elegant buggies. He annually sells a large number of mules and does generally a very flourishing business.

Spencer & Easterby, two progressive young men, also run a first-class livery stable. They do a large business and make a specialty in selling mules and horses.

Some six months ago the Alliance of this township, or rather the consolidated Alliances of fourteen precincts, formed a joint stock company with a capital stock of $2,000. There are a thousand shares at $2 a share, and each Sub-Alliance took as many shares as it desired. Capt. John R. Jefferies of Union County is president, and Mr. W.C. Lipscomb is trade agent, while Mr. W.G. Austell is the Alliance cotton weigher for Gaffney City. A neat and commodious warehouse for the Alliance has been built alongside the railroad track. Capt. Jefferies is a wide-awake, progressive farmer and sound business man, and under his management the Alliance stores here will mete out the greatest benefit to the farmers.

There are two excellent hotels here. Mr. J.I. Sarratt is proprietor of one, and Mr. W.S. Lipscomb is the jovial host of the other. Both the hotels are situated within a few steps of the railroad. Attentive porters always meet every train, and passengers who stop over in this place are always shown the best of civilities and attention. There are also innumerable smaller boarding houses in various parts of the town.

At a recent election the following municipal officers were chosen: Intendant, Nathan Lipscomb; wardens, W.C. Carpenter, W.H. Richardson, C.C. Harris, and T.G. McGraw. The revenues of the town are raised by the licensing of bar rooms at the rate of $1,000 each. Until recently the sale of whiskey was prohibited here and all the revenue was made up by town taxation. Now there are no city taxes, and the money paid in by the bar rooms is entirely sufficient to defray all the expenses of the town government. By a recent act of the Legislature the limits of Gaffney City have been extended considerably. The Limestone Springs, over a mile distant, are now included within the confines of the place. Capt. B.F. Camp is the chief of police here and preserves absolute order. The streets are well lighted with oil lamps, and in fact everything that tends to the prosperity of the townspeople is afforded by the city fathers.

While it is a patent fact that there is very little contention and, as some of the denizens term it, "lawin'" in this section, yet there are two trial justices here. One is "Squire" H.G. Gaffney and the other is Mr. James E. Webster. Both attend to their duties faithfully and well. There are also four lawyers here: Col. W. Waddy

Thompson, James E. Webster, Col. T. Stobo Farrow, and J.C. Jefferies. The high standing of these lawyers is well known outside of their town and county.

Whatever may be said of the building of Gaffney City and the people who made it what it is today, there is no denying the fact that the Atlanta and Charlotte Air Line Railroad has done more to build up the place than all other factors combined. The present able superintendent of the road, Col. E. Berkeley, has done and is still doing all that is within his power to aid in anything that is conducive to the general welfare of the place. Recently a very pretty passenger depot and ticket office has been erected here. In this building is situated the ticket and telegraph offices. Directly opposite is the freight depot. It is commodious and amply affords all the room necessary. Mr. R.M. Gaffney is the depot agent, and Mr. Charlie Christman is the faithful and efficient telegraph operator and ticket agent.

Another railroad to this place will likely be built. It is being surveyed, and there is every reason to believe that it will be completed. This road will be called "The Camden, Cheraw, and Gaffney City Railroad." At least that is its present name, but it will likely be changed to that of "The Atlantic, Thermal Belt, and Knoxville Railroad" when it is completed from Florence to Knoxville. The officers of the road are as follows: President, J.V. Sarratt, Gaffney City; secretary and treasurer, S.B. Latham, Chester; financial agent, A.N. Wood, Gaffney City; directors, J.K. Henry, Col. J.R. Culp, S.M. Wiley, and J.W. Wilkes, all of Chester, and A.N. Wood, J.A. Carroll, D.A. Thomas, R.C. Thomson, and J.V. Sarratt from Gaffney City. Capt. C.L. Kingsley is the engineer in charge of the survey of the road, which will afford another direct outlet to the West for the eastern section of the State.

The famous Three C's Railroad will run within a few miles of this place, and direct communication will be given by this great trunk line, which will be built to Augusta from Blacksburg by the first of the coming year. When all these roads are finished, this place, with the excellent facilities that it has already, will become a railroad centre of importance.

Of all the various industries that go to make up the prosperity of this place the lime manufacturing business is, perhaps, the greatest. The limestone quarries are situated within a few rods of the famous Limestone Spring and are practically inexhaustible. Two different firms are now working the quarries and making carloads every day. One part of the quarries is owned by Simon Brothers, and is said to be the best paving business in this section of the State. The other part is owned and worked by Capt. W.H. Richardson and he is said to be making a large amount of money each year by selling the product of his quarries and kilns.

In point of educational advantages and facilities Gaffney City has no superior in the State, and, indeed, very few equals. Away back yonder in the year 1845 the Limestone Springs Female High School was founded by the Rev. Dr. Thomas Curtis and his son, Wm. Curtis, of England, both of whom were celebrated for their piety and learning and ability as teachers.

A number of gentlemen had formed themselves into a joint stock company for the purpose of making Limestone one of the grandest watering places in the South. At a cost of between sixty and seventy-five thousand dollars a structure capable of accommodating up to three hundred boarders was erected. But Limestone was then in the backwoods of South Carolina, and the whole Piedmont region was but little known to the health and pleasure-seekers of the world. As a consequence the patronage received as a watering place was not commensurate with the expectations of the company, and, as stated, Dr. Curtis and his son purchased it and fitted it up for a "female high school." The school soon reached a remarkable degree of prosperity. But in 1859 Dr. Thomas Curtis was lost in the wreck of the steamer, *North Carolina,* bound from Baltimore to Norfolk. Then the war came with all its upheavals and disasters. Dr. Wm. Curtis's health failed, his property was swept away by the tide of revolution, and the "Limestone Springs Female High School," which had become a household name all over this sunny land, was closed in gloom and became a thing of the past.

After the termination of the war the property changed hands several times, until finally it came into the possession of that great philanthropist, the Hon. Peter Cooper, of New York, who in 1880 donated it to the Spartanburg Baptist Association for educational purposes. The present principal was elected by trustees appointed by that body, and the school opened on the 3rd of October, 1881. In the past season it had seventy-three boarding pupils.

The main school building is 240 feet long by 40 feet wide, four stories high, and contains above the ground about 100 rooms. Many of these rooms are 20 by 18 feet, are provided with comfortable fireplaces, stationary wardrobes, convenient closets, and two or more large windows each. The school room, chapel, and recitation rooms are all on the first floor and are large and well ventilated. The entire building has been recently repaired and renovated. It has a new tin roof well painted. The interior has been freshly kalsomined and supplied with new furniture of the most approved modern style, and the building in all respects is as good as it ever was and in many respects better.

The grounds are enclosed with a new plank fence and contain about eight acres set in grass and shaded by rows of magnificent elms and water oaks. The famous Limestone Spring is just outside of the enclosure, bubbling up over sixty gallons of pure, sparkling water every minute, and is approached by an avenue of magnificent water oaks extending down from the campus.

The board of instruction and the officers of the college are: M.P. Griffith, principal, intellectual and moral philosophy, English literature, rhetoric, and physical science; the Rev. I.W. Wingo, chaplain, algebra, trigonometry, and geometry; Mrs. M.E. Nowell, vocal and instrumental music and French; Miss Nannie Sexton, assistant in instrumental music; Miss Mamie Rogers, arithmetic, Latin, and history; Miss Phoebe Fuller, English, Latin, and emotional calisthenics; Mrs. George Center, preparatory; Dr. J.D. Westervelt, resident physician and telegraphy; Miss Hattie Kendrick, drawing and painting; Miss Nannie Hudson,

Students at Cooper-Limestone Institute, March 2, 1887. *Courtesy of Limestone College. South Caroliniana Library.*

secretary; Mrs. A.P. Griffith, matron; and Miss Lizzie Scruggs, housekeeper. The board of trustees is composed of the following gentlemen: Capt. J.H. Montgomery, president; the Hon. A.B. Woodruff, secretary; J.A. Carroll, treasurer; the Rev. W.P. Smith, the Hon. K.S. Allen, Nathan Lipscomb, the Hon. John Earle Bomar, and Dr. J.B.O. Landrum.

Another excellent institution situated in the very heart of the place is the Gaffney City Male and Female Seminary. The principals are W.F. McArthur, J.M. Tankersley, and R.O. Sams, and the corps of instructors is as follows: W.F. McArthur, English, moral and mental science; J.M. Tankersley, Latin, Greek, and mathematics; R.O. Sams, mathematics, French, and natural science; Miss Mary E. Lynn (late of the State Normal School, Fredonia, N.Y.), preparatory department; Miss Carrie O. Sams, primary work; Miss Johnnie Sanders, music department; and Miss E.C. Black, drawing and painting.

The seminary comprehends two cooperative departments—the preparatory and the collegiate. Each has a splendid curriculum and the manner that the pupils are taught is excellent. All the boys over 14 years of age are members of the military company unless excused from some physical weakness. Military tactics are taught and the company is daily examined in that excellent discipline that is characteristic of all well regulated military schools. The armory is well supplied with light breech-loading cadet rifles and with corresponding accoutrements. All the cadets are uniformed in the regulation Confederate gray. Fully three hundred pupils can be accommodated and all these can be boarded in the immediate vicinity of the seminary and under the direct supervision of the professors and principals. The boys and girls while at work, and except on stated occasions, are kept separately, and the greatest harmony and good will always prevail. Capt. R.O. Sams, one of the principals and a graduate of the Citadel, has command of the military company, and if those who are under him now shall make the man and the soldier that he has always been in time of war and of peace, then the work of this excellent institution will be more than well done.

There are two literary societies connected with the seminary. The Phi Sigma, male, and the Kappa Chi, female, are both well organized societies and meet weekly for debate and other literary improvement. The seminary has a distinguished board of visitors: the Rev. A.A. Marshal, Anderson; the Rev. J.G. Galloway, Yorkville; Judge W.S. Thompson, Spartanburg; Mr. Elias Inman, Bullock's Creek; and the Rev. A.A. Gilbert, Gaffney City.

There is still another school of high standing here: the Gaffney City High School. It has been running very successfully for the last five years and today is in a very flourishing condition. It is designed for both boys and girls and has a very high grade curriculum. The principal is the Rev. F.C. Hickson, famous as a preacher and a missionary to China. His assistants are Miss Ella Whitlock of Union, who is in charge of the young ladies, and Miss Dorsett of New York, who is the teacher of French and music. At present there are about seventy-five pupils in attendance at this school.

The colored people, as is their custom, are not behind in the matter of education here. There are two colored schools, both of which are well attended. Thus, as an educational centre, Gaffney City stands in a superior position, and the day is not very far distant when pupils will flock here from all portions of the State.

There are two Masonic lodges here (old Limestone and Grenard), the Knights and Ladies of Honor, the Knights of the Golden Rule, and the Knights of Honor, all in a flourishing condition.*

The climate of this beautiful village is very conducive to good health and is mild and invigorating. It is in some degree exempt from the withering heat and stinging mosquitoes of the summer season and the extremely cold weather of the winters. The health of the place is very good, and no material disorders belong to the town. Nevertheless, there are four good doctors here: Drs. H.M. Holmes, formerly of Charleston, J.D. Westervelt, M. Bonner, and M.W. Smith.

There are four churches here and each has a very large and interesting congregation. The Baptist Church, a handsome building, with the Rev. I.W. Wingo for its pastor, is in a very flourishing condition. The Methodist Church is a modern structure and is ably presided over by the Rev. A.A. Gilbert. The Presbyterian Church is likewise a very neat and commodious building, and the Rev. J.W. Query is the eloquent pastor. The Episcopal Church, with a goodly congregation, has

---

*McKissick supplies the names of the officers of some of these groups. See the *News and Courier,* April 21, 1890.

for its rector the Rev. J.D. McCollough, a man of deep piety and erudition. There are also two colored churches here.

With a population of about 1,600 souls, with the best of railroad facilities and a fertile surrounding country, with many advantages that a majority of the towns and villages of the interior do not possess, there is every reason why Gaffney City should have a cotton factory. About a year ago a movement was started to build a cotton factory here, and Mr. A.N. Wood was made president. Fully $50,000 was subscribed, but as that much additional was needed it has never been built. But there is a decided desire that a cotton mill shall be built here, and with such a man as "Dolph" Wood at the head of the movement there is every reason to believe that the factory will be built in the near future. It ought to be built, and the men of this place who have its interests at their hearts will sooner or later see to it that the factory is built. This place also needs the railroad that is now being projected from Knoxville in Tennessee to Florence in South Carolina. There is no reckoning the vast benefit that this place will derive from it.

News and Courier, April 21, 1890. E.P.M'K.

Georgetown: New Life in an Old City

Reporter Matthew Tighe found Georgetown a strange mix of old and new in February of 1888. He obviously was intrigued by relics of colonial times, shad fishing, and the economic impact of new railroad lines. Yet it still was a land in which malaria was a fact of daily life, a place where "a little care and more quinine" might be necessary for good health.

* * *

The city of Georgetown is situated on the north side of the Sampit River and near its junction with the Black River, where both of these rivers empty into Winyah Bay, ten miles from the Atlantic Ocean. It is reached either by the water from Charleston or by rail on the Atlantic Coast Line to Lane's Station, and thence by the Georgetown and Northwestern Railroad. The approach to the city from the west is by the railroad, and the first glimpse as the train reaches the station is neither exhilarating nor prepossessing.

The outskirts are composed of scattered houses, which have all the appearances of having been built before the Revolutionary War. They are mostly small, one-story buildings that have been innocent of paint or whitewash certainly beyond the recollection of the last two generations. The illusion is at once conveyed from this point of observation of a dead, certainly a sleeping, city, but the fancy is at once dispelled by the hum of the machinery and the clouds of smoke from the magnificent building of the Georgetown Rice Milling Company.

The outbuildings, too, the smaller ones, are in all stages of decay, with rapidly disappearing roofs, weather-beaten and sun-cracked walls, and a degree of architectural abandon that is in vivid contrast with other towns and cities in South Carolina, and especially at this stage of industrial and commercial life.

There is nothing peculiar about the architecture of Georgetown with the exception, perhaps, of piazzas that were intended originally to cover as much of the pavement as possible. This is an old, very old style, which has not lately been followed in the new houses that have been erected since the war. The business street, called Front Street, runs along the Sampit water front. With this a half a dozen or more streets run parallel, and the others are perpendicular to this base line. But these streets are of exceeding beauty. They are wide and on either side are low rows of white oaks as a rule. One of these, High Market Street, is perhaps the most picturesque in South Carolina, and in the spring and summer must present a view of unrivalled beauty.

Practically the city is at the confluence of the Sampit, the Waccamaw, and the Black rivers, the latter of which is joined above Georgetown by the Pee Dee. The

Cotton on wharves at Georgetown in the 1890s. *South Caroliniana Library.*

waters of these form the magnificent Winyah Bay, ten miles long and about two miles wide, forming a united highway out to the Atlantic Ocean. Once upon a time these rivers poured their golden agricultural harvest into the lap of Georgetown. Rice was the royal crop, and it succeeded the indigo crops, which have passed out of history save in the records of the time-honored Winyah Indigo Society, a distinctive literary and social bed-rock institution of South Carolina. The wealth and magnificence of those times are now, however, only recollections. Except in a few instances the rice field of today is a small affair compared with the rice estates of the early and middle years of this century. The contrast of what was and what is may best be understood from the fact given by an old planter that before the war the rice crop of the country amounted to 120,000 barrels and that this day it averages about 35,000 barrels.

Yet there has been an awakening. Other industries were found to be profitable, among them, shingles, crossties, fish, oysters, game, cotton, lumber, rosin, and turpentine. The first streak of the dawn was the Georgetown and Lane's Railroad, the work of constructing which was begun in November, 1882. At the Georgetown terminus of the road, which is only thirty-six miles in length, there has been built an ample wharf, alongside of which the largest steamers can anchor. Besides this, a side track has been built to the Georgetown Rice Mills, through which passes a very large portion of the rice product of the county. From Georgetown to Lane's the road passes through a fine belt of pine forest, and along this line there are already hamlets such as Irio, Sampit, and Harper's springing up into business notoriety.

It is claimed by the management of the road that they have already divided the transportation of rice to Charleston with the steamship line and credit themselves with having shipped 4,000 barrels to Charleston last year. Besides this, they offer through rates to New York and come into active competition with the packet lines for nearly all classes of freight. The fish trade to New York, Philadelphia, and generally North is virtually controlled by this road, and the value of their trade, including oysters and game, is valued at about $75,000 for the present year. The lumber trade and the crosstie business of the road is also very large. The road is fairly well equipped for business, being well supplied with freight cars, and the passenger accommodations are now admirable.

It gives to the people of Georgetown a double daily mail, a luxury that was impossible before the road was built, the trip from Georgetown to Lane's being accomplished in one hour and twenty minutes. Formerly the few commercial men who visited Georgetown drove across the country from Kingstree, a distance of about forty miles. Nowadays the hotel here is crowded with these harbingers of prosperity from one end of the week to the other.

It is said that the ultimate aim of the road is to reach out into central and northern South Carolina and divert to Georgetown whatever trade goes at this time to Wilmington and thence further north. However true or feasible this may be, it is certain that the owners of the road are making an effort to continue the line by sea from Georgetown to New York by means of the steamship line which has just been established. The object of this new movement is two-fold. First, to compete with the two packet lines in which J. Kamanski & Co. and Congdon, Hazard & Co. of this place are largely interested; and, secondly, in the perhaps remote future to transport freights that now go to Wilmington. There will doubtless be a war of rates between the packet lines and the new steamer, which, it is said, will only end with the withdrawal of either.

Standing on any one of the wharves along the river front the signs of progress are everywhere visible. On the south is to be seen the building of the Palmetto Lumber Company, and north the imposing structure of the Georgetown Rice Mills, and just beyond the latter the wharf of the Georgetown and Northwestern Railroad. At the railway wharf there are coastwise vessels at anchor, and at every wharf along the river there are light-draft river steamers and schooners loading and unloading.

Everybody is busy; everybody, in fact, is taking part in the revival, and to an outsider the appearances are that everybody is terribly in earnest. Four years ago Georgetown beat its own $3,000,000 business record of ante-bellum days when the bay and the Sampit River floated in the business season a fleet of from forty to fifty schooners. The last trustworthy statistics were carefully compiled by Mr. Walter Hazard, of the *Enquirer,* in 1883, of the gross amount of the city's trade, and it footed up to $4,516,280. What rapid strides have been taken since then may be inferred from U.S. government statistics for the calendar year 1886 which show a total of $5,052,000, a difference of about half a million dollars.

This amount of business will appear to be almost phenomenal when it is taken into account that the population of Georgetown is only about 3,000, of which, it is said, only the third part is white. All the business is done on Front Street, which suffered during and after the war by fire. The merchants number, perhaps, about sixty and, as may be inferred from the amount of business, carry fine stocks. Among the most important and extensive dealers are H. Kaminski & Co., wholesale and retail groceries, rice, and naval stores, a handsome, three-story brick store and stocked from the cellar to the roof; Congdon & Hazard, same line of business; Butler & Lowenthal, general merchandise; John Voss, groceries, fish, game, and crossties; I. Sittenfield, general merchandise; G.A. Lohr, general merchandise; S. Brilles, fancy goods; F. Young, merchandise and bakery; L.G. Emanuel, general merchandise; Marks, Moses & Bro., general merchandise; Butler & Scheck, general merchandise; C.H. Ortman, groceries; Dr. T.B. Bailey, drug store; and J.A. Iseman, the Norman Drug Store. Only recently the merchants have formed themselves into a board of trade, and it is expected that within the year every merchant in the city will have become a member.

A by no means unimportant part of the business of Georgetown is the shad fisheries. The fishing begins about the middle of January and continues from two and a half to three months. The fishermen are permitted by law to fish from Tuesday morning until sunset on Thursday of each week, the rest of the week being reserved to give the fish free access to the upper waters of the bay.

The method of capturing the fish is very simple. A net sometimes three hundred yards in length and from twelve to fourteen feet in depth is floated by means of bobbins. The off end of the net is floated by a buoy, and the near end is attached to a small boat in which there are two fishermen. The net by means of leads rests in the water perpendicularly, the whole trap being permitted to drift up and down with the tides.

As the bay is about two miles wide, or about 3,520 yards, it would require about a dozen of the largest nets to span the sheet of water and shut out the shad from upward progress at least through a depth of fourteen feet. Two trips were made over the bay by this correspondent and in no case was anything approaching such an arrangement noted. The nets appeared to be disposed haphazard. The line of the net in the majority of cases almost doubled in upon itself and reduced its length practically about one-third, not withstanding the effort to keep it perpendicular to the shore. The off ends of the net are kept well off shore to avoid snags and other obstructions. The shad that runs into the net usually gets entangled by the gills and the meshes and he is caught. As a greater part of the fishing must necessarily be done in water deeper than fourteen feet, it is argued that the shad may escape under the nets or between the lines of nets on either side. There are no steel nets to be seen anywhere, and the people here say that the story about steel nets is a myth.

There are about one hundred and fifty men engaged as fishermen, many of whom are white. The value of the trade is now estimated at from $60,000 to $75,000. The fishermen get about twenty-five cents apiece for the fish. The trade is practically controlled in bulk by John Voss and the resident agents of Philadelphia and New York houses. The oyster and game proportion of the trade is small compared to that of shad.

The municipal and social economy of Georgetown possesses all the material elements of progress. The intendant is Mr. L.S. Ehrich, a bustling, active, and energetic young man, who is president of the Palmetto Lumber Company for the manufacture of cypress shingles. This is said to be the best equipped establishment of the kind in the South and has a capacity of from 20,000 to 25,000 shingles per day. It is expected that the company will soon provide the mill with electric lights so as to run night and day.

The wardens are Mr. T.M. Merriman, F. Young, and J.A. Jackson and C.H. Sperry, the latter two being colored. The council controls about $18,000 annual revenue, $3,500 of which is raised from liquor licenses at $500 each, the rest being raised by a tax of 1½ per cent, which includes the retirement of $80,000 of railway bonds. There are also market fees and licenses for vehicles, &c.

The following is a list of other officials: Chief of Police, S.W. Rouquie, Jr.; Chief of Fire Department, A.P. Hazard; Assistants, P.E. Twiggs, John Voss, Anthony Jordan, and Moses Myers; Fire Companies—Winyah Steam F.E. Company, J.B. Steele, president; Salamander H. and L. Company, T.W. Brightman, president; Heston F.E. Company, colored, W.J. Moultrie, president; Star F.E. Company, colored, J.B. Baxter, president; Clerk of the Fire Department, R.C. Davis; Engineer, R.W. Mustard; Portwardens—H.A. Munnerlyn, W.W. Taylor, and James Mitchell; Chairman of Board of Health, Dr. G.E.T. Sparkman; Collector of Customs, B.H. Ward; Deputy Collector, Julius Levy; Postmaster, S.M. Ward; Assistant Postmaster, W.T. Tubberville.*

The schools are now run as graded schools and supply a special district of about three miles from the centre of the town. The school for white children is taught in the Winyah Indigo Society building. The superintendent is Mr. S.McB. Hamby, a courtly gentleman and an elegant scholar who has charge of the academic course. The pupils here are assisted by the benevolent funds of the Winyah Indigo Society. The society of today is the lineal descendant of the organization chartered in 1755 by King George. Among the incorporators was Robert Pawley,

*The *News and Courier* (February 14, 1888) also contains the officers of these companies and associations: Georgetown Rice Milling Company, Georgetown Building and Loan Association, Georgetown Land Association, Georgetown Telegraph Company, Winyah Indigo Society, Palmetto Club, Board of Trade, Survivors' Association, Pilot Commissioners, Masonic Lodge, American Legion of Honor, Knights of Honor, Georgetown and Western Railroad, Gilbert Dredge Company, and Mosquito Creek Canal Dredge Company, as well as considerable information concerning river and ocean-going steamers active in the Georgetown area. Reporter Tighe notes that Georgetown has two brass bands—the Centennial and the Cornet Club—both black organizations.

for whom Pawley's Island was named. Apart from its care of the free schools in provincial times, the Winyah Society was a social and literary organization.

The library, a small part of which has survived, is still in the old building in this city and it is a very interesting collection. The finest books are said to have been carried off by the officers of Willard's negro troops after the war. The literature is of the old style of reading, Pope, Dryden, Steele, Addison, &c., books of travel and old histories, and the Delphin edition of the classics. A very rare edition of Aristotle has been presented to the University of the South. Only recently through the instrumentality of ex-Governor Magrath, of Charleston, was recovered an autograph address of Gen. Washington to the citizens of Georgetown while on his Southern tour after the adoption of the Constitution. The present president of the society is H. Dozier, one of the vieille roche* of Georgetown. The present building was erected in 1858. The anniversary is the first Friday in May. The library contains about 2,500 volumes.

To return to the school: The principal is Mr. T.P. Bailey, Jr., a bright young scholar, his assistants being Miss L.R. Burckmeyer, Miss Isabella Monteith, and Miss S.I. Knight. These young ladies are well equipped for the work they have undertaken, and the people here speak in glowing terms of the institution and its teachers. The roll of pupils numbers about 130.

The colored school is under the supervision of P.E. Drayton, a colored man, who enjoys the reputation of being well qualified for the position. He is assisted by four teachers, the attendance being about 350.

The white churches are Prince George Winyah Episcopal, rector the Rev. Stuart McQueen; Methodist, pastor the Rev. A.H. Lester; and Baptist, without a resident pastor. There are four colored churches of as many denominations. Prince George's Church is said to have been built in 1700. It is an edifice built of English brick, rectangular in form with Roman arch window caps. The tower is octagonal, capped by a dome and containing a belfry and a clock tower. Inside the architecture is Tuscan, there being no galleries, and the pews are so arranged that it is possible to sit with one's back to the rector, to sleep, perchance to dream, to hear no more. The chancel roof is vaulted, the painted design being a blue sky over a wave-beaten rocky shore, with the sun, typical of the eye of Providence, looking down from the centre of the picture.

The churchyard is surrounded by a thick brick wall, which is here and there covered with ivy. The clock stopped at 25 minutes after 5 some time ago and has not been in tune since. The chancel has a beautiful window of cathedral glass, which is also the material of the transoms of the side doors of the church. The panels of the church are in buff and brown. On the lectern lie the Book of Prayer, old type, date 1795, and the Bible, date 1743.

In the graveyard are the graves and vaults of all of the old families of the

*The good old stock ... of the old school.

parish. A companion church to this beautiful relic is All Saints' Church on Waccamaw Neck, about eighteen miles distant. The church as it stands was built by funds given by Mrs. Mary Huger in 1843. A view of these two churches alone is worth a much longer journey than from Charleston to Georgetown.

On Waccamaw Neck are many of the plantations of the indigo planters, of which there is nothing now left but an embankment here and there, probably the dividing lines of the estates. The Neck is covered by second growth of forest which is stocked with deer, turkeys, partridges, snipe, ducks, and woodcock, making it one of the finest game preserves in the world.

The Waccamaw Neck is to be the section in which the truck farming industry is one day to be developed. The country to the northwest of Georgetown is also said to be a desirable district for this purpose, and there is talk of introducing the planting of vegetables on a large scale. All of this, by the way, is the result of the big commercial boom that has only recently been inaugurated.

It is conceded here all around that Georgetown is under the influence of an atmosphere charged at certain seasons of the year with the miasma from the rice fields. In other words, that it is a malarial district. It is even said that every wind, except from the northwest, floats the miasmatic vapor over the city. Yet, for all this, the people do not die here by the hecatombs, nor are the cemeteries filled any faster than they are in any other city of equal population. Whatever may be their internal economy, the people of this city are just as healthy looking as they are, for instance, in Columbia. There are no sallow skins and lack-luster eyes as are to be seen in the inland fever districts of Colleton, Beaufort, or Berkeley counties. It might be said that the people here are acclimated. So they are and the process does not appear to be dangerous. A little fever "to start with" may or may not be expected by every visitor. Even if he or she gets a touch of it, it will not be followed by prostration or demoralization. A little care and more quinine appear to make Georgetown as fair a place to dwell as any other similarly situated city on the coast.

News and Courier, February 13–15, 1888. M.F.T.

Greenville: Progress Is the Watchword

During the 1880s, three *News and Courier* reporters tried to capture the essence of "The Pearl of the Piedmont." Ambrose Gonzales, author of this sketch, stresses the same themes delineated by James C. Hemphill (May 13, 1882) and Matthew F. Tighe (August 22, 1887)—progress, industry, growth. At times during the decade, burgeoning Greenville caused some uneasiness among business leaders at the state capital, fearful this Up Country upstart might divert trade and commerce from their community. But whenever controversy arose, they could count upon the Columbia bureau of the *News and Courier* to spring to their defense.

* * *

Early in the present century Greenville became famous as a summer resort. Many wealthy residents of Charleston and the low country owned summer seats here, and those who passed through to the mountains beyond almost invariably spent a week or two here both going and returning.

Notwithstanding Greenville's splendid climate and fine tributary country, the expense of marketing her produce in the distant cities of Charleston and Augusta was so great that she was still a village in 1853 when the completion of the Greenville and Columbia Railroad gave her an outlet to the sea. Immediately she awakened into new life and became the distributing point for a large section of country extending far into North Carolina, Georgia, and Tennessee. The caravans, instead of passing through to Augusta, stopped in Greenville to sell their produce and buy their return loads. Much of this mountain trade is retained to this day, and on Saturdays the streets are filled with wagons laden with apples, cabbages, hides, etc. hauled here from points fifty miles away.

For many years before the war Greenville was a stronghold of the Union party, which steadfastly supported Governor B.F. Perry in his persistent struggle against the tide of secession, which for so many years threatened and finally overwhelmed South Carolina. When the war came, however, Greenville County responded gallantly to the call for volunteers, and, with a voting population of 2,200 in 1860, she furnished more than 2,500 troops.

At the close of the war Greenville County, not having been in the line of Sherman's march, recuperated rapidly. The men returned to their fields, and the use of commercial fertilizers having become general, cotton culture was engaged in extensively and profitably. Many farmers here raise a bale to the acre, and the acreage is being largely increased each year. Nor is cotton the only profitable crop grown here. The many creek bottoms in the county yield heavy crops of corn;

most of the farmers raise their own wheat, while fields of oats, rye, and barley are seen everywhere.

The city of Greenville is built on both sides of Reedy River at a considerable elevation above the bed of the stream, which brawls noisily over the rocky shallows and tumbles with a roar down two falls of thirty feet each, turning as it goes the turbines of the upper and lower mills of the Camperdown Company, and adding to the sound of the rushing waters the hum of ten thousand spindles. Into this swift stream the rock drains and terra cotta sewerage pipes of the city lead. The drainage of Greenville is therefore perfect.

The broad streets of Greenville are well graded and macadamized. The sidewalks are principally of brick and granite, but some of the property owners along Main Street have supplemented the municipal appropriation and aided in the construction of beautifully smooth concrete pavements, which are at once an ornament to the great thoroughfare and a delight to the pedestrian. Most of the streets are shaded by elms, oaks, and mimosas, and there are many lovely blue grass lawns and flower gardens surrounding handsome residences.

The writer is assured by Dr. G.T. Swandale, chairman of the board of health, that the city enjoys absolute immunity from epidemics of every kind. There is no malaria, of course, and no cases of intermittent fever are ever recorded here. For persons afflicted with throat and lung troubles this climate is peculiarly well adapted, especially during the spring and autumn months.

For years before the war the Mansion House was a favorite resort of the wealthy planters of lower Carolina. Three years ago, the owners having expended $27,000 in remodeling, enlarging, and equipping the building in modern style, it became, under the management of A.A. Gates, the most popular hostelry between Charleston and Asheville, and by many of the travelling men, who are competent to judge, the fare and attendance is compared very favorably with that of the vaunted Kimball House in Atlanta. The building is of brick, three stories high, and is centrally located on Main Street. It is provided with fine parlors, reception and reading rooms, and sample rooms for commercial men. On the first floor are well-appointed barber shops, bath rooms, bar and billiard parlors. C.J. Holloway, a well-known Charlestonian, presides over the barber shop. The office and main entrance of the Mansion House are finished in natural woods. The walls are frescoed and the floors laid with marble tiling. The rooms, seventy in number, are comfortably furnished, and many of them, fronting on Main Street and Court Square, admit the mountain breezes in the summer and the warm sunshine in winter. Most of the rooms are en suite, with open fireplaces for wood or coal fires. A 'bus meets all trains and a livery stable is connected with the hotel. The house is lighted throughout with electricity, both the arc and incandescent lights being used. Mr. Gates is a thorough hotel man and the office is in charge of W.C. Earnhardt, an accomplished clerk, assisted by the versatile and ubiquitous James Swandale.

In connection with the Mansion House is a first-class steam laundry fitted

Looking up the river from Main Street, Greenville, c. 1890. *South Caroliniana Library.*

with Troy machinery and working ten operatives. Agencies have been established in all of the neighboring towns, and the laundry, having acquired a reputation for fine work, is increasing its business rapidly.

The Exchange Hotel, on Washington Street, is managed by Capt. W.R. White, a native of Abbeville, and a genial and entertaining host. There are 35 bedrooms, with high ceilings, admirably ventilated, and well carpeted and furnished. Capt. White is deservedly popular with the travelling public, and the Exchange Hotel is liberally patronized.

The Goodwin House, on Main and Washington streets, is a fine building with large, airy rooms and a convenient and central location. It is conducted by Miss Mary Latimer.

The Central Hotel is, as its name indicates, located on Main Street in the heart of the city. The proprietor is A.M. Stephens.

The boarding houses in Greenville are too numerous to mention.

The Hotel Altamonte, which is being built on the top of Paris Mountain by a company of Greenville capitalists, will be opened to the public on July 15. The design of the building is unique and beautiful. There will be a view from every window, and the rooms will be handsomely and comfortably furnished. A complete system of water-works and electric call bells has been provided, and there is telephone connection with Greenville. A line of hacks will ply constantly between the city and the Altamonte, and the drive is an easy one of fifty minutes. Certainly there is no mountain resort in this section that is so accessible or that gives promise of being more popular than the Altamonte. Mr. A.H. French will manage the hotel.

The National Bank of Greenville, established in 1872, has had a most successful career and occupies a prominent place among the financial institutions of South Carolina. The officers and directors are men of the highest character and commercial standing: President, Hamlin Beattie; cashier, W.E. Beattie; teller, Eustice M. Bolton; bookkeeper, F.F. Capers; collector, James Lewis. The directors are Hamlin Beattie, Wm. H. Perry, Wm. Wilkins, H.C. Markley, H.P. Hammet, and Alexander McBee.

The bank occupies a handsome and substantial brick building, centrally located on Main Street. The vaults are fitted with burglar-proof chests, time-locks, etc.

The People's Bank of Greenville, established in 1887, occupies the beautiful Ferguson & Miller building at the corner of Main and Washington streets. The offices are tastefully fitted up, and the vaults, safes, time-locks, etc. are built in the most approved modern style. The officers of the bank are: Frank Hammond, president, Jas. A. Hoyt, vice president; Wm. C. Beacham, cashier. The directors are: Frank Hammond, Jas. L. Orr, Jas. A. Hoyt, E.H. Fulenweider, O.P. Mills, H.F. Means, W.M. Hagood and F.W. Poe.

The Greenville Savings Bank, which also conducts a general banking business, was established one year ago, and has been managed so successfully that the bank has already earned about 12 per cent on the capital stock, which has been increased from $25,000 to $50,000. The president is J. Wilkins Norwood and the cashier is W.L. Gassaway. The directors are: H.C. Markley, Jas. L. Orr, Theo. B. Hayne, Wm. C. Cleveland, T.Q. Donaldson, Jas. H. Maxwell, Julius H. Heyward, John Slattery, and J. Wilkins Norwood.

The population of Greenville was 2,757 in 1870, 6,160 in 1880, and today there are between 10,000 and 11,000 people within the corporate limits. During the past two years hundreds of houses have been built in every part of the city and still the demand for dwellings is unprecedented. Real estate is rapidly increasing in value, keeping pace with the growth of the city. The municipal revenues are derived from a moderate tax on real and personal property, and from the sale of liquor licenses, which, under the wise high license law in force here, yield the city upwards of $10,000 per annum.

Greenville is lighted by forty-six Brush electric arc lights of 2,000 candle-power each. The plant is owned by the city, which supplies six hundred incandescent lights to individuals. There is also a plant operating the Thomson-Houston system, controlled by Messrs. Asbury & Son, who furnish both arc and incandescent lights to mills, hotels, and merchants.

In addition to the large number of fire wells and public cisterns in Greenville, there is an excellent system of water-works owned by Ferguson & Miller. The water is pumped by steam from rock springs on their property and supplied to

Main Street, Greenville, c. 1890. *South Caroliniana Library.*

the city through hydrants on Main Street and also to the Mansion House and the Ferguson & Miller Hall.

The mayor of Greenville is S.A. Towns, and the aldermen are L.M. McBee, W.J. Smith, James McPherson, Alex Finley, James T. Williams, and James McDaniel. The corporation counsel is Major W.A. Williams, the city clerk and treasurer is C.W. D'Oyley, the street overseer is Frank Hunt, and the superintendent of the cemetery is J.G. Morris.

The chief of police is Capt. R.H. Kennedy, who, with a force of ten men, rigorously enforces the law and maintains order in the city. The Greenville Fire Department has four companies, two white and two colored, under the control of Fire Chief J.C. Kirkpatrick. Each company receives $20 a month from the city treasurer.*

The Greenville Y.M.C.A. is in a very flourishing condition. The rooms occupied by them in the Record Building are unquestionably the finest and best arranged in the State. The ladies of Greenville have very generally interested themselves in the Association. They have carpeted, furnished, and appropriately decorated the parlors, and the walls are adorned with paintings and engravings contributed by them. The parlor contains an organ and the reading room is supplied with the best newspapers and magazines. The gymnasium is completely equipped, and bath rooms and recreation rooms are also fitted in the building. The officers are J.A. McCullough, president; P.T. Hayne, vice president; Wm.

*See the *News and Courier* (July 8, 1889) for the names of the officers of these companies, as well as those of the board of firemasters.

Goldsmith, Jr., treasurer; Lewis W. Parker, secretary; and C.R. Hardy, general secretary.

Several months ago, in order to utilize the musical talent of Greenville, the Greenville Musical Association was organized, with A.E. Smyth, president; B.A. Morgan, secretary and treasurer; and Mrs. R.H. Kennedy, musical directress. The association has recently purchased a $1,000 concert grand Knabe piano and has leased Duncan's Hall for rehearsals and concerts. The plan of organization is similar to that of the Charleston Musical Association and under Mrs. Kennedy's direction the young association will doubtless achieve many musical triumphs.

The Greenville Cotillion Club, although organized not very long ago, includes in its membership most of the society men of Greenville. The club gives three balls during the season under the management of president E.A. Smyth, vice president J.L. Orr, and secretary and treasurer W.E. Beattie. Those already given have been brilliant society events and have attracted a large number of visitors from other cities.

The Greenville Club offers its members a delightful retreat, with rooms for quiet reading, rooms for billiards, rooms with papers and magazines, and rooms with Chick Springs water. The ruling spirits of this masculine paradise are R.G. McPherson, Jr., president; J.F. Richardson, vice president; and F.F. Capers, secretary and treasurer.

The Greenville chapter of the Society for the Prevention of Cruelty to Animals, under the efficient presidency of William Elliott Johnstone, has done much to check the barbarity with which many persons seem to consider themselves privileged to treat horses and other animals that are so unfortunate as to come into their possession. The pitiable scarecrows and starved horses and mules that are brought for swapping purposes to most country towns on sales days are no longer seen in Greenville. Anyone appearing with such an animal is promptly arrested, subjected to fine or imprisonment, and the maltreated animal is stabled and cared for or destroyed if too far gone.

It is a pity that societies of this kind were not organized in every town in South Carolina. The inhuman treatment of live stock by brutal negroes and ruffianly white men is a blot upon our alleged civilization. It is no uncommon thing for an abandoned drunkard to rush into a village or town, urging under whip and spur a galled, starved horse and leave him hitched to a picket fence, without food and water, for perhaps thirty-six hours, while the owner continues his debauch. It is questionable whether a man should be allowed to keep in his possession an animal that he either will not or cannot feed and care for, and if the law should be rigidly enforced, 50 per cent of the horses and mules owned in this State by negroes would be confiscated for fines or destroyed. President Johnstone is ably seconded in his work by P.T. Hayne, secretary, and R.S. Morgan, treasurer of the society.

There are two crack military organizations in Greenville, the Butler Guards and the Greenville Guards.

The various secret societies are well represented here. They include Recovery Lodge, No. 31, A.F.M. (sixty-five members); R.E. Lee Lodge, No. 3, A.O.U.W. (sixty-five members); I.O.O.F. (fifty members); the Knights of the Golden Rule (fifty members); and Waverly Lodge, No. 30, K. of H. (fifty-four members).* The colored societies are innumerable.

The Baptist Church, a fine brick edifice on McBee Avenue, is the largest in Greenville, with the largest attendance. The pastor is the Rev. J.A. Mundy, D.D., a native of Virginia and a popular and powerful preacher.

The Methodist Church is on Buncombe Street, built of brick and surrounded by a pretty grove. The pastor is the Rev. J.O. Wilson.

The Presbyterians completed four years ago a beautiful brick church on Washington Street. The pastor is the Rev. L.H. Cline.

The Episcopalians of Greenville own one of the most valuable church properties in the South. The grounds are very extensive and beautiful. The present rector is the Rev. Byron Holly, an eloquent and accomplished man.

Near the Episcopal Church, and supported by its members, is the Christ Church Home, where the needy sick of all denominations are cared for free of charge by the ladies of the Episcopal congregation and attended gratuitously by Drs. Rutledge and Trescot. The building and the handsome grounds surrounding it was the gift of Mrs. Tench Coxe, a woman whose charities are unnumbered—here. The Home is a perfectly appointed hospital and the matron in charge is Mrs. Rantin.

St. Mary's Catholic Church is a pretty little wooden building in charge of Father A. Hirschmeyer, who has beautified the grounds with flowers and shrubbery. Services are held in the Camperdown Baptist Church by the Rev. Dr. Bailey.

There are six colored churches in Greenville. The Mattson Presbyterian Church, with a mission school attached, in charge of the Rev. B.F. McDowell. The Springfield Baptist Church, the Rev. J.N. Watkins, pastor. The Mount Zion Baptist Church, the Rev. Fred Brown, pastor. The Methodist Episcopal Church, the Rev. J.A. Brown, pastor. The African Methodist Church, the Rev. J.F. Jackson, pastor, and the Philadelphia Baptist Church, the Rev. I.V. Jones, pastor.

The Gilreath Opera House, under the management of B.T. Whitmore, has during the past two seasons, presented many standard theatrical attractions to the people of Greenville. The building is centrally located on Main and Coffee streets. It is well equipped with scenery and stage appliances, and the seating capacity is about 800.

Ferguson & Miller's new hall on Main Street is, perhaps, the largest, as it certainly is one of the handsomest, in the State. Unfortunately for the amusement-loving public it has been temporarily leased to the United States Government for use as a court room. When the new public building shall have been completed,

---

*See the *News and Courier* (July 8, 1889) for the names of the officers of these various organizations.

however, the hall will be available for balls, concerts, etc., the purposes for which it was built.

Gower & Reilly's Hall has long been a popular assembly room for entertainments of various kinds. The other public halls are Williams's and Sloan & Duncan's.

On a beautiful wooded slope overlooking all Greenville and the surrounding country stands Furman University, one of the handsomest college buildings in the State and an institution dear to the heart of every Baptist within its borders. For more than a generation the University has graduated and sent out to careers of usefulness and honor men who attribute all their successful achievements to the mental and moral training given them in their alma mater in the Mountain City. The University is prosperous, and there are about one hundred students enrolled for the next session.

The faculty members are: Charles Manly, D.D., president and professor of English language and literature; J.C. Furman, D.D., professor of intellectual and moral philosophy and logic; C.H. Hudson, LL.D., professor of mathematics and mechanical philosophy; H.T. Cook, A.M., professor of ancient languages; W.M. Watson, A.M., professor of physics and chemistry; H.H. Watkins, A.M., principal, preparatory school; and W.M. Clyde, A.M., assistant.

The Greenville Female College, founded in 1854, has increased in popularity and usefulness from year to year, and under the signally successful administration of President Townes the number of pupils enrolled during the past session was 227, a very gratifying exhibit even for the largest female seminary in the State. The buildings are beautifully located in the centre of extensive grounds. Connected with the College is the conservatory of music, the handsomest building of its kind in South Carolina. Like Furman University, the Greenville Female College is under the auspices of the Baptist Church.

The faculty members are: A.S. Townes, president, English, Latin, moral and mental science; Miss Mary C. Judson, lady principal, logic, physical sciences, elocution, and calisthenics; Miss Caroline D. Dawson, French, mathematics, and history; Miss Bessie Bagby, English, Latin, and mathematics; Miss Lucy R. Hoyt, composition, arithmetic, and English; Miss Georgia E. Ackerman, physical science, mathematics, and history; Prof. W.M. Watson, professor of chemistry and physics in Furman University, special lecturer in physics and chemistry; Prof. J.M. Perry, penmanship and bookkeeping; Miss F.G. Bibb, principal of academic department; Miss Mamie E. Goggeshall, assistant; Miss Maggie G. Griffith, principal of primary department; Mrs. M.G. DeCamps, principal of music department, theory of music, harmony, vocalization, piano forte, guitar, organ, and violin; Miss Emma E. Werts, theory of music and tho mass [thorough bass]; Miss Helen R. Platt, principal of art department; Miss F.G. Bibb, lady principal of the boarding department; and Mrs. M.M. Lynes, matron.*

*See the *News and Courier* (July 8, 1889) for names of the boards of trustees of Furman University and the Greenville Female College, as well as a list of the latter's graduating class of 1889.

The splendid graded schools of Greenville have, under the control of Prof. W.S. Morrison, superintendent of the city schools, attained a degree of excellence that should be very gratifying to those who, two years ago, persistently fought the opposition to the issuance of school bonds for the erection of buildings and the establishment of free schools in Greenville. The opposition was overcome, however, and the legislative consent was obtained to the issuance of city school bonds in the amount of $18,000. Two brick buildings were erected, one in East Greenville and the other in West Greenville. Twenty thousand dollars was expended in the construction of the buildings and their equipment, which is complete in every detail.

The East End School is built on the highest elevation in Greenville, commanding a fine view of mountains and valley. There are ten recitation rooms besides offices and assembly room, all furnished with modern combination desks, blackboards, etc. Surrounding the handsome building is the play ground, three acres in extent. The average enrolment of pupils for the past year was 402.

The teachers are: W.S. Morrison, acting superintendent; Miss Sallie Dorroh, Miss Lizzie Easley, Miss Nellie Hoyt, Miss Mamie Stuart, Miss Lucie Charles, Miss Eliza Powers, Miss Hattie Goldsmith, and Miss Mittie Marshall.

The West End School building contains four rooms. The average attendance is 125 pupils. The principal is W.T. Slaughter and his assistants are Miss Jennie Irvine and Miss Nannie Williams. To this school also a large play ground is attached.

The colored schools are two in number. A. Robertson is the principal of the East End School, which has an enrolment of 265 pupils. The West End School has an attendance of 350 pupils and the principal is Elias B. Holloway.

Both the white and the colored schools are under the supervision of Prof. Morrison and the following board of trustees: T.C. Gower, chairman; Dr. J.F. Dorroh, A.H. Cureton, H.T. Cook, E.F.S. Rowley, and P.T. Hayne, secretary.

It is impossible to overestimate the value to this city of the *Greenville Daily News,* published by the Greenville News Company and edited by A.B. Williams, a brilliant and fearless writer, who in his editorial utterances is always forcible and always honest.

The *News* has, in the nine years of its existence under the present management, labored increasingly for the development of Greenville and the Piedmont section of South Carolina, and its efforts deserve the gratitude and support of the people for whom it has striven. Mr. Williams is assisted by T.E. Horton, city editor, and W.W. Price, local reporter. The company is organized with J.F. Richardson, manager and treasurer, and Jas. L. Orr, president. The directors are: H.P. Hammet, A.B. Williams, E.A. Smyth, W.H. Perry, John Ferguson, Wm. Wilkins, J.H. Morgan, P.H. Reilly, and Jas. L. Orr. The bookkeeper is R.S. Morgan.

The capital stock of the Greenville News Company is $25,000. Their publications are the *Daily News,* a handsome, four-page, eight-column paper, with Associated Press dispatches, specials, and full local news, and the *Weekly News,* a four-page, nine-column paper adapted specially to the farmers of Greenville

County. The presses are run by steam, and a complete job printing establishment is connected with the office.

Messrs. Jas. A. Hoyt and W.W. Keys publish and edit the *Baptist Courier* and the *Cotton Plant,* the only agricultural paper in the State. The *Courier* is published weekly, four pages and eight columns. The *Cotton Plant* is a five-column, eight-page, semi-monthly publication. Messrs. Hoyt & Keys have an extensive job printing establishment and publish the reports of the State Department of Agriculture.

Three months ago Mr. J.S. Daley formed a co-partnership with Mr. W.S. Killingsworth for the publication of the *South Atlantic,* an industrial monthly magazine, which, while giving space to current literature and the news of the day, eschews politics and is especially devoted to the material advancement of Greenville and the Piedmont country in general.

The oldest country paper in the State is the *Enterprise and Mountaineer,* a weekly paper, owned and edited by John C. Bailey. The *Mountaineer,* which was established in 1824, was at one time edited by Governor B.F. Perry, and at another by Judge Campbell. It was in 1873 consolidated with the *Enterprise,* a journal founded in 1854. The present paper is one of the most extensively circulated country papers in the State and has a liberal advertising patronage.

The job printing establishment of Messrs. Shannon & Co. is supplied with modern presses, new type, and every facility for the execution of first-class work.

The manufactures of Greenville have increased from $400,000 in 1880 to $1,283,000 in 1889.

Foremost in importance is the Camperdown Manufacturing Company, operating two mills located on the falls of Reedy River. The capital stock is $100,000. The president is H.P. Hammet and the treasurer is E.F. Patterson. Eleven thousand spindles are run by water and steam power. Two engines of 125 and 250 horse power and two Victor turbines are in use, and 4,700 bales of cotton are annually manufactured into carpet yarns, hosiery yarns, and other yarns of various kinds; 235 operatives are employed, and the electric light is used in the mills.

The Huguenot Mills, built also on the banks of Reedy River, employ 175 operatives in the manufacture of overall ducks, cottonades and other dyed goods. The motive power is supplied by a Harris-Corliss engine of 125 horse power, which runs 2,000 spindles and 184 looms. The president of the company is E.H. Fulenweider, the treasurer is H.E. Fulenweider, and the superintendent of the mills is W.J. Fulenweider. The capital stock is $60,000. The mill is lighted by electricity.

A perfectly appointed little mill is that of the Lanneau Manufacturing Company, C.H. Lanneau, president. The capital stock is $25,000. Eleven hundred spindles and 30 operatives are employed in the manufacture of soft cotton yarns of the highest grades. The mill is lighted with the Loomis incandescent light, and the engine used is a 50 horse power "Ball" pattern with Harrison safety boilers.

The capital stock of the Greenville Cotton Seed Oil and Ice Company is $42,840.

A.H. Cureton is manager and treasurer, A.S. Duncan, president, and A.C. McFall, superintendent. The capacity of the mills is being increased to 80 tons per day; large ware houses have been erected and others rented for storage purposes. The oil is shipped to Providence, R.I., refineries.

Many years ago Dr. J.M. Westmoreland came into possession of a formula for the manufacture of a tonic that even with limited advertising has become famous in the malarial regions of the Southern States. Dr. Westmoreland recently formed a company, which, with ample capital, will manufacture on a large scale and extensively advertise the Westmoreland Calisaya Tonic. A spacious laboratory has been fitted up on Washington Street, and here, surrounded by bales of Peruvian bark, packages of gentian, and barrels of high grade whiskey, Dr. Westmoreland manufactures hundreds of cases of the tonic, which is already being shipped to agencies and depositories in New Orleans, Memphis, Mobile, and other cities.

The organization of the company is as follows: J.M. Westmoreland, M.D., president; W.H. Westmoreland, secretary; Frank Hammond, treasurer; directors, Dr. J.M. Westmoreland, Jas. L. Orr, Jas. Maxwell, J.M. McGee, Wm. Wilkins, W.S. Gray, and Frank Hammond.

The Greenville Coach Factory, established in 1835 by Cox and Gower, has, for more than half a century, sustained its early acquired reputation for thoroughly reliable work. Buggies, carriages, wagons, and vehicles of all kinds are manufactured here out of the best materials and in the most substantial manner. The wood and iron working machinery is run by an overshot wheel in the upper Reedy River, and a large number of hands are employed. The present owner of the factory is Mr. H.C. Markley and the superintendent is Mr. G.W. Sirrine.

Beard, Long & Co. employ 15 hands in the manufacture and repair of boilers, engines, etc. at the Palmetto Iron Works. Castings are made in brass and iron, and the works are equipped with modern iron-working machinery.

R.M. McDonald's Iron Foundry is completely equipped for all kinds of iron work in building and repairing. Fifteen hands are employed.

The tannery of Messrs. Gower, Reilly & Goodlett has been in successful operation for a number of years and utilizes advantageously the hides of all the beef cattle brought to this market, as well as the supply hauled from the mountain country above. The leather manufactured is of excellent quality and commands ready sale and profitable prices in Baltimore, Boston, and other shoe manufacturing centres.

A new industry has recently been added to the manufactures of Greenville in the bottling works of Ligon & Co., who manufacture soda water, ginger ale, and other summer drinks.

The Piedmont Ice Company is running day and night to supply the Piedmont demand for ice, which is shipped all over this section and as far west as Elberton, Ga. The capacity of the factory is seven tons per day. The president is John B. Marshall and the superintendent is J.S. Marshall.

The candy factory of W.M. Boyst supplies, not only Greenville, but all of the neighboring towns with candies of all kinds.

There are four planing mills in Greenville operated by J.W. Cagle, Case & Litton, W.T. Shumate & Co., and W.D. Goodwin.

Taylor's furniture factory has been equipped with new machinery for the manufacture of all grades of furniture.

Brick yards are owned by W.D. Goodwin (pressed brick), Grady & Murray, Wm. Johnson, and Harry Moseley.

The Greenville Pants Factory commenced work two years ago and has been one of the most successful of Greenville's younger industries. Travelling salesmen are employed, and the products are sold through all the Piedmont country. The manager is Mr. T. Davis.

J.C. Fitzgerald's beautiful photographic studio is on the second floor of Mauldin's Block, corner of Main and Washington streets. L.C. Wheeler also has a studio in Greenville.

The harness manufacturers are Gower, Reilly & Goodlett, McDaniel & McBee, and Geo. Heldman.

There are two grist mills, McCarter's and K. McGowan's.

A prominent factor in the industrial development of Greenville is the board of trade. The president is Capt. E.A. Smyth; vice president, W.E. Beattie; and secretary-treasurer, Wm. Lee. Through their special agent, Mr. T.E. Horton, the board is now advertising Greenville's climate and resources at the Paris Exposition, with the special object of attracting French grape growers to this section.

The grape industry, which a few years ago was in its infancy here, is rapidly becoming one of great importance. Among the many vineyards hereabouts are those of M. David, H.G. Gilreath, the famous Carpin vineyard leased by G.T. Willis, Duncan & Weldon, H.B. Buist, A.M. Howell, P. Jaffeux, Mme. Garraux, F. Hahn, L.G. Cole, Jas. McPherson, and Esquire McBee.

Just beyond the city limits south of Greenville is "Millsdale," the beautiful dairy farm of O.P. Mills. Mr. Mills breeds Jersey cattle for sale, and his splendid dairy supplies a large number of persons with milk and butter.

At Sans Souci, the lovely home of the Perry family three miles northwest of Greenville, Messrs. William H. and B.F. Perry are raising thoroughbred stock of all kinds. These gentlemen were the largest exhibitors at the last State Fair and their stock took many premiums. Having recently determined to breed trotting horses on an extensive scale, they attended the breeders' sales in Kentucky and purchased fifteen standard bred mares, several of them with records of 2.26 or better.

The cotton receipts of Greenville are 19,000 bales per annum. They would be 40,000 bales except for the proximity of the great mills at Piedmont and Pelzer. The cotton buyers are: Theo. B. Hayne, W.E. Johnstone, John Slattery, Carroll & Stacy, J.B. Henry, and Cely Bros.

The annual receipts of fertilizers are 4,000 tons. The dealers are Julius C.

Smith, A.H. Jenkins & Son, C.L. Yates, W.T.J. Woodward & Son, John Slattery, John Ferguson, and the brokers generally.

The business houses of the city, classified by type with their estimated annual receipts, are as follows:

Groceries ($1,378,000)—Ferguson & Miller, R.F. Allen & Bro., Lipscomb & Russell, Finlay Bros., John Slattery, Ellison & Finlay, Cely Brothers, W.A. Jennings, J.T. Nix (two stores), King & Browning, M.E. Gaines & Co., C.L. Foster & Bro., R.C. Foster, D. Mills Hoke, B.F. Madden, D.H. Bull, T.J. Price, Gray & Sullivan, B.M. McGee, T.D. Harris, W.B. Freeman, D.C. Moore, E.B. Wells, J.L. Reeves, J.G. Perry, Wm. Lee, J.L.F. Jones, and J.A. Parker.

Produce Brokers ($550,000)—W.T.J. Woodward & Son, L.M. McBee, A.H. Jenkins & Son, Briggs Brothers, S.C. Clyde, J.P. Mahoney, and J.C. Boyd.

Dry Goods ($515,000)—J.H. Morgan & Bro., Stradley & Barr, McAllister & Benz, T.A. Walker & Bro., F.P. Mimnaugh, E.W. Marshall & Co., Earle & Willson, Henry M. Shumate, John Slattery, S. Robinson, and the Bee Hive Racket Store.

Clothing and Hats ($175,000)—F.W. Poe & Co., L. Rothschild, Isaac Weil, H. Endel, and H.C. Mark.

Hardware, Guns, Etc. ($215,000)—Wilkins, Poe & Co., James F. Williams & Co., and H.C. Markley.

Drugs, Paints, and Oils ($75,000)—Sloan Bros., D.T. Bacot & Co., Westmoreland Bros., George Legge, and S.M. Reynolds.

Jewelry, Watches, and Clocks ($26,000)—S.M. Snider & Co., Gilreath & Patton, W.R. Hale, and Miss Belle Black.

Furniture and Undertaking ($65,000)—Turner & Mackey, George L. Dantzler, and Thomas Steen.

Crockery and Glassware ($90,000)—Gilreath & Patton, G.D. Barr & Son, and S.P. Burbage.

Millinery and Dressmaking ($30,000)—Mrs. Isaac Weil, the Misses Ross, the Misses McKay, T.A. Walker & Brother, Miss Betty Garraux, Miss N.A. Green, and Miss Ella Pepper.

Boots and Shoes ($150,000)—W.C. Humphreys, F.W. Poe & Co., and J.H. Morgan & Bro.

Wines and Liquors ($140,000)—Mansion House bar, Tork & Legon, Holcombe & Simmons, Williams & Hogg, J.W. Burgess, Geo. Black, Simon Turner, N. Trebardt, C. Randall, H. Knebel, C.B. McIntyre, Jas. A. Payne, W.S. Hill, Zion Collins, H. Hoff, Lynn & Collins, and S. McKinney.

Livery and Sale Stables ($150,000)—J.A. Goodwin, W.C. Hillhouse, John B. Parks, John McNab, and J.P. Charles.

Wagons, Carriages, Etc. ($100,000)—Bates & Ferguson, H.C. Markley, and Julius C. Smith.

Books and Stationery ($20,000)—R.G. McPherson, Jr., and H.J. Felton.

Confectionery, Fruits, and Vegetables ($25,000)—Mrs. E. Garraux and Charles Richardson.

Bakers ($10,000)—J.F. Roessler and H. Sussman.

Pianos and Musical Instruments ($18,000)—Miss Belle Black and J.L. Haynie and daughter.

Butchers, Meats ($30,000)—D.T. Rounds, D. Speegle & Co., Atkinson & Carter, and John Thompson.

Lime and Cement ($9,000)—Gower & Reilly.

Wood and Coal ($25,000)—Gower & Reilly.

Doors, Sash, and Blinds ($10,000)—Gower & Reilly, J.W. Cagle, and W.T. Shumate & Co.

Insurance ($35,000)—A.B. Jenkins & Son, Julius C. Smith, John Ferguson, E.M. Bollin, C.L. Yates, Gower & Reilly, L.M. McBee, R.C. Goodlett, and King & Browning.

The real estate dealers are: Julius C. Smith, George H. Chapin, A.H. Jenkins & Son, Daley & Clyde, and Mitchell & Furman.

The members of the local Bar are: Wells & Orr, Perry & Heyward, Donaldson & Donaldson, Cothran, Ansel & Morgan, Westmoreland & Haynesworth, Shuman & Mayfield, Nix, Dill & Nix, Blythe & McCullough, Irvine & Mooney, Isaac M. Bryan, Jno. R. Bellinger, Jno. G. Capers, Lewis W. Parker, G.W. Taylor, A.H. Dean, Wm. A. Williams, Robert Fleming, John I. Earle, Thos. Earle, F.B. McBee, E.A. McBee, Edward Croft, Adam C. Welborn, Geo. B. Thruston, L.K. Clyde, D.P. Verner, C.M. Furman, A.G. Furman, Thompson H. Cooke, W.D. Mayfield, and David A. Speer.

The members of the medical profession are: Geo F. Trescot, John H. Maxwell, H.R. Rutledge, T.T. Earle, J.F. Dorroh, F.F.S. Rowley, W.R. Jones, C.C. Jones, G.T. Swandale, J.R. Wilkinson, Davis Furman, F.A. Miles, L.H. Peebles, Jas. B. Earle, F.W. Bailey, W.E. Wright, C.A. Simpson, J.W. Hewell, and J.W. Hewell, Jr.

The dentists are: A.M. Hill, R.T. Welborn, J.W. Norwood, W.M. Norwood, and J.P. Carlisle.

County officers are as follows: P.D. Gilreath, sheriff; A.J. Moseley, clerk of court; W.F. Thackston, treasurer; W.K. Grant, auditor; P.W.B. Freeman, judge of probate; D.P. Verner, master; John G. Capers, school commissioner; J.P. Goodwin, J.W. Bowling, and George W. Richardson, county commissioners; L.K. Clyde, clerk.

Greenville's railroad facilities are first-class. The Columbia and Greenville Railway connects her with Charleston and the entire State of South Carolina. The Atlanta and Charlotte Air Line gives communication with the North and West, and the Greenville and Laurens Railroad connects at Laurens with the lines of the Georgia Central system for Port Royal and Savannah. Greenville has been hoping for a great deal from the Carolina, Knoxville, and Western Railroad, which a year ago built twelve miles of road from Greenville to Marietta, a point northwest of Greenville, in the direction of Caesar's Head. Everything looked promising at first, but the company was overtaken by financial difficulties and work was suspended. There is a prospect, however, of speedily putting matters on a satisfactory basis, when work will be resumed, and Greenville at no distant day put into communication with Knoxville and the West.

Annual Value of Manufactures

Cotton mills	$ 585,000
Oil mill	368,000
Calisaya Tonic	60,000
Tannery	25,000
Foundries	25,000
Ice factory	8,000
Brick yards	25,000
Planing mills	28,000
Coach factory	30,000
Pants factory	40,000
Printing, publishing and binding	40,000
Photography	3,000
Candy factory	7,000
Marble and granite	10,000
Soda water	4,000
Furniture factory	15,000
Harness factories	10,000
Total	$1,283,000

Recapitulation

Annual value of manufactures	$1,283,000
Commercial business	3,941,000
Hotels	40,000
Cotton, 19,000 bales	950,000
Total	$6,114,000*

If the loans of the banks, amounting to $560,000, and the amount collected for freight and passenger business at the three railroad agencies here ($390,000) are included, the business would be $7,064,000.

With such a splendid commercial and industrial exhibit, with her magnificent location, fine climate, perfect health, powerful and intelligent press, sound financial institutions, splendid schools, colleges, and churches, there is no height in the social, industrial, and commercial world to which her hopeful, thrifty, and energetic people may not elevate the Pearl of the Piedmont.

*Total should be $6,214,000.

News and Courier, July 8, 1889. A.E.G.

The Growth of Greenwood

Greenwood, originally a fifty-cent meal stop on the Columbia and Greenville Railroad, almost disappeared when a schedule change shifted the eating time to nearby Ninety Six. But in the 1880s, thanks to new railroad connections generated for the most part by residents of Greenwood itself, the town's population rose from 745 to 1,326, making it the second-largest community in Abbeville County. This anonymous report describes Greenwood in December of 1889.*

* * *

Some one has said that the history of Greenwood began fifty years ago when the daily trains on the Columbia and Greenville Road would stop at the town and the passengers could get for fifty cents one of the best meals to be had in the State. Many are the travellers from lower Carolina who remember the little town by the roadside where such fine dinners were to be had. But the schedule of the trains was changed and the dinner station was moved to the famous town of Ninety-Six. So the history of Greenwood was cut short and the town nearly ceased to be, and never was heard of except as the location of a good female school. The time was not yet ripe for Greenwood to show the latent energy within her bounds and to make plain how a few sound-minded, enterprising men could build up a community and set in motion wheels of progress whose velocity increases with time. Greenwood has no history. It is making its record in the present, and a record, too, of which it can be proud.

Without any natural advantages, Greenwood is fast becoming one of the busiest marts in South Carolina and is destined to be one of the best distributing points in the upper section of the State. Nature gave health, Greenwood has done and is doing the rest. The town is pre-eminently an example of what can be accomplished by unremitting energy and boundless self-reliance. The Columbia and Greenville Railroad was diverted from its natural and most direct route on its way from the Capital of the State to the Mountain City and made to circle round to Greenwood by the enterprising efforts of the townspeople. The Augusta and Knoxville Road was built solely by the people of Greenwood and a few of those living along the line. Work was commenced on this road when there was but one thousand dollars subscribed towards the enterprise and it was built to completion amidst the jeers of hundreds. It was at first owned almost entirely by persons in and around Greenwood and was operated by them until it was bought by the

---

*See other columns on Greenwood which appeared in the *News and Courier* on July 19, 1887, and April 20, 1891. *Note:* Ninety Six usually was referred to as "Ninety-Six" in the nineteenth century.

Central of Georgia. There never was a road built under such fearful odds and with so little encouragement from outsiders, and yet there are few roads which pass from the possession of the first stockholders with as little loss as did the old Greenwood and Augusta Road.

The next road projected from Greenwood was the "Greenwood and Abbeville, with the privilege to extend cither way, east or west." The charter for it was then altered so as to allow it to run to Chester, and then again to Monroe, N.C., and Atlanta, Ga., where the name was changed and it was known as the Georgia, Carolina, and Northern. It will be one of the best roads in the South, running as it does through a section of country ripe for development. Thus Greenwood has become a railroad centre, well knowing that in our fertile Southland where there were the outlets for traffic that there would spring up very soon a traffic to let out. In the case of Greenwood this has proved itself true. Enterprise after enterprise has been begun. As a cotton market the town has grown till now it far exceeds in wealth and prosperity any town in the State of its own age and has few peers among those of twice or thrice its age.

The town is governed by an intendant and a board of wardens. As the town is, so are its rulers, young and enterprising. Mr. Joel S. Bailey is the intendant and the wardens are: J.W. Duckett, B.R. Calhoun, C.W. Crews, and Lewis Waller (colored). Greenwood is a dry town and needs no peace officers and has only a night watchman. There is a nominal town tax of one and one-half mills.

The Greenwood Bank, with a paid in capital stock of $40,000, commenced business on September 15, 1888, and since that time has been doing a thriving business. Last August it declared a dividend of 8 per cent and carried $3,000 to the surplus fund. Its stock is not on the market and cannot be bought except at a very great advance. The business of the bank is increasing rapidly, and it is probable that next year's dividend will greatly exceed that of this year. The officers of the bank are: J.K. Durst, president; D.A.P. Jordan, vice president; J.W. Greene, cashier; J.F. Davis, assistant cashier. The directors are Dr. W.B. Millwee, R.W. Majors, H.P. McGhee, H.M. Spikes, and T.C. Duncan.

The Greenwood Cotton Mill will begin work next season. The present capital stock is $100,000, but it is probable that this will be doubled, and the buildings are being constructed with this view. The mill is being built on the co-operative plan, and no money is allowed to lie idle but is called for just as it is needed.

About the mill site the company owns twenty acres of land on which the cottages of the operatives will be built. A side track runs from the mill site to the Richmond and Danville Railroad, which has connection with the Augusta and Knoxville. The mill will make the coarser grades of cotton, and if the Alliance decide to use cotton bagging for another year, machinery for making this article will be put in the mill.*

*The Farmers' Alliance was fighting the "jute trust" at this time, and its members were refusing to use jute bagging for cotton.

Mr. W.L. Durst, one of the most enterprising men of the town, is the president of the cotton mill company, and Mr. Joel S. Bailey is the secretary and treasurer. The directors are W.L. Durst, Dr. J.C. Maxwell, Dr. W.B. Millwee, G.A. Barksdale, J.T. Simmons, H.P. McGhee, and W.H. Bailey.

The cotton seed oil mill was completed a few weeks ago and is now in active operation. It is a twenty-ton mill with a capital stock of $30,000. It is conveniently situated to the railroads. The mill is one of the best constructed small mills in the State, and has been so pronounced by experts. The Smith-Vail machinery with Carver linters are the kind used in it, and the most careful attention has been given its construction and equipment by its president, Dr. W.B. Millwee. The directors of the company are Dr. W.B. Millwee, Dr. J.C. Maxwell, J.T. Simmons, J.P. Mickler, J.S. Morse, T.F. Riley, and H.B. Reynolds.

The only cotton compress in the State outside of Charleston and Columbia is in Greenwood. A company of capitalists have put it here, after critically examining the whole State for a favorable location. It is situated near the side track to the cotton mill and convenient to the three railroads.

Messrs. Johnson and Wilkerson of North Carolina have been operating a door, blind, and sash factory for the past two years, but so far have not been able to do more than satisfy the local patronage, which, however, has been considerable owing to the number of buildings being put up in Greenwood.

Messrs. Giles L. Wilson and R.B. Wilson of Gastonia, N.C., graduates of Wofford and of Erskine, respectively, began last year the Greenwood Male High School. They are both young men of talent and energy and are founding a school which will honor them and the town. The school is receiving patronage from Abbeville and neighboring counties and bids fair to be one of the best high schools in this part of the State.

The Misses Giles have under their charges a very flourishing female school located at Greenwood. Their school has been in successful operation for some years past and it is yet on the gain. The Misses Giles are highly accomplished ladies and are devoted to their profession. The Female school is one of Greenwood's most prized institutions and is very generously patronized.

Since last May the Presbyterian Company, formerly of Due West, has been located here. They publish the *Associate Reformed Presbyterian*, the official organ of the church of that name, the *Little Banner*, and the *Greenwood Times*, and have very successfully conducted a general publishing business. The *Associate Reformed Presbyterian* and *Little Banner* have been bought by a company at Due West and will be published at that place after June 1, 1880. The *Times* will not be published longer by its present owners, but it is probable that others will continue to do so.

Messrs. Mays & Weeks, contractors, are making large quantities of brick from clay, of which there is abundance in the vicinity of the town. The brick made have been pronounced to be of superior quality, and the industry is growing. They have not been able to supply the demand for brick which has come from all sections.

Public square, Greenwood, c. 1890. *South Caroliniana Library.*

There are only three churches in Greenwood, Presbyterian, Methodist, and Baptist. This is due to the youth of the town and not sufficient time for other denominations to occupy the field. Each church has a large number of members, and services are always well attended. It will not be long before other denominations will come in, as the members of other churches are rapidly increasing in numbers.

While Greenwood is a remarkably healthy town, free from malaria and on a high ridge, with a climate strikingly like Aiken, there are a number of physicians here, most of whom, however, have other sources of livelihood besides their profession. The doctors are: J.C. Maxwell, G.P. Neel, S.L. Swygert, W.L. Hood, M.C. Taggart, J.B. Huey, and B.W. Cobb. This is the only profession in Greenwood that can lay claim to being crowded.

For the size of Greenwood there are very few lawyers, due no doubt to its not being a county seat. The lawyers are W.K. Blake, who is also a trial justice, E.S.F. Giles, and F.H. McMaster.

Dr. M.A. Bailey is the only dentist. He is a rising young practitioner, who is thoroughly master of his art.

Every traveller in the State has stopped at Riley's Hotel, which has made for itself the same reputation that was once given to the dinner house located here. Mr. J.F. Riley is the genial proprietor of the hotel and he has done as much as any other man in Greenwood to make the town what it is. He keeps a fine hotel and it is a famous "lay over" for commercial travellers. There are a large number of boarding houses in the town where the accommodations are good and the rates very cheap.

The merchants of Greenwood are doing a fine business, both wholesale and retail, and their thrift and enterprise would do justice to a place of much more note. As will be seen, the merchants are all young and have not been in business long. Prominent in every business enterprise and in all things to advance the interests of Greenwood are the Dursts, J.K. and W.L., two brothers from Edgefield, who began business here in September 1884. The firm is known as J.K. Durst & Co. and is composed of J.K. Durst, W.L. Durst, and S.P. Matthews, three as fine business men as one often meets. They have two large stores in Greenwood and do a wholesale and retail trade in groceries, dry goods, clothing, notions, and millinery. Their territory is not confined to Abbeville, but extends into neighboring counties. For the fiscal year ending July 31, 1889, this firm did business of $142,321.28.

The firm of Bailey, Barksdale & Co., composed of G.A. Barksdale and Joel S. Bailey, is one of the oldest and most substantial in Greenwood. They began business in 1875 and have since that time done a very large business. They have two stores and do a wholesale and retail business in groceries and general merchandise. They have a well-established trade and are widely known for their fine business qualifications.

Mr. J.W. Duckett began business in October 1888 and named his store the New York Store. He deals in dry goods, shoes, and notions, and there is no more thriving business in the town than his. A young man, quiet in demeanor, he has established a growing trade of which he may be proud. His sales during the year of 1889 so far have averaged $5,000 a month.

Mr. A. Rosenberg is a young man who began business in Greenwood in the fall of 1888. He is doing a large business and his store is continually filled with customers. He carries a $35,000 stock of dry goods and since his coming to Greenwood has made much money. His business is increasing daily and Mr. Rosenberg is happy that his lot fell in Greenwood.

Jervey & Co. is composed of Eugene P. Jervey, Lewis S. Jervey, and Robert S. Sparkman. The first two named are well-known merchants of Charleston, and Mr. Sparkman is the manager here. They are dealers in farmers' supplies, cotton, and rice. The firm is doing a thriving business in supplies and is the wholesale dealer in rice for the up-country, besides handling much cotton every season.

Messrs. A. St. Clair Lee and W.R. Bailey deal in drugs, paints, and oils and in the summer time wholesale and retail ice to the trade in this section. They own one of the few granite-front buildings in this part of the State and are doing a prosperous business. They commenced business in 1884.

F.F. Dunbar & Co. is composed of F.F. Dunbar and Idis Brabham, both of Hattieville, Barnwell County. They commenced business here this fall and are well pleased with their success so far and with the prospects ahead. They deal in general merchandise.

Greenwood boasts of the finest carriage emporium in the State outside of Charleston. It is owned by J.T. Simmons, who began business here in January 1883. The repository is a two-story brick building 30 by 120 feet and most carefully constructed. Mr. Simmons has on hand always a stock of vehicles that fills both floors of his repository and a large ware house besides. He has a branch establishment at Lowndesville and at Mount Carmel.

Other business houses include Blythe & Wells, furniture dealers and undertakers; J.C. Sproles, stoves, tinware, and roofing; Calhoun Bros., groceries; D.C. Du Pre, drugs, paints, oils, and stationery; Lee & Hodges, insurance and fertilizers; W.C. Strawhorne, general merchandise; J.C. Nichels, confectionery and general merchandise; J.T. Youngblood, general merchandise; J.W. Greene & Co., general merchandise; A.McD. Singleton, fancy groceries; B.W. Cobb, drugs; P.B. Reynolds, general merchandise; J.S. Cummings, groceries and building materials; Hartzog & Hays, livestock, horses, and mules; and D.J. Raborn, general merchandise.

Thus, as briefly as possible, is given an account of what is to be found at Greenwood, which is undoubtedly one of the most progressive towns in South Carolina. Besides the enterprises set forth are some of minor importance. There are two building and loan associations, through whose workings a number of the homes in the town have been built. They are still in successful operation.

With a fair soil and unexcelled climate Greenwood, with her railroad facilities and the other enterprises that are to be found in the town, bids fair to be a city at no very distant day. It offers many advantages to young men and capitalists. There is no place in the State where an artisan has better opportunities for success. Its people are hospitable and progressive. It extends a welcome to all who may come to it.

News and Courier, December 26, 1889.

Hampton County: Lumber and Rich Farmlands

One of South Carolina's most rural counties, Hampton in 1880 could boast of only two villages, Brunson and Hampton, each with fewer than 170 inhabitants. During the next ten years county population rose a bit (from 18,741 to 20,554), and this growth enabled Brunson and Hampton to double in size and also created a third village, Varnville (population 553). Yet Matthew F. Tighe, who visited Hampton County in July 1885, seemed more intrigued by a fourth community, Crockettville, which had disappeared and was "a town of mere reminiscences."

*　　　*　　　*

The marvellous progress of Hampton County, of late years, but more especially in regard to the development of its natural resources as an agricultural district, is an indisputable fact, and one that would forcibly impress even the most casual observer. It is not a mere optical delusion. The keen edge of the ploughshare has engraved in its valleys and on its green hillsides the certain signs of advancement, and, at this season of the year, may be seen on all sides the maturing and bountiful harvests of prosperous and intelligent industry.

Not many years ago Hampton County, or rather that part of Beaufort which is now known as Hampton, was monopolized by the lumber men, except in certain sections of the county which by nature were as garden spots, and which courted just that modicum of labor which made them what they are today. A general knowledge of the incomparable richness and fertility of the soil in other than these specially favored places is a thing of comparatively recent date. Not more than twelve or fifteen years ago the people began in a general sense to wake up to the advantages by which they were surrounded, and farming then received the impulse which has continued to the present time. It is not to be inferred, however, that the occupation of the hewers of wood is gone. On the contrary, the supply of timber of the country is well nigh inexhaustible, and the operations in that branch of labor are being conducted as generally and as extensively as in former years. Side by side with the lumber trade there is growing up a rival and ever increasing industry which is making strides that in a few years will bring Hampton County up to the level of the richest counties in the State.

The topography of the county and its railroad facilities are exceptionally fine and they, in every respect, are of incalculable advantage to the interest of the farmer in the prerequisites for successful operation. The county therefore is naturally capable of boundless agricultural development. Along the entire eastern boundary of the county runs the Saltkehatchie. On the west it is skirted by the Savannah River, and within the county are Whippy Swamp, Caw-Caw Swamp, Jackson's Branch, and other water courses furnishing all that the most exacting farmer could desire in the way of bases of operations. The whole southern boundary is the Charleston and Savannah Railway, and through the county runs the Port Royal and Augusta Railway. Besides the latter shipping facilities, the Savannah River is one of the chief commercial highways of the county and the Saltkehatchie is now being opened up by the United States service to small craft and is being made a stream of rapid transit for the lumber trade. The rivers, swamps, and internal streams are bordered with belts, of varying width, of alluvial soil of a naturally fertile character. Just outside of this is the harder, firmer, and more clayey soil, and then come the pine woods extending interminably towards the centre of the county. The "pine barrens," as they are called, certainly by misnomer, in this county at least, are dotted here and there with oases, so to speak, of farms and plantations, which, although requiring the aid of foreign substance to produce good crops, are in many respects the best farming localities in the county.

The glowing reports which have been current for the past few weeks, as to the exceedingly bountiful crops of Hampton County and their prosperous condition, induced a correspondent of the *News and Courier* to visit the county and make a personal inspection of its crops and their prospects.

Just immediately around the town of Hampton there is very little to indicate the resources that lie at some distance beyond the town limits. Within the incorporation there are, however, a few farms on which much labor and expense have been lavished, and on these are to be found some phenomenal specimens of the corn and cotton crop. Notably among these is the farm of Col. Geo. H. Hoover, near the Courthouse. On this farm is a piece of about eight acres of cotton which is in a highly advanced condition. It is fruiting well and will doubtless produce about ten or eleven bales of cotton, which will be harvested at a very early day. Col. Hoover also has a noteworthy field of corn, from which a most bounteous crop is expected.

On Monday morning a party consisting of Col. Hoover, Mr. D.H. Ellis, Mr. E.F. Warren, and the correspondent of the *News and Courier* left the county seat to visit the plantations in the northern section of the county. Crossing a pine belt which extends for about five or six miles to the north one arrives by the Crockettville Road at a section of the county where live some of the largest planters. In passing it may be of interest to know that Crockettville has undergone a radical change within the past fifteen years. In fact, there is now no Crockettville to speak of.

It was formerly a crossroads village where was the muster ground and the camping ground for political canvassers and where people who were so inclined went to "fight it out" when sufficiently braced up with the kind of whiskey that was sold or given away at Crockettville. The village and its ante-bellum institutions have all been swept away and where there were four or five barrooms there are now two churches and a school-house.

About a mile and a half from this town of mere reminiscences, one of the most fertile and thickly settled districts of the county is reached. Among the prominent and wealthy barons of the county who are planting on a large scale there are Major W.J. Gooding, John A. Lightsey, W.H. Tuten, John Miley, Geo. W. Brunson, Jacob A. Lightsey, and Jacob L. Fulk. The above-named planters are situated on Whippy Swamp and plant each one hundred acres of cotton or more, and at least an equal number of acres of corn. Their cotton crops are now in the most flourishing condition, and although planted somewhat later in the season than those in the Lawtonville section, are well up and making rapid headway towards maturity. The farms and plantations in this locality are models of agricultural perfection, and there is a constant tendency towards yearly improvement and extension, which manifests itself at a glance.

On Caw-Caw Swamp will be found such intelligent and extensive farmers as Col. George H. Hoover, H.M. Sauls, Col. H.M. Ulmer, W.T. Ulmer, Rev. W.F. Hogarth, W.P. and E.H. Hogarth, and G.M. Bowers. These planters also cultivate a hundred or more acres of cotton each and have bestowed such an amount of attention on their farming interests that they will undoubtedly be rewarded with a most bountiful and profitable yield. On the Saltkehatchie there are farms upon farms innumerable, from among which are selected those of D.T. Moore, Nick Williams, Jake Gooding, Henry Miley, and James Miley, as being representative both as to their extent and the forward condition of their crops of cotton and corn.

All of the above mentioned farmers have been enabled through the employment of labor-saving machinery to plant more largely than their neighbors, but it is also a fact that there are hundreds of small farms around them on which there are some of the finest crops in the country as a result of harder labor, but equally intelligent and progressive work. It may be stated generally in reference to the condition of these crops that, if no unforeseen contingencies interfere, the harvest will be the most abundant within the last five years.

On Tuesday your correspondent, accompanied by Major W.H. Mauldin, made a visit to the Lawtonville section, which is par excellence the garden spot of the county. It is situated about fifteen miles west and southwest of the Courthouse, and is reached by a new and well-kept road from the Courthouse. Before arriving at this farmers' paradise, however, there is a splendid district known as Peeplesville where there are some plantations that vie with any in the county. Foremost among these is the plantation of Mr. H.H. Peeples, about twelve miles from Hampton on the Lawtonville Road. He has under the most perfect mode of cultivation one hundred and forty acres of cotton and in the neighborhood of a hundred acres of corn. There is not a stump to be seen in his cotton field, and the crop is perhaps just a little behind those of the wide-awake farmers around Lawtonville. He is this year experimenting with the "Jones's prolific" seed. Among his thrifty and well-to-do neighbors who are planting cotton on a large scale are Messrs. D.I. Peeples and Dr. Johnson. Leaving this section of the country and going southwest the road is through an avenue of fields of cotton bursting into bloom and waving fields of corn. About two and a half miles from Peeplesville is Lawtonville, under which

Huspah Primitive Baptist Church, Hampton County, c. 1890. *South Caroliniana Library.*

name is comprised a very large territory which extends as far as the Savannah River.

The farmers of this part of the county are operating on the extensive and expensive style, and have been famous agriculturalists from time immemorial. They are the earliest in the market, and lead in the matter of scientific cultivation of the cotton crop. They are blessed with a soil that is without an equal in any part of the State, and it is loaded with fertilizer enough to completely change the original character of the soil. Every one of the farmers, and there is a whole host of them, is supplied with labor-saving machinery, and a stump in a field is one of the rarest sights imaginable. Lawtonville is the home of the great cotton kings of the county, and of the large royal following who have made it famous as a planting district. The most extensive operators in cotton-growing, perhaps, are John Lawton, Wilcox & Gibbes, William Preacher, Capt. E.H. Peeples, and J.W. Peeples. Around Brighton, Stafford's, and Robertsville there are also some large planters, such as Dr. Southworth Smith, Walter Smith, Frank Mayne, J.C. Richardson, and Major William Lawton.

Around Lawtonville the planters pursue a course of heavy fertilizing to recuperate their lands, which they are thus enabled to plant from year to year, while in other parts of the county the policy of the alternate planting and resting of fields is carried out with much practical advantage, and chiefly in the respect of a reduction of the annual expense of fertilizing. It is not to be supposed, of course, that too much attention is being paid to cotton alone. The more substantial crops intended for home consumption, such as peas, corn, and oats, are planted on a sufficiently large scale to supply the wants of the whole county, and it is only in the rarest instances that such products are now imported into the county.

It is a significant fact that it is almost impossible to buy a single acre of land in the county which has received the benefits of cultivation and improvement. There are, however, thousands upon thousands of acres of virgin land in every direction throughout the county that are obtainable at very reasonable figures. In more than a half-dozen instances inquiry was made as to the original value of lands now under cultivation, and it was found that they were bought about eight or nine years ago at prices varying from three to five dollars an acre, and are now considered worth from thirty to fifty dollars an acre, but are not for sale. The great body of land which is now outlying as forest land, it may be stated, is in great proportion of the same quality and character as that on which a phenomenal or fancy valuation is now placed by the successful planters of the county.

Much attention is of late being turned to the raising of improved stock. Major Mauldin is experimenting on a small scale with the Devon and Jersey stock. Mr. H.H. Peeples has a fine herd of Devons and an excellent stock of Berkshire hogs, while Mr. J.C. Richardson, of Robertsville, owns quite a considerable number of Jerseys.

It will be seen, therefore, that all along the line Hampton is moving with great progressive strides, and is looming up as an important county in the State. In educational matters the people are now moving in a direction that will be both creditable and highly beneficial to the social interests of the county in the near future.

There is now on foot in the county a project for the establishment of a female graded school at Hampton Courthouse. Some time ago a meeting was held and the following trustees of the school were elected: Col. Geo. H. Hoover, chairman; Gen. J.W. Moore, John Lawton, W.J. Causey, M.B. McSweeney, E.F. Warren, and Major W.H. Mauldin, secretary. The proposed building is now in course of erection, and will have an accommodating capacity for about one hundred students. It will be exclusively for girls, and it is expected that it will be in operation about the first of September, by which time a competent corps of teachers will have been secured.

In this matter, as in every other, the county is endeavoring to keep abreast of the times, and there is scarcely a doubt that within the next five years Hampton will have assumed a foremost place on the roll of progressive counties in the way of internal and general social and industrial improvement.

News and Courier, July 17, 1885. M.F.T.

Johnston—Capital of the "Ridge"

Situated in eastern Edgefield County near the headwaters of the Edisto, Savannah, and Saluda rivers, Johnston was an ambitious little community filled with the same yearnings felt by much larger towns and cities of the late 1880s. Convinced that they lived in one of South Carolina's garden spots, Johnstonians dreamed of a big winter resort hotel, better rail connections, lower interest rates, and a bumper crop of cotton and fruit. Edgefield Court House admittedly was much older and larger, but they were certain that Johnston some day would rival towns such as Greenwood and Rock Hill.*

*   *   *

There are few places in South Carolina which possess greater natural advantages than Johnston, yet the assertion is ventured that there are few towns in the State concerning which there is less known. Without stopping to speculate on the reasons for this last statement, I will simply endeavor to give some description of Johnston and its chances for commercial development.

Johnston is situated in the eastern section of Edgefield County on the line of the Charlotte, Columbia, and Augusta Railroad. It is claimed to be the largest town and chief centre of business in the county, although Edgefield Court House exceeds it in point of population and in the number of its imposing buildings. Edgefield also has the advantage in age, being almost ready to celebrate its centennial, while Johnston is, comparatively speaking, still in its swaddling clothes. The town has advantages, however, in point of location, which, if backed up by local energy and push, promise some day to make it the rival of such thriving towns as Greenwood, Rock Hill, and others.

Situated in the very heart of one of the finest cotton-growing sections of the State, Johnston commands the trade and is the outlet for the cotton of the farmers living within a radius of many miles. Last season the shipment of cotton from here aggregated between 8,000 and 9,000 bales, and it is confidently expected that these figures will be exceeded this season, the shipments up to date amounting to over 500 bales. The price of the staple is also holding up well, one sale of the Allen fibre, an unusually fine grade of cotton, having been made last Saturday at twelve cents a pound.

A large part of this cotton is grown on what is known as the "Ridge," better

---

*However, the author of this sketch ("R. M. S."), presumably Robert M. Solomons, a former *News and Courier* staff member who had been studying with his brother—"one of the most skilful and successful dentists in the State"—preferred Charleston and soon was departing for that city.

cotton land than which is not to be found perhaps anywhere in the State. The "Ridge" comprises an elevated roll or border of land extending across the eastern section of the county, from Trenton on one end to Leesville on the other. Here centre the head-waters of all three rivers, and here is felt almost every rain that strikes the county. The land consists of sand on top with clay sub-soil and just sufficient roll to give good drainage without washing. It is the dividing line between an extensive clay country on the west and a large sand area on the east. It is said that no finer farming country can be found anywhere.

Col. J.H. Rice, the well-known State superintendent of education, is credited with having said on one occasion up here that the men who planted on the "Ridge" were very largely indebted to their fine lands for their success as farmers, and there seems to be a great deal of truth in the statement, for nowhere are the farmers more prosperous and well-to-do than in the country hereabouts. The grumblers are few and far between: as a rule they make good average crops every year, and the majority of them seem to be ahead of the world.

After what has been said concerning the "Ridge," it is almost needless to add that it is one of the garden spots of the State, and Johnston has the good fortune to be located in the midst of it. The town stands about 82 feet higher than Aiken and, by reason of its superior elevation, claims climatic advantages over that well-known winter resort for Northern tourists and invalids. Like Charleston, Johnston has her pet hotel scheme and is convinced that if someone would only erect a fine hostelry on the main street, wealthy Northerners could easily be induced to come here with their money bags.

That the town is healthy and a desirable place to live is proved by the fact that there is not an empty house in the place and that there are a number of families who would move in tomorrow if they could get houses to live in.

The population at present is said to be about 1,000, with indications of a steady increase, and that the town is steadily improving is shown by the number of new buildings constantly going up. The latest additions to the taxable property of the town are two brick stores just completed on Main Street, next to the corner of Mims Avenue. One was erected by Mr. J.M. Smiley for his own use, while the other was put up by Mr. D.T. Ouzts for Messrs. Crouch & Hazel, one of the youngest, but most enterprising and go-ahead firms in the place, by whom it has just been occupied.

The most imposing building in the town is the Bank of Johnston, a two-story structure, on the corner of Main Street and Mims Avenue, with a handsome front of native granite and red pressed brick. The first floor is used by the bank, while the second story is occupied by Dr. J.R. Solomons, the well-known dentist. The latter is a native of Charleston, but has been engaged here in the practice of his profession for the past three years, and it is no exaggeration to say that he is one of the most skilful and successful dentists in the State.

The bank is not yet a year old, having been opened for business on October 15, 1888, but is already one of the most prosperous institutions of the kind in the State. It has a capital of $30,000, on which it will show a dividend of about 10 per cent at the end of the first year. Its officers are: President, State Senator W.J. Ready; vice president, R.A. Turner; directors, W.G. Kernaghan, Benjamin Boatwright, T.R. Denny, J.H. Bouknight, and A.J. Salinas of Charleston; cashier, D.F. Ouzts; assistant cashier, W.S. Wills.

Another institution of which the Johnstonians are justly proud is the Johnston Male and Female Institute, the largest institution of learning in the county and one of the most admirably conducted town schools in the State. It is run on the free school system and has a corps of five teachers, of which Prof. Brown is principal. It opened on the 1st of September with about one hundred and twenty-five matriculates, which number it is expected will be increased to two hundred during the course of the school term.

In point of railroad facilities, Johnston is entirely dependent upon the Richmond and Danville system, the Charlotte, Columbia, and Augusta Railroad being its sole connection with the outside world, the Charleston, Cumberland Gap, and Chicago Railroad passing it at Trenton, seven miles distant, on its way from Aiken to Edgefield. Under such a condition of things the bulk of Johnston's business naturally goes to Augusta and Columbia, but the people here are well disposed towards Charleston and are eagerly looking forward to the time when they shall have direct communication with the City by the Sea. Their greatest hopes towards this end are centred in the Blackville, Newberry, and Alston Railroad, of which Mr. George A. Wagener of Charleston is president, and the Carolina, Knoxville, and Western Railroad, a projected line from Greenville to Knoxville, Tenn., by way of Ninety-Six.

The Blackville, Newberry, and Alston Railroad is now in operation as far as the kaolin mines of the company and is reaching out for some connecting point in this section, Johnston, Greenwood, and Batesburg being the places under consideration for this purpose. Should the first named place be selected, this road will be the means of giving Johnston direct connection with Charleston and of opening up one of the finest cotton-growing sections to the metropolis of the State.

The Carolina, Knoxville, and Western Railroad, which was originally chartered as the Atlantic, Greenville, and Knoxville Railroad, is already graded from Augusta to Greenville by way of Johnston and Ninety-Six. The greater part of this work was done about three years ago, since which time operations have been mostly suspended pending the result of various litigations.

There seems, however, to be a fair prospect that something will soon be done with the road. The hope is here that the Blackville, Newberry, and Alston Railroad will take it, as the kaolin mines which form the present terminus of their line are only twenty-seven miles in a direct line from Johnston.

The Three C's people are also said to be after the road. On the other hand, I was informed today by Capt. T.R. Denny, intendant of Johnston and a former director of the road, that a Boston syndicate now have their eyes on the road and will in all probability buy it if a favorable report is received from an engineer whom they now have employed examining the line of the route.

From what has been written it will be seen that Johnston has a bright future before it, provided the tide of its affairs is taken at the flood and pushed on to fortune. Her present prospects are certainly very promising. The farmers, for the most part, have been successful with their crops and seem happy and contented everywhere as they busily reap the fruits of their labors. I am told that the cotton crop in Edgefield County will be equal to that of last season and that the corn crop will be about double.

The early cotton crop is now coming in splendidly, but there does not seem to be much expected of the late crop, consisting mostly of cotton that was replanted in consequence of the April drought, unless there should be a late fall. The warm, dry weather of the past five weeks, while just the right thing for the early crop, was

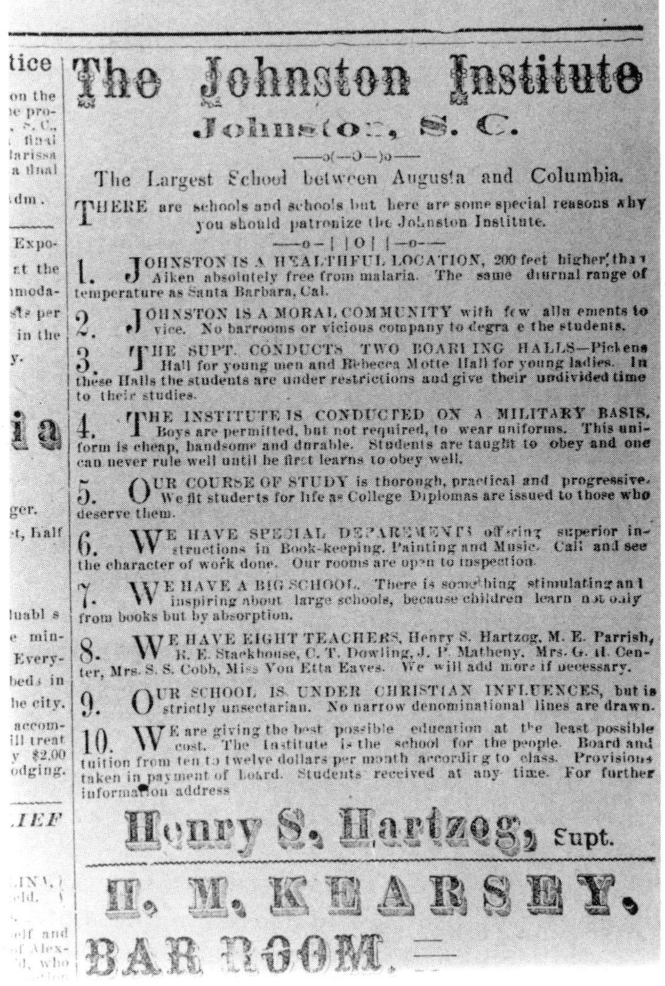

The Johnston Institute

Johnston, S. C.

The Largest School between Augusta and Columbia.

THERE are schools and schools but here are some special reasons why you should patronize the Johnston Institute.

1. JOHNSTON IS A HEALTHFUL LOCATION, 200 feet higher than Aiken absolutely free from malaria. The same diurnal range of temperature as Santa Barbara, Cal.

2. JOHNSTON IS A MORAL COMMUNITY with few allurements to vice. No barrooms or vicious company to degrade the students.

3. THE SUPT. CONDUCTS TWO BOARDING HALLS—Pickens Hall for young men and Rebecca Motte Hall for young ladies. In these Halls the students are under restrictions and give their undivided time to their studies.

4. THE INSTITUTE IS CONDUCTED ON A MILITARY BASIS. Boys are permitted, but not required, to wear uniforms. This uniform is cheap, handsome and durable. Students are taught to obey and one can never rule well until he first learns to obey well.

5. OUR COURSE OF STUDY is thorough, practical and progressive. We fit students for life as College Diplomas are issued to those who deserve them.

6. WE HAVE SPECIAL DEPAREMENTS offering superior instructions in Book-keeping, Painting and Music. Call and see the character of work done. Our rooms are open to inspection.

7. WE HAVE A BIG SCHOOL. There is something stimulating and inspiring about large schools, because children learn not only from books but by absorption.

8. WE HAVE EIGHT TEACHERS, Henry S. Hartzog, M. E. Parrish, R. E. Stackhouse, C. T. Dowling, J. P. Matheny, Mrs. G. H. Center, Mrs. S. S. Cobb, Miss Von Etta Eaves. We will add more if necessary.

9. OUR SCHOOL IS UNDER CHRISTIAN INFLUENCES, but is strictly unsectarian. No narrow denominational lines are drawn.

10. WE are giving the best possible education at the least possible cost. The Institute is the school for the people. Board and tuition from ten to twelve dollars per month according to class. Provisions taken in payment of board. Students received at any time. For further information address

Henry S. Hartzog, Supt.

H. M. KEARSEY.

BAR ROOM.

Advertisement in the *Edgefield Weekly Monitor,* October 24, 1895. *South Caroliniana Library.*

not good for the late cotton. The latter will be much benefited, however, by the rains of today. The corn crop is said to be phenomenal in point of size, and many of the farmers will have the grain to carry over next season.

Other advantages operating in favor of the farmers here this season are the ability to obtain money at a better rate of interest, owing to the improved banking facilities, the drop in the prices of provisions last spring, and the high figures now offering for cotton. On the whole it would seem that the farmers have every reason to be satisfied, and most of them expect to have "corn a plenty and cotton to spare," which is about all that any farmer could ask for.

The peach and melon crops about here this season have also been a great success. I was told the other day of a farmer in this neighborhood who made $3,000 on his peach crop, notwithstanding the fact that the fruit was a terrible drug on the market.

But this rather rambling account of Johnston would be incomplete without some tribute, however feeble it might be, to the young ladies of the place. As a young man prominent in society remarked the other day, "It's the dear girls that make a place," and perhaps there is more truth in the remark than some of us would care to admit. If such be the case, then Johnston's future is already assured, for she has more than a fair proportion of pretty girls. No less than three of them have become the wives of Charlestonians within the past two or three years, which goes to show that their charms are not altogether superficial.

Personal Notes

Editor McLenna of the *Edgefield Monitor* has been seriously ill here for some time, but is now on the road to recovery. During his sickness the paper has been under the sole management of his son, Alvin McLenna, who is undoubtedly one of the rising young journalists of the State.

Mr. Robert M. Solomons, of Charleston, a former member of the staff of the *News and Courier,* has been up here for some time studying dentistry with his brother, Dr. J.R. Solomons, but will leave for home next week.

One of the latest additions to the resident population of Johnston is Dr. J.W. Wyman, a popular and promising young physician, who moved here with his family from Graniteville some time ago.

Two Specimen Farmers

Capt. "Clint" Ward, the father and founder of Ward's Station, a prosperous little village about four miles from here, is probably one of the most successful grape cultivators in the State. The captain has grown this year about fifty different kinds of grapes, including such choice Northern varieties as the Oneida, Delaware, and Concord and the native scuppernong and muscadine, the last two in immense quantities. The captain is also a successful farmer and one of the most hospitable men in the country. In the last respect he has a worthy rival in Capt. Dan Purifoy, whose farm house at Havirdville, twenty-two miles from here, is known throughout the county for the free and hearty hospitality of its genial host. Capt. Purifoy has represented Edgefield in the Legislature for two terms and will in all probability be returned for a third term next year.

News and Courier, September 26, 1889. R.M.S.

Lovely Little Lancaster

Lancaster, we are told in this brief survey by "R.E.P.," was beginning to bestir itself in 1887. Its population had doubled during the 1880s, new financial institutions were appearing, and the familiar sounds of progress were heard throughout the community. And among its prominent citizens, "R.E.P." saw many who were "worthy followers" of Lancaster's most famous son, Andrew Jackson. For yet another quick look at Lancaster, see a column by Ambrose Gonzales that appeared in the *News and Courier* on August 28, 1888.

* * *

In the setting of towns that adorn the State of South Carolina Lancaster is not the least brilliant. After years of quiet repose, undisturbed by the whistle of the locomotive or the racket of the carpenter's hammer, at last she has aroused herself and is now in the front rank of the progressive Southern towns. First, the whistle of the baby engine on the Cheraw and Chester Narrow Gauge Railway, awakening the sleeping valley and silent hill tops, brought out all Lancaster to see this emblem of forward improvement. Ever since then the quiet little hamlet of eight hundred inhabitants has been pushing forward on every line of improvement. Today its inhabitants number fifteen hundred or two thousand, having more than doubled in less than ten years. On all sides signs of life may be seen. The carpenter's hammer, the whistle of the mill engine and the locomotive on a grand trunk line of railway, the Charleston, Cincinnati, and Chicago, the bustling drays and busses, and the busy merchants, these do not fail to tell their own tale.

Among recent manufacturing enterprises may be mentioned a spoke and handle factory with Mr. L.C. Payseur as president, a manufacturing and repair factory by J.M. Hood & Co., and flour and grist mill by J.A. Chisolm.

Another new enterprise is the Bank of Lancaster, Leroy Springs, president; D.A. Williams, vice president; and W.C. Thompson, cashier. The books of subscription to the People's Loan and Savings Bank are now open. In this enterprise Senator J.B. Erwin, Capt. H.B. Patrick, and W.D. Lemmond are active. The first of these expects to be ready for business by August the 15th, and it is hoped that the other will soon be opened.

A cotton mill is being discussed, and perhaps a cotton seed oil mill will come in due time.

The municipal government is in the hands of Lancaster's most wide-awake citizens: Mayor, L.C. Payseur; wardens, W.W. Perry, M.F. Jones, T.S. McManus, and J.F. Hunter. The postmaster recently appointed has taken charge of the office, which will continue to be managed by Capt. John W. Hamel.

Courthouse steps in Lancaster. *South Caroliniana Library.*

There are two weekly newspapers published here, the *Lancaster Review* and the *Lancaster Ledger.* The *Review* is owned by Riddle & Connors and edited by Major Charles T. Connors. The *Ledger* is owned and edited by D.J. & L.S. Carter. They are both model country newspapers. The *Ledger* has recently put in a large Campbell cylinder press. Major Connors, of the *Review,* is a popular Representative in the Legislature, in which he has done effective service for his county and made an enviable name for himself. A still higher sphere of usefulness is predicted for him by those who know him.

The Lancaster Guards, Capt. John W. Hamel, is a credit to the town.

The following firms transact a large volume of business: T.M. Fitzpatrick & Bro.; Heath, Springs & Co.; Wm. Ganson; W.D. Lemmond; L.C. Payseur; Cunningham Bros.; Cloud & Abison [Allison]; Racket Store, W.B. Knight, manager; J.E. Taylor; W.H. Crockett; Jones & Co.; G.F. Payseur; T.H. Davis; W.A. Davis, artist; T.S. McManus, millinery; Miss Jane Stevens, millinery; J.F. Mackey & Co., drugs; Crawford Bros., drugs; Long & West, bar; Clark & Wharlow, bar; S.C. Schaffer, bar; H.J. Gregory & Co., livery and sale; J.M. Hood, livery and sale; Hickson & Walker, livery and sale; F.A. Dual, repair shop; W.D. Drennan, repair shop; Richard Young, market; and J.M. Summey, barber.

The Catawba House, J.J. Perry, proprietor, and the Crockett House, Jones Crockett, proprietor, furnish ample accommodations for the travelling public.

At the Lancaster Bar may be found as bright talent as there is in the State. R.E. Allison, J.D. Wylie are the oldest. Then come sons of such worthy scions, R.B. Allison and R.E. Wylie. Others are Ernest Moore, M.J. Hough, Charles T. Connors, T.S. Carter, Ira B. Jones, B.J. Witherspoon, who is trial justice, and T.Y. Williams.

The physicians are: J.F. Mackey, Mart P. Crawford, W.M. Crawford, T.J. Strait, J.H. Witherspoon, and Robert P. Witherspoon.

The educational interests are in a prosperous condition. The Franklin Institute, President J.B. Baird, has closed a prosperous year. The building is being enlarged, and the friends of the school expect a material increase of patronage the coming session. Prof. Baird is doing excellent work.

The pride of Lancaster is her churches. There are four white and two colored. The Methodists have recently erected a handsome brick structure, and they are having, under the pastorship of the popular, eloquent Rev. P.F. King, a most prosperous year. Their Sunday-school is under M.F. Jones, superintendent.

The Baptists are growing under the effective labors of the devoted Rev. A.J. Stough. Mr. W.J. Long is superintendent of the Sunday-school.

The Presbyterians, the Rev. C.W. Humphries, pastor, are moving along with the others. R.T. Beaty, superintendent of Sunday-school.

The Associate Reformed Presbyterians have lost their pastor, the Rev. R.Z. Mills, by death, and have not yet secured another. Ira B. Jones has charge of the Sunday-school.

There is one colored Baptist Church and one A.M.E. Zion Church.

Lancaster is surrounded by fertile farms and rich mines. Her prosperity is solid and the heights not yet reached.

The town has produced the illustrious Dr. J. Marion Sims,* and the county claims the birthplace of "Old Hickory," the brave Andrew Jackson. In the persons of Lancaster's prominent citizens I see worthy followers of these great men.

*Sims (1813—1883), a pioneer gynecologist, won fame in both America and Europe for his research and operating techniques. Much honored, he lived in Paris in the 1860s and later returned during the Franco-Prussian War to organize an ambulance corps. A bronze statue to his memory was erected in New York City's Bryant Park, and his autobiography, *The Story of My Life* (edited by his son), was published in 1884.

News and Courier, July 18, 1889. R.E.P.

There Are No Croakers in Laurens

A tournament held in Greenwood on July 20, 1887, lured both Matthew Tighe and Narcisco Gonzales to that community, and according to an account the latter published on the 21st it was a lively affair indeed. Some four thousand spectators watched twenty-three knights (some of them in gorgeous costumes) gallop over a three-ring course, saw Miss Lou Breazeale crowned queen in ceremonies held on the hotel piazza, and then gorged themselves at heavily laden barbecue tables. At 4 P.M. the "Columbias" and the "Greenvilles" clashed in baseball, Greenville winning 7-6 in a game that nearly ended in a riot. Gonzales wrote that only this bit of "ruffianism" marred a near-perfect day, which ended with a grand ball at Durst's Hall (admission $1). As for Tighe, he was busy with a series of town portraits, visiting not only Greenwood but also Newberry and Laurens before returning to Charleston. Here are his observations concerning Laurens, a growing community situated, not on seven hills, but two.*

* * *

This town will, fortunately for many centuries to come, escape from the affliction of being described as the "loveliest village of the plain" for the reason chiefly that it was originally located on a hill through the wisdom of it founders. Strictly speaking, and to be geographically correct, Laurens covers two hills which are separated from each other by a valley through which flows the mazy Little River. The town "crowns the heights," and it would be difficult, indeed, to select another town in the State in the surroundings of which there is so much to admire.

The people of Laurens do not boast much of the importance or greatness of Little River. It bears a modest, unassuming name, but without it there would be a void that both for aesthetic and sanitary reasons could scarcely be satisfactorily filled. It runs through a forest-clad valley in a southeasterly direction, through the corporate limits, the section of the town lying to the east and west of the dividing stream.

The city proper is divided into three parts: Laurens proper, "Brooklyn," and "Jersey City." These latter divisions are so named with humorous reference to some famous suburbs of New York. Only five years ago there was nothing but the forest primeval where "Jersey City" now smiles on its neighbor across the valley. It is now all of an independent town in which $40,000 have been invested in residences, in which the merchant and farmer princes of Laurens have found cosy, attractive, and comfortable homes. "Brooklyn," too, is fast rising into ambitious prominence with

---

*Another descriptive column on Laurens appeared in the *News and Courier* on June 29, 1889.

its flourishing neighbor. Nine houses have already been erected, and if the promises of the present hold out there is little doubt that Laurens soon will find its rival towns within its borders.

Few towns in the State enjoy so many railroad facilities as Laurens. It has the benefit first, of the Greenville, Laurens, and Spartanburg Road, which enters the town about 400 yards from the public square; second, the Greenville and Laurens Road, which passes within a hundred yards of the square, and the Laurens and Newberry, which comes into the town about 200 yards from that square. The depots of these lines of railway are, therefore, at convenient distances from the business centre of Laurens, both for passenger and for freight traffic. The roads run through the most productive sections of the county and attract to Laurens, therefore, a very large proportion of the agricultural products.

The current history of Laurens is something to which its people may point with pardonable pride. The town has practically been built since 1882. At that time there were not many fine houses on the streets which now enclose the public square, which is now densely surrounded with the handsomest buildings. On this great business and social resort the larger proportion of the business is done. There are about forty stores in the town, and quite a number are credited with doing a $100,000 business. Not only, however, on the public square are the indications to be found of a big stride having been made since 1882. Main Street for the distance of about a mile is lined on either side with pretty dwelling houses, each house almost invariably adorned with a well-kept flower garden. In proportion to its length the town is very narrow, and on account of the hilly, sloping nature of the site of the town the place is, of course, well drained and needs but little expenditure in that respect by its town council.

That body is composed of Intendant Dr. B.E. Martin and Wardens D.M. Patton, J.R. Cooper, W.J. Hunter, and J.J. Pluss. It has been found that two policemen under normal conditions are sufficient for the police force of Laurens. One of these officers is paid $50 a month and the other $40 a month. On sales days or on any occasion when disturbances may be expected to arise the force is usually increased. In the winter season there is employed a night watchman.

The fire department is about as well equipped and trained as that of perhaps any country town in the State. The "steamer" is in charge of a company that was organized in April last with Mr. J.F. Johnston as president and Prof. Frank Evans as captain. The engine cost $3,000 and had the first trial about two weeks ago when, by a quick response of the volunteers, $50,000 worth of property was saved. The fire was under control in twenty minutes after the alarm was given. Besides the steamer there is a hook and ladder company, which is composed of colored firemen, and they are highly spoken of by the white citizens of the town for their active and energetic service. The two companies mentioned are under the control of the fire department, of which Mr. J.J. Pluss is the chief and Mr. R.H. Hudgens assistant chief.

The revenue of the town is largely drawn from the licenses from the sale of whiskey. There are in the corporate limits five barrooms, which pay each a license of $800 annually. This gives the town a fund of about $4,000, which is increased by an income tax, licenses to carry on the professions, taxes on realty and personalty, and a commission tax to a total revenue of about $7,000. This money is spent largely, and in the right direction, on the streets, which are being now macadamized as far as the finances will permit. As much work in this line could not be done this year as was desired on account of the outlay for the new fire engine, which had become an absolute necessity, but the general appearance of the roads and streets is a credit to the town council.

Among the noteworthy institutions of Laurens are the Female College and the Male Academy. The former is now under the presidency of Prof. T.M. McCaslan, who will, at the opening of the next collegiate term, have five assistants. He is spoken of, not only in Laurens, but every place where he is known, as a man of equal executive and scholarly attainments. The general opinion in the town is that the future of the college will be even more bright and prosperous than heretofore.

The Male Academy is in charge of Prof. Frank Evans, to whose popularity the success of the institution is largely due. He has one assistant. There is also a free common school in "Jersey City" and one in "Brooklyn." The Laurens Seminary has been discontinued since April last.

The churches of Laurens are the Methodist, in charge of the Rev. J.M. Carlisle; the Baptist, in charge of the Rev. John D. Pitts; the Presbyterian, in charge of the Rev. E.O. Frierson; and the Episcopal Church, which has no local pastor. There are two colored churches in town, one of the Presbyterian and the other of the Methodist faith.

So far as the financial institutions for doing business are concerned, Laurens is in splendid position. The merchants have the benefit of both the National Bank of Laurens and the People's Loan and Exchange Bank. The former has been in operation since July 1886. The president of the bank is Dr. J.A. Barksdale. A dividend of four per cent was declared in the early part of the present month. The capital stock of the concern is $63,000, which it is understood will soon be increased to $100,000.

The People's Loan and Exchange Bank was organized on the 4th of the present July and has not yet made a history for itself. The president of the bank is Capt. Albert Dial.

The Building and Loan Association began operation in January 1886 and is now considered to be on a sound financial basis. Of this institution Dr. J.A. Barksdale is also president. A very considerable proportion of the houses put up since January 1886 is entirely due to the existence of this association, and the young men of the town are availing themselves very generally of its easy terms.

One of the most important industries of the place is the brick manufactory, which carries only a capital stock of $5,000 but uses the most improved machinery for the manufacture of the brick. It is expected that this industry will be called upon at no very distant day to furnish the material for the long talked-of and much-desired "Laurens Cotton Factory." The scheme is to have erected by September 1888

Cotton mill, Laurens, c. 1890. *South Caroliniana Library.*

a first-class factory at an estimated cost of about $200,000. Of this amount $63,000 has already been put up, and the likelihood is that the factory will assume definite shape within the time limited for its construction. When the factory is built at least one-half of the cotton that goes by the Richmond and Danville to West Point and by the Georgia Central to Augusta and Savannah will remain at home. The average shipment from Laurens is about 11,000 to 12,000 bales [per year].

Real estate within the corporate limits is held at a very stiff figure, as is always the case with rapidly progressing towns. There is nothing prohibitory, however, in the prices asked, the average being $300 an acre, although not very long ago a half acre fronting on the public square was sold for $6,000.

It will be seen from even this short review of the advantages of the town of Laurens that it is entitled to a prominent place among the towns of the hill country of South Carolina. There is nothing wanting there in the way of facilities, either for the transaction of business or the education of its people.

There are no croakers in Laurens. Whenever the inevitable comes the business community accept it with philosophic grace and begin the new year as confidently as ever. Judging from the magnificent progress made by Laurens within even the last two years and looking at what the people there now propose to do, one scarcely need be told that the town is determined and destined to achieve a satisfactory industrial and commercial name for itself in the very near future.

News and Courier, July 27, 1887. M.F.T.

The Making of Manning

In January of 1890, Clarendon's county seat was—thanks to railroads, lumber, and diversified farming—a sturdy little community. It had a Collegiate Institute, several fine stores, a bank, a building and loan association (with headquarters in Alabama), a unique dime savings scheme, two newspapers, two hotels, six physicians, and seven lawyers, one of them a black man. Good land could be purchased in the immediate vicinity for $4 to $8 an acre, and since liquor revenues paid all municipal expenses, Manning levied no taxes.

* * *

On every hand I see possibilities which might have been realities years ago but for lack of opportunity. Remembering what the condition of the whole State was only a decade ago, it does not take a prophet to see what the future of this section will be. Of all who are seeking a home in the "Palmetto State," the people of this place ask an investigation of the town's claims. A fine climate, fine water, schools and churches, a refined and hospitable society, and cheap living are among the town's inducements.

To those who are seeking good lands susceptible of the highest improvement this county offers a practically unlimited field. There is not, probably, elsewhere in the State a section of country whose land of the same grade is as cheap as that in this county. The soil is light but deep and will grow as great a variety of crops as that in any section of the South. The healthiness of this section is attributable to the porosity of the soil and the large forests of pine which cover a large portion of the county. There is not a crop of the South which cannot be grown here—from the wheat of the hill country to the cotton of the middle country and the rice and sugar cane of the seashore. A great inducement to agriculture is, first, the price of the land; second, the lightness of the soil; and third, the cheapness of the labor. It is an inexplicable fact, the like of which, however, has been observed elsewhere time and again, that although fruits and vegetables flourish here with little or no cultivation, only a small portion of the people pay attention to them.

The county is crossed by Black River, and Pocotaligo River, one of its branches, passes close to the town. On the south and west the county is bounded by the Santee, the great river of this section of the State. There are other streams too small to be named on most of the maps, but in whose valleys flourish forests of gigantic hard-wood trees. These forests are a resource of vast wealth. There are more saw mills in this county than in any other county in the State, and their number is constantly increasing; but the demand for yellow pine lumber is so great that when all the pine forests are cut the prices will be even higher than they are today.

It is a common belief that when a forest is cut it is destroyed. On the contrary, there are many trees in every forest which the lumber man cannot use, because of their small size or defect. One of the large mill men here is cutting timber now from forests which were cut by his father twenty-five years ago. These forests also produce large quantities of turpentine and rosin.

It is in the hard-wood forests—the great river swamps—that development is backward. However, a large business is being done in cypress shingles, which find a ready market both North and South. These great swamps will soon be developed. New York and Chicago capitalists have already invested many thousands of dollars in them and are still purchasing. They can be bought now for "almost a song," but are steadily advancing in price. Every railroad that is built enhances their value.

But this is all about the county—Clarendon County by the way. Let us have a look at the county seat, the nucleus around which the wealth of the county as it is developed will gather. Manning stands on a bluff near [the] Pocotaligo River. It is about seventy-five miles from Charleston and is reached by the Central Railroad. It is beautifully laid out, and the streets are broad and shaded. The population is about 1,500.

Some people judge a town by its size, for what reason it would be interesting to know. Why a town of 2,500 people should possess more possibilities than one of 1,000 people is a question upon which no one has given any information. The history of the development of the State since the war will show that, as a rule, the smaller towns have done more than the larger ones. It is the resources which surround a town—not the number of people in it—which is the source of its progress. But while on the subject of population it may be well to note the things which retarded both the growth of the town and the development of the county. There was no railroad here until about six years ago. The great forests were almost as valueless as treasures at the bottom of the sea, and cotton, the principal crop of the county, had to be carted many miles to market. Isolated thus, how could the town be developed? The wonder is not that it did not develop, but that it did not stagnate completely.

In 1855 the county of Clarendon was formed out of a portion of Sumter district. The town was in its infancy when the war came, but was large enough to attract the attention of Gen. [Edward E.] Potter while on his well-remembered raid. The result was the burning of the Court House, jail, academy, and private buildings. When the war ended there was no business being done here. The first man who began business was Mr. Moses Levi, the present merchant prince of the town. Mr. Levi's beginning, to put it mildly, was very modest, and the fact that he accumulated a fortune and built up one of the largest businesses in this section of the State speaks well for the possibilities of the place. Steadily growing and developing in the face of great obstacles and drawbacks, the town has come to what it is. Let us look at its people and its institutions.

The people of Manning have utilized these opportunities, as anyone who knew the place before the railroad was built will testify. They are as kindly as they are progressive, and live in such harmony that Manning might appropriately be called "a town of brotherly love." The Methodists, Baptists, and Presbyterians have churches, and there is a fine school for children of both sexes.

The Collegiate Institute was opened last Christmas with a fine corps of teachers: Prof. William Simons, principal, and Mr. J.M. Knight and Miss Sadie Householder, assistants. The Institute is a very pretty building, admirably located, and has a large attendance, between seventy-five and a hundred. There are besides several private schools.

While there are not a large number of business houses, there is more diversity of trade than one would expect in so small a place.

Mr. Moses Levi's store is one of the largest in the State, and his business is in proportion. Mr. Levi deals in general merchandise, cotton, fertilizers, and furniture. His main store is a two-story building, 160 feet long by 85 feet wide. His furniture store is a two-story building, 100 feet long and 35 feet wide. The other business houses are as follows: General Merchandise—S.A. Rigby, Louis Lyons, B.A. Walker, A. Weinberg, H.A. Lowry, M. Kalisky, C. Karesh, and M. Karesh; Drugs, Paints, and Oils—J.G. Dinkins & Co. and W.E. Brown & Co.; Tobacco, Liquors, etc.—S. Walkoviskie and Henry Weinberg; Millinery—Mrs. Mary O. Burgess; Bakery—Mrs. O.E. Edwards.

As already noticed, there are a great many saw mills in the county, and, of course, they add a great deal to the trade of the town. There is a large saw mill in town, however, and a small grist mill. The saw mill is owned by Messrs. C.R. & W.S. Harvin. About $20,000 is invested in the business, and the annual output amounts to about $40,000.

Messrs. Legg & Bell have extensive stables and do a large sale and livery business. Mr. D.M. Bradham has recently opened a sale stable, which has proven a success.

That the trade of the town is flourishing may be seen from the condition of the Bank of Manning. This institution commenced business on September 8, last year, with $6,000, the first instalment of its capital stock. The authorized capital is $40,000 and the subscribed capital $30,000, which was paid in four instalments. This bank makes a specialty of collecting, and its rates of exchange are as low as those of any other bank in the State. The officers are: A. Levi, president; J.P. Brock, vice president; Joseph Sprott, Jr., cashier; directors, A. Levi, S.A. Rigby, J.C. Simonds, S.M. Nixson, M. Levi, J.P. Brock, and O.F. Wieters, of Charleston.

The Southern Building and Loan Association of Huntsville, Alabama, organized a branch here last November with 350 shares taken.

The Dime Savings Association was organized on the first of last month, and the subscription books will be open until February 1. The plan of this association is unique. Every shareholder pays ten cents a day for one thousand days, when the business is settled, and the profits are divided up. The officers are: W.E. Brown, president; J.M. Knight, vice president; L.I. Bagnall, secretary-treasurer; directors, W.E. Brown, S.A. Nettles, Joseph Sprott, Jr., J.T. Stubbs, and J.M. Knight.

The Young Men's Building and Loan Association has just been organized and will begin business February 1. The prospects are bright.

There are two progressive papers here under the management of young men who are able and energetic, and who are thoroughly identified with the welfare of the community. The *Times* was founded in 1884. It is now owned by Mr. S.A. Nettles, who has improved it in every department. The *Enterprise* was established twenty-two years ago. After many changes it came under the control of Messrs. Lesesne & Lowery, who have made it a power for much good.

Advertisement in the *Manning Times,* May 15, 1889.
South Caroliniana Library.

The lawyers of the town, several of whom have wide reputations, are: B. Pressely Barrow, J.F. Rhame, John S. Wilson, A. Levi, M.C. Galluchat, J.E. Scott, and R.A. Stuart, colored.

There are two hotels which afford the traveller every comfort. The Central, under the hospitable Capt. K. Bell, is the principal house. It is conveniently located and has connected with it a fine system of livery. To parties coming South for the winter Manning offers many attractions, for the shooting throughout the county is as fine as there is in the State. The Benbow House, Mr. P.G. Benbow, is the other house and is also conveniently located.

The municipal officers are: W.K. Bell, intendant; and [wardens] W. Scott Harvin, P.B. Thomas, D.M. Bradham, and Theodore Harvin, colored. This council has shown itself alive to the best interest of the place. No municipal tax is levied as the liquor revenue pays all expenses.

The Manning Rifles, organized in 1887, Capt. A. Levi, commander, is a soldierly body of forty members.

The Masons and Knights of Pythias have lodges here, which are flourishing.

A canning factory and opera house have been proposed, and it is probable that they will be erected at an early day. As one can readily see, there is no reason why factories which will utilize any of the raw materials in which the county abounds would not succeed. To those who think of purchasing land in the State for agricultural purposes, it may be well to state that such men as Capt. Peterkin and Mr. Stackhouse of the Farmers' Alliance have said there is no better anywhere than in this county. Good land can be purchased at from four to eight dollars [per acre].

In conclusion, I would bespeak for this place a reasonable and impartial investigation. Do not judge it by what it has not done, for the causes which have retarded its growth have been given. To any sensible person who thinks for himself, it is evident that much may be accomplished here with a small investment. The lumberman, the agriculturalist, and manufacturer will each find a good field here and a warm welcome.

News and Courier, January 29, 1890. J.I.G.

Marion: The City of Elms

Ambrose Gonzales found Marion, county seat of what was once known as Craven County, to be a very pleasant place in April of 1889. It had fine schools and churches, streets lighted by gasoline lamps, extensive fairgrounds, two newspapers, and a very impressive forge and machine shop. Gonzales conceded that the Marion of old had not been known for its business enterprise, but conditions seemed to be changing. In addition to explaining how this had come about, he also provides a rather amusing tale of how Marion got its beautiful elms.*

* * *

Very appropriately has this little municipality been styled the City of Elms, for to these lovely trees which shade her wide level streets Marion owes much of her attractiveness. The town is a very pretty one, with many handsome residences and extensive flower gardens. The environing country is level, with some fine yellow pine timber, and along the swamps quantities of valuable cypress, juniper, and other woods are found. The arable lands are very fertile, those lying along both the Great and the Little Pee Dee rivers equaling any perhaps in the world. One hundred bushels of corn per acre is no uncommon yield on these river bottoms, and the uplands, which are in the great cotton belt extending through Marlboro and Darlington, yield very heavy crops. Mr. E.H. Gasque, a prominent merchant of this place, who is also an intensive farmer, picked last year ten bales of cotton from a four acre plot, and it was not a good year for cotton either.

Marion was originally Craven County, formed from a portion of old Liberty County. The name was subsequently changed in honor of Gen. Francis Marion, whose fastnesses during the Revolutionary War were in the Pee Dee swamps. On "Snow's Island," in the Great Pee Dee River, immense saw mills are now running on the very spot where Gen. Marion improvised his famous sweet potato banquet, and the stump of the giant cypress log upon which he sat was still standing a year or two ago.

Tarleton and Marion met in a serious conflict at Bowling Green, four miles from Marion Court House, and at the "Blue Savannah," on the Little Pee Dee, a severe battle was fought between the same commanders. Here only a few years ago quantities of human bones and other relics of the conflict were found.

The lumber interest on both the Pee Dee rivers is a very extensive one. The cypress timber is magnificent, and there are some tracts of immense juniper trees yielding a highly prized lumber. Most of the timber is floated to mills on the

---

*See also John I. Green's sketch of Marion which appeared in the *News and Courier,* January 15, 1890.

Waccamaw and at Georgetown, but some of it is sawed on the spot and rafted to Georgetown for export. The obstructions in the Little Pee Dee River interfere seriously with this traffic, and it is to be hoped that they will be removed in the near future.

In 1800 the first Court House was built here. The edifice, a small wooden structure, is still standing, although long since superseded by the capacious brick building now in use.

In 1817 the Marion Academy Society was formed and an academy was established here, employing eminent instructors and giving a great impetus to education throughout this section. The full classical course was taught, with English and mathematics, and young men came from a distance and families having boys to educate moved here to avail themselves of the educational advantages afforded. The influence of this society has extended to succeeding generations, and Marion has given many sons to the State who have distinguished themselves on her battlefields and in her councils.

The population of Marion is 1,500. The intendant is Mr. C.E. Evans, and the wardens are W.A. Witcover, Dr. J.C. McMillan, E.W. McKay, and T.E. Taylor (colored). The marshal is Mr. G.W. Wall.

The streets are kept in excellent order, the sidewalks are good, and the town is splendidly drained. All of the streets are well lighted with gasoline lamps.

The town went "dry" in 1883, and by a legislative enactment will be dry for twenty years. Time was when it was otherwise, and there is a story that many years ago three young planters upon one occasion made a night of it in the quiet little town and were next morning fined $300 for their fun. The money was applied to planting elm trees on Main Street, and the cold water drinkers of Marion profit today by the folly of the last generation.

The Marion graded school is unquestionably one of the finest in the State. Two years ago a handsome brick building was erected on a spacious and conveniently located lot, at a cost of $8,000. Prof. Julius E. Leigh, of Virginia, a teacher of fine attainments, was chosen principal. His assistants are Miss Grace Griffith, of Greenville, Miss Helen Young, of Abbeville, Mrs. Johnson, of Charleston, and Mrs. A.W. Tenhet, of Marion, a splendid corps of teachers, and the two hundred pupils who are in daily attendance are fortunate indeed. The colored schools are excellent and are controlled by the same board of trustees which is composed of the following gentlemen: C.A. Wood, chairman; G.A. Norwood, J.W. Johnson, Dr. D.S. Price, and J.P. Davis, secretary and treasurer.

Four religious denominations are represented in Marion. Some of the churches are large and handsome edifices. The Methodist Church and congregation is the largest here. The pastor is the Rev. W.A. Rogers. The pastor of the Baptist Church is the Rev. T.D.D. Clark; the Presbyterian pastor is the Rev. J.E. Dunlop; and the Episcopalians are cared for by the Rev. W.A. Guerry.

The Bank of Marion, organized under a State charter in January, 1884, has been highly successful. It commenced at once to pay 8 per cent dividends and has besides

Clinton Masonic Lodge Building, Marion. The basement of this structure, erected in 1810, was used as a classroom until a graded school was built in 1887. *Photograph by Carl Julien, reproduced by permission of the University of South Carolina Press from* Pee Dee Panorama. *South Caroliniana Library.*

accumulated a handsome surplus. The officers are: G.A. Norwood, president; D. Murchison, vice president; and W.H. Cross, cashier. The directors are: G.A. Norwood, D. Murchison, J.M. Johnson, J.W. Holliday, C.A. Woods, and H.C. Graham. The last quarterly statement showed deposits of $69,072.56 and $13,633.92 in cash on hand.

The Marion Fair Company owns extensive and handsome grounds on the outskirts of the town. It has constructed a beautifully level and well drained half mile track, and has erected a commodious grand stand and all necessary stables and outbuildings. The Association pays a 7 per cent dividend and has a considerable surplus in the treasury. The location of a good race track here has stimulated the rearing and handling of trotting horses in this neighborhood, and there are more three-minute horses here, it is claimed, that in any other town in the State except Charleston. It is certain that there are twelve or fifteen well-bred and speedy trotters and roadsters owned and kept in Marion.

The directors of the Fair Company are: W.A. Brown, president; Dr. F.M. Monroe, W.J. Montgomery, B.R. Mullins, H.C. Graham, L.B. Rogers, J.G. Haseiden, W.H. Ellerbee, J.S. Scott, J.D. Montgomery, and R.J. Blackwell, who is also secretary and treasurer.

Marion is at last going to have a cotton mill, which, while making a modest beginning, it is hoped will prove profitable enough to warrant the speedy enlargement of its plant. The company has just been organized with $25,000 capital for the manufacture of cotton yarn. The lot has been selected and work on the building will commence at once. The directors are: W.M. Monroe, president; W.J. Montgomery, J.E. Ellerbee, C.A. Willcox, B.F. Elliot, C.A. Woods, and H.C. Graham.

A cotton seed oil mill too will be built in time for the next cotton season. A company has been formed with $20,000 capital, and work will begin at once. The directors are: G.A. Norwood, president; J.D. Montgomery, secretary and treasurer; H.C. Graham, B.R. Mullins, C.A. Woods, B.G. Smith, and J.W. Holliday.

There is also an excellent prospect of building a factory for the manufacture of pine straw bagging, but nothing definite has been arranged.

Marion has two newspapers. The *Star* was established in 1846, is printed at home, and under the management of Messrs. W.J. McKerrall & J.H. Evans, has built up a fine circulation in this and contiguous counties, and deserves and receives liberal advertising patronage.

The *Pee Dee Index* was started in 1882. It is owned and edited by Messrs. Macfarlan & Hamer. Like the *Star,* it is printed at home and is well supported. An excellent job office is connected with the paper.

The Planters' Hotel is conveniently located near the railroad depot and contains thirty rooms. The proprietors, Messrs. J.W. Holliday & Son, are courteous and attentive, and they have all the travelling patronage. The Marion Hotel is run as a boarding house by Mrs. Martha Smith.

Through the agency of the Building and Loan Association, organized here last September, several new dwellings are being constructed and the association is doing remarkably well. There are five hundred shares, and the president is Mr. W.J. Montgomery, with Mr. W.H. Cross, secretary and treasurer.

The Marion Machine Shops will repay a visit. Mr. Emerson McDuffie, a young man of this county, came here a year or two ago and established a small forge and machine shop. His ability and energy compelled success, and he has now a very complete establishment, fitted with new and improved iron working machinery. Twelve hands are employed and the shops turn out everything that may be called for, from a plough bolt to a 50-horse engine or a steel boiler. Mr. McDuffie is a mechanical genius and models many of his castings from designs of his own. The works are being enlarged by the addition of wood-working shops, etc., and altogether the establishment is a credit to the town.

The cotton receipts of Marion are 10,000 bales per annum, and 2,500 tons of guano are distributed from here.

The following is the business directory: R.J. Blackwell & Co., dealers in general merchandise; W.H. Bethea, general merchandise; A. Witcover, general merchandise; B.R. Mullins, general merchandise; F.H. Gasque, general merchandise; H.C. Graham, general merchandise; B. Hartz, general merchandise; W.M. Monroe, general merchandise; J.W. Holliday & Son, livery and sale stables; C.A. Willcox, general merchandise; J.E. Middleton, general merchandise; W.S. Taxworth, general merchandise; C.A. Willcox & Co., furniture; J. Stackhouse, livery and sale stables; B.F. Elliott, livery stables; W.R. Rogers, general merchandise; Mrs. C. Witcover, Sr., general merchandise; Mrs. S. Iseman, general merchandise; J. Brown & Bro., general merchandise; P.S. Wall & Bro., general merchandise; W.C. McMillan, furniture; E.H. Gasque, millinery; Mrs. A.J. Godbold, millinery; Mrs. Florence McEachern, millinery; Dr. D.S. Price, pharmacist; W.C. McMillan, druggist; H.J. Gasque, druggist; Dr. E.L. Brown, pharmacist; J.H. Davis & Son, jewellers; W.K. Hamilton, photographer; O.D. Crawford, fruiterer; S.L. McQueen, fruiterer; W.B. Tillman, fruiterer; S.C. Whiteheart, groceries, billiard and pool room; J.M. Williams, barber shops; T.E. Taylor, barber; W.W. McEachern and J.A. Williams, blacksmiths and wagon builders. The cotton buyers are R.J. Blackwell and W.L. Gregg.

Mr. A. Campbell is the agent of the Coast Line Railway and Southern Express Company here and is also manager of the Western Telegraph Company.

The postmaster is Mrs. M. Sue Sellers, a very efficient public official.

The lawyers are: Chancellor W.D. Johnson, and Messrs. C.O. Woods, J.M. Johnson (solicitor), C.D. Evans, J.W. Johnson, J.H. Evans, F.D. Bryant, W.W. Sellers, P.B. Sellers, P.B. Hamer, R. Macfarlan, and W.J. Montgomery.

The physicians are: D.S. Price, J.C. Mullins, A. McIntyre, R.L. Brown, and S.C. McMillan.

The county officers are: W.A. Wall, sheriff; John Willcox, Jr., clerk of court; J.D.

McLucas, probate judge and master; J.P. Davis, treasurer; J.B. White, school commissioner; P.Y. Bethea, auditor; and J.C. Finkles, A.B. Oliver, and Gilbert Carmichael, county commissioners.

Marion has been noted heretofore rather more for her health, her society, and her educational institutions than for her business enterprises. Her resources having been purely agricultural and the last three or four crop seasons having been unfavorable, it is natural that she should not have made the material progress that her citizens hoped for. Now the conditions are changed, however. Marion holds high trumps in her newly inaugurated manufacturing enterprises; and, backed up by her strong agricultural suit, she will take, let us hope, many tricks in the great game of industrial life.

News and Courier, April 29, 1889. A.E.G.

Newberry, the City That Has Everything

While other communities struggled to get water power, factories, railroads, and schools, Newberry, in the opinion of Ambrose E. Gonzales, had "everything." In 1889 it could boast of several hotels, a stunning Opera House, a fine municipal market, a flourishing cotton mill, and a thriving college. It also had an extensive retail and wholesale trade, at least seven saloons, and a modern dairy farm that Gonzales describes in great detail. (For yet another view of Newberry, see an account by Matthew F. Tighe published in the *News and Courier*, July 29, 1887.)

* * *

Beautifully situated on a cluster of hills overlooking a fertile, well-watered, agricultural region, this thriving midland city has everything to commend it as a most suitable place for residence, for business, and for investment. The rich country surrounding the city has long been famed for the heavy crops of cotton it produced, and the bottoms lying along the many creeks and smaller streams that flow through the country yield, freshets permitting, magnificent corn crops. Many of the finest grasses, notably Lucerne and Bermuda grass, grow here to perfection, and the rearing of live stock is an important industry in this section. Some fine trotting and thoroughbred colts and horses are to be seen on the streets of Newberry, and the dairy interest is quite an extensive one.

Newberry is handsomely laid out, and the streets, many of them macadamized and all of them provided with excellent sidewalks, are shaded by mulberry, elm, and other trees. Most of the business houses are clustered around the public square, and the solid blocks of buildings present quite a metropolitan appearance.

The cotton receipts of Newberry are heavy, aggregating 20,000 bales. The cotton mill consumes 5,500 bales annually, and the remainder is shipped to Charleston, Liverpool, and other points. There are several buyers here during the fall and winter months, and liberal prices are paid the farmers for the staple.

The population of Newberry numbers upwards of 4,000 and is rapidly increasing. The mayor is Mr. George B. Cromer. The aldermen are Messrs. E.C. Jones, M.D., Edward Scholtz, George McWhirter, and B.H. Cline. The clerk of the board is Mr. John S. Fair, and the chief of police is Capt. J.H. Chappell. The head of the fire department is J.E. Brown, with S.B. McCaughrin and S.B. Jones assistant chiefs. They are provided with a first-class La France steamer manned by the young white men of Newberry, who take a great interest in their work and are prompt and efficient. The steamer company is supplemented by a colored hand engine and a colored hook and ladder company, the whole combining to make the department one of the best equipped and most efficient in the State.

Newberry is well provided with churches. The Episcopalians have a pretty little brick edifice in charge of the Rev. W.H. Hanckel. The Baptist Church is a wooden building and the pastor is the Rev. C.P. Scott. The Lutheran congregation is a large one. Their pastor is the Rev. W.C. Schaeffer. The pastor of the Methodist Church is the Rev. W.S. Wightman, and the pastor of the Presbyterian Church is the Rev. J.S. Cosby. The Associate Reformed Presbyterians have also a church and the Rev. E.P. McClintock is their pastor. There are three colored churches in Newberry—Baptist, Methodist, and Presbyterian.

Newberry is also amply provided with educational facilities. First of all is, of course, the Newberry College, a Lutheran institution of thirty years' standing. The present handsome College building was erected ten years ago and is located in the centre of an extensive campus, on a hill in the northern part of town and commanding a fine view of the place and surrounding country. The building cost $20,000 and is admirably arranged with spacious lecture and class rooms. The College is in a prosperous condition and there are now one hundred and twenty pupils in attendance. The faculty includes the Rev. G.W. Holland, president and professor of mental and moral science and English literature; Mr. O.B. Mayer, professor of physiology and hygiene; the Rev. A.G. Voigt, professor of modern languages and literature; the Rev. Junius B. Fox, professor of mathematics and natural science; and Mr. Thos. H. Dreher, professor and principal of the primary department. A school of technology has recently been added and is in charge of Prof. Schott.

Then there is the Newberry Male Academy, John P. Glasgow, principal, with excellent instructors and a large attendance. The Female Academy is ably presided over by Miss O.E. Garlington. This institution is liberally patronized, and the course of instruction is all that could be desired. There is also an excellent private school (primary) taught by Miss McIntosh. The colored schools are ample and some of them, notably the Hoge Institute, are largely attended.

Newberry's especial pride is the Opera House, built by the town in 1881 at a cost of $30,000. The structure is of brick, surmounted by a tall and graceful clock tower. It is an ornament to the public square. The interior of the Opera House is handsomely decorated. The stage is ample, the scenery good, and the chairs and fittings are modern and comfortable. Another municipal feature is the market, which is built of brick, and is unquestionably the most extensive and best arranged in the up-country.

The Newberry Building and Loan Association, incorporated three years ago, has been highly successful. The president is Dr. James McIntosh; the vice president, John O. Peoples; and the secretary and treasurer, J.W.M. Simmons.

The Newberry Hotel, a handsome and commodious brick building situated on the public square, is admirably kept by Mr. P.N. Crouch and affords ample accommodation for the travelling public. There are several minor hotels and boarding houses. The Crotwell is kept by Mrs. Emma F. Blease, and boarding houses are conducted by Mrs. Fant, A.J. Sproles, H.H. Blease, and B. H. Lovelace.

Mill village for workers at Newberry Cotton Mills, c. 1890. *South Caroliniana Library.*

The National Bank of Newberry, one of the most prosperous in the State, has a capital of $150,000. The deposits are very heavy, and the business of the bank extends not only over all of Newberry County but also to portions of Edgefield, Fairfield, and other contiguous counties. The officers of this thriving institution are: R.L. McCaughrin, president; R.S. Duncan, cashier; T.J. McCrary, assistant cashier; J.W.M. Simmons, bookkeeper; and John F. Carwile, clerk.

For three or four years past the traveller, as he wound slowly around the erratic curves of the Columbia and Greenville Railroad, may have observed when nearing this favored spot a dark cloud hanging over the fair little town. Paradoxical as it might seem, that cloud was in reality a sign of industrial promise. To use a Westernism, he was only "watching McCaughrin's smoke" as it poured from the tall chimney of the Newberry Cotton Mills. The factory is an imposing structure, four stories high, located near the depot, and built of the tough salmon-colored brick for which Newberry is famous. The offices are handsome and luxuriously fitted up, and the mills are splendidly equipped and supplied with modern machinery and every appliance conducive to the safety and comfort of the employees. The safeguards against fire are especially complete. Great water tanks are kept constantly filled, and by a system of pipes and sprays every room in the mill can be deluged at a moment's notice.

The president of the mills is R.L. McCaughrin, and Mr. H.C. Robertson of Charleston is treasurer and general manager. The capital employed is $243,000 and operatives number 250. The mills contain 10,112 spindles and 330 looms (36 by 40 inch). They work full-time and manufacture 5,500 bales of cotton annually into brown shirtings and sheetings. A great deal of their cloth is sent to Northern bleacheries, whence it is sold in its whitened form as interlinings extensively used in the manufacture of linen collars and cuffs. Shipments from these mills have recently been made to China. The company is daily improving its plant, new cottages have recently been built for the operatives, and on the 1st of January last a dividend of 2½ per cent was declared, a precursor, we may be sure, of many dividends to follow.

Among the many places of interest in and around Newberry none will better repay a visit than the Innesfallen dairy farm owned by Mr. A.J. McCaughrin and managed by G.M. Berry. The buildings are located upon a knob or hill to the southwest of the city. Within the barbed wires encircling the farm one hundred and fifteen acres are contained. Other fences subdivide them into conveniently sized lots for pasture and for the growing of grain, hay, and forage crops. Upwards of forty milch cows are kept upon the premises. Some of them are thoroughbred Jerseys of the most approved strains.

Around three sides of the barnyard the cow houses are built, the doors opening toward the barn, which is in the centre of the lot. Each stall is numbered and each cow knows her own habitation. The barn is a spacious building, two stories high. The upper portion is devoted to the storing of hay and dry forage, while the lower story contains the grain bins, cutter, and tool rooms, and four immense silos, sixteen feet square and twenty feet deep.

These are built into the ground eight or ten feet and rise ten or twelve feet above the floor of the barn, so that they have to be filled from the second story of the building. The sides are made of dressed tongued and grooved plank, two inches thick, set perpendicularly. The outer seams are covered with paper and slatted, so that the silos are practically air tight. The four pits have an aggregate capacity for storing the product of sixty acres of green forage. The ensilage crop of the Innesfallen farm is either corn, sown in drills and cut when the ears are half ripe, or milo maize and other varieties of the eighteen non-saccharine sorghums. The green stuff is cut close to the ground and hauled to the barn where it is passed through a Ross feedcutter, run by hand or steam power, and cut into half-inch lengths. As soon as cut, the ensilage is packed in the bins, which, when filled, are covered with plank and weighted down. With no other treatment the mass is left to ferment; and, in the winter when it is needed for food, the plank covering is removed and the well-cured ensilage is fed out to the cattle, about twelve pounds per day being the average ration. When cured the stuff is of a light green color, sweet to the taste and is greedily relished by cattle and horses. The economy of ensilage forage is great, one acre so cured being estimated as worth five acres of dry-cured forage.

The dairy and milk vault at Innesfallen are models of convenience. The small, one-storied building covers a cellar twenty feet deep. You descend by a winding staircase to the bottom, which is bricked and cemented. Here on broad shelves the milk is kept in metal pans holding from three to five gallons each and covered with light muslin to exclude dust, &c. The temperature in this vault is never above 60° in summer and is kept at the same point in winter by means of an oil lamp. The milk pans are taken up and down on a small elevator, and the skimming and churning is done in the upper room. At this season of the year very litle butter is made; however, the fresh milk is in great demand in Newberry at 10 cents a quart, a highly remunerative price. The enterprise is a very successful one, and Mr. McCaughrin deserves his success.

There is a quarry of very fine granite within a mile of Newberry, owned and quarried by Messrs. Leavell & Speers. Some of this dressed granite is being shipped to Augusta for the new Government building and to Anderson for the facings of the hotel.

A large Newberry enterprise is brick-making. Messrs. Poole & Poole manufacture a handsome salmon-colored brick, which is in great demand not only for local building but for export to various railroad points in the up-country.

The Newberry Board of Trade, under President John O. Peoples, is doing excellent work for the advancement of the business interests of the city. The men who do business in Newberry are: W.E. Pelham, druggist and pharmacist; W.H. Harris, groceries; J.S. Russell, general merchandise; B.H. Cline, groceries; M. Foot, Jr. & Co., general merchandise and furniture; B.H. Lovelace, groceries and confectionery; J.W. Fant, saloon and restaurant; J. Mittelle, groceries and confectionery; Gary, Cook & Carwile, dry goods and notions; Wooten & McWhirter, dry goods and furniture; Minter & Jamieson, dry goods and furniture; J.W. Chapman, books and stationery; L. Crede, confectioner and baker; D.M. Ward & Co., general merchandise and saloon; J. Mann, general merchandise; D.R. Phifer, livery and sale stables; Geo. McWhirter, wholesale grocer; Thos. F. Harmon, groceries; A.L. Knighton, groceries; H.C. Summers, groceries and saloon; Jos. Brown, clothing, dry goods, and general merchandise; A.M. Bowers, groceries and saloon; Edward Scholtz, jeweller and optician; M.S. Epstin, dry goods; Floyd & Purcell, general merchandise; Davis & Goggans, dry goods; J.W. Kibler & Co., groceries; Smith & Warren, clothing and gentlemen's furnishing goods; S.P. Boozer & Son, hardware and guns; Cofield & Lyons, wholesale druggists; S.B. Jones, confectionery and restaurant; Summer Brothers, dry goods; C.L. Havird, dry goods; Thomas F. Tarrant, dry goods and millinery; Proctor Todd, groceries and confectionery; C. & G.S. Mower, dry goods; W.A. Kinard, groceries and confectionery; Paul Johnstone, dry goods; J.W. White, gunsmith; L.P.W. Riser, groceries, dry goods, and millinery; Leavell & Speers, marble yards; O.K. Klettner, groceries and saloon; John Donahoe, groceries; W.T. Tarrant, general merchandise; J.W. Montgomery, jeweller; J.N. Martin, wholesale grocer; J.B. Martin, carriages, wagon, and buggies; R.C. Williams, art store; R.C. Chapman, undertaker; R.Y. Leavell, furniture; L.M. Speers, undertaker; F.R. Wallace & Co., groceries; J.D. Smith, livery and sale stable; Fant & Buford, carriages, buggies, &c.; A.J. McCaughrin, dealer in fertilizers; Peoples & Johnson, hardware; Wright & J.W. Coppock, clothing; W.H. Hunt, Jr., books and stationery; O.H.P. Fant, wholesale groceries; Summers Brothers, groceries; Jordan Green, saloon; Peter Robinson, drugs; Aull & Houseal, job printing, T.F. Greneker, books and stationery; T.Q. Boozer, groceries and saloon; Caldwell Brothers, groceries; F.A. Schumpert, carriages and buggies; D.B. Wheeler, sewing machines; M.J. Scott, tin shop; A.J. Sproles, tinware; W.T. Davis, sash, door, and blind factory; J.T. Taylor, wagon and carriage factory; Dominick & Lovelace, grist mills; B.H. Blease, livery stable; W.H. Blatts, shoe shop; Harbey Reese, barber; Tom Williams, blacksmith; Elijah Phillips, blacksmith; Charles Cannon, blacksmith; Joe Hines, blacksmith; and O.McR. Holmes, fertilizers.

The cotton buyers are Messrs. W.H. Stapleton, O.McR. Holmes, J.N. Martin, J.W. Lake, and Mr. Hicks. The cotton weighers are Wm. M. Lane and S.B. Aull. Messrs. Carlisle & Lane are real estate agents. The insurance agents are Messrs. S.P. Boozer & Son, E.A. Scott, James F. Glenn, W.T. Tarrant, James F. Todd, and J.A. Burton, who is also a commission merchant.

The Newberry Bar is particularly strong. Among the attorneys are Messrs. Y.J. Pope, Johnstone & Cromer, Suber & Caldwell, O.L. Schumpert, George S. Moser, Jones & Jones, Milton A. Carlisle, J.Y. Culbreath, Goggans & Hunt, T.S. Moorman, G.G. Sale, and H.H. Blease, Jr.

The press of Newberry is a credit to the city and county. The *Observer,* published by Messrs. Wallace and Kinard, is edited by W.H. Wallace, an able, thoughtful, and fearless writer. The news is admirably selected and classified; the paper is well printed and deserves its large circulation. The *News and Herald,* owned and edited by E.H. Aull, is a bright, well-arranged paper, full of news and advertising, and is deservedly popular.

In addition to her thrifty population, prosperous bank, successful factory, excellent newspapers, splendid schools and churches, good hotels, handsome Opera House, fine stores, and enterprising merchants, Newberry is blessed with a fine climate and almost perfect health. Dr. O.B. Mayer, Jr., the president of the board of health, declares that pneumonia and typhoid fever are practically unknown, and the general health of the city never has been as good as at present.

In view of Dr. Mayer's assurances it may fairly be expected that the great majority of Newberry's present population will live to see their numbers multiplied and the town, its industries, and institutions expanded to the wide extent which is assured by the wise and liberal tendencies of its industrial and commercial life.

News and Courier, February 21, 1889. A.E.G.

Orangeburg, the City on the Edisto

This is last of three surveys of Orangeburg that appeared in the *News and Courier* in the 1880s.* The author of the first, native-son August Kohn, paid special tribute to Claflin University, while noting that local blacks referred to his honor the mayor as "ten days or five dollars." Twenty-four months later Orangeburg had developed a mile-long street railway to serve the city's business district and was thinking of lighting its principal thoroughfares with electricity. Also, like so many South Carolina towns and cities, Orangeburg had fallen victim to the "health resort" virus and was convinced that it badly needed more rail connections and a huge hotel suitable for Northern tourists.

* * *

Orangeburg has certainly been on a boom during the past year. Enterprises have been springing up here and there, improvements have been going on, new buildings being erected, until now the friends of the City on the Edisto see that she means to be second to no town in the State. Orangeburg has a thriving and happy population, numbering in all about five thousand. They encourage anything that looks to the welfare of the place and are most hospitable to visitors. Year by year the town has extended its confines, and to say that the growth of the place is lasting and steady is merely clothing in words an unquestionable fact.

The first step forward just now to something great in the way of railroad facilities is the South-Bound Railroad, which will run from Savannah to Blackville and thence to Sumter via Orangeburg. Columbia is putting forth all her energies to induce the road to come to that city, but the Capital City might as well be quiet—Orangeburg wants the proposed route to run through this place, and its citizens will do all in their power to accomplish that aim. The leading men of our city are deeply interested in this matter and would make any reasonable inducements for the road to come here. If the road should take to Orangeburg it would open a new country through which there is no railroad and would give a shorter route for Northerners who are bound for Florida. No railroad can afford to ignore established centres, and the South-Bound would certainly be doing so should it ignore Orangeburg.

After we get this railroad, we want a large hotel, something on the order of the Dorchester of Summerville to accommodate Northern visitors who flock down South every winter. A number of these health-seekers from the other side

*See also the issues of August 16, 1887, and May 29, 1888. Interestingly, in both of these years Orangeburg had at least one black alderman on its city council.

of the Mason and Dixon's line come to our town and stop with families from the North who have located here. They say that scores of others would come here if Orangeburg only had the accommodations. They will not have to wait long. Several of our enterprising men see the necessity for establishing a palatial hotel here, and it will be only a short time before we have one.

Besides these things already mentioned which are to come, it is understood that the city authorities are discussing the advisability of lighting the streets with electricity. The cotton factory at this place is lit by the electric lights, and it is thought that an arrangement can be made with Mr. Cornelson, the proprietor of the mills, by which this light can be shed abroad on our thoroughfares. Another new enterprise to be started here is an ice factory. The machinery for the factory has already been ordered and everything is expected to be ready for work by April 1, 1890.

One of the principal signs of the city's prosperity is the fact that so many health-seekers and pleasure-loving people flock to our hospitable little inland city, the number of visitors during the year far exceeding any past record. People are finding out that this is a healthy place, and consequently numbers come here for their health and to spend their vacation. The climate is salubrious, the well water good, and the hospitality of the people is so well known that no comment upon it is needed. A heavy pine timbering, all the way from the extreme western Barnwell boundary, passes through the city, the railroad cut conducts a draught of ocean breeze towards sunset, and these, with the openness of the settlements, give a mild climate. The city and surroundings possess all the essentials necessary to health, such as elevation, drainage, and an invigorating and dry atmosphere. The place is free from malaria, and the climate is especially adapted to those suffering from pulmonary diseases. One of our prominent medical practitioners remarked to your correspondent that the observations of practicing physicians establish the death rate at not above five to the thousand. The blizzard is unknown, and even severe winters are unusual. The water supply is drawn from wells of the average depth of thirty feet and is abundant, healthful, and unobjectionable to sight or taste. The germs of epidemical disease find here no congenial soil.

The city is in a sound and satisfactorily [sic] financial condition. It has no public debt, and licenses and taxes are not necessarily high. The value of the taxable property of the city, both real and personal, amounts to about $1,000,000. The tax for this year of grace is 7½ mills, giving a revenue of about $7,500. Local licenses and fines (including the liquor revenue) amount to $3,600.

The greatest improvement that has been made in the past year is the establishment of the Orangeburg City Street Railway. Through the untiring efforts of Messrs. J.W.H. Dukes and L.H. Wannamaker, together with the other members of the board of co-operators, Messrs. J.W. Lowman, B.H. Moss, O.R. Lowman, M.B. Randle, and D.E. Dukes, the building of the road was at last begun on July 1st. The contract was awarded to J.W. Craig of Charleston, and on the first day of September the road was completed at a cost of something over $10,000. The road is a little over a mile in length and has turnouts running into the yards of the principal mercantile houses. Three flat cars for the hauling of freight are used and are kept running all of the time. Two passenger cars were bought by the company, but only one is used regularly, the other being kept in reserve for extra occasions. Since the road has been in operation it has done a good business, and the stockholders feel assured of making fair dividends on their investment, even in the first year. The officers are: President, J.W.H. Dukes; secretary and treasurer, B.H. Moss; freight agent, Alex. N. Brunson; directors, J.W.H. Dukes, G.H. Cornelson, L.H. Wannamaker, N.H. Bull , G.W. Brunson, M.B. Randle, W.M. Sain, O.B. Lowman, and E.N. Scovill.

Another enterprise recently chartered is the Orangeburg Wood and Material Company. This company will manufacture doors, sash, and blinds and will run a planing department. In addition to this, they will keep on hand all supplies for building purposes. This is a much-needed establishment and will add materially to the business of the city. It is officered by E.F. Slater as president and D.W. Ayers, one of the largest contractors of the State, as general manager and secretary and treasurer. The directors are E.F. Slater, J.E. Bull, D.W. Ayers, Samuel Dibble, James F. Izlar, C.G. Dantzler, J.S. Rowe, and O.R. Lowman.

During the year just ended a great deal has been done toward obtaining an ample supply of water for fire and other purposes. The water-works, which are now owned by Mr. G.H. Cornelson, have been extended all over the city. Six-inch pipes have been laid through the principal streets, with one hundred and two double hydrants at intervals of from 150 to 200 feet. The stand-pipe was raised 24 feet high and now towers majestically toward the heavens to a height of 96 feet. It holds 40,000 gallons, and with the mains all full the capacity is about 80,000 gallons. A stream of water can be thrown 65 feet high through a 24-inch hose connected with any hydrant. This water is used for fire purposes and the watering of the streets, and then families can have the works extended into their households by paying the usual fee. Besides this, there are seven cisterns in the city with a capacity of about 150,000 gallons, and Mr. Cornelson's Artesian well, which stands ready to fill the stand-pipe and the cisterns at a moment's notice. In this connection it is well to mention that our fire department is a most efficient one. Mr. F.A. Schiffley is chief, with Messrs. R.F. Bryant and L.H. Wannamaker as first and second assistant chiefs respectively. The department consists of one steamer, one truck, one hand engine, and five reel organizations, all in different parts of the city. These organizations are all voluntary ones, but the members thereof render valuable service in times of fire.

Orangeburg has an extensive retail business and carries on, to a limited extent, a jobbing trade also. The report of business for the year 1888-89 certainly shows up well. A number of merchants feel some delicacy in disclosing their sales, but with the reports handed in by some of the principal business men and a careful estimate it can be safely said that the following is a very near approximation of the business done here from September 1888 to September 1889:

Building material	$ 18,500
Books and stationery	8,250
Buggies, carts, and wagons	54,000
Clothing	68,000
Crockery and tinware	9,500
Cotton sales	800,000
Drugs, oils, and paints	68,000
Dry goods	348,000
Fertilizers	42,000
Grain and hay	8,000
Groceries	427,000
Hardware, stoves, etc.	58,000
Liquors, cigars, and tobacco	55,000
Machinery, gins, etc.	20,000
Millinery	4,500
Mules and horses	55,000
Newspapers, printing, etc.	12,000
Shoes and hats	104,000
Sewing machines	20,000
Miscellaneous	25,000
Total	$2,204,750

This is certainly a good showing, $161,577 more than in 1887-88, and doubtless the report of next year will show another handsome increase. The above summary does not embrace the amount of freight, express, postoffice or agency business done in Orangeburg. The business at the Orangeburg depot has increased at least 17 per cent, and the express gross receipts also foot up very favorably.

As an indication of the growth of the city the postmaster states that the bulk of the mail matter received here has about doubled in four years. This office has become the distributing point for the entire county. There are six star routes in operation, some of them running daily, which serve about twenty-five offices. The money order business has had a corresponding increase. Mr. F.A. Schiffley is the excellent postmaster, and Mr. W. Hutson Bailey is his assistant. So well and systematically are the duties of the office attended to that it is seldom any reports of irregularities in the mails at this point occur.

The Bank of Orangeburg, which is officered by Gen. James F. Izlar as president and Mr. J.E. Bull as cashier, was organized February 23, 1887. Since its organization it has been doing a thriving business, and has already paid two dividends, and has a good surplus on hand. The par value of shares are $100; they are quoted on the market at $130.

The Edisto Savings Bank is a new institution. It was opened in May last on a subscribed capital of $30,000 in 1,200 shares, nearly two-thirds of which is already paid in, and the remainder is payable in instalments on the first day of each month. The officers are: Samuel Dibble, president; W.B. Thompson, vice president; Theodore Kohn, L.H. Wannamaker, B.H. Moss, J.W. Lowman, G.W. Brunson, F. DeMars, and John W. Fairey, directors. Mr. E. Courtenay Dibble is cashier. This bank, in addition to its savings department, does a general banking business and adds materially to the commercial facilities of our city.

The Orangeburg Building and Loan Association is another institution of the almighty dollar which is proving successful. It has been running four years and has invested principally in real estate $47,500. The amount paid in on each share up to date is $48, and the shares are today worth $63. The investment has earned 15 per cent annually. All of the capital of the Association is invested.

The Orange Cotton Mills, which is owned and controlled by Mr. Geo. H. Cornelson, is doing a flourishing business. It ranks among the largest manufactories of the State, employing about one hundred and sixty hands. It is engaged in the manufacture of yarns and ropes, and is now running six thousand spindles. Under the excellent management of Superintendent Monarch the factory works up about seventy-five bales of cotton a week, which is about 10,800 pounds of yarn.

The Dr. J.G. Wannamaker Manufacturing Company is among the chief industries of the city. This company conducts one of the largest drug stores in the State and in addition to their retail business is engaged in the manufacture of medicines. Their large and commodious laboratory, in the rear of the drug store, is kept constantly busy in the manufacture of their special preparations, as well as a full line of the non-secrets. They are building up a large business in this and other States.

Mr. Patrick Doyle runs a big buggy and wagon manufactory here. He has experienced workmen in every department and does good work. Some of the buggies manufactured by Mr. Doyle are as good in looks, style, and quality as any of the Western buggies brought here for sale.

Mr. Harpin Riggs also runs a carriage factory. He does a great deal of work in repairing, etc., and adds greatly to the business of the city. Other minor blacksmith shops make up very good wagons and do excellent repairing.

Orangeburg can justly boast of having the best private schools of the State. During the past year they have been well attended, and for the coming season just begun the outlook is most promising. The Sheridan Classical School is a school of a considerable reputation. It is well patronized by the school population of the city, and numbers attend from adjoining counties. The faculty is a most excellent one and consists of Capt. H.G. Sheridan, principal; Prof. H.G. Sheridan, Jr., and Miss Lizzie Dexter, assistants.

The Mellichamp High School is another institution of learning which has done much good in our midst. It has been in operation for nearly twenty years,

Old Dixie Club Library, an ante-bellum structure that once stood on Orangeburg's public square. The building now belongs to the Orangeburg Historical Society.

and many of the city's "grown up" boys and ladies owe their preliminary training to this school. It is also well patronized by this and other counties. The following constitute the corps of teachers who are earnest and painstaking in their work: Prof. Stiles R. Mellichamp, principal; Miss F.L. and E.R. Mellichamp, assistants; Miss Carrie Moss, teacher of drawing; Prof. Anton Berg, instructor of music.

The art perservative [sic] of the city consists of three weeklies— the *Times and Democrat*, the *Spectator*, and the *Plain Speaker.*

The *Times and Democrat* is an eight-page paper, well edited, and always full of the latest and brightest locals. It has about the largest circulation of any county paper in the State. Mr. James L. Sims is the editor and proprietor.

The *Spectator* is run by a chartered company, with Mr. H.S. Cunningham as editor. It looks well after the interests of the city and contains some spicy reading matter.

The *Plain Speaker* is a Republican journal run by a joint stock company. Its writers are all colored men, but they look well after the interests of their race in the columns of their paper.

The *Carolina School Journal*, edited by Prof. S.R. Mellichamp, is published here by Mr. R. Lewis Berry. The *Journal* was adopted by the recent State Teachers' Institute as the organ of the teachers of South Carolina.

An extensive job printing establishment is carried on by Mr. R. Lewis Berry. Mr. Berry has recently associated with him Mr. C.L. Howell and has ordered a large Cottrell cylinder press to keep apace with his growing trade. The press will run by steam.

The Orangeburg Hotel is a model place of rest for travellers. It is run by Capt. John W. Fairey, and the genial landlord does all in his power to accommodate his guests and to satisfy the aspiration of their palates.

Mrs. Howell will soon open a large hotel in the old Slater Building on Russell Street. The building is now being enlarged and repaired and will soon be ready for the accommodation of guests.

Now, in conclusion, let a word of praise be put in this account for our excellent city fathers. They have in their past administration accomplished a deal of good for the city. They have, in fact, done more for the welfare of the place than any previous administration. Some of the improvements made by them are given here: the widening and straightening of Russell Street gives us a thoroughfare worthy of any city; the extension of the water-works cannot be too highly valued; and, with the opening of the canal on Sunnyside [and] the good order and peace which reigns on our streets and other good things, we are wont to feel that this council is one of the most efficient and public-spirited that the city has ever had. The Hon. J. Schmidt Albergotti is mayor, with the assistance of the following aldermen: the Hons. W.B. Thompson, John W. Fairey, P.G. Cannon, Frank DeMars, W.M. Sain, and James A. Williams. The council recently elected consists of the above named with the exception of Messrs. Cannon and DeMars. Capt. G.W. Brunson and the Rev. E.C. Brown succeed them.

News and Courier, September 16, 1889. F.W.

Pawley's Island, a Summer Paradise

While visiting in Georgetown in February of 1888, reporter Matthew F. Tighe decided to investigate the rustic charms of Pawley's Island. According to this account, the first building was erected there in 1822, and some six decades later only fourteen more had been added, four of them owned by one family. It was, in brief, long the playground of a few well-to-do planters, although others were beginning to become aware of the island's many attractions, so many that an excursion line of steamships connected Pawley's with Georgetown and Waverley Plantation.

* * *

In the summer time the people of Georgetown have within easy reach one of the most delightful resorts on the Atlantic Coast, Pawley's Island. A trip to the city would be incomplete without taking a look at Pawley's Island, which is coming into some notoriety as a summer resort. It is a small island about three miles long and varying from zero to a quarter of a mile in width. It is about nine miles north of the Georgetown harbor by sea. It is reached now, however, by a trip on an excursion steamer, the *Sadie,* Capt. Munnerlyn, from Georgetown first to Waverley Plantation on the Waccamaw and thence across the Neck about three miles to a bridge which connects the south end of the island with the mainland.

The eastern shore of the island is composed of a range of sand hills and sand dunes, which are covered by a growth of sea oats. From the base of this line of hills there is a fine beach. About three-quarters of a mile of the south end of the beach is marred and broken by long rifts and by lagoons. From the north end towards the south, however, there is a continuous stretch of beach, which slopes gradually from the sand hills out to any depth at sea. At low tide the exposed part of the beach varies from three hundred to four hundred yards. At high tide the waves break almost at the base of the hills, leaving only a good carriage drive at that stage of the water.

Off shore are the famous coral reef fishing banks, the small boats fishing there being always in sight of shore. The fish caught here are bass, sheephead, sailor's choice, &c. Bathing on such a beach can scarcely be excelled anywhere. The west shore of the island is bounded by a marsh which separates the island from Waccamaw Neck.

All the "summer resort" houses are built along this west shore, and on account of the sand hills on the east the ocean to a majority of them is invisible. The view from the "back beach" is therefore to the mainland of Waccamaw Neck and its dense

Sea oats in the wind, Pawley's Island. *Photograph by Carl Julien. South Caroliniana Library.*

forests, which are only distant about a quarter of a mile. The houses are built among stunted growths of cedar and myrtle and are all quite old.

The first building put up on the island was erected in 1822. Since that time only fourteen additional houses were put up, four of which belong to members of the Lachicotte family, and the rest belong to Dr. Henry Tucker, Dr. B.G. Fraser, Joe Blythe Allston, Mrs. Governor Alston, Capt. Plowden Weston, B.G. Ward, John La Bruce, Col. Ralph Nesbit, and S. Martineau Ward. Since 1822, and probably before, the island has been the resort of the planters of the Neck. The best hunting grounds in the State are just west of the Island, and equally fine fishing grounds are on the east. The houses on the island have no pretensions to style, with the exception perhaps of the Hagley House, which was run last summer as the Ocean View Hotel.

Some of the houses have a peculiar tortoise shell look from the fact that they are shingled from the ground to the ridgeboard on the roof. Last season it is estimated that about one hundred and fifty people visited the island for the bathing and fishing. They were from Florence, Sumter, Columbia, and other interior cities and towns. Nearly everybody in Georgetown and on the Neck who was spoken to on the subject was ready to make an affidavit that not a single mosquito could be found on the whole island from May until the close of the season in October.

There is just now some talk of building a suitable hotel for the resort. This will not be done for the present season, although the new railroad and steamship management favor the enterprise. At any rate there is quite a crowd expected next summer, and an excursion line of steamers has already been put on between Georgetown and Waverley.

Nine miles below Pawley's Island are North Island and South Island, the distance between which is 4,200 feet. At this point the next work of the U.S. government will be done for Georgetown. It is proposed to construct a stone dike from the east end of North Island nearly a mile in length, the object of which is to prevent the waste of water to the north and direct its force into a new channel, thus removing a sand bar obstruction. The channel proposed would practically be a new one. It is estimated that this work will cost about $275,000. If completed as indicated, there will be a commercial revolution in Georgetown.

News and Courier, February 15, 1888. M.F.T.

Pelzer, a Company Town

Pelzer, an Anderson County mill town planned and developed by Charleston industrialists, appeared almost as if by magic in the early 1880s. What once was farmland became a bustling hubbub of activity. According to this report, written in the summer of 1885, Pelzer was a near-perfect community—no liquor, no dogs, no rent, a church, a school, a hotel, four stores, and a spacious mill equipped with the most modern machinery. Yet this hymn of praise to the virtues of capitalism cannot disguise long hours, hard work, considerable drudgery, and an existence dictated entirely by "the Mill."

* * *

Here, within three years, has grown up as if by magic a thriving and prosperous town of fourteen hundred inhabitants. In it stands one of the finest cotton mills in the South, and the increasing hum and roar of its machinery, the diligent and business-like step of its people, the unmistakable evidences of thrift and industry to be seen on every hand tell of the happy copartnership between capital and labor.

Pelzer is situated in Anderson County 127 miles north of Columbia and ten miles south of Greenville. At the railroad station there is a handsome little depot with ticket and telegraph offices. Pelzer Cotton Mill lies on the west bank of the Saluda River, a half mile away, where the stream makes its way between the hills of Anderson and Greenville counties. The first work done toward its erection was the building of a solid rock dam across the river from the Greenville to the Anderson side. The dam is eighteen feet wide at its base, tapering up to ten inches at the top. It is 300 feet long and 21 feet high and, completely stemming the whole stream, turns its main force into a canal forty-two feet wide and seventeen feet deep. This canal runs under the building and furnishes the tremendous power that whirls the machinery of the great mill.

The water pours over the dam for its entire length in a constant, roaring cataract that tells of a vast amount of power that could yet be acquired were it ever to be needed. But as it stands, 1,000 horse power has been developed, and of this only 600 horse power is requisite to run the ponderous driving machinery.

The Pelzer Mill is essentially a Charleston enterprise. Its origin was in the mind of Mr. F.J. Pelzer, and to his foresight, energy, public spirit, and business sagacity the State is indebted for the thriving town and splendid manufacturing establishment we are about to describe. The first organization was as follows: President and treasurer, Capt. Ellison A. Smyth; directors, F.J. Pelzer, William Lebby, W.B. Smith, and David Lopez, all well-known Charleston men. Mr. Lebby afterwards died and was succeeded by Senator A.T. Smythe, and Mr. Lopez, whose death created another vacancy, has been succeeded by Capt. Wm. A. Courtenay, now mayor of Charleston.

The work of securing the water power having been finished, the task of building and completing the mill and all of its essential adjuncts was next begun. A regularly laid broad-gauge railroad was constructed from Pelzer Station, connecting there with the track of the Columbia and Greenville Railroad and running directly to the factory site. Shops were erected and in these all of the doors and windows and much more of the woodwork of the mill was built. Brickyards were started, and the five million bricks necessary for the erection of the factory building and warehouses were made on the spot. Hundreds of hands were employed, wages were promptly paid in cash, and Pelzer at once became the scene of active business life.

The large tract of land purchased by the company contained previously a few dilapidated cabins and a farmhouse of little value. Buildings for the factory and homes for the president, the superintendent, and the operatives went up on all sides. The railroad, at once a great economizer of time, labor, and expense, delivered carloads of lumber and machinery at the factory doors; skilled workmen placed them in position, and the work went systematically on until the original model of Pelzer was finished.

Pelzer Cotton Mill is approached through Lebby Street, named in honor of the late Wm. Lebby. To the right runs Courtenay Street, named for Mayor Courtenay. To the left, at a point overlooking the factory, stands the residence of President Smyth, a handsome building of modern design. The railroad passes directly in front of it. To the right, approaching the mill, stand prominently the neat cottage residences of the overseers. To the right again we see the substantial depot used for the reception and storing of oil, starch, and other material used at the mill. Farther up the hill stand two large brick warehouses of a capacity of 8,000 bales. From these warehouses truckways lead to the picker room, which is on the factory's second floor. These truckways afford a level and easy way over which cotton is carried directly into the picker room, where bales are opened and the cotton fed into the picker machines.

The factory building, a splendid, four-story brick edifice, stands on the bank of the river, a short distance below. The company's office occupies a commanding position. From its entrance on the side next to the factory a full view of the mill and the warehouses is had. The office is a commodious and well-appointed building, containing a piazza on its front, a large sitting room, the president's office, the secretary's office, one or two smaller rooms, and a back porch which faces the mill. It is automatically supplied with pure spring water and is an open, cool building, beautifully situated under branching oaks. The view from the president's private office and from that of the secretary is even romantic. It takes in the river above the dam where, deepened by the back-water, it is open and unobstructed for three-quarters of a mile. Such a splendid sheet of water, upon

Pelzer Cotton Mill, c. 1890. *South Caroliniana Library.*

which pleasure boats are seen to gracefully glide unhindered by the current and over which come cool and gentle breezes, is hardly to be found elsewhere in the up-country.

The village proper lies a short distance north of the factory. It is approached through Smythe Street, named in honor of Senator A.T. Smythe of Charleston. This street is the only inlet to the town where the operatives dwell in comfortable houses of four and six rooms, built for them by the company and which they occupy free of rent. There are one hundred and fifty of these comfortable cottages, all occupied.* The town is beautifully laid off on an elevated plain, which overlooks the river and much of the surrounding country. In its centre is preserved an open square, upon which the company will soon erect a village school-house. A flourishing school of which Mr. P.B. Langston, a graduate of Wofford College, is principal, is regularly kept open and occupies at present a building nearby. The salary of the teacher and the greater part of the expenses of the school are paid by the Pelzer Manufacturing Company, and it is "free and open" not only to the children of the factory people but to those of the adjacent country.

From the Central Square radiate the streets of the town. A drive through the village reveals a population of contented people. The families which supply the mill operatives are people of respectability and worth. They dress neatly, look

*Fourteen hundred people in 150 cottages indicates an average of about ten people per cottage.

bright and cheerful, and have everything about them in tidy condition. No disreputable characters are tolerated or allowed to dwell in Pelzer. The people of the town drink pure water, breathe pure air, and have good health. Around their dwellings are noticeable evidences of taste and refinement. Flowers grow about the doors and good vegetable gardens adjoin most of the cottage yards.

Beyond the northern extremity of the town is enclosed with wire fencing a verdant pasture of 175 acres. This pasture is upon the company's land and is set apart for grazing milch cows, a considerable number of which are owned by the village people, who enjoy the use of the pasture without charge.

A handsome church edifice occupies a convenient location in the town, just opposite the hotel, which is kept in a way that reflects credit upon Pelzer. The church is decidedly a handsome one—one of the handsomest in South Carolina. It is the Queen Anne style of architecture, designed by Mr. Valk of New York, the architect who has planned other churches in the State. Its seating capacity is 600. It is well arranged with Sunday-school and class-rooms and has an inclined floor, neat and comfortable pews, high arched ceilings, stained glass windows, and good ventilation. It is provided with an excellent church organ, and the Sabbath's worship is attended with good music by a well-practiced choir. The church in its completed and finished form was a present to the Pelzer Manufacturing Company from Mr. F.J. Pelzer, who paid its entire cost of $5,000 out of his own pocket. It is what is termed a free church—open to all denominations. Four denominations worship in it—Presbyterians, Methodists, Baptists, and Episcopalians—who take it on alternate Sundays, and the people to a considerable extent worship all together.

Four general merchandise stores supply Pelzer and the surrounding country with general lines of merchantable goods. The buildings are owned by the Pelzer Manufacturing Company and are rented from the company by the occupants. The Pelzer Company does no merchandise business and has no interest in any that is carried on, but pays cash to its operatives and cash for its cotton, leaving the people to trade where they please and get the benefits of competition in trade.

In close proximity to the cotton mill the company has in operation a large flour mill and corn mill and cotton gin. Hundreds of bales of cotton from the farms close by are ginned here yearly, and large quantities of grain ground into flour, grits, and meal. This mill is run by water power and is situated on the Greenville side of the river at the entrance to the splendid covered bridge which spans the river.

Pelzer is under the supervision of a town marshal appointed by the Governor. The marshal is endowed with authority to arrest persons for disorderly conduct and for misdemeanors. Offenders are taken before the nearest trial justice and prosecuted, as Pelzer is not an incorporated town with an officer of judicial authority. The salary of the marshal is paid by the Pelzer Company.

No dogs are allowed in Pelzer. In this particular, as well as in others, Pelzer is a pioneer town, leading in a good cause and setting a good example for more pretentious towns and cities. After a trial of this abstinence its untold blessings are generally felt, and the fact that dogs are in ninety-nine cases out of a hundred worthless and troublesome has been fully established.

Another inestimable blessing that rests upon Pelzer is the absence of drinking saloons. The law disallows the sale of intoxicating drinks within three miles of the town. There is, in consequence, no drunkenness, no midnight broils to disturb the peace and quiet of its sober and orderly people. Pelzer has one drug store and one resident physician, Dr. M.P. Ravenel, formerly of Charleston.

So, in all the requisites of life—religious, educational, social, and industrial—Pelzer is a complete little city. The country around it is rich in agricultural and horticultural products, and here is a market for them. Country produce wagons are common on the streets, and the stores of the town supply in exchange or for cash all household goods. A close and convenient cotton market is also created and the highest market prices are paid for the staple. Eight thousand bales were purchased in Pelzer last year.

But let us take a glance at the factory. The building is an immense one of four stories above the wheel-pit. Into the latter place the water rushes with great velocity from the canal. A Boyden turbine water-wheel of 550-horse power, supplemented by another wheel of 175-horse power, supplies the force that propels the machinery of the mill. These wheels are situated far underground in a pit encased with solid masonry. The waterfall is twenty-four and a half feet, and the outlet is so ample that the water rushes through the foaming madness into the river below. The power of the two wheels is transmitted to three ponderous driving pulleys 13 feet in diameter and thence to the shafting of the mill above and to the spindles, looms, and other machinery.

The entrance to the mill is upon the ground floor. In this respect Pelzer Mill, built at the base of a steep hill, has an advantage over many other mills. Mills built partly underground feel the inconvenience of being partly shut out from the light, and artificial lights become necessary even in day time. Extra provision for light was also made at Pelzer in the size and construction of its windows. These are wide and high and double, with slender center-columns between the two sides. The windows have each four sashes and are made to slide up and down so as to furnish a great amount of light, to furnish it where it is needed, and in addition to this to furnish an abundance of ventilation.

The two spacious lower floors are devoted to weaving and the two upper floors to spinning. The entire mill, whose floors would cover several acres of land, is chock full of busy machinery of the most improved makes. Everything is in systematic order and runs with an evenness, a smoothness, a regularity, and rapidity that inspires one with the idea of concentrated power, industry, and ingenuity. The mill is supplied also with all requisite machinery for baling and packing its products, which consist entirely of cloth goods. The bales are compact and neat and handy for shipment to any part of the world. They are loaded on flat cars at the mill and quickly transported by the use of mules over the Pelzer Railroad to the depot at Pelzer Station.

The arrangements for protection against fire are ample and complete. A tank of twelve thousand gallons of water is on the top of the factory building. In an instant this water, with its powerful pressure, can be turned into the mill by means of automatic sprinklers. The mill is also supplied with electric light for use when it is operated at night. Two Weston Dynamo Electric machines are in use. They are of easy connection with the driving machinery of the mill, and when operated furnish a most brilliant light throughout the building. The president's office and residence and depot are connected by telephone.

Pelzer Mill employs five hundred operatives and pays out in wages about $8,000 a month or about $100,000 a year. A large number of the operatives are girls and women. With houses to live in free of rent and with all of the advantages of a thriving and prosperous town and the country surrounding it, where the cost of living is so small, there is every chance for these people to prosper and live a life of contentment.

One of the needs of all manufacturing centres like Pelzer is a savings bank. Such an institution would greatly encourage economy and the accumulation of means by the people.

The consumption of cotton by the mill accounts to about 10,000 to 11,000 bales per annum. Pelzer goods find ready sale in the principal markets of the country, and many of them are exported directly to foreign countries.

The benefits conferred upon the State cannot be more than approximately estimated. One hundred thousand dollars a year are earned by the labor of the people who would otherwise be to a great extent a burden upon the country. A good living, if nothing more, is afforded fourteen hundred people. The cost of manufacturing eleven thousand bales of cotton is kept in the pockets of the poor people at home, property is increasing in value in consequence of the infusion of life into the industries of the people, and, lastly but not leastly, a property which cost a half million dollars (the capital stock of the company) is added to the taxable values of the State and of the county in which it is situated. Before the building of Pelzer land was selling in the neighborhood for $6 to $9 per acre. Now prices range from $13 to $20, and the tendency is upward.

A point that should afford food for thought is this: Pelzer is a living monument to the wisdom of the Exemption Law. I am told by Capt. Smyth that, had it not been for the law, the Pelzer Mill would not have been built. The property is, of course, not taxable until after ten years of its establishment. But that time will soon pass, and its five hundred thousand dollars will pay its pro rata share of the taxes of the State.

The question arises: Is Pelzer making money? I am not at liberty to give figures or statements, but there are two facts that seem to point to a successful business. The one is that the mill has made no stop during the past year of business depression, and the other is that it is known that the stockholders are well-satisfied with the management of their property. Another noticeable point is the absence of an accumulation of stock, which would likely be the case if the goods did not find an easy market at satisfactory prices. The mill is in full blast, working with a full force of hands on full time. There is nothing dull about its daily work. The place is alive with business and everything is of cheerful aspect and pushing business activity.

News and Courier, July 9, 1885. A.M.H.

The Selling of Port Royal

Tucked away on Saint Helena Island in the most southern part of the state, Port Royal has had a turbulent history, some of which this anonymous correspondent describes in the sketch that follows. He is, however, more concerned with the rumored development of the little town by an English syndicate. Unlike most such articles published by the *News and Courier* during the 1880s, this one was profusely illustrated, presumably by the author himself.

* * *

Port Royal is a name that has been on many lips of late, and yet to many it is little more than a name. But small as it is, Port Royal has a way of its own of making itself known that might be envied by larger and more prestigious places. Some years ago Mr. Peter Papin and Daniel F. Appleton made a great stir and laid their plans for the building of a city, the metes and boundaries of which may still be traced upon some of the local maps of the period.* The huge elevator and cotton compresses and a warehouse of enormous length right on the water front, with a double line of railroad track running by it, stand as monuments to the energy and faith of those who hoped against hope; for the railroads which were to have been built to the West have never been constructed, and the ocean is waiting for the fleets that have never come in.

But in the breasts of the good people of Port Royal "hope springs eternal," and Peter Papin passed away only to be succeeded by other and more promising schemers and schemes. About a year ago, Vanderbilt's splendid yacht steamed into the harbor of Port Royal. It went there to get coal and to put Mr. Vanderbilt's party ashore so that they might travel to New York by rail and in this way escape the perilous passage of Hatteras, but this was enough to start the speculators speculating, and lo! another city loomed up like a mirage in the desert.

The Vanderbilt sensation likewise speedily passed away, to be succeeded by the latest and most promising perhaps of all the splendid things which have elated the people of Port Royal. A little over a month ago, the report was circulated that the town had been sold to the representatives of English capitalists who have money without limit and who intend to spend the money for the development of Port Royal and its marvelous resources.

When it is said that the whole town has been sold, of course, only the share of it owned by Appleton is meant, but this really includes nearly the whole place, or at least the whole of the most desirable part of it. To find out the "true inward-

*For details of the Appleton scheme and its demise see the *News and Courier,* September 22, 1885.

ness" of this rumor and also to see exactly what sort of place Port Royal is, a special artist and correspondent was recently dispatched to see the city that has been and may be. At Yemassee the passenger is switched off to the Port Royal Road. The style of motion on this road gives one the idea that the engineer is thinking pensively of the girl he left behind and can't persuade himself to put on steam. It is only twenty-five miles from Yemassee to Port Royal, however, so there is plenty of time to get there in the course of a day. Port Royal is the next station to Beaufort. The first indication of the city is the big warehouse. Over it a glimpse is obtained of the top of the old grain elevator, and in front the waters of Battery Creek dance and glitter in the bright sunlight. The people here have been disappointed so often before that one could have expected much difficulty in getting anyone to talk. But not so. Everybody has something to say about the subject and nearly all had this or that reason for saying that Port Royal this time is beyond doubt upon the edge of a great and lasting revival. Now just what has touched off the mental thermometer of the people here and sent the mercury flying up to anything over fever heat is this.

About a month ago, or to be exact, on the 14th of November, Edmund Flynn and his wife, from New York, registered at the Live Oak Hotel. Mr. Flynn was quiet and impressed everyone as being a fine specimen of a "strictly business" man. Still he let fall, in unguarded moments it is to be supposed, remarks which are treasured up like virgin gold. From these remarks it is inferred that Mr. Flynn had an enormous amount of capital at his back in England and that he intended to use it shortly in the interest of Port Royal. Mr. Flynn and his wife stayed at Port Royal for about two weeks. Both expressed themselves much impressed with the place, particularly the latter, who purchased a site for a residence on the place known as the "Old Fort Plantation," about a mile from town. Mrs. Flynn had visited Port Royal several years ago when she went there for the benefit of her health, and at that time she was much impressed with its great natural advantages.

Mr. Flynn procured the services of a well-known Charleston civil engineer to make a survey of the place. He also got a party from Beaufort to make a drawing of the water front with its warehouses, elevators, &c. upon it and also to add additional sheds and wharves that have no existence except upon the map. Many in Port Royal saw the map and describe it as having been a beautiful piece of drawing. This drawing, report adds, Mr. Flynn has taken with him to England. In conversing with several of the most prominent citizens of Port Royal, they all expressed themselves as feeling confident that Flynn was more than a mere speculator and that the effects of the recent purchase by him would soon be felt. Of course, just when or how this would be done is no more than mere conjecture. Some think that as early as January the good work will begin, while others deem it more probable that nothing will be done before April next and perhaps on the first day of that month as a surprise.

Port Royal is a very small place. It does not take long to go all over it. Nearly every prominent person there is a strong believer in the future of the town. It is hard, however, to get a thoroughly unbiased opinion in a place where a person's judgment must inevitably be affected by his interests. So it was determined to go to Beaufort and feel the pulse of public opinion there. This beautiful old town is but five miles distant and the road leading to it is a charming one. The foliage has a very tropical look and palmetto trees and the Spanish dagger are abundant.

Mr. Flynn is a Cape Cod man and a retired sea captain. I had heard there was a gentleman in Beaufort who came from a neighboring town in Massachusetts to the place in which Mr. Flynn first saw the light of day, and I went over to see him. This gentleman, who holds a most responsible position and besides owns much real estate near Beaufort, was found in his office.

He stated that he had known Flynn's father and family for years, and this knowledge gave him more confidence in the latest Port Royal sensation than anything else. "For," he went on to say, "they have always been noted for their uprightness and strict business dealings." Flynn, he said, had retired from the sea about fifteen years ago and since then had been living in New York. Here, his keen judgment and business sense, had enabled him to accumulate considerable means. "In fact," added the Beaufort oracle, "the only thing that shakes my faith in this whole business at all is the enormous amount of the mortgage upon the property, which would seem to indicate that barely one thousand dollars had passed hands, which upon so large a sale is absurd."

A gentleman who has the reputation of possessing solid sense and a judgment never influenced by his wishes said, "Well, don't give it as coming from me, but in my opinion this whole sale is nothing but a huge spec. Now, mind, I don't say it is so, but why couldn't Flynn and Appleton have made some mutual arrangement about this sale, and now Flynn is going over to try and work up an interest in the subject in England?" It was suggested in reply that Appleton might be afraid of affecting the real value of his property here by getting up a false sale. "Not a bit of it. I tell you, and the books in the auditor's office will prove it, that Mr. Appleton has made money and lots of it, too, already on his property here, and he is willing to risk a little now."

An old sea captain lives in Beaufort who grew up with Flynn and knew him well. When someone mentioned to him that Flynn had bought Port Royal, he threw up his hands and gave a deep and briny oath—"What, Neddy Flynn buy a town—why, I was a captain in the same shipping company with Flynn for years, and I'll be ——— ——— if I believe he has enough money to buy a drink, let alone a town!" This may be taken as the extreme pessimistic view of the boom.

At the office of the mesne conveyance at the Court House in Beaufort, the registrar, who, by the way, is a colored man but thoroughly courteous and polite, gave every facility in looking over the deeds relating to the recent sale of Port Royal. There are two deeds of conveyance, one for $100,000, the other for $40,000. In these deeds the whole of Appleton's property is conveyed by Daniel F. Appleton to Edmund Flynn. Upon this property there is a mortgage of $139,200. The record is also given of the purchase of the "Grove" at the Old Fort Plantation by Mrs. Flynn. She paid $10,000 for the property and gave a mortgage upon it for $9,800. All of these deeds are dated the 21st of October, 1887, and were recorded at Beaufort on the 15th of November, which was the day after Mr. Flynn had registered at Port Royal. An effort was made to get Flynn's views about the railroad, for of course it is only by means of a railroad run in the interest of Port Royal that the town can be built up. But on this point it was impossible to find out anything for the reason that Flynn did not express his views about it. All the facts to be had have been given, and anything more that could be stated would be simple surmise and conjecture, of which there is a very abundant quantity floating around both Port Royal and Beaufort just at this time. In fact, there is a perfect fog of surmise here, and its only effect is to make it more difficult to form a correct opinion.

Old elevator and wharf at Port Royal, a drawing in the *News and Courier*, December 28, 1887. *South Caroliniana Library.*

But talking aside and looking simply at Port Royal with all of its natural beauties and advantages of position, the outlook is more pleasant and encouraging. It is a beautiful little place, as all of South Carolina's seacoast towns are. It has none of the pert freshness that most small places have but possesses rather a sedate individuality of its own. Perhaps the massive elevator and pier, rapidly falling into decay, help to add to this appearance. The town is situated on a neck of land running out between Battery Creek on the one hand and Beaufort River on the other. On the former is the wharf frontage, and between the latter and the town is a wide strip of marsh land, which would have to be filled up before it could be utilized. The town is eighteen miles from the ocean, but at the bar there is a depth of twenty-one feet at low water, and it is an acknowledged fact that it has the deepest entrance and largest roadstead on the coast from Maine to Florida.

As one gets off the cars at the neat little depot and looks around, the point that strikes his attention first is the immense wharf front with the long, low warehouse running the whole length of it. There's room here easily for three thousand feet of wharf front. There is a double track running by this which is within twenty feet of the water. In this way every facility is furnished for the loading and unloading of vessels. The water at the head of the wharf is of a depth to allow the deepest draft steamships to approach with ease. This pier is in want of repair but could be fixed at a comparatively small outlay. The superintendent in charge of the warehouse says that there is about three thousand bales of cotton there at this time. So small a supply of cotton, however, together with a lot of miscellaneous freight, gave the capacious warehouse a rather bare and empty appearance.

A few minutes' walk will enable one to see the whole town. The houses are scattered, but there is much order in the manner in which the town is laid out. The roadways are spoken of as avenues and are lined on both sides with the handsomest live oaks. Port Royal has about four hundred and fifty inhabitants, of which 125 are white. Within a few miles of the town are three large phosphate mining companies and two fertilizer companies.

There are here a church in which every sect is allowed to preach, one school admirably conducted by a young lady from St. John's Berkeley, one newspaper is published here whose editor is a man of recognized talent the State over, a post office with regular daily mails, several fine stores, and an excellent hotel. There is also a line of steamers running to the North, one leaving and arriving every week. The temperature is delightful the year round and the climate perfectly healthy in the summer. This is accounted for by the large bodies of salt water all around. In the winter no better resort could be found for anyone desiring a mild, bracing climate, and for those wishing to combine with these advantages the pleasures of hunting, Port Royal offers every advantage; game of all kind is to be found in the country around in abundance.

On my way homeward in the cars I mused over the checkered career this little town has met with. Centuries ago, in 1562, it was settled by the French under Ribault. He with two vessels was searching for the "Jordan," as the river Combahee was then called. A storm came up and, being driven apart, one of the vessels was supposed to have been lost. This was not the case, as it proved, for it had anchored in a bay which from its size they judged must be the outlet of some large stream. To this bay, "because of the fairnesse and largenesse thereof," Ribault gave the name of Port Royale. This settlement was destroyed by Spanish hatred and jealousy. In 1670 the English under William Sayle settled here, but again the proximity of the Spanish and their constant inroads and piracies broke up this settlement also.

The Union Church at Port Royal, a drawing in the *News and Courier,* December 28, 1887. *South Caroliniana Library.*

To pass over a long period of time and come down to more recent events: About fifteen years ago the place was built up and prosperity seemed assured, when once more the jealousy this time of a neighboring town blighted the prospects of the rising young commercial centre. Now it is hoped that the long looked-for peace and success have come at last. Whether it has or not no one can more than conjecture, but it is certain that although it may not be in a few months, as the sanguine hope, still it is nothing but a matter of time until Port Royal will be a successful seaport.

When Mr. W.G. Raoul was president of the Georgia Central Railroad he made a hard struggle to develop the commercial advantages of Port Royal. The grain elevator was there, and rates on grain and cotton were made as low as by any other route. An effort was even made to bring a cargo of cotton to the ships; but, after sustaining great loss, Mr. Raoul reached the conclusion that trade could not be forced out of its natural channels, and so the effort to build up Port Royal was abandoned. The railroad leading to the town was greatly improved, and the seed sown from which, perhaps, the great Flynn syndicate may reap the harvest.

Of one thing, however, Port Royal and its brave and patient people may rest assured: When the fullness of the time comes, the long looked-for city will be built, and South Carolina will rejoice with them in their well-earned prosperity.

News and Courier, December 28, 1887.

The Prosperity of Prosperity

Once known as Frog Level, by the close of 1888 this aptly named Newberry County community was, according to Ambrose Gonzales, a thriving place. It had a high school, a fine hook-and-ladder company, two hotels, and dreams of becoming a resort center. In addition, Prosperity soon would be the crossroads of two rail lines, a development that could only increase business and commercial activity.

* * *

Perhaps nowhere in South Carolina can there be found a more remarkable instance of industrial progress than is evidenced in the evolution of the ancient hamlet of Frog Level into the town of Prosperity. Situated in the lower part of Newberry County on the line of the Columbia and Greenville Railroad forty miles above Columbia, this thriving town transacts a mercantile and cotton business that would astonish those who knew it only as an euphonism of early travel on the Columbia and Greenville line.

The population of Prosperity is about 800. The intendant is Major George G. De Walt; the wardens are Messrs. William Bowers, T.L. Shumpert, G.A. Moffett, and D.I. Sheeley; and the clerk and treasurer is Mr. A.M. Lester. The town is out of debt, has no municipal tax, and as a majority of its citizens are Prohibitionists from principle and not for political reasons, their town is probably as dry as any in the State. A few years ago Prosperity received but twenty-five hundred bales of cotton. Today her receipts average nine thousand bales per annum. The total business of her merchants, including cotton, aggregates nine hundred thousand dollars yearly.

The territory tributary to Prosperity contains some of the best lands in Newberry and Lexington counties, densely peopled with thrifty and industrious white farmers, many of whom are advanced agriculturalists and get the best possible yields from their land.

If the surrounding farmers are thrifty, the merchants of Prosperity are not less so, and a more alert business community can hardly be found anywhere. The firm of Wheeler & Moseley has done much to build up, develop, and properly advertise the town, and they have prospered in every undertaking. Commencing business in 1866 in a primitive wooden building, they have twice outgrown their stores, and two years ago the firm erected a ten thousand dollar brick structure containing two large stores, banking offices, and extensive ware rooms.

A few months ago Messrs. Wheeler & Moseley established a private bank with ample capital for the transaction of the banking business of Prosperity. The cashier is Mr. Joseph H. Hunter. The deposits are already very large and the bank is flourishing.

The churches of Prosperity are: the Lutheran, the Rev. C.A. Marks, rector; the Methodist, the Rev. M.M. Brabham, pastor; and the Baptist, the Rev. W.B. Elkin, pastor. The Associated Reformed Presbyterians are building a handsome new church, and their pastor is the Rev. J.C. Boyd.

Prosperity is proud of her high school building, which is handsome and commodious and is fitted with modern desks, heating apparatus, &c. The Rev. A.J. Bowers is principal. Mr. John E. Edwards is first assistant and Miss Lilian Luther, second assistant. One hundred scholars are in regular attendance.

There are two hotels: the Prosperity Hotel, conducted by Capt. W.H. Dickert, and Messrs. Wise & Birge's Hotel. There is a fine hook-and-ladder company in Prosperity and fires are infrequent.

The health of Prosperity is excellent. Malarial fevers are comparatively unknown, and the town, built on rolling land, is perfectly drained. The municipality owns a well of very fine mineral water which approximates in analysis the waters of the famous Glenn Springs. The well is on the public square and the town authorities are about to erect over it a handsome spring house and beautify its surroundings.

The *Press and Reporter* is a lively newspaper and has done a great deal to advertise the town. It is edited by Mr. F.V. Capers.

Eight miles below Prosperity, on the line of the Columbia, Newberry, and Laurens Railroad, the Piedmont Land Improvement and Investment Company has purchased a valuable body of timber and arable lands, including the "Little Mountain" of local celebrity. This mountain rises to a height of four or five hun-

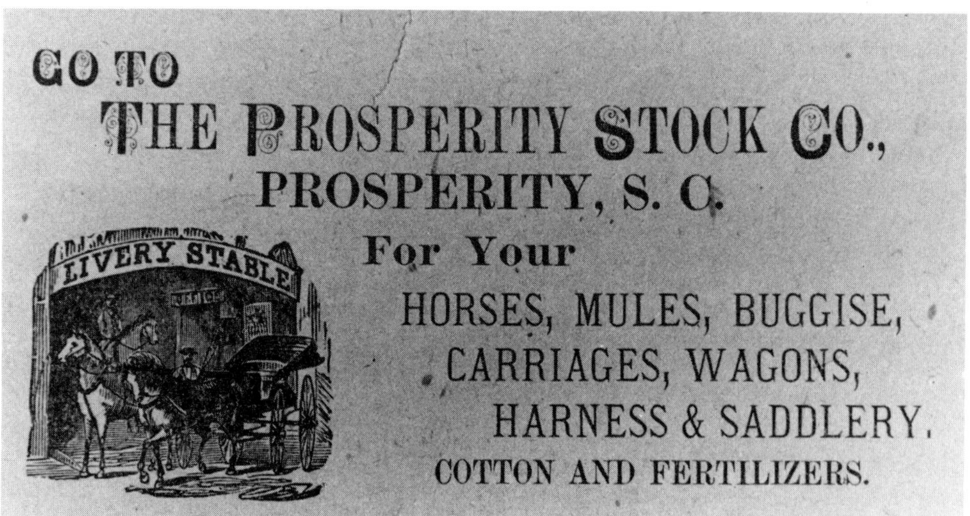

Advertisement in Prosperity's *Eagle Eye,* January 15, 1902. *South Caroliniana Library.*

dred feet above the surrounding country. Its sides are seamed with granite and dotted with pine trees. At its foot are copious springs from which it is proposed to conduct water in pipes to the summit of the mountain where the company will erect a hotel for summer and winter resort. The president of this investment company is Mr. C.J. Iredell, and the directors are Messrs. M.A. Carlisle, H.C. Moseley, and J.E. Desportes.

Among the merchants of Prosperity are: Messrs. Wheeler & Moseley, dealers in cotton, fertilizers, and general merchandise; Wise Brothers, dealers in general merchandise; Luther & Langford, cotton and general merchandise; A.H. Kohn, dealer in general merchandise; S.J. Kohn & Co., general merchandise; S.J. Kohn, general merchandise; Crook & Bankright, general merchandise; A.H. Kohn, dealer in drugs; R.E. Norman, dealer in drugs; H.A. Moffett, groceries and confectionery; and T.L. Shumpert, dealer in fancy groceries and confectionery.

The Columbia, Newberry, and Laurens Railroad, now under construction, will intersect the Columbia and Greenville Railroad at Prosperity, giving competitive rates and still further augmenting the business of an already prosperous town.

News and Courier, December 29, 1888. A.E.G.

Rock Hill, a Wide-Awake Town

The population of Rock Hill, merely a railroad depot in 1870, more than tripled in the 1880s, rising from 809 to 2,744. This growth, naturally enough, attracted the attention of the *News and Courier.* The first survey of Rock Hill, an anonymous report published on September 12, 1887, told how this plucky little town had continued to grow despite several disastrous fires. It also heaped special praise upon J. Henry Toole, a black man, who had managed the village barber shop for the past eighteen years

> except for two months, when, in 1871, he was placed in jail with a number of our citizens for alleged Kukluxing. Henry's allegiance to the Democracy of South Carolina and his gentility has won for him the esteem of the entire community.

Another report (August 27, 1888), written by Ambrose E. Gonzales, added still more details concerning Rock Hill's growth and development, and a third, published in June of 1890, was a profusely illustrated overview covering more than two pages. The work of Edward P. McKissick, it is reproduced here in slightly abbreviated form.

* * *

In 1881 the foundation for the future material advancement of the place was laid by the establishment of the Rock Hill Cotton Factory. The principal promoters were Capt. W.L. Roddey and A.E. Hutchinson. These men are as progressive merchants and capitalists as can be found in South Carolina. They started the movement that has made Rock Hill what she is today. In 1886 the educational advantages were of the most primitive nature, and only the rudiments of a common school education were obtainable. Whatever business was transacted had its source in the territory immediately surrounding Rock Hill. Scarcely $100,000 was invested in mercantile business of the place, and the annual trade did not amount to over $500,000. In addition to this the cotton business amounted to annually about $400,000. There was only one factory and one bank. What a wonderful change has taken place!

Rock Hill today is a model city. Its educational advantages compare favorably with those of any city of its size in the South. The sale of spirituous intoxicating liquors is prohibited, and today lawlessness and rowdyism are kept in bounds by a vigilant policeman, whose daily duties scarcely amount to more than looking after the streets and reading the *News and Courier.* A few years ago a very handsome and serviceable steam fire engine was purchased at a cost of $3,000, and since then has literally paid for itself. There is also a hook and ladder company here and a hand engine. The result is that Rock Hill has the same insurance rates afforded much larger places, and thus the merchants enjoy an exceptional advantage in the insurance line.

Another notable advantage that Rock Hill has is that the streets are in excellent condition. The sidewalks are curbed with dressed granite, while the pavement is made of the same material. The streets are macadamized, and the presence of mud or slush is very rare. Rock Hill has a municipal debt of about $12,000. A tax of about four mills is required to pay the interest on this debt and to meet the current expenses of city government.

The location and plan of the city of Rock Hill, its artificial advantages, and its natural commercial position are indeed very favorable. It is situated in the northeastern portion of the State and in the eastern part of York County near the Indian reservation. It is 84 miles distant from Columbia and within 25 miles of Charlotte. Yorkville, the county seat, is fifteen miles distant, and with all these points Rock Hill is connected by railroads. The *Yorkville Enquirer,* in a review published in October 1888, had these comments concerning the birth and growth of Rock Hill.

> The location was platted in 1853 by John Roddey, father of Capt. W.L. Roddey, who was then deputy surveyor for that section. The plat provided for only twenty-three lots, ranged on both sides of what was then the Charlotte and South Carolina Railroad. This plan, however, has long since become inadequate to the growth of the town, which, although still compact, leaves the railroad for a considerable distance on each side. Although no more extensive plan has since been agreed upon, much system has been preserved in the laying off of streets, and the town is building up in convenient shape.

The government of Rock Hill is all that could be desired. Its health and sanitary laws are strictly enforced, while the municipal regulations are carried out to the very letter. The members of the city council are: Capt. J.M. Cherry, mayor; R.T. Fewell, J.J. Hagin, A.D. Holler, and D.C. Williams, aldermen. All of these gentlemen are progressive and thrifty citizens who have the interests of the place at heart.

Rock Hill was incorporated as a town in February 1870 with corporate limits radiating one-half mile from what was then known as the Gordon Hotel. By an act of the last session of the Legislature the city was authorized to enlarge its limits, and this has been done. Now the total area is four square miles.

There are four churches and a factory chapel here, and another church is being built. The Presbyterian denomination predominates, while the Methodists come in for a good second. The Baptist congregation is also very strong, and the Episcopal flock has increased considerably in the recent past. The Rev. W.M. Anderson is pastor of the Presbyterian Church. It has a very large congregation, which has so greatly increased that another church is being erected. It will have for its pastor, rumor says, the Rev. J.S. White, who has a distinguished reputation as a preacher of eminent worth and ability. This church, Second Presbyterian Church, will be built in the suburbs. The Rev. R.A. Child, formerly of Pickens, is pastor of the Methodist Church. The Baptist Church has as pastor the Rev. J.Q. Adams, while the Rev. Mr. Bradley is rector of the Episcopal Church. The Episcopalians have built a chapel for the colored people and also have a mission school. The colored people also have good churches. They are all well contented and, of course, have very large congregations.

A short distance from Rock Hill, in that lovely little suburb of the city, Ebenezer, is the oldest church in upper South Carolina. Its name is Ebenezer Church, and it was founded before the Revolutionary War. In the graveyard adjoining the church are to be seen tombstones erected during the Revolution, and some are so very old that one cannot decipher the inscriptions contained thereon.

One of the most popular institutions in Rock Hill is the public library, which has been very appropriately named "The People's Pet." This institution of itself is an ornament to the town. The Library Association was founded in June 1884, and since that time has grown in influence and importance each year. There are now over 150 members who pay annual dues of two dollars each. Shortly after the organization of the Association the corner stone of the library building was laid. The cost of the building was about $3,000. The officers of the Library Association are as follows: President, the Rev. J.S. White; vice president, the Rev. J.Q. Adams; directors, J.J. Hull, J.R. London, W.J. Roddey, D. Hutchinson, and J.G. Andrews.

The ladies have a very great pride in the library, and each week donations are made to the supply of books and magazines of the institution. Donations are also made of a more substantial nature, and every now and then money is given to the library. It is the repository for public documents for the Fifth Congressional District, and valuable public papers are sent here almost every week. At the present time it has over 1,500 volumes of judiciously selected books. All the periodicals of any importance can be always found here, and every paper of any note is always on file here. The *News and Courier* can be found here at all times.

Perhaps the greatest improvement and advancement that has been made within the past three years is the establishment of a system of graded schools. Those who were able sent their children to school in other places, but then the change came. As the result of a popular movement a public meeting was held. At this meeting, which will go down into the history of this place as one of the most notable and most important ones ever held in the State, it was decided that over $7,000 was needed to build a school building and a residence for the principal. An appropriation was then made by the town authorities, and the Legislature passed a bill for the levy of a tax of two mills additional for the school district. The original amount of $7,000 was supplemented by an additional subscription of $1,500 by the citizens of the place, besides some money obtained from the sale of some old school property.

To the Rev. J.S. White was entrusted the entire sum of money and the erection of the buildings was left to his wisdom and care. That this was a very judicious act of the citizens is manifest and can be seen in the splendid school building and

Main Street, Rock Hill, c. 1890. *South Caroliniana Library.*

the home of the principal. The good judgment of Mr. White is to be seen on every hand. The school building was constructed at a cost of about $5,500, and the cost of the residence of the principal was about $2,000. The furniture of the school cost about $1,000. The first floor of the building is divided into seven apartments, which are all used as classrooms. The second story is given up entirely to a very large auditorium. In spite of the roominess of this building, it is expected that its capacity will have to be increased very soon on account of an overflow of pupils.

The course of study is varied and thorough. This is a model institution, and in it is taught every branch of study that is needful to prepare the student for the higher colleges and seminaries. The following is a list of the teachers: Prof. A.R. Banks, principal; J.L. Douglass, W.W. Lewis, Miss E.J. Roach, Miss Manassas Withers, Miss Mary Clarkson, and Miss Anna Rawlinson.

The school was opened September 3, 1888, with an enrolment of 125 pupils. There are now 325 pupils. The board of trustees are: the Rev. J.S. White, chairman; Capt. W.L. Roddey, W.B. Wilson, Jr., A.E. Smith, C.J. Sharp, W.S. Creighton, and Iredell Jones.

In the *Rock Hill Herald* this community has one of the best and brightest weekly newspapers to be found anywhere in the South. It was established in 1876 by Col. J.M. Ivy and has grown up to be a first-class Democratic newspaper. It is a newsy and well-edited journal and reflects credit on the city of Rock Hill. The editor is Col. J.J. Hull, one of the handsomest and most jovial editors in the State.

The soil of the country contiguous to Rock Hill is very rich and productive. All sorts of grains are raised here, while cotton and corn are both largely cultivated. This place has a very wide reputation as a cotton market, and the business that the cotton from other counties brings here annually adds a very considerable amount. Again, the railroad facilities here are very fine and afford every convenience to the shipper as well as to the producer. The annual sales of cotton at this place amount to about fifteen to sixteen thousand bales.

The standing of the merchants is high. They are all prosperous and are the very bone and sinew of this land. The amount of annual business being done in banking, manufacturing, general business, and cotton amounts to at least $1,500,000. A well-known merchant has an estimate, which I here make use of to show what a very large sum of money is invested here. At the present time there is invested in taxable property about $1,335,000, in general business $200,000, in banking concerns $215,000, in manufactures $400,000; amount of general business transacted about $950,000; amount of cotton and manufacturing business done yearly about $1,450,000.

The business houses are all built of brick; and, as in a majority of the towns in the interior, they face a main street. The Rock Hill store houses are in many instances superior to many to be found in the larger cities of the Atlantic slope. For instance, the Roddey Building is one of the handsomest that can be found anywhere in the South; it is, in fact, the largest building of its kind north of Columbia in the State. The average depth of the stores is about 125 feet and the width about 50 feet, and as a rule they are only two stories high.

Here is a list of the merchants of Rock Hill. W.L. Roddey & Co., a larger wholesale and retail trade than any other firm outside of Charleston, also cotton and millinery; A.E. Smith & Co., general merchants, Mr. Smith also is State agent of the Catawba Indians, whose reservation is about seven miles distant; A. Friedheim & Bro., one of the largest retail and wholesale businesses in this section of the State; Holler & Anderson, carriages, wagons, and buggies; Frew Brothers, general merchandise (the elder Mr. Frew is agent for the *News and Courier* at Rock Hill); Creighton, Sherfesce & Co., furniture, buggies, wagons, carriages, and vehicle repair; F.O. London & Co., groceries and confectioneries; Bryant & Avery, groceries, canned goods, cigars, tobacco, confectioneries, and fruit; J.J. Hagin & Co., drugs, paints, and oils; Hope & Codo, drugs (Dr. Hope, senior partner, is the oldest practicing physician in this section and was the first physician to settle in Rock Hill); Fewell & Kendall, drugs, paints, and oils; J.B. Johnson, drugs, oils, paints, cigars, tobaccos, and onion sets; S.T. Frew & Co., furniture, stoves, tinware, and coffins; Iredell Jones, machinery and agricultural implements; B.N. Craig, groceries, confectioneries, and apples; W.H. Roumillat & Co., drugs; D.P. & W.M. Steele (formerly J.R. Allen), general merchandise; Robertson Bros., the Racket Store; W.S. Faulk, B.B. Gordon & Co., and George Beach, jewelry and watchmaking; S.J. Kimball & Co., fancy and heavy groceries; T.P. Roddey, heavy and fancy groceries; M. Johnson, saddlery, harness, and whips; J.B. Kennedy, general merchandise; Mallard Bros., general produce; and W.B. McFadden, keeps city market, meats, and country produce.

W.P. Evans keeps a restaurant near the Charlotte, Columbia, and Augusta depot.

F.H. London, the efficient correspondent of the *News and Courier* at this place, deals in all sorts of general brokerage and is also the representative of a number of fire and insurance companies.

The sale of live stock, or rather mules and horses, has become one of the fixed industries of this place. There are four livery stables in the town owned by J. Edward Poag, John Ratteree, Heath & Kimball, and A. Friedheim & Co. The livery stable of J. Edward Poag is by far the handsomest in the upper section of South Carolina. The other stables are well appointed and do a very good business even in the dull season.

One of the most important firms in Rock Hill and one that will in the very near future bring new honors to her gate is that of Roddey & Whitner, civil engineers and contractors. They do all sorts of engineering and contract work such as the construction of water-works, railroads, and canals. At present this firm is erecting the water-works at Anderson. This young firm built a large portion of the Three C's Road, and Mr. Whitner built the bridge over the Catawba River, where the road crosses it.

Jenkins and Gelzer will open up a first-class hardware store here in August. This firm is composed of young men from Charleston, who are live and progressive and deserve the encouragement and support of the people of this place.

The industry of raising blooded stock has been begun here by Col. John C. Witherspoon. He has a very fine set of horses and intends enlarging his facilities for raising blooded animals. Speaking of the raising of blooded horses, Col. Witherspoon says, "It is just as cheap to raise a finely blooded horse as a common plug."

There are two of the best banking institutions in the State here. Both are well established and operated with the greatest care. The older of the two is the First National Bank, which was chartered in 1887. Not a cent, so the writer was informed, has been lost by this bank since its doors were first opened. It has a capital stock of $50,000 and total resources of about $140,000. The officers are: Capt. W.L. Roddey, president; W.J. Roddey, vice president; J.H. Miller, cashier; R. Lee Kerr, teller; directors, Capt. W.L. Roddey, John R. London, W.J. Roddey, J.E. Roddey, W.M. Frew, J.H. Miller, and A.F. Ruff.

The other bank is the Savings Bank of Rock Hill, which has grown out of the Young Men's Loan and Trust Company, founded in 1882. This institution began with 228 shares, representing $100 each, to be paid on the instalment plan at one dollar per share per month. Launching operations with $228, the company met with such success as to encourage its conversion into a savings bank in December 1886.

The building used by the bank is a fine, two-story brick structure with a beautiful iron and plate glass front, while the inside is elegantly fitted up with expensive and convenient bank furniture. Inside of a spacious fireproof vault is what is guaranteed to be an absolutely burglar-proof safe constructed with alternate layers of iron and case-hardened steel. The manufacturers claim that the introduction of powder is impossible and that the steel is as hard as any cutting instrument that could be applied.

The bank now has total resources of about $110,000. The officers are: David Hutchinson, president; John R. London, vice president; J.M. Cherry, cashier; directors, D. Hutchinson, J.R. London, R.T. Fewell, N.P. Alexander, T.L. Johnson, T.A. Crawford, and W.C. Hutchinson.

Another very prosperous institution is the Southern Loan and Investment Company, organized in 1888. The purpose of this company, capitalized at $75,000, is the investment of money in real estate and the general improvement of the city. The officers are: Capt. W.L. Roddey, president; W.J. Roddey, manager and treasurer; directors, W.L. Roddey, W.J. Roddey, S.L. Reid, J.E. Roddey, J.H. Miller, and J.R. Reid.

There is still another financial institution in Rock Hill, the Rock Hill Real Estate and Loan Company. It has a capital stock of $200,000, of which a greater portion has been paid in. The officers are as follows: David Hutchinson, president; N.P. Alexander, vice president; J.M. Cherry, secretary and treasurer; directors, the Rev. J.Q. Adams, David Hutchinson, R.T. Fewell, J.R. London, N.P. Alexander, T.L. Johnson, J.M. Cherry, and W.J. Rawlinson.

There are also several building and loan associations here, all of which are said to be in a fine condition.

Rock Hill's board of trade would reflect a great deal of credit upon a much more prestigious city. It was organized some time ago and has always been alive to the best interests of the place and will always strive to build up the city in any way that is offered. The officers are: W.J. Roddey, president; R.T. Fewell, vice president; W.J. Cherry, secretary and treasurer. These are all young men, sterling business men, and upon them rests the responsibility of building up the place still more.

It is a curious fact that the real estate here has never been on a boom, but it has always commanded a very good price. At this time real estate is comparatively high, and in spite of this there is a ready demand for all good building lots. The average price of a lot in the suburbs is $165.

About 1880, Capt. W.L. Roddey, the late Capt. J.M. Ivy, Capt. A.F. Hutchinson, and a few other enterprising citizens began a movement to build a cotton mill. In a very short time a company was organized with a capital of $120,000, and in 1881 the Rock Hill Cotton Factory began operation. It has been one of the best paying investments in the South. Its machinery is run by steam power, and it is worthy of note that this factory was the fourth in South Carolina to be run by steam. The stock of this company cannot be purchased and has never been on the market.

The factory, situated a few rods from the Charlotte, Columbia, and Augusta Railroad and about the same distance from the Three C's Railroad, has about 8,000 spindles and annually consumes 3,000 bales of cotton. Its annual output is 900,000 pounds of yarn. The officers of the company are: A.E. Hutchinson, president; D. Hutchinson, secretary and treasurer; directors, A.E. Hutchinson, W.L. Roddey, J.S. White, J.R. London, A.H. White, John Gill of Baltimore, and F.J. Pelzer of Charleston. The factory operatives are comfortably quartered in neat cottages around the factory. They have never given any trouble and represent the best class of that kind of labor. Mr. J.R. Nessler is the efficient superintendent of the factory.

A short while after this factory began operation another factory was started. Its father was W.J. Roddey, a remarkably progressive and thorough business man and the son of Capt. W.L. Roddey. It was his genius that originated the idea of erecting a factory on the instalment plan, a scheme which ought to be copied by other towns in the State which want to build a cotton factory and have not the capital. The plan Mr. Roddey conceived was a weekly assessment of fifty cents per share. Any subscriber who paid in full and in advance received 7 per cent interest. In a very short time building of the factory commenced. The purpose of this establishment, the Standard Cotton Mill, is the manufacture of yarn into fine ginghams and calicoes. The quality of the goods is very fine, and several young ladies of this city now are wearing dresses made from goods produced at this mill. There are now 225 looms of the celebrated Crampton manufacture in operation. The daily output is about 12,000 yards, and the mill is making money very rapidly. The officers are: John R. London, president; W.M. Frew, secretary and treasurer; directors, W.J. Roddey, A.E. Smith, A. Friedheim, W.M. Frew, R.T. Fewell, J.R. London, W.J. Rawlinson, and T.A. Crawford.

Not satisfied, the people of Rock Hill soon organized a third cotton factory. A charter was obtained for the Globe Cotton Mill and the capital stock of $100,000 speedily subscribed. The officers are: John R. London, president and general manager; W.L. Roddey, secretary and treasurer; directors, John R. London, A.F. Ruff, W.L. Roddey, W.E. Trainer, A.E. Smith, A. Friedheim, and J.M. Trainer. The building, 335 feet long and 85 feet wide, is situated within easy access of both railroads. Ten thousand spindles will be operated and the annual output of the mill will be about one million pounds of yarn.

It is through the excellent advertising facilities of the *News and Courier* that this mill was built. It will be remembered that some months ago an advertisement appeared in this paper offering to put in a complete mechanical outfit for a first-class cotton mill and so much capital stock, provided that a commensurate amount of capital stock was subscribed by any town in the South. The advertisement created considerable activity in a great many manufacturing centres, and a number of bids were made for this excellent offer. Rock Hill, with its indomitable pluck and superb enterprise, sent to the Messrs. Trainer the best offer. The result was the cotton factory that has been built here, and the people of Rock Hill are accordingly grateful to the *News and Courier* for its share in securing this valuable acquisition to the manufacturing interests of the State. No factory has a better prospect of success than the Globe Cotton Mill.

Another prominent enterprise is the Rock Hill Cotton Seed Oil and Fertilizer Company, which was organized in one hour by Capt. W.L. Roddey over a year ago. The capital stock of this enterprise is $35,000. It is expected that twenty-five tons of seed will be consumed daily, and of course the output will be considerable. The officers are: A.F. Ruff, president; W.L. Roddey, vice president; directors, W.L. Roddey, A.F. Ruff, A.H. White, W.J. Rawlinson, and R.T. Fewell.

Perhaps the best paying investment in the smaller industries is found in the Rock Hill Construction Company, which began business last year with a capital stock of $15,000. The purpose of the company is to manufacture doors, sashes, and blinds, construct residences, build all sorts of houses, and deal generally in lumber. The officers of the company are as follows: W.M. Frew, president; W.H. Stuart, manager; directors, W.L. Roddey, J.B. Johnson, A. Friedheim, R.T. Fewell, W.M. Frew, D. Hutchinson, and W.J. Reid.

Another splendid industry here is the Davis Canning and Candy Company, which commenced business last year with a capital stock of $5,000. The purpose of the company is the canning of vegetables and fruits and the wholesale manufacture of candy. The annual output of 40,000 cans will be increased gradually. The company plans to cultivate fruit on a large and extensive scale, and when this is done the outlook will be very materially augmented. The officers are: A.H. White, president; L.M. Davis, manager; J.M. Cherry, secretary and treasurer; directors, J.M. Cherry, R.T. Fewell, A.H. White, L.M. Davis, W.C. Hutchinson, E.B. Mobley, and D. Hutchinson.

The Rock Hill Machine Works, owned by Creighton, Sherfesce & Co., is a first-class operation. Some 130 employees do all sorts of iron and wood working and manufacture wagons, buggies, and carriages. There is also a repair department. Four forges are constantly employed. Nearly all of the timber used in the manufacture of buggies at this place is found in this county.

Another like establishment is that of Holler & Anderson, who manufacture buggies, wagons, and harness on a large scale. They also manufacture axe handles, shuttle blocks, and similar articles used in the manufacture of buggies. The business of manufacturing brick and tile is also carried on here with success.

A soap factory is being talked of, and it is very likely that it will be established. Mr. John T. Roddey is the prime mover in this enterprise. It will doubtless be as successful as any other small enterprise in this city.

The general agency for the famous Equitable Life Insurance Association of New York for the States of North and South Carolina is placed here. Its agent is Mr. W.J. Roddey, vice president of the First National Bank and a stockholder in nearly every other enterprise in Rock Hill. Mr. Roddey employs a very large number of agents for both States, and nearly all of his time is taken up dictating to his corps of stenographers. His office has been nicely fitted up in the Roddey Building adjoining the bank, and it is one of the neatest and best appointed offices that can be found outside of New York. It consists of three separate apartments finished in native woods and varnished oak. All the furniture, including the desks and other paraphernalia, is of the lastest designs, while the carpets and rugs are of the most costly character. Besides representing the Equitable Company, Mr. Roddey is the agent for about forty other insurance companies.

The other insurance agents here are Fred H. London, J.M. Cherry, David Hutchinson, and M.P. Alexander, all of whom do a very good business.

The old military spirit still prevails here, and Rock Hill has one of the best military companies in the State. The Catawba Rifles was organized in 1887, and the esprit de corps is excellent. The officers are: Captain A.E. Smith, First Lieutenant J.F. Reid, and Second Lieutenant R.T. Fewell. The company has been uniformed in the State regulation uniform, and wherever they have appeared they have always created a splendid impression.

The health of the place is so good that the physicians who live here find a greater part of their practice in the country and have very few patients in the city. The physicians are: R.H. Hope, who has been here since the place was founded, T.A. Crawford, J.M. Hunter, T.L. Cornwell, and J.W. Fewell. There are four good dentists: Isaiah Simpson, J.B. Patrick, J.A. Glenn, and W.A. Black.

The lawyers have done their share in building up this section, and one of their number, Col. W.B. Wilson, Jr., has been the man who has developed the mineral resources of the county more than anyone else, at least who lives here. The lawyers here are: John C. Witherspoon, J.C. Wilborn, Wilson & McDow, Hart & Cherry, and Spencer & Waters.

There are two hotels. The Carolina Hotel, of which Mr. Howell Cobb is the proprietor, is a first-class one in every respect and is run on a very strict business plan. The other is the Central Hotel, which is an old landmark. Its proprietor is Mr. David Gordon, who has kept the hotel here since the war. The Carolina Hotel is in the Roddey Building and has every convenience that can be found in a well-regulated hotel.

There are four cotton buyers here and they are all live, energetic men. Their names are: T.L. Johnson, who buys for W.L. Roddey & Co.; Edward Fewell, who buys for R.T. Fewell & Co.; E.H. Byers, who represents Carroll & Stacey of Gaffney City; and E. Biggers, who represents Heath, Fairly & Heath of Charlotte.

A sketch of Rock Hill would be incomplete without even a meagre mention of the handsome residences. As a rule they are all commodious and well arranged, while the general architectural style is of the latest pattern. They are not confined to any particular street, but are scattered throughout the various parts of the place. Notable among the handsome and striking residences here are those of the following gentlemen: John T. Roddey, Col. John C. Witherspoon, Capt. W.L. Roddey, Rev. J.S. White, Ben Fewell, E.B. Mobley, A.F. Ruff, A. Friedheim, W.G. Reid, David Hutchinson, W.J. Rawlinson, J.H. Neely, Dr. Patrick, and a very great many others.

But the most striking structure in Rock Hill is the celebrated Roddey Building. This structure was erected in 1888 and is, perhaps, the largest building of its kind outside of Charleston. The part occupied by the store alone is 123 feet wide and 150 feet deep. This includes, of course, the room allowed for the First National Bank. The building is three stories high and well constructed of the best quality brick. Recently an addition was made to the store, and in part of this is situated the insurance office of W.J. Roddey. The building also includes the Carolina Hotel, which alone claims a very great portion of the building, using over forty rooms. The building was constructed by Capt. W.L. Roddey, who owns the entire property, at a cost of nearly $20,000.

The railroad facilities of Rock Hill are excellent. The Charlotte, Columbia, and Augusta Railroad and the Charleston, Cincinnati, and Chicago Railroad both run through this place and afford every facility for the shipment of goods as well as the transportation of the travelling public. Mr. E.B. Rock is the agent for the Charlotte, Columbia, and Augusta Railroad. Mr. Emil Worth is the genial and efficient agent of the Three C's. These two lines are in a measure strong competitors, and in this way the place is afforded a great many facilities and good freight rates that other places have not. Both roads are attentive to the wants of the people.

The two suburban hamlets of Rock Hill are Ebenezer—one of the oldest settlements in this section of the country—and Johnstown, which is of more recent growth and which was named in honor of Mr. John T. Roddey. The former place is built up of old-fashioned, hospitable homes, and at one time there was a considerable amount of business done here. In the building of Rock Hill, Ebenezer has lost its former prestige as a business centre for the surrounding country. Johnstown is a small and conspicuous hamlet one mile from the business centre of Rock Hill. It consists of a few well-built houses, and the entire town is the property of Mr. J.T. Roddey. Both of these hamlets are in easy access of the city. The drive to Ebenezer and to the old church nearby, for which the place is named, is such a delightful one that it is very popular for health-seekers, as well as seekers after summer romances.

News and Courier, June 7, 1890. E.P. McKissick.

Saint Matthews Wants a Court House

Echoing a cry heard throughout American history, in the 1890s, Saint Matthews—then spelled "St. Matthew's"—mounted a campaign to become the capital of a proposed new entity, Calhoun County. An anonymous portrait of this would-be county seat describes not only the commercial and social life of Saint Matthews (population 524, according to the 1890 census), but also tells us about two subdivisions that were taking shape. This land, we are informed, was "as good as gold and a safe investment, even at advanced prices."

* * *

Within the past four or five years a great deal of attention has been directed to the thriving and prosperous town of St. Matthew's, and just at this time the place is growing with remarkable rapidity. The situation of St. Matthew's is almost perfect, and while it retains to some extent the "taint and travail of antiquity," it has all the earmarks of progressive ideas and achievement.

St. Matthew's was incorporated about 1870, when the location was selected on account of its being in the centre of a fertile belt. Good schools were instituted in St. Matthew's about the same time. The place grew slowly, and notwithstanding the fact that the South Carolina Railway passes through the place, it was only a very small country village until about eight or ten years ago. A greater portion of the trade that belonged legitimately to St. Matthew's was, and is now to some extent, given to Orangeburg, the county seat; but that trade will all come to St. Matthew's as soon as we secure the proposed new county of Calhoun. There is a movement on foot now to form a joint stock company and erect a $2,500 school building at this place, and it will undoubtedly be a success. The building will be ready to be occupied by September. St. Matthew's is not a very large place now, but it has a healthy climate and a homogeneous, thrifty, pushing population.

It has long been conceded that Orangeburg County is one among the best agricultural sections in the State, that its fertile hills, plains, and valleys respond to the touch of the farmer as nicely as in any part of the State. St. Matthew's is situated in the centre of the richest section of Orangeburg County, and has, therefore, all the agricultural advantages that could be desired. Cotton and corn are the staple products, while rice, oats, rye, and all other cereals are produced around very largely. Hay and all sorts of forage grow in this section in profusion, while fruits of all kinds are thrown in for good measure. The climatic conditions of this section are especially conducive to the production of fine crops and moreover to the good health of the masses. In the matter of healthfulness the people of St.

Matthew's have exceptional advantages. The water is very good here and the natural drainage of the town and surrounding country is unexcelled. There is scarcely any serious sickness and epidemics of any kind are not known in this section. In short, the health of St. Matthew's is one of its strong points. The atmosphere, generally speaking, is crisp, dry, and invigorating. To the seeker after health, to those who desire farming lands, to those who seek a first-class commercial centre, to those whose desire is to establish industries of any sort, St. Matthew's offers advantages seldom found.

There is little to be said about the railroad advantages as we have a poor and uncomfortable depot, but it is not the fault of the people of St. Matthew's, for they have struggled and striven to get the railroad company to erect a new and commodious depot here, but the railroad officials thus far have refused to give in. The business done by the railroad at this place is very large, well warranting a new and elegant depot. It would not only be a great advantage to the business people of this place, but it would add to the convenience and comfort of this whole country and would tend to increase the railroad's business.

St. Matthew's will be in the future a large manufacturing centre. Already, since the new county movement has been started, a large cotton factory is being prominently spoken of by our thriving business men, and it is generally known that a canning factory will be started here this winter. The St. Matthew's Manufacturing and Ware House Company has been pronounced by prominent mechanics to be one of the best in the State. It is built of brick, admirably constructed, and very conveniently situated, right opposite the depot. During the cotton season it is kept busy all the time, and its output of crude cotton and oil meal and fertilizers is sold as fast as manufactured. F.J. Buyck is president, and C.F. Zeigler superintendent. The largest portion of the stock of the company is owned in St. Matthew's. It earned last season over 10 per cent on its capital stock of $25,000. The directors have declared a dividend of 5 per cent. The oldest grist mill and ginnery of this place is owned and conducted by Col. A.P. Amaker. This mill has been in successful operation for more than fifteen years, and it still receives a liberal patronage.

There are four or five saw mills in and near St. Matthew's. The first belongs to Mr. C.F. Zeigler, and is situated in the western part of the town. He also has a planing machine connected with his saw mill. All kinds of lumber are planed by this machine and shipped to various points in this State. The other mills are near the town, and are owned by J.A. Banks, J.E. Wannamaker, Jessie Zeigler, and I.H. Zimmerman, who have a full share of the lumber business here.

St. Matthew's now has three machine shops, which do a very large business, and the outlook for a steady increase in this direction is very bright.

It is generally known that St. Matthew's does more [cotton] business than any other town in South Carolina of the same size. In 1875 the cotton receipts amounted to about 3,000 bales. Fifteen years later, during the past year, the cotton receipts from this place amounted to about 15,000 bales. In the last decade the volume of trade in St. Matthew's has grown from $100,000 to $800,000. These are facts and figures that cannot be controverted.

It will be proper here to show in succession what has been done by the business men of St. Matthew's in the establishment of various enterprises. First comes the St. Matthew's Savings Bank, which was established in August, 1889, and has up to this time done a prosperous business. The officers of the bank are: P. Rich, Sr., president; J.E. Wannamaker, vice president; J.W. Zimmerman, cashier; W.F. Spigener, assistant cashier; and the following directors: W.T.C. Bates, F.J. Buyck, J.H. Loryea, W.P. Cain, and J.A. Banks. The bank has never lost a cent and has been up to this time a paying investment.

Another institution that is having a great deal to do with building up St. Matthew's and its trade is the St. Matthew's Building and Loan Association, which was established in December, 1889. The officers of the association are: J.H. Loryea, president; Dr. W.L. Pou, vice president; J.W. Zimmerman, secretary and treasurer; Philip Rich, Sr., W.T.C. Bates, E. Wimberly, W.L. Pou, L.M. Whaley, and C.F. Zeigler, directors; M.O. Dantzler, solicitor. The association is in a very prosperous condition. The money is sold at a good premium.

The largest mercantile establishment in St. Matthew's is that of F.J. Buyck & Co's, in the centre of the business part of the town. It is built of brick and is two stories high. The store is handsomely fitted up in every way and will compare with any store of the same size between Charleston and Columbia. The firm is composed of excellent business men and does a very large cash and credit business.

The firm of Banks & Wimberly, retail dealers in groceries, plantation supplies, hardware, dry goods, and notions, do a large business. The firm is composed of J.A. Banks and E. Wimberly, both of whom are excellent business men and thorough gentlemen. The firm does a very large cotton business. The store is situated in the centre of the town and in the business part. It is nicely fitted up inside and is an ornament to St. Matthew's.

One of the best arranged stores here is that of Philip Rich, Sr., whose sterling worth and integrity, with his enterprise as a merchant, make him one of the notable men of St. Matthew's. He keeps a general line of merchandise, including dry goods, clothing, shoes, millinery, notions, glassware, tinware, furniture and, in fact, everything else found in a well regulated mercantile establishment.

J.H. Loryea does a very large business in all lines of merchandise. He occupies a store on the corner of Bridge Street and East Railroad Avenue, and in this everything that can be desired at home, on farm, on railroad, or anywhere else may be purchased. Mr. Loryea stands very high financially and is president of the St. Matthew's Building and Loan Association.

Dr. H.N. Fair is the leading druggist here, and he does a large and lucrative business. Dr. Fair is a prosperous, progressive business man, fully alive to the demands of this progressive age. His establishment is one of the most attractive here, and in it can be found everything that a first-class drug establishment keeps.

In connection with his drug store he keeps a full line of choice fancy groceries. During the summer months Dr. Fair makes a specialty of ice cold soda water and milk shakes, of which he sells an abundance. He also keeps a nice line of school books. In room No. 3 in Dr. Fair's store will be found the office of Drs. W.L. Pou and L.B. Bates. They are two prominent physicians of this place.

M. Jarecky, who is one of the enterprising merchants here, does a large and extensive trade in groceries, plantation supplies, dry goods, hardware, furniture, shoes, hats, and caps. His store occupies a space twenty feet long and twenty-five feet wide.

J. Lewishon deals in groceries, fruits, dry goods, hats, and notions. He recently moved here from Germany, but still he has his share of trade, and it is increasing.

W.P. Cain & Co., an old established firm, are dealers in all kinds of merchandise, such as groceries, dry goods, clothing, shoes, hats, caps, notions, hardware, and furniture. This store occupies a space about ninety feet long, thirty feet wide, and two stories. The store is an ornament to St. Matthew's. Mr. Cain is owner of one of St. Matthew's handsome hotels, which is situated in the northwestern portion of the town.

L. Jarecky keeps a general merchandise store and does a very nice business.

B. Jacobson & Son, another enterprising and progressive firm, do a thriving and extensive business. They keep on hand an elegant stock of clothing, dry goods, millinery, shoes, hardware, furniture, groceries, and liquors of all kind.

Cleckley & Robinson, colored, one of our new firms, do a large business. The firm is composed of C.D. Cleckley and George Robinson.

Smith & Co. have just established themselves here in the liquor business.

The firm of Herlong & Co., retail dealers in groceries, plantation supplies, hardware, dry goods, shoes and hats, do a large business. The company is composed of D.W. Herlong, D.D. Herlong, and J.W. Buyck, all of whom are excellent business men.

Mr. J.W. Buyck is the proprietor of Buyck's Hotel. The hotel is situated on the eastern end of Bridge Street. It is a commodious building with large rooms.

J.W.B. Chaplin, another enterprising and progressive business man, does a thriving and increasing business. He keeps the largest saloon in the place. He also keeps on hand a stock of clothing, dry goods, shoes, hardware, and groceries.

T.L. Buyck & Co., another newly established firm, are dealers in all kinds of merchandise. Their establishment is in the centre of the business section of the town and is well stocked.

S. Elosser deals in general merchandise, fruits, and vegetables, and he always keeps fresh bakers' bread on hand.

S.M. Weatherhorn deals altogether in liquors and cigars.

Lewis Herlong is another saloon-keeper. He also sells ice.

Autley & Prickett are dealers in groceries, dry goods, millinery, and plantation

Drugstore in St. Matthews, c. 1900. *South Caroliniana Library.*

supplies. The firm is composed of J.D. Autley and F.M. Prickett. Mr. Prickett is the postmaster here.

Next is the establishment of Drs. Able & Able, physicians and druggists. The men who compose this firm are Drs. A.R. and L.M. Able. They are both progressive men, who take an interest in everything that pertains to the welfare of St. Matthew's and Calhoun County.

L.B. Rast deals in general merchandise and has a well established business.

St. Matthew's can also boast of as fine livery and sales stables as any town in the State outside of Charleston and Columbia. These stables are owned and conducted by Geo. W. Arthur. The principal business firms have been given above, but there are a few others which claim their share of trade. Here are their names and business: G.V. Patrick, groceries and beef market; D.F. Joyner, general merchandise; and W.L. Buyck, beef market.

There is really very little need of any physicians here, but all healthy places are generally supplied with them. St. Matthew's has its share of good physicians, and their names are as follows: W.L. Pou, L.B. Bates, A.R. Able, and L.M. Able. Dr. W.H. Ott is the only dentist here and he has his office neatly fitted up.

There are also two lawyers here who do a very large business. Their names are: M.O. Dantzler and J.B. McLauchlin.

There are a few gentlemen here who are agents. Here is a list of their names: J.H. Loryea, life and fire insurance; Wheeler & Wilson, sewing machines; J.W. Zimmerman, life insurance; Buyck & Co., fertilizers; and Banks & Wimberly, fertilizers.

St. Matthew's is sufficiently supplied with churches, and her people, generally speaking, are church-going citizens. There are two white churches here, the Baptist and Methodist. The Rev. D.H. Crosland is pastor of the Baptist Church, and the Rev. W.P. Meadors is pastor of the Methodist Church. The Young Men's Christian Association here is in a flourishing condition. Its officers are: J.W. Zimmerman, president; John McLauchlin, vice president; J.R. Paulling, secretary; and P.P. Patrick, treasurer.

Another progressive enterprise is that of the *St. Matthew's Herald,* edited by G.J. Brown. The *Herald* has a large circulation and is becoming very popular in this section.

Recently the citizens of St. Matthew's assembled in a mass meeting to decide the matter of having a graded school here. It was voted down. Immediately after this meeting several of the citizens decided to form a joint stock company and to build a handsome school house and employ teachers to manage it. All the stock has been subscribed and the building will soon begin. At present there is a well-regulated academy here under the management of the Rev. D.H. Crosland, who has as his assistant, Miss Minnie Wroe. The high school of this place is a well-regulated institution and is under the management of Prof. W.S. Murray. Miss Lillie Malone also has a small school.

It will be seen from the foregoing sketch of the industries, manufactures, and other causes of the remarkable growth of St. Matthew's that there is every reason to predict that the town is just now commencing its era of prosperity. No one who has visited St. Matthew's in the past few years will deny that the place is built on a sound, substantial basis. It is not surprising, therefore, that real estate is increasing in value very fast. The people here are holding on to their land, but still there is always some for sale. It is as good as gold and is a safe investment, even at advanced prices. There are two tracts of land that have been divided into convenient lots, one in the southeastern portion of the town, owned by T.A. Amaker, who has it subdivided into handsome lots of seventy feet front and one hundred and fifty feet deep. The streets that divide these lots are all seventy feet wide. Several of these lots have been sold, but still there are several desirable ones on the market. Handsome buildings are now being erected on some of them. The other tract is on the western side of town, and is under the management of W.H. Pennon. He has it divided into handsome building lots. His streets have been laid off with three rows of trees, which are very attractive.

News and Courier, June 22, 1891.

Spartanburg, Hub of the Piedmont

For reasons unknown, the *News and Courier* largely ignored the growth of Spartanburg until mid-1890. Then, in a staggering avalanche of verbose prose, statistics, and illustrations encompassing nearly seven pages (41 columns, compared to an average of two or three columns for other towns and cities), Spartanburg received coverage such as never was lavished even upon Charleston itself during these years. The result, the labor of Edward P. McKissick, is a compendium unequaled among these community portraits. It appears here in much reduced form, of course, and anyone interested in the history of Spartanburg and Spartanburg County in the late nineteenth century should seek out the original, which abounds with biographical data and historical tidbits found nowhere else.*

* * *

Like all inland towns, Spartanburg grew very slowly. Its trade was local, and no manufactures startled the inhabitants with the buzzing of machinery. A few stores, blacksmiths' shops, bar rooms (called groceries in those days), the town hotel, and a doctor's shop made up the business part of the town. According to Robert Mills, in 1825 there were twenty-six houses, including three law offices, one saddler's, one tailor's, and three blacksmiths' shops. The growth was gradual for many years. It was not more attractive as a place of trade than the crossroads stores, for all merchants then bought in the same markets and had to haul their goods in wagons.

When people began to look at Spartanburg as an educational centre it increased in importance. The village academies were ably managed, and then about 1850 the Rev. Benjamin Wofford, a native of Spartanburg and a Methodist preacher, left $100,000 for the erection of a college. This was completed and the first classes began work in 1854. The location of the college here gave property an upward tendency; people bought on speculation and also to build in order that they might educate their children. About the same time the old wooden stores began to yield to brick and mortar and Spartanburg's prosperity was assured.

At the close of the war Spartanburg began to look up as a commercial centre. It soon became one of the best cotton markets in the country. The merchants were noted for their enterprise. So great was the increase in business that by 1878 it was difficult to rent a store or a dwelling-house, and stores, especially the smaller ones, rented for about one-third of their cost. These high rates generated a build-

*This may have been the culmination of McKissick's series of articles on towns and cities. According to the *News and Courier* (February 17, 1895), McKissick was born near Glenn Springs in 1867, educated at South Carolina College, and edited a Union newspaper before joining the *News and Courier* for eight years. However, by 1895 he had abandoned journalism and was managing Asheville's famed Battery Park Hotel.

ing spirit, and between 1878 and 1882 about twenty-nine large store houses were erected. The streets were macadamized and, while irregular, are very attractive, not only for riding but for walking. Within the past decade Spartanburg has increased in wealth, business, manufactures, educational facilities, and in fact in every way in a marvelous manner. Today it is a growing city, and, as will be shown hereafter, has a particularly bright future.

The climate of this section, and especially of this city, has a reputation which reaches all over this broad land. The city is on a ridge at an elevation of about eight hundred feet above the level of the sea. The drainage is all natural and is of the best character. There is an abundant supply of mineral water in the immediate vicinity, the most notable water being that of the famous Glenn Springs, which is always kept on draught here.

Spartanburg was incorporated as a city in 1880. The members of the current city council are: J.A. Henneman, mayor; aldermen, Capt. J.H. Montgomery, W.B. Hallett, M. Carlson, C.P. Sanders, J.F. Floyd, and Thomas Bomar. The last named man is one of the representative colored men of this place and is highly respected by those who know him. The clerk and treasurer is Major Joseph M. Elford. The income of the city last year was $18,900, which includes $7,250 from real and personal property valued at an estimated $1,500,000 and assessed at 5 mills and $8,000 from the retail liquor licenses of eight saloons.

The fire department is one of the best in the South and perhaps one of the most unique. The height of the standpipe is such that a hose attached to any hydrant will throw water with sufficient force to enable the city to dispense with its steam fire engine. The chief of the department is Mr. M. Greenewald, and the assistant chief is Capt. R.E. Brewton. Under them are four white companies, two colored companies, and one colored hook and ladder company.

The chief of the police department is John H. Hill. His assistants are Thomas Caldwell, E.D. Gentry, John Miller, and Jess Crook. There are also two colored policemen who do duty as night watchmen and perform other duties assigned to them.

The Board of Trade was organized on September 15, 1885. Since that time it has been instrumental in securing the completion of the Spartanburg and Asheville Railroad, the construction of a commodious passenger depot, the connection of the Georgia Central Air Line tracks, and the organization of a cotton mill within the city limits. The present officers are: Charles H. Carlisle, president; S.T. McCravy, vice president; and Edwin Kerrison, secretary and treasurer. The members of the executive committee are: Chairman J.B. Liles, W.E. Burnett, T.H. Cannon, W.E. Lucas, and J.H. Sloan. The Board of Trade holds monthly meetings in its handsomely furnished hall on the second floor of the Kennedy Library building. There are now ninety-one active members.

The Bar of Spartanburg is one of the ablest in the State and its reputation is well known. In the Supreme Court of the United States the lawyers of this place who have appeared there have always held their own and created a good impression. There is rarely any bitterness among the lawyers here, and everyone seems to be in good fellowship with the others. The firms are as follows: Carlisle & Hydrick, Bomar & Simpson, Nicholls & Moore, Duncan & Sanders, and the following who practice alone: S.T. McCravy, David Johnson, Jr., H. Edmund Ravenel, T.B. Thackston, Ralph K. Carson, H.B. Carlisle, Arch B. Calvert, Stayarne Wilson, J.K. Jennings, J.J. Burnett, J.M. Elford, H.L. Farley, G.H. Hinnant, W.S. Thompson, Edwin Kerrison, and Charles P. Barrett.

The high sheriff of the county is John M. Nicholls, who as a boy served with distinguished gallantry and on one occasion gave wounded and dying soldiers water while standing between the fire of his own men and that of the enemy. His deputies are Capt. R.E. Brewton, an old Confederate soldier, and J.E. Vernon, who is a very capable officer. The other county officials are: Capt. T.R. Trimmier, clerk of court; John Sevier (great-grandson of Captain Sevier who was killed at King's Mountain), deputy clerk of court; W.S. Thomason, probate judge; G.W. Bomar, assistant probate judge; Col. H.D. Floyd, treasurer; B.B. Chapman, school commissioner; Capt. Edmund Bacon, auditor; Howard B. Carlisle, master; T.B. Thackston and G.H. Hinnant, trial justices for the city; J.M. James, coroner; and C.A. Barry, A.J. Caldwell, and J.L. Howell, county commissioners. The Senator from the county is Dr. Robert M. Smith. The Representatives are Dr. S.T.D. Lancaster, W.G. Austen, Judge W.G. Britton, and H.H. Arnold.

The Opera House, which is owned by the city, is one of the best and most conveniently arranged in the State. It has a seating capacity of seven hundred and a stage and set of dressing rooms fully large enough to accommodate any company that travels in the Southern States. The Opera House, situated in the central portion of the City Hall, is leased by J.B. Liles.

The Merchants' Hotel, erected in 1880, has no superior in this section of the State. Since 1888 it has been under the excellent management of C.C. Chase, who is well known among the travelling public and universally popular. The Merchants' Hotel has about seventy-five sleeping rooms, all of which are admirably furnished and lighted with gas. Electric bells and in fact every convenience is afforded here. Its cuisine is all that could be desired.

The Central Hotel has been reopened by P.N. Crouch, an old hotel man, who recently kept the Newberry Hotel. It is opposite the Merchants' Hotel and is eligibly situated. There are several other smaller hotels, the best of which is the Arlington, kept by J.L. Tinsley. It is near the Opera House and has a good reputation.

In 1870 the census of this place was only 1,080. It is now estimated at about 7,000. It had increased to 3,300 by the census of 1880, and since then it has multiplied in a marvelous manner. So upon this calculation it will be seen that the population of Spartanburg has increased over 600 per cent within the last twenty years.

To a great extent this growth has resulted from the development of railroads which have made Spartanburg the hub of the Piedmont. Spartanburg has shown

Public square, Spartanburg, c. 1890. *South Caroliniana Library.*

her faith in railroads by assuming a heavy load of bonded indebtedness in order to secure these highways of commerce. The Atlanta and Charlotte Air Line is the great freight-carrying way of this region. The Spartanburg and Columbia branch of the Richmond and Danville system has recently made noticeable improvements in its road beds, train service, and rolling stock. Better time is made, and the road is upon a decidedly more profitable basis. And, by the way, the Asheville and Spartanburg is now doing a marvelous freight business. The branch of the Port Royal and Western Carolina that joins us with Augusta is the last road built to Spartanburg. Its business is steadily growing. Lately it has proved a favorite route alike for summer tourists to the Land of the Sky [the North Carolina mountains] and winter tourists toward the Land of Flowers [Florida]. There is much good feeling between Spartanburg and the railroad men. She is their staunch friend and always will be.

There is no county in any of the Southern States which has as many manufacturing enterprises as Spartanburg. It is the manufacturing centre of the State and will, in a few years, be the most important in this line in the South. There are already sixteen cotton factories in the county, representing a total of 200,000 spindles.

Glendale might well be called the "Mother of Mills." It was one of the first cotton mills in this section of the State before the war and was then known as "Bivingsville." After the war it struggled along quietly when suddenly its proprietors commenced to improve the factory and its lovely surroundings. The impetus given old Bivingsville by Mr. Converse and his right bower, Mr. Twitchell, infused new life into the mill interests in this county. Then Mr. Converse took hold of the old rolling mills and made Clifton what it is today. The name of Bivingsville was changed to Glendale, and now that name is well known wherever cotton goods find a market.

Just a few years prior to the beginning of the war, Mr. Converse and Mr. Twitchell came to Bivingsville and held positions in the old factory. When the war came on these two gentlemen, natives of the North, volunteered in the Confederate services, and for four long years fought a good fight. After the war they returned to Bivingsville and took their old positions. Later on they bought an interest in the factory, and since then they have been steadily successful.

The present officers of the company are: D.E. Converse, president; A.H. Twitchell, secretary and treasurer; directors, D.E. Converse, C.W. Zimmerman, and A.H. Twitchell. The product of the mill is about one million pounds of cloth per year, consisting of heavy sheeting and drills. About twenty-four hundred bales of cotton are consumed annually. Four thousand and one hundred and thirty spindles and one hundred and thirty-six looms are in use daily. There are two water wheels, and their combined force is 160 horse power. The main building, which is of brick, is 180 feet long and 50 feet wide and three stories and a half high.

The operatives are intelligent and orderly. They live in seventy-five tenement houses, neatly built and with an eye to comfort. All are painted and attractively fitted up and present a striking appearance. A new church, free to all denominations, has been built with a seating capacity of 300. Near the church is a new school house, which has been fitted up comfortably with modern desks and all the necessary appliances for a well-regulated school. A public hall has also been built and the operatives have free use of it at any time they may desire.

Perhaps the greatest factor in the future development of the resources of Spartanburg will be the immense Spartan Mills, which commenced operations recently. In 1888 the Spartan Mills were organized with a capital stock of $150,000, payable in shares of $100 upon the cooperative plan of one dollar a month on each share. This plan was found to be slow and unsatisfactory, but work began in April 1889 with a view to erect a mill of ten thousand spindles.

Then a proposal came from Northern capitalists to join the Spartan Mills on the condition that the Spartanburg people would increase their subscription to create a capital stock of $500,000. The company was speedily organized with these officers: John H. Montgomery, president and treasurer; W.E. Burnett, vice president; Alvin Green, superintendent; directors, J.H. Montgomery, A.H. Twitchell, John B. Cleveland, D.R. Duncan, W.E. Burnett, J.L.H. Cobb of Lewiston, Me., Stephen Green of Newburyport, Mass., S.M. Milliken of New York, and G.W. Donaldson of Providence, R.I.

The main building, which catches the eye of perhaps every passenger who travels over the Piedmont Air Line Railroad, is 420 feet long and 101 feet wide. It is four stories high, each story being fifteen feet in height. Power is provided by ten boilers of 120 horse power each. Next to the boiler room is the heating arrangement which is entirely new in this section. Instead of steam pipes running through the mill, two large fans are used to drive hot air through flues built in the wall and into each room. By this arrangement during hot weather cold air is driven into the compartments—the same machine thus serving two purposes, that of ventilating as well as heating.

The smoke stack is the highest structure of the kind in the State. It is 178 feet in height, and its base is 40 feet in diameter. Furthermore, it is probably the only round chimney in the South. The company owns about 60 acres of land, all within the corporate limits of the city. Upon this property has been built the largest and best equipped cotton mill in the Southern States.

Nearby is Montgomeryville, made up of 150 neat cottages, with four rooms each, in which will live the operatives. There are still 24 acres of untouched land. These tenements are intended for one family only to each house. They are built of dressed lumber, ceiled throughout, and have been neatly painted a drab color with brown borderings. About fifty of these houses are already occupied, and families are moving in as the mills near completion. With a population of 1,500 souls this little village will be a valuable adjunct to the already prosperous municipality of Spartanburg.

Spartan Mills, the largest in the State, will consume about one-third of the cotton crop raised in the county. The company has now put in 3,500 spindles and 1,100 looms and will yet have ample space of fully 5,000 additional spindles and several hundred looms. The mills will be lighted with the Thomson-Houston system of incandescent electric lights. Recently the stock of the company has been increased to one million dollars.

On the banks of the Pacolet River, seven miles east of the city of Spartanburg, is to be found the Clifton Manufacturing Company. This company was organized in 1880 with a capital stock of $500,000, which was increased to $700,000 in 1887. The plant really consists of two mills connected by a railroad operated by the company. Together the two mills have 50,000 spinning spindles, 1,460 twister spindles, 1,460 looms, 364 cards, 37 lappers, and other machinery in proportion. The power for driving this machinery is made up of seven water wheels representing 1,950 horse power, two steam engines representing 600 horse power, and nine steam boilers representing 700 horse power.

In addition to ten ware houses with a storage capacity of 25,000 bales, there are 126 six-room and 150 four-room tenement houses, a church with a seating capacity of 1,000, and two public school houses furnished by the company. Four teachers are employed from eight to ten months of the year, the company paying more than half of the salary of each teacher.

The class of goods manufactured by this company consists of coarse and fine sheeting drills and carpet warp. The monthly product of coarse cloth is 700,000 yards, 1,000,000 yards of fine cloth, and 150,000 pounds of carpet warp, making an annual product of 20,000,000 yards or 8,000,000 pounds. These mills consume

21,500 bales of cotton annually. The number of hands is 1,300, the amount of wages paid ranges from twenty cents to four dollars a day, and the monthly pay roll amounts to $17,000.

D.E. Converse is president of these mills, and A.W. Twitchell is secretary and treasurer. The superintendent is H.D. Wheat, a native South Carolinian, who passed his early life in the Saluda Mill of Columbia.

The Pacolet Manufacturing Company, which also consists of two mills, commenced operations in December 1883. The officers are: John H. Montgomery, president and treasurer; directors, John B. Cleveland, Joseph Walker, Stephen Green, John H. Montgomery, Frank E. Taylor, C.E. Fleming, R.K. Carson, and John D. Murchison. The capital stock is now $450,000. The product of the two mills per day is 50,000 yards. Some of this is in sheeting and the other in brown drills. About 10,550 bales of cotton are consumed each year.

The pay roll of the operatives, not including the salaries of various officers of the company, amounts to over $100,000 annually. There are no strikers or quarrelsome disturbers among the operatives, and if the writer had to search for an intelligent body of people, combining the qualities of good citizenship, he would make a requisition on the operatives who have done so much to make this manufacturing centre the attractive and lovely place it is. There are 107 tenement houses, all of which have been built by the company with an eye single to the comfort and convenience of those who live in them. A very handsome church has been built in the middle of the town where all denominations worship.

The most notable building, apart from the two mills, is the store, which is owned and operated by the Pacolet Manufacturing Company. About $15,000 is invested in the store, and, under the management of D. Baxter Wood, it has always been a paying investment. The store is 90 feet long by 30 feet wide, and in it is kept everything that could be desired. There are on the outskirts four smaller stores which are also said to do a good business. There are two skilled physicians here: Dr. C.C. Roy and Dr. S.H. Griffith.

The school here is one of the best factory schools in South Carolina. It runs ten months in the year and has an average attendance of 130 pupils. Mr. A.B. Stalworth is the principal, assisted by his sister, Miss Sallie Stalworth. The school is a free school, and the $200 that is due each year from the county is handsomely supplemented by the company.

There are three secret societies here: the Knights of Honor, the Knights and Ladies of Honor, and Trough Shoals Masonic Lodge No. 228 B. There is also a brass band with thirteen members, of which Mr. C.E. Thomas is captain.

The Whitney Manufacturing Company, capital stock $193,000, is another one of those magnificent industries within a mile of Spartanburg which sprang into existence almost within a fortnight. These mills began operations in April of last year and have had unprecedented success. The officers are: Dr. C.E. Fleming, president and treasurer; directors, Col. Joseph Walker, J.B. Cleveland, J.H. Sloan,

L.P. Walker, A.H. Foster, J.H. Montgomery, J.A. Henneman, and C.E. Fleming. R.L. Cumnock is superintendent.

The mills are on the old Harris Mill site and the water power is excellent. The main building of the mills is 263 feet long and 78 feet wide and three stories high. The two hundred operatives are comfortably housed in about forty tenements. A school and a handsome church are also provided by the company.

The Enoree Manufacturing Company is situated on the Enoree River at Mountain Shoals. It is about the same size as the Charleston Cotton Mills. The capital stock is $400,000. There are 20,000 spindles and 576 looms in the mill. About 400 operatives are employed and the character of the labor is excellent. The operatives live in tenement houses, numbering about one hundred comfortable homes. A well-appointed school house has been erected and a handsome church is about being completed.

The officers of the company are: Grange S. Coffin, president and treasurer; F. Enzel, secretary; directors, A.B. Rose, William E. Huger, F.J. Pelzer, and A.R. Guerard; superintendent, K. McGowan. It will be seen that these officers and directors, with one exception, are Charlestonians, and distinguished for their business enterprise and wealth. In fact, this factory may well be called a Charleston factory, for nearly [all] if not all of the capital stock is owned by Charleston capitalists.

The village of Enoree is progressing rapidly. Besides the homes of the operatives, there are several handsome residences, which are occupied by Mr. Coffin and the other officers of the company. There are three stores here, which do a good business.

A year ago the people of Cowpens, located ten miles from this city, determined to build a cotton factory. Within a short time the Cowpens Manufacturing Company was organized with capital stock of $60,000. The officers are: R.R. Brown, president and treasurer; directors, A.B. Calvert, S.B. Wilkins, John Dewberry, R.R. Brown, J.T. Wilkins, F.H. Cash, and C.L. Burnett.

A very handsome brick building has been erected with a capacity of 8,000 spindles, but for the moment only 3,000 spindles are used. About 1,500 bales of cotton will be consumed annually. The daily output will be about 1,400 pounds of yarn, and nothing but yarns will be manufactured for the present. There will be about 75 operatives, who will be comfortably quartered in the commodious tenement houses.

The Crawfordsville Manufacturing Company is another one of the new enterprises within the limits of this county. Before the war this property (the water power) was developed by Dr. William Bivings, whose name is so intimately associated with the cotton factories of the old regime. It afterwards passed into the hands of the Morgan brothers, who operated it for a time until they failed. The old mill has been purchased by Messrs. Harris and Dillard, who have formed a company with $20,000 in capital stock and are putting up a handsome and very commodious building. It is expected that the mill will use about twenty-five bales of cotton per week, producing nothing but yarns. There will be about fifty operatives, and the proprietors are determined to have the best quality of labor.

Other operations in the area include the Fingerville Manufacturing Company (capital stock $50,000), which is now under construction; the Valley Falls Yarn Mill near Lawson's Fork, one of the region's oldest mills; the Beaumont Factory, which is also being erected at this time; the Produco Mills, a cotton seed oil and fertilizer enterprise organized only two months ago; the Pelham Cotton Mills, located in the western portion of the county; and the Arlington Mills, situated in the extreme northwestern part of the county. A cotton factory will soon be built at Wellford, and another probably will be erected at Gaffney City.

In addition to cotton manufacturing, these enterprises are also found in Spartanburg County: Morgan Manufacturing Company—brick, tiles, etc., as well as doors, sash, and blinds, and a general lumber business; Fowler & Robinson—buggies, wagons, coffins, and caskets; Cantrell & Co.—wagons, buggies, carriages, and vehicle repair; Morgan Iron Works—a first-class foundry; the Piedmont Bottling Factory—bottling of carbonated beverages, manufacture of cider, and bottling of beer for export; and the Palmetto Ice Factory—manufactures ice all year around and sells coal and wood in the winter. It is possible that a bobbin factory and a soap factory also will be opened here in the near future.

In all, the merchants of this place do a business of about $5,000,000 a year. Here is a list of what was done in 1889:

Groceries and provisions	$ 620,000
Hardware	200,000
Dry goods and notions	450,000
Harness and saddlery	35,000
Clothing, shoes and hats	150,000
Fruits and confectioneries	45,000
Crockery, tinware and stoves	42,000
Drugs and medicines	45,000
Furniture and coffins	62,000
Manufactures	150,000
Books, printing, &c.	45,000
Liquors and wines	75,000
Fertilizers	120,000
Livery and stock	50,000
Commission business	220,000
Other kinds	200,000
Cotton business	2,525,000
Grand total	$5,034,000

This does not include the business done by the manufacturers outside of the city, nor does it comprehend the amount of business transacted by the various railroads, nor the postoffice, nor even the banks.

As a rule the stores of Spartanburg are built of brick, although there are a few of the old ante-bellum style still in existence. There is one principal thoroughfare of business in the city, and this is known as the public square, from which diverge different streets upon which are some very neat and attractive stores. Here is a list of the business establishments:

J.A. Lee & Son (two stores), dry goods, millinery, and ladies' dress goods; R.L. Bowden, dry goods, shoes, and hats; James Geddes & Co., ladies' dress goods, house furnishings, carpets, rugs, shoes, and millinery; J.N. Cudd & Co. (two stores), general merchandise, fine groceries, and farm supplies; P.A. Gardner, dry goods, notions, jewelry, and china; the Augusta Cash Store, dry goods, notions, shoes and boots, hats, trunks, etc.; Liles & Floyd, men's clothing; M. Greenwald, men's clothing, hats, and underwear; Lethco & Montgomery, wholesale and retail dealers in hardware, guns, cutlery, engines, saw mill outfits, gins, stoves, and tinware; J.S. Cloud, men's clothing, hats, shoes, etc.; D.P. Posey, dry goods, notions, house furnishings, and millinery; Harris, Thompson & Co., dry goods and general merchandise; Wm. K. Blake, general merchandise and farm supplies and implements; W.C. Cannon, hardware and groceries; Warren Du Pré's Bookstore, books, magazines, newspapers, job printing, and the latest copies of paintings from the London and Parisian art emporiums; S.R. Ezell, hardware, groceries, and farm implements; J.O. Erwin, dry goods, notions, and fancy dress goods; L.P. Walker, staple and fancy groceries, tobacco and cigars, bagging and ties, etc.; J. Walter Allen, fancy groceries, fruits, tobacco and cigars, and crockery; J.C. McCorkle, crockery, glassware, china, lamps, housekeeper's supplies, silverware, etc.; T.H. Cannon, boots, shoes, and hats; R.A. Oliphant, boots and shoes; W.F. Gilliland, general merchandise, groceries, and dry goods; C.D. Whitman, tinware, stoves, and house furnishings; Carlisle & Cannon, furniture, carpets, and lumber supplies; J.F. Floyd & Co., furniture, coffins, and caskets; Thomas J. Trimmier, books, periodicals, newspapers, job printing, and agent for Glenn Springs water (also on draught); B.F. Shockley, heavy and fancy groceries; J.A. Henneman's Monumental Jewelry Store, jewelry, watches, clocks, and silverware; W.J. Wingo, staple and fancy groceries; A.G. Floyd, general merchandise; James Pola, confectioneries, fruits, candies, etc.; S. Becker's Palmetto Corner Store, confectioneries, tobacco, and cigars ... one of the best soda fountains in the State in which gather the beauty and chivalry to partake of his delicious ice cream ... in the winter this dish is changed to oysters; Hill, Dawkins & Co., drugs, medicines, and paints; Arthur Irwin, drugs, medicines, oils, paints, and varnishes; H.E. Heintish & Co., drug store; H.A. Ligon's emporium known as "The Immense Drug and Paint Establishment," also agent for Glenn Springs water; S.B. Reid, heavy and fancy groceries; J.K. Stuckey, groceries, grain, flour, hay, and lime; W.A. Burnett, groceries and tobacco; Sorg & Zimmerman, meats, oysters, and fresh fish; C.J. Brede, candy and cakes; Foster & Harris, sewing machines, organs, pianos, etc.; David W. Moore, harness and leather goods; M. Heldman, harness and leather goods; P.M. Petty, confectioneries and groceries; W.H. Vandiver, groceries; J.S. Johnson, groceries, tobacco, and confectioneries; E.C. Wrightson, fresh meats; G.W. Traylor, tinware and repair; W.A. Milster, tinware and repair; Preston, Bell & Co., furniture and undertaking; Mrs. A.A. Kendall's New York Racket Store, dry goods and notions; W.J. Shirley, groceries; Fred Christman & Bros., general merchandise; S.N. Neighbors, groceries and general merchandise; Dr. Asbury Turner, drug store; M. Propes, watchmaker and jeweler; J.C. Archer, harness and leather goods; John Geddes, marble, granite, and tombstones; S.C. Mouzon and M. Cooper, photographers; J.W. Harden, groceries and general merchandise; J.W. King, groceries and general merchandise; S.B. Calcutt, groceries and general merchandise; A. Duck, W.D. Archer, Alfred Keene, John McCall, and R.M. Young, tonsorial artists; T. Dickson, tailor; Mrs. E.S. Lockwood, Miss Simpson, Miss Reed, Mrs. Springs, the Misses Farrows, the Misses Hampton, and Mrs. Bain, milliners and mantuamakers; W.R. Brown, groceries; S. Eiseman & Co., dry goods, boots, shoes, and clothing; C.C. Bomar (colored), groceries, cigars, and tobacco; Nathan Eiseman & Co., dry goods, clothing, millinery, etc.; J.T. McMillen, groceries; S.J. Nesbitt, groceries; G.O. Fike, lumber, doors, sash, blinds, and shingles; Vass & Harty, fresh meats and fish in season; J.P. Stevens, groceries and confectioneries; Bomar Brothers, fresh meats and country produce; W.J. Gilmore, sewing machines; F. Biquely, watchmaker and jeweler; J.H. Lindsay, engine and shotgun repair; and J.B. Liles & Co., wagons, buggies, harness, and fertilizers.

There are three brokerage and commission establishments here: F.S. Smith & Co., John E. Holmes, formerly of Charleston, and T.P. Sims.

For some years Spartanburg was a "dry" town, and no whiskey was sold except on the sly. This order of things was changed about two years ago, and now there are a number of bar rooms here. J.Q. Little is proprietor of two handsome metropolitan bar rooms which sell whiskey both wholesale and retail. W.R. Nolen also runs two first-class bar rooms and billiard parlors. J.R. Huseman, T.O. Monk, L.E. Cox, and L. Reibling are also proprietors of bar rooms and billiard parlors. R.E. Brewton is proprietor of a first-class restaurant. The Robert Portner Brewing Company of Alexandria, Va., has recently established a branch bottling establishment near the Main Street crossing under the management of J.B. Williams. Beer is shipped here in carload lots and then distributed throughout the State.

The insurance agents are: Joseph M. Elford, C.H. Carlisle, John F. Holmes, Alex White, H.S. Ball, J.P. Goodlett, James Cofield & Co., and Walker, Fleming & Sloan.

The shoemakers are: Joshua P. Mullinax, S. Steinberg, George Mills, Amos Pilgrim, W.M. Moss, and E.A. Wigger.

M. Carlson is a popular and skilled contractor who does all sorts of house building and general work.

There is now on deposit in the banks of this city over $300,000. The National Bank of Spartanburg was organized in 1871 with a capital stock of $100,000. The president of the bank, Mr. George Cofield, has been with the institution since that time, beginning as cashier. The other officers are: Gabriel Cannon, vice president; Capt. W.E. Burnett, cashier; J.C. Evins, teller; John Adger, bookkeeper; and R.E. Lucas, law and collection clerk; directors, George Cofield, J.W. Carlisle, J.B. Cleveland, Joseph Walker, W.E. Burnett, J.H. Montgomery, D.E. Converse, Gabriel Cannon, and R.H.F. Chapman.

The Fidelity Loan and Trust Company was organized in March 1887 with a capital stock of $30,000. Interest at the rate of 4 per cent is paid on all deposits semi-annually. The officers are: George Cofield, president; W.E. Burnett, cashier; directors, D.E. Converse, T.C. Duncan of Union, George Cofield, W.S. Manning, John B. Cleveland, Joseph Walker, W.E. Burnett, and George W. Nicholls.

The youngest bank in Spartanburg is the Merchants' and Farmers' Bank, which began business just a little over a year ago. The capital stock has already been increased from $50,000 to $100,000. The officers are: Joseph Walker (senior partner of Walker, Fleming & Sloan), president; L.C. Cannon, cashier; A.L. White, assistant cashier; L.K. Anderson, bookkeeper; directors, Joseph Walker, Geo. W. Nicholls, J.H. Sloan, W.F. Smith, A.G. Floyd, H.A. Ligon, A.N. Wood of Gaffney City, and Wm. A. Law.

There are also a number of building and loan associations here, and all of them are doing very well. The oldest is the Mechanics' Building and Loan Association, which has paid up two series and has two more series running at present. The People's Building and Loan Association was organized last November, and all of its first series of shares have been taken up by merchants, lawyers, and farmers of this county. There are also a number of foreign building and loan associations with branches here, among them, the Southern Building and Loan Association of Huntsville, Alabama, and the Old Dominion Building and Loan Association of Richmond, Va.

Two real estate agencies are doing a fine business here: Major Joseph M. Elford and A.J. Gwynn. There is plenty of room for other real estate agencies and now is the time to come and invest in Spartanburg. Land is comparatively cheap, but each day marks the rise in prices.

The amount of business transacted annually by the various lines of railroad has increased wonderfully within the past few years. The largest amount is, of course, done by the Richmond and Danville Company, which owns or controls all the railroads, with the exception of one. The agent here is W.P. Irwin. The Port Royal and Western Carolina Railway does a good business also. The agent of this road is J.B. Carlisle, a very efficient and obliging gentleman.

J.T. Gray, formerly of Richmond, Va., has been manager of the office of the Western Union Telegraph Company here for nine years. When he took charge there were only two wires in Spartanburg—the railroad wire and one short commercial wire to Charlotte. At present, however, there are eight wires running in every direction from the city, and this does not include the railroad wires. There are now handled at this office three to four thousand messages a month, and Spartanburg has become a distributing point for the smaller offices in the up country.

The works of the Spartanburg Gas Company are situated near the Main Street railroad crossing on the east side of the city. The present company purchased the plant from a Yorkville syndicate two years ago. The works run day and night and are one of the largest and most complete in the State, all of which is due to the energy and long experience of the president, Col. A.H. Leftwich.

Notwithstanding the superior quality of the gas now manufactured, the people are anxious to have the streets lighted by electricity, and to meet this want the company has put up a Schuyler electric light plant with a fifty light dynamo and engine. The light is fifteen hundred candle power, and owing to its superiority over gas for street lighting has been adopted by the city council.

Spartanburg has special advantages for social and literary culture. Wofford College, with its Fitting School for the Methodist Church, Converse College for young ladies, the city graded school, the Kennedy Library, the Musical Association, the various Chautauqua circles, together with a number of social and literary clubs, all make this beautiful city a very desirable community of highest culture and refinement.

Converse College is situated on a high hill, facing on Main Street, about one mile from the public square, and is surrounded by a beautiful oak grove covering forty acres. The main building of the college, containing 110 rooms and costing $50,000, will be completed by September 1st of this year. It contains a chapel, art studio, recitation rooms, infirmary, parlors, dining rooms, bath rooms, and student rooms. The latter are eighteen by sixteen feet and furnished with a marble-top washstand and dressing case, wardrobe, bed with wire woven springs, moss hair mattress, feather pillows, two rocking chairs, table, and carpeted floor.

The entire building is heated by steam. This part of the work was done by specialists at a cost of $5,000. A radiator is placed in each dormitory, so that the students can increase or diminish the temperature by simply turning a valve. The building is supplied with gas from the city gas factory and with water from the city reservoir. Fire escapes are also provided. Neither time, energy, nor money have been spared to make everything about the college as complete as possible.

The faculty is composed as follows: the Rev. B.F. Wilson, president, mental and moral science; Prof. D.A. DuPré of Wofford College, physical science; the Rev. A. Coke Smith of Wofford College, mental science; the Rev. T.D. Bratton, history and political science; Geo. Heintish, M.D., anatomy and physiology; Prof. Carl S. Gaertner, director of music; Miss Mattie B. Gamewell, Latin and academic department; Miss Nannie Gary Blackwell, Latin and modern languages; Miss Mary V. Woodward, English language and literature; Miss Fannie A. Camp, mathematics; Miss Helen M. Albaugh, elocution and calisthenics; Miss Eleanor S. Long, art department; Miss Cora Steele, primary department; and Mrs. Lula Butler Thompson, matron. Stenography, telegraphy, and typewriting will be taught, and there will be complete gymnasium and calisthenic departments.

Wofford College, created by the Rev. Benjamin Wofford's bequest of $100,000, began its work in 1854. The high moral tone of Wofford College students has always been a subject of congratulations to the board of trustees and faculty. There are at present 103 students in attendance.

The faculty is as follows: James H. Carlisle, president, mathematics and astronomy; the Rev. Whitefoord Smith, emeritus professor of English literature and elocution; Daniel A. DuPré, chemistry, physics, and geology; J.A. Gamewell, Latin; Granville Goodloe, Greek; the Rev. A. Coke Smith, metaphysics and political science; Augustus W. Long, English language and literature; J.H. Marshall, French and German; and the Rev. John C. Kilgo, financial agent.

The Wofford Fitting School, located in the old Spartanburg Female College property, was organized in 1887 to prepare students for higher education. The enrolment books for the current year show the handsome sum total of 105 matriculates. Headmaster A.G. Rembert is assisted by William G. Blake and E.D. Smith.

Up to 1884 the public schools of Spartanburg were in a very unsatisfactory condition, separated as they were and running only three or four months each year. Realizing this, the city voted a local two-mill tax, and with proceeds from this and the State tax set in operation the system of graded schools. The city has recently erected a new school, a handsome building on Magnolia Street, which is an ornament of the city. It has ten large recitation rooms which will accommodate about 500 pupils. Eight teachers, four of whom are graduates of normal schools, are under the direction of Superintendent D.F. Houston, former tutor of ancient languages at South Carolina College. The enrolment in both white and colored schools is between 750 and 800. Until recently, on account of the want of room, attendance has not been as large as it would have been otherwise.

The Deaf, Dumb, and Blind Institution, located four miles south of the city at Cedar Springs, was founded many years ago by the father of the present superintendent. Originally a private facility, it now has been taken over by the State, which annually appropriates about $12,000 for its support. At present there are seventy-four deaf mutes and thirty blind in the institution. Besides the white department, there is a colored department into which colored people are admitted under certain conditions. The present superintendent, N.F. Walker, is assisted by a staff of sixteen.*

The Kennedy Library, established seven years ago on land given to the city by the widow of Lionel Chalmers Kennedy, is the pride of the literary folk of Spartanburg and the admiration of everyone else. A free library, it was formally opened to the public on October 17, 1885. Mrs. E.E. Evins is librarian.

*See the *News and Courier* (June 27, 1901) for an extensive article on this institution and its work.

The churches of Spartanburg are: Central Methodist Church, the Rev. W.R. Richardson, pastor; Bethel Methodist Church, the Rev. S.J. Bethea, pastor; Baptist Church, the Rev. W.T. Derieux, pastor; Episcopal Church, the Rev. Theodore D. Bratton, rector; Presbyterian Church, the Rev. B.F. Wilson, pastor; and Catholic Church, which is in charge of Father Hirschmeyer of Greenville. The Methodists are about to erect a third church in the west end of the city, and the Baptists and Presbyterians also contemplate building in that same area. There are several colored churches here, which are comparatively quiet in their demonstrations in acquiring religion.

Active social groups include the Y.M.C.A., which has a nicely-fitted up gymnasium with a shower bath arrangement and reading rooms, the Musical Association under the management of Prof. A.D. DuPré, and the Morgan Rifles, commanded by Capt. Edmund Bacon. The Masons, Knights of Pythias, Knights of Honor, Knights of the Golden Rule, Knights and Ladies of Honor, Good Templars, and Ancient Order of United Workmen each have a substantial membership here.

The Spartanburg Farmers' Alliance is one of the largest in the State. The best farmers in the county are members and the rolls are increasing. The chief officers are: N.F. Walker of Cedar Springs, president; H.E. Williams of Glenn Springs, secretary; F.S. Smith of Glenn Springs, treasurer; executive committee, R.M. Smith of Reidville, S.T.D. Lancaster of Glenn Springs, and J.R. Dadgett of Poole's. The Alliance is well organized and has headquarters and a supply depot in Spartanburg. From there all the Sub-Alliances are supplied with merchandise. The manager of the depot is W. McK. Zimmerman. The Alliance store, 120 feet long and 30 feet wide, is directly under the Merchants' Hotel. In it can always be purchased the best grades of farm and home supplies and a very large business is carried on.

By common consent, the grounds and buildings of the Farmers' Encampment, held here for two years, have been sold to the city and will become a public park. A great deal of money was spent on the Inter-State Fair, but the scheme was never as successful as it should have been.

There are two weekly papers here. The *Carolina Spartan*, established in 1843, is edited by Capt. Charles Perry, a forcible writer who takes considerable interest in the production of field and garden crops. The *Spartanburg Herald* is edited by Wm. M. Jones, who also has a very large job printing business. Associated with the *Herald* is the Inter-State Ready Print Company, which furnishes what is known as "patent outsiders" for twenty-six newspapers in this and other states. John S. Reynolds is editor of this service used by many county newspapers.

The physicians of Spartanburg are: Drs. J. Nott Moore, T. Sumter Means, Geo. R. Dean, W.T. Russell, T.F. Nott, George Means, G.W. Heintish, W.A. Hill, W.B. Nott, J.T. Boyd, J.W. Quillian, and Asbury Turner. The dental firms are Calvert & Oeland and Lee & Lee.

Spartanburg, a city of handsome residences, is located in a county filled with growing towns and villages, bountiful farms, and numerous popular springs overflowing with sparkling mineral waters. One thing badly needed, however, is a dummy line or an electric railway connecting Spartanburg with the manufacturing towns of Clifton, Glendale, Whitney, and Beaumont.

The conspicuous evidence of rapid and sure progress has been presented herein. No one with the facts that have been given can deny that Spartanburg has a grand future, pregnant with the brightest and best possibilities the South affords.

News and Courier, July 28, 1890. Edward P. McKissick.

Springfield and Salley: New Towns in the Wilderness

Late in December of 1887, reporter Matthew Tighe accompanied various officials of the Blackville, Alston, and Newberry Railroad on a tour of the line, traveling in the private car of Colonel J.H. Averill, superintendent of construction. The goal of this yet-to-be-completed project, built in part with convict labor, was kaolin mines in Aiken County; in fact, the railroad's board of directors owned those mines. Tighe, much impressed with what he saw, had this to say concerning two new towns along the route.

* * *

The first of these is Springfield, which was incorporated at the last session of the Legislature. The town came into existence with a single building towards the end of last summer. It is being built on a healthy pine ridge ten and a half miles from Blackville. The greater part of the tract on which it is situated is the property of Col. M. Brown. It has partially been divided into building lots, which have trebled in value since the boom of the Blackville, Alston, and Newberry was inaugurated. It is one of the busiest and most thriving towns imaginable. The circular saw is going day and night, frames of dwellings now being erected are seen everywhere in the woods, the yards and gardens are being cleared up, and the stores which have already been erected are doing a brisk trade. There is already a neat postoffice building, a Baptist church, and the following stores: Mike Brown & Bro., general merchandise; Mike Brown & Bro., furniture, livery stable, and sales stable; Miller & Miller, general merchandise; Porter & Miller, general merchandise; W. Strickland, blacksmith and wheelwright; Dr. F.A. Oden, pharmacy; and W.C. Tumper, saw mill.

There are two new stores being now erected, one to be run by W.C. Tumper and the other by W.K. Smith. There are in all about twenty buildings in the town, all new, and all quite pretentious in style. The stores of Messrs. Brown & Bro. are quite handsome and were evidently built with reference to a great town after not many days. Mr. Brown has already brought in about 500 bales of cotton, and the other merchants about an equal number, making about 1,000 bales which have gravitated to what not very long ago was veritably a howling wilderness. It is the intention of this city, so to speak, to have an election ordered soon for intendant and wardens, and it is said that Mr. Charles Brown will be the coming man.

Springfield is in the centre of a big farming district, with big farms and big

The Springfield Town Museum, nearly 100 years old, has been a dwelling, telephone exchange, barber shop, printing shop, cafe, and fish shop. *Courtesy of Jacqueline Cooper, author of* Springfield, South Carolina: A Small Town Saga.

farmers. Lumber is cheap, being about $7 a thousand, and builders have but little difficulty in making their "claims" good.

The more remarkable of the two towns is, however, Salley's.* It was first known as Johntown when it was no town at all; then it was known as Salleyville, in honor of Capt. D.H. Salley, and now it has been incorporated simply as Salley's; and a miraculous town it is. It is built on a pine plateau, which is traversed by the railroad nearly due north and south. Railroad Avenue is the principal street, perpendicular to which and parallel to which are the other streets, regularly laid out. The streets parallel with the avenues are Duncan, Aldrich, Gordon, Brown, and Porter. The cross streets are Walnut, Poplar, Locust, Magnolia, Maple, and Cedar.

Railroad Avenue is now flanked on either side by a row of fine stores, where, in August last, there was nothing to be seen but the virgin forest of long-leaf pine. Among the more important of these stores are those of Salley & Riley, Dr. H.J. Salley, Everett Steadman, Abel & Bros., Phin Storne, J.A. Gunter & Bros., Dr. Milhous, Levi Gunter, Martin Corbett, and A. Polin. Most of these stores are general merchandise. Among these is a jeweller's store, a saw mill, and a planing

*Cited as "Sallys" in the 1890 census and now called "Salley."

The home of Dr. Homer Salley, built c. 1885 and, from a later era, the community's first automobile.

mill. There is also a hotel being built to contain about a dozen rooms, the proprietor of which will be Mr. John M. Price. Most of the stores are also dwelling houses, or rather their second stories are used as such. The buildings erected number twenty-five, with quite a number "on the ground."

When Col. Averill's car arrived at Salley's yesterday morning at about 8 o'clock, there was nobody in town but the inhabitants. It appeared, however, that the woods were full of 'em, for about midday the whole country came to town and the place was made quite lively. This correspondent saw about 200 bales of cotton lying around about the place where the depot is to be built and about an equal number of barrels of rosin and turpentine. The assurance was given that the very first trains run to Blackville and Charleston will take away not less than 1,000 bales of cotton and about 3,000 barrels of rosin.

These are, perhaps, facts and figures enough to show what manner of towns they are building along the line of the Blackville, Alston, and Newberry Railroad and what kind of railroad runs along these flourishing towns that have sprung into prominence at a municipal bound. As at Springfield, the country around Salley's is inhabited by a thrifty race of farmers, who know how to make cotton and will make more of it henceforward.

Another industry that is sure to be developed and very quickly is the growing of watermelons. Both Mr. [Thomas] Hughes and Col. Averill said yesterday that the land at a great many places along the railroad is identical in character with that of the well-known watermelon belt, and that the railroad and the facilities it offers for shipment will induce general attention to this crop and perhaps others during the growing season. The possibilities of the lumber and rosin trade of the country traversed by the railroad are almost incredible and might have lain dormant forever without the railroad.

At Salley's, which is only about fifteen miles from the kaolin mines, they think and talk chalk. The kaolin at the mines has been pronounced to be of the finest quality and is practically inexhaustible. At one place there is a tract of about thirty acres on which the vein is from ten to thirty to forty feet thick. Specimens of the kaolin have been sent to be manufactured in Europe, New Jersey, Massachusetts, &c., and some of the articles rival in many respects the Dresden china. The material is worth from $11 to $22 a ton, and it is claimed that ready sale can be had for it in all the manufacturing centres.

Col. Brown said tonight that there probably will be established a manufactory at the mines, but that certainly shipments of the crude stuff could be made in the spring. The uses of kaolin are well-known in candies, soaps, pottery, flours, &c., and the demand is constant. The mines will doubtless be all of the bonanza which they are claimed to be.

News and Courier, January 3, 1888. M.F.T.

Sullivan's Island—the New Brighton Hotel

This article, rather than describing the commercial and social life of a community, details construction of a grand new edifice, which, it was hoped, would lure both summer and winter visitors to the Charleston area. The three-story New Brighton Hotel, a seaside wonder and precursor of the many structures that now dot South Carolina's famed "Grand Strand," provided 112 "matted" rooms, musical entertainment, semi-detached cottages fitted out with speaking tubes and electric bells, and bathing houses for ladies and gentlemen.

> A wooden plankway will take the bather directly to the surf and enable him to reach his dressing-room without wading through the sand. Both houses will be supplied with bath-tubs and fresh water by a complete system of water-works connected with the main system. They will also be lighted with gas.

What more could one ask for?

* * *

The advantages of Sullivan's Island as a summer resort are pretty well known all over the South. With its broad beach, affording a clean drive of over three miles, its bracing salt sea breezes, its contiguity to the city and the facilities offered in the way of communication, it offers attractions for those who would escape from the heat of the summer such as are to be found at very few watering places in the South. While the residents of Charleston, however, have not hesitated to avail themselves of these advantages, very little in the way of attracting visitors from abroad has heretofore been done. The want of proper hotel accommodations has been the most serious drawback in the way of the advancement of the material prosperity of the Island. But this want has at last been supplied, and yesterday the Stars and Stripes and the Palmetto flag were floating on the breeze from the flagstaff over the tower of the New Brighton Hotel at Ocean Park, indicating the substantial completion of the new house and the dawn of a new era for our suburb on the sea.

The New Brighton is built on the front beach, about 500 yards to the east and south of Centennial Hall and the present terminus of the Street Railway track. It is a handsome and imposing structure, stands over nine feet above high water level, and faces the sea. It will be formally opened for the accommodation of boarders on the 18th of June, of which date there will be positively no postponement. The owner, Mr. J.F. Burnham, a Northern gentleman of means, undertook the building of the hotel and its establishment as a matter of investment and has every confidence in the success of the enterprise. The contract for the lumber was given out on the 15th of December last and the contractors, Messrs. Dorney &

Carter of Savannah, broke ground for the work in the latter part of January following. The original plans and estimates contemplated a building to cost about $25,000, but Mr. Burnham, who has been in constant supervision of the work in all its details, has made improvements and changes in the plans which will probably nearly double that amount, the idea being to erect a handsome, permanent, substantial, and storm-proof structure. Since the commencement of the work seven lumber mills have been kept constantly employed in furnishing materials, and an average force of one hundred men has been engaged upon the work. Mr. Burnham has lived on the Island during this time, and the contractors have not let the grass grow under their feet. Under such circumstances the rapid progress that has been made in the work is not surprising.

The accompanying diagram will give an idea of the situation and extent of the improvements that are contemplated:

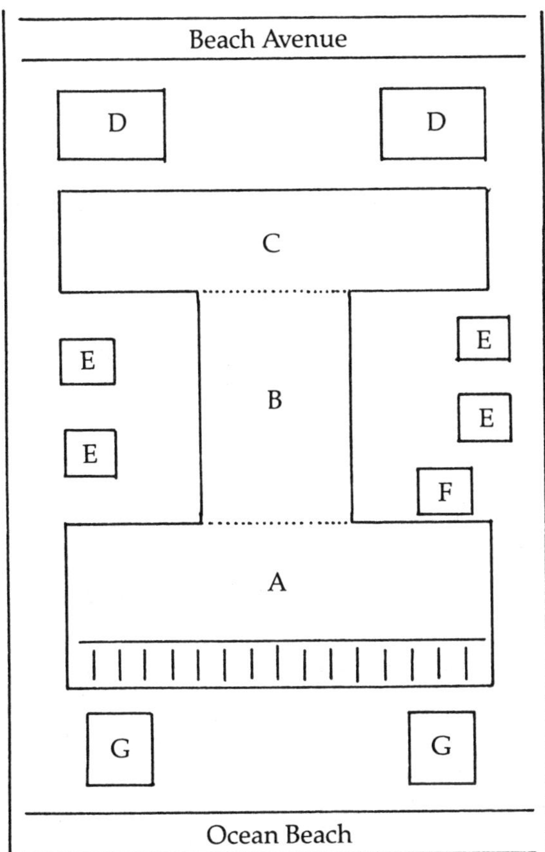

A—Main building of hotel and veranda, 120 x 40 feet.
B—Dining room, 90 x 40 feet.
C—Casino, 120 x 40 feet.
D—Kitchens and servants' quarters.
E—Cottages.
F—Water tower and water-works.
G—Bathing-houses.

The hotel is built upon brick pillars which rest upon a solid concrete foundation. The main building has a front of 120 feet and is three stories high, with a Mansard roof and dormer windows. One hundred and forty-five thousand bricks were used in the foundation. The brick pillars upon which the structure rests are six feet square at the base and rise seven feet, being about four feet above the surface. Through these strong iron rods are run beneath the concrete foundation and are clamped to the bottom of huge timbers which form the sills and to the joists under the flooring. Iron trusses run through the building from the foundation to the roof and secure the structure, making it as strong as human ingenuity can make it. In fact, it would seem impossible that any accident from storms could occur save by such a wind as would tear the building up by the roots, so to speak, and turn it over foundation and all. The main building, as has been stated, is three stories in height. A spacious piazza 15 feet wide extends the entire length of the building, the roof of the piazza projecting from the top of the second floor. Adjustable blinds will shut out the glare. The French windows on the second floor, some ten in number, open upon small balconies, one to each room, which will give the occupants of the rooms the opportunity of enjoying the sea breezes without the necessity of joining the throng on the general promenade. On the first floor are the office, the reading room, ladies' parlor, reception room, nursery, and baggage-room. A branch of the Middle Street Railway track will run directly to the doors of the hotel and will land passengers on the spot. Three new cars have been purchased which will run over the Middle Street Railway exclusively for the guests of the house and in close connection with the boats of the ferry company. Broad hallways run through the building in every direction, ensuring the most thorough ventilation and the circulation of the sea breeze. The sleeping rooms, of which there are 112, will be fitted up in the most thorough and comfortable manner. The entire house will be matted except for the parlors, which will be carpeted, and the wainscotting and finishings of the interior will be handsome and appropriate.

The dining room is entered from the Casino and from the main building by folding doors. This room is 40 x 90 feet, with a ceiling fifteen feet high. It is lighted and ventilated by eighteen windows. The walls and ceiling will be panelled and the place thoroughly equipped. Under the dining room, and extending about half its length, is a monster cistern, with a capacity of 65,000 gallons. The water will be forced up from this to a tank on a tower situated near the eastern end of the building, whence it will be distributed through the house by a complete system of water pipes. Adjoining the cistern under the dining room is a cellar 40 x 45 feet, built of solid brick and Portland cement, and to be used for the storing of provisions, wines, &c. The building in which is the dining room connects the main building with the Casino and is two stories in height with a shelving tin roof. The second floor is divided into sleeping rooms and opens into the main building. There will be two flights of stairs leading to the second and third floors, one at each end of the main building.

The Casino, the building in the rear of the dining room, will be of the same style and size as that on the front beach. The first floor will be devoted to amusements. It will consist of a hall capable of seating 500 or more persons and provided with a stage, scenery, &c. It is proposed during the summer to give a series of musical and dramatic entertainments, and arrangements will be made which will enable the city people to run over to the Island, attend a concert or ball, or whatever is in progress, and return to the city for about the same amount as is charged for admission to the Academy of Music.

The celebrated Reaves American Band and Orchestra of 25 instrumentalists has been engaged to open the season with a series of concerts commencing on June 18 and lasting probably two weeks. This band and orchestra is probably one of the finest in the country. It is said to be, with one exception, certainly the finest military band in America and has visited professionally all of the principal cities of the country, save perhaps Charleston. In the ranks of its membership are the following artists: Mr. Bowen R. Church, cornet virtuoso; Mr. Harry Whittier, the world's greatest euphonium soloist; Mr. Fred Padley, piccolo soloist; Mr. E.A. Bosworth, solo clarionet; Mr. Lafricain, premier cornet; Mr. Scott, base clarionet; Mr. Fookes, bombardon. During their engagement, which has been effected at a cost of $1,800 per week, excluding travelling expenses and board, two concerts will be given daily at the New Brighton Casino—an afternoon concert by the military band and an instrumental concert at night by the orchestra. They will be followed by the famous Vienna female orchestra, whose admirable concerts at the

Ad for the New Brighton Hotel, c. 1889. *South Caroliniana Library.*

Atlantic Gardens in New York have probably been heard by many Charlestonians, and who have also an engagement of about two weeks. In this building will also be the billiard rooms, pool rooms, saloons, &c. The upper stories will be divided into sleeping rooms.

The buildings to be used as kitchens and servants' quarters will be detached from the hotel proper. The kitchen will be 48 x 30 feet and will be connected with the dining room by a covered way. It will be fitted up with one of the best ranges from Bramhall & Dean, with portable brick ovens and large hot-water tanks and boilers.

The plan of the hotel contemplates the erection of a number of "semi-detached" cottages on the premises, although the work on these have not yet been commenced. These will be built to the east and west of the main building within the enclosure and will contain eight or ten rooms each. They will be connected with the hotel office by means of electric bells, speaking tubes, &c. and, like the rooms in the hotel proper, will be handsomely furnished with all the latest and most improved conveniences.

The lumber for the bathing houses is all upon the ground, and these important adjuncts to a seaside hotel will be finished and ready for use when the doors of the hotel are thrown open to the public. There will be two of these, as indicated in the diagram published herewith, one for ladies and the other for gentlemen. They will be built so as to permit their removal in the winter season. The houses will stand near the high water mark on the beach. They will be divided into dressing-rooms neatly and comfortably furnished, bathing suits will be provided, and in each house will be an office in which a safe will be kept for the deposit of the valuables of the bathers. A wooden plankway will take the bather directly to the surf and enable him to reach his dressing-room without wading through the sand. Both houses will be supplied with bath-tubs and fresh water by a complete system of water-works connected with the main system. They will also be lighted with gas.

As has been stated, the work has progressed with wonderful rapidity. The buildings will require nearly 300,000 feet of lumber, which was furnished by seven mills. At this time the front section and dining room are almost completed. The remaining buildings will be put up at once. The entire villa will be lighted with gas manufactured on the spot by a 500 light Springfield gas machine, and the fixtures and conveniences will be of the latest improved style and make. Mr. Burnham and the contractors think that the buildings will be completely finished not later than the 25th of May, and the New Brighton Hotel, under the management of that veteran caterer and hotel man, Mr. George T. Alford, will be formally thrown open to the public on the 18th of June with appropriate ceremonies and observances, the details of which will be announced hereafter.

While the New Brighton intends to attract visitors from the South during the summer and to get a fair share of patronage from Charleston residents, it will be kept open in the winter for the accommodation of the large number of Northern tourists who annually travel southward to avoid the bleak and frosty winds of the North and Northwest, and who will find at the New Brighton a splendid modern edifice, with all the comforts and conveniences required by modern civilization, upon an historic and attractive spot, with balmy breezes and mild temperatures.

News and Courier, March 17, 1884.

Summerville, Suburbia Among the Pines

This anonymous report, published in the summer of 1884, turned the spotlight upon a community where more and more Charlestonians were making their homes. In short, thanks to improvements in rail travel, they were becoming commuters, working in city offices by day but returning to the rustic quiet of Summerville each evening.

* * *

The Summervillians are just now revelling on the sea of social glory which the summer season always brings to the gay country capital. This "summer" season, albeit somewhat paradoxically, begins in the early spring and ends late in the autumn when the grand army of free lances vanishes like the leaves and birds of our forests, but almost invariably comes again. The come-again practice is, however, gradually and pleasantly going out of fashion, most people nowadays coming to stay; and with that healthy change of sentiment better days have come and a brighter future is in store for Charleston's progressive suburb. There can no longer be a rational doubt about the fact that Summerville is fast looming up as a most important place as far as Charleston is concerned. To speak in expressive modern English, the town is celebrating an immense boom, a boom in social as well as in civil interests, and of this fact the citizens are very righteously although not inordinately proud. As a daughter of the City by the Sea, in the direct (railroad) line, the town is intimately connected with the city, and their interests are daily becoming more closely allied and blended. The fact is that the professional life of the town, so to speak, is passed in the city, and the other life is very discreetly and sensibly spent at home. It would possibly be a matter of surprise to the people of Charleston if they were officially informed of the numbers who have left the city and made their homes in Summerville. On this point the judgment here is almost unanimous that the colonists from Charleston have acted in the premises with a rare degree of sound sense and an eye single to the fitness of human things and places. And the good work is going on and probably will continue until the modest but model town has developed into a stately and rival city.

The progress of Summerville is certainly somewhat remarkable, and the change for the better both rapid and sudden. The last five years have been marked by improvements in every respect, but more especially by an almost magical building up of the waste places and a regeneration of the old. Formerly, with a good show of reason, people spoke of the place as "Sleepy Hollow," "Frog Level," the "missing municipal link," &c., and of its people as a race of lotos-eaters and effete do-nothings. The all-sufficient commentary is, however, plainly written today in the vast deal that has been accomplished towards wheeling the Rip Van Winkles into line and pushing the place forward in the rank of progressive towns.

Perhaps the surest and most substantial indication of our latter-day development is found in the phenomenal advance in the value of real estate. What not many years ago would have been considered fabulous prices must be paid today for lands that were originally bought for a song. The present march of progress is, however, accompanied with more expensive music. From $800 to $1,500 is now asked for an acre of land which was bought for but a little more than the valuation placed upon it by the Westoe proprietors and other Indian landlords. As an example of the comparative prices of land it may be mentioned that a tract of four acres originally bought for $47 was sold six years ago for $1,700 and cannot now be bought for $3,500. Another parcel of two acres was formerly purchased for a lawyer's fee of $12 and was sold not long ago for $300. (It may also be stated as a matter of justice in this connection that the local lawyers' fees have "gone up" in the same proportion.) The last mentioned sale does not, however, show the actual value of property, as the land in question is not situated in an eligible part of the town. As a general thing the value of real estate is now ten times what it was ten or twelve years ago. Compared with that time, this shows an enormous increase in valuation and also the activity of competition for purchase. Strangely enough, the demand is now for lots near the depot, a locality which, in the old days, was shunned with holy terror. Everybody and everything now are gravitating to that centre and for apparent reasons. It is on account of the addition of new Summerville to the incorporation.

The business centre of the town is regularly laid out in building squares and is fast putting on a municipal appearance. It may not be so well known as it should be that Summerville is divided into two distinct sections, separated by a stream appropriately called Pike Hole Branch. This stream is the natural dividing line of property values in the town. On the "Old Summerville" side, or that most remote from the railroad section, land is not considered to be as valuable as on the more favored "side of the creek." In the old town an acre may be bought for from five to six hundred dollars. This valuation, however, will not long remain as the indications are that property there will soon reach the figures asked in New Summerville. The "old town," too, is by all odds the prettier section of the town, and singularity of its "lay-out" being considered more of an attraction than a depreciation. It has all the combined effects of town and country, and considering the almost universal tendency to settle near the depot, is making marked progress in the way of buildings and general improvement.

Many things have contributed to the new departure in Summerville, but none more visibly that the facilities of communication with Charleston and other places offered by the South Carolina Railway Company. There is possibly no place in the State which has so frequent communication with other places as Summerville. All that could be done for the growth and development of a station has been done for the town, and general advantage is being taken of the facilities offered. The Summerville train, like the "Island boat," is a kind of rolling exchange between

Summerville and Charleston. It is one of the town's oldest institutions, and in its improved shape, speed, and design is in marked contrast to the "Accommodation train" in the days of coffee-pot boilers and trips that consumed an hour and a half or more between Charleston and Summerville. The schedule time is now thirty-five minutes, and so frequent are the trips that one may visit Charleston half a dozen times a day. The telegraph facilities, too, are all that could be desired. For a long time this was only a day office, but when the station became an important one in railroad circles, a night operator was stationed here, giving the citizens the benefit of night and day telegraph service.

Besides what has been done in other respects by the railway company toward advancing the interests of the town, Mr. J.H. Averill, trainmaster of the road, has recently thrown open for the use of the citizens as a public park a part of the company's reservation near the depot. The square has been neatly inclosed and furnishes a very excellent retreat in these red-hot days. According to the law of compensation the business of the company here has been immensely increased. The cargoes of freight consigned here in a week are probably as great as those sent here in six months before the new order of things.

The mercantile trade of the town also has taken rapid strides in the past few years, the volume of trade having been increased ten-fold. Among the prominent business men at present here are: W.L. Lowery, dry goods and groceries; J.J. Borger, general merchandise; F.C. Borner, same; Henry Struhs & Co., general merchandise; H.W. Kriete, groceries; Emanuel Bros., dry goods and groceries; J.W. McLaughlin & Co., dry goods and groceries; Dr. H.C. Guerin, groceries; and W. Sassard, general merchandise. Some of these have the usual rum attachment which is supposed to be an indispensable attraction for the country trade. There are, of course, scores of small shops that drive a thriving business in all sorts of ways and with all sorts of people.

The population of the town is variously estimated at from 2,500 to 3,000 souls. This population is as "variegated" as it could well be, the German element, as usual, controlling the trade, and their fellow citizens paying the price of their protection. There are seven "saloons" in town, which also do a conspicuously fine business. On these it is rumored that an aggressive warfare is soon to be waged. It is said that they are now under the strict surveillance of a vigilance committee on the enforcement of the Sunday law and that the days of Sunday refreshment are well nigh over. This will no doubt be a sad blow to the gilded youth, who will be obliged to seek both revenge and consolation in foreign saloons. A remarkable fact in connection with the time-honored existence of bar-rooms in the town is that there has not been a single crime committed in them, except the equally time-honored crime of getting drunk, for the past thirty-five years. In fact, our gin-mill corporations have escaped the odium that attaches to the guild of less favored places where people shoot and carve each other as a "post-brandial" recreation.

As an antithesis and antidote to this subject there are six churches in Summerville, which are not so numerously attended as the other places of public resort, notwithstanding the fact that the congregations of most of them are very large. Of these the colored Baptist congregation is the most numerous, the Methodist congregation next, the Episcopal third, and the Catholic the smallest in numbers. The Presbyterian Church, for a long while without a resident minister, has secured the services of the Rev. Mr. Taylor, and services are regularly held in that church at present. The Catholic congregation have no resident priest, mass being celebrated monthly by the Rev. P.L. Wilson, who is in charge of the mission. The Rev. L.F. Guerry has charge of the Episcopal Church and the Rev. J.M. Pike of the Methodist Church. The Rev. Anthony Allston, colored, is in charge of the Baptist Church.

In the way of amusements the town is fully provided. The Musical and Dramatic Association is composed of a corps of excellent musical and dramatic amateurs, who have earned a well-deserved reputation, at least from the Summerville public. There is also a musical combination known as the Berkeley Minstrels, which is just the kind of combination for the people who like that kind of entertainment. The great increase in population has made necessary the building of a proper hall for dramatic and concert purposes, and a company has undertaken to provide such a building in the near future. The site for the proposed building has already been obtained, and the work of erection will be commenced as soon as the necessary arrangements can be made.

Summerville has no reason, however, to be proud of its public buildings. The town hall is the smallest building of the kind in the State, considering the size and population of the place, and the "market" is not much larger than an ordinary log cabin. The present town council is composed of Intendant J.W. Perry, Wardens George Gibbs, F.M. Emanuel, Dr. A.B. Muckenfuss, L.C. Stoll, and T.W. Stanland. Very little had been left undone by the previous council in the nature of street improvements, and the energies of the present council have been directed to the keeping of the old works in repair. Two new streets have been opened by the present board which are generally considered of questionable utility. The destruction of the large number of trees necessary for the construction of the streets is also commented upon unfavorably, whatever use there may have been for the new streets being more than counterbalanced by the injudicious and wholesale slaughter of our pine-tree protectors. The town is now, nevertheless, absolutely healthy in every respect. The drainage is not as thorough as it might be, but there is very little to be desired to make it as complete as requirements demand. The gradual clearing away of the undergrowth will, however, in a few years make necessary the construction of many more drains than now exist as a set off to the danger incurred by baring the swamp lands to the action of the sun. If this is not done Summerville will soon degenerate in point of healthfulness to the reputation for which its progress to a great degree is due.

A great deal, good, bad, and indifferent, has of late years been written about Summerville and its surroundings for the Northern press. While a great deal of such criticism has been adverse, it has not been denied that the climate here is a specific remedy for the varied forms of lung and bronchial diseases. In this respect

The Dorchester Hotel, Summerville, c. 1888. *South Caroliniana Library.*

the town enjoys an extensive reputation, which might be immeasurably increased by a moderate amount of judicious advertising and providing for the accommodation of Northern travellers.

A "hotel for Summerville" has been a theme and a dream of our citizens for any given number of years, but the project is as near completion today as the famous castles in Spain. The want of such a hotel is a serious drawback to the place and is being felt more and more every year.* Taking into consideration the absence of an enterprise with that style and character of accommodation required by the average Northern and Western tourist, it is surprising how many of that class of travellers remain here during the winter. There has been, however, no increase in the number for many years, but there can be no doubt that under other circumstances the town would receive much of the public patronage that is given to less attractive resorts. There are boarding houses without number in the town, most of which are constantly filled. There is also the Paradise Hotel, in one of the most charming locations imaginable, which is well kept and is fairly patronized, but what is required is a building *a la* New Brighton, at least that is what the hotel enthusiasts have to say on that most important subject. With a good hotel Summerville would soon loom up as a dangerous rival to the Island, on which it is now casting a jealous and rapacious eye.

The topography of the town is as agreeable as could be desired. The latest discovery in that line is that the town is built or rather is being built on seven hills,

*Summerville finally got its grand hotel four years later. According to a drawing and description of the "Dorchester" in the *News and Courier* (October 19, 1888), this four-story structure was to be built on the "Ford lot" at a cost of about $35,000. One special feature was a winter conservatory filled with "the rarest exotic plants, mosses, ferns, potted plants, the view being very similar to that which has often been seen in Charleston at the local Floral Fair. This custom appears to be demanded by the taste of the Northern travellers, and especially the lady invalids who on many days, even in Southern Georgia and in Florida, cannot go out into the fields or even out of the hotel."

like a certain famous eternal city. This augurs well, but the nomenclature of the hills is sadly marred in the modern version. In place of the Aventine, the Pincian, the Esquiline, &c., we have such horrid hills as Buzzard's Roost, Monkey's Mount, Red Hill, Hickory Hill, and other common places that would not be tolerated in a third-rate classical dictionary. All these hillsides are nevertheless dotted with fine private buildings, and notably so Hickory Hill. This is the latest hill that has been colonized and is considered the most beautiful location in town. Among the many fine residences there are those of Messrs. W.A. Gammell, Wm. C. Chisolm, W.K. Pelzer, H.A.M. Smith, T.B. Huger, W.S. Hastie, Jr., and others in course of erection. The names of the dwellers on Monkey's Mount and Buzzard's Roost are not herein chronicled for good and obvious reasons.

The social life of the average Summervillian, male or female, is not a very complex or ostentatious affair. In summer it is gay and fashionable, and in winter people are happy in the knowledge that the next season will be gayer and livelier than the last. This has been the rule without exception for a number of consecutive years and will most likely be the order of business for the future.

As to the prospects of the place, they were never brighter or with more show and assurance of realization than now. The notable influx of population during the last half decade will in the nature of things be proportionally increased during the next. Taking into consideration that in 1880 the population was only 1,300 and that the most reliable information now places it near 3,000, it may safely be predicted that at the end of Cleveland's term of office it will be at least 5,000. There is nothing just now either probable or contingent to forestall the consummation of this modest prediction, and it is to be hoped that its verification will redound to the credit of a prophet in his own country.

News and Courier, July 20, 1884.

Sumter, the Gamecock City

Originally Sumterville in Clarendon District, both that region and its seat of government experienced a change of names in the 1850s when a local legislator decided to honor more directly the memory of General Thomas Sumter, a Revolutionary War hero, who once owned much of the land in and around Sumter. John I. Green, who visited there in November of 1889, found a community not unlike many others throughout South Carolina—a commercial life based upon a diversified agriculture of sorts but still heavily dependent upon cotton, substantial forest resources, a yearning for better rail connections and a bigger hotel, and churches and schools in which local residents took considerable pride. Yet in one respect Sumter was different, for its streets were now lighted each night by thirty-five arc lights, each with 800 more candlepower than found in either Charleston or Columbia!*

* * *

The location of this place is admirable. On one side is Turkey Creek and on the other Green Swamp. These streams, connected with an inexpensive system of sewerage, keep the city thoroughly drained. The soil here is very porous and therefore readily absorbs the rainfall. These are some of the causes of the city's healthiness. The atmosphere is balmy and dry and is thoroughly impregnated by the ozone from the immense pine forests which stretch away for miles in every direction. This feature of the climate explains the rareness of pulmonary diseases here and affords an asylum for all who suffer from the rigors of a severer climate. But the reader must not think that these pine lands are unbroken fastnesses. A large portion of the soil has for many years been literally "fields of abundance." There is a double reason for this: the fertility of the land and the intelligence of the planters. Strangers always remark upon the degree of culture attained by the majority of the people in this county. There is as little—not to say less— illiteracy here as there is in any county in the South. Throughout the county there are comfortable farm houses, and in many fields the most improved labor-saving machines are at work. Cotton is the staple crop of commerce, but large crops of corn, hay, oats, wheat, peas, and sorghum are grown in all sections of the county. It is estimated that there is sold annually in the city of Sumter, for local consumption, several thousand dollars' worth of county-raised hay. But it is its cotton crop in which the county takes so much pride. At least 50,000 bales are grown here annually, and the quality is of the finest. Twenty-three thousand bales are sold in this city, thus giving it from one source alone a

*For a slightly earlier survey of Sumter, see the *News and Courier,* August 8, 1887.

trade of over a million dollars. There are two other large industries which contribute many thousands to the city's business—the distillation of turpentine and the manufacture of lumber. Throughout every portion of the county turpentine "farms" are scattered, and the song of the saw mills sounds along all the timber belts.

There are rare facilities for marketing this great wealth, but they are constantly being improved. Many years before the war the Wilmington, Columbia, and Augusta Railroad was completed, connecting Sumter with Columbia and the North. The Northeastern Road gave a line via Florence to Charleston. As this placed the metropolis one hundred and forty miles away, the Central Road was built about eight years ago, affording this city a direct line, ninety miles long, to the "City by the Sea." Standing on the high road to great marts of the West and North and being nearer to Charleston than any inland town its size, Sumter occupies an enviable position.

But being a progressive city she is by no means satisfied with her facilities for transportation. Only recently she donated land to the Eutawville Railroad for depots and workshops. This road gives another line to Charleston and will connect at Cheraw with the Robinson system of railways, giving two lines to the North which will compete with each other. The Atlantic Coast Line has begun an extension to Augusta, and this will be completed as soon as the Coast Line's contract with the Charlotte, Columbia, and Augusta Road expires. This will give two lines to Florida and the Southwest. In the efforts for the development of this city the plan for securing the construction of a road to Camden to connect with the Three C's Road is second to none. This would give Sumter a competing line to the West, which is needed now and will be needed more in the future. For everything from the West (and what vast purchases we make in that section!) this city and all the other towns of North and South Carolina are dependent upon the roads of the Richmond Terminal system. If Sumter could get the Charleston, Cincinnati, and Chicago Railroad to connect here with the Coast Line, she would have a short line to the coal and iron fields of Tennessee and the grain and meat markets of the West.

This city will doubtless be a great manufacturing centre in the near future, and then the matter of cheap fuel will be a momentous one. This is an age of competition and small profits, and no manufacturing enterprise can succeed unless the cost of production is reduced to a minimum. Eighteen months ago the general manager of the Three C's proposed to build his road to Sumter, provided $80,000 was subscribed to it by this county. Only a few months ago President Coxe informed the writer that the offer was still open. It is to be hoped that the people here will avail themselves of it.

Two years ago Sumter was made a city, and the corporate limits were extended a quarter of a mile. After this was done there was a population of 4,000, which has since grown to at least 4,500. The streets were improved, several thousand dollars were expended in improving the drainage, and soon the place was a city in appearance as well as in name.

In 1882 the total value of real and personal property was $675,000. Now it is, including the manufacturing enterprises which have been built since 1882, $1,580,000. A very large part of this increase has been caused by the rise in real estate values, which has recently been phenomenal. Only a few weeks ago a lot 100 feet deep with a 30-foot frontage on Main Street sold for three thousand dollars! Every sort of property has been improved, and the building fever which set in several years ago has not abated a whit. There are several long streets on which the larger number of the residences have been built within the past eight years. In five years the amount invested in mercantile enterprises has been increased at least 30 percent.

Five years ago there was nothing here in the line of factories save several shops for the repairing of vehicles and a few grist mills. In 1885 the Sumter Cotton Mills began work with 1,900 spindles. This plant cost about $70,000 and was built with local capital. Eight hundred spindles were added three years ago, when the company was reoganized. These mills run twenty-one hours a day and produce 21,000 pounds of yarn per week. One hundred and twenty-five operatives are employed. The officers of the company are: D. James Winn, president and general manager; A. Moses, secretary and treasurer; directors, R.M. Wallace, E.W. Moise, C.T. Mason, Jr., D. James Winn, A. Moses, E.H. Holman, and M.G. Ryttenberg.

Last summer Lukens and Reifanyder established here the most extensive planing mills and dry kilns in the State. The plant cost over $15,000 and is run in connection with the large lumber mills at Harvin's, which are owned by the same firm. But it takes the output of several large mills to keep the planing mills and kilns running on full time. Mr. J.T. Laughery is the manager of this enterprise and will take pleasure in giving lumbermen any information which they may desire about Sumter's advantages as a point for purchasing stock.

Only twelve miles to the west are the hard wood forests of the Wateree, where millions of dollars' worth of oak, walnut, boxwood, poplar, and cypress await the enterprising capitalist. On the whole, this is probably the most advantageous point in the State for the establishment of a large sash, door, and blind factory or furniture works. Mr. J.A. McClure, who has managed extensive lumber interests here for several years is of this opinion. He has travelled over the greater part of the South and is therefore a capable judge of a place's merits.

The Curtis Carriage Company has been in business here for many years, and its trade has grown with the city's progress. R.W. Bradham, a year or two ago, began the manufacture of vehicles and has found it necessary to increase his plant.

As the city has grown, the opportunities which it offered over other places were increased, and even those who sold their cotton at other places came here to spend their money. The large houses here have as expert buyers in all lines as there are in the State, and these visit the great markets North and West every season. Such enterprise could result but one way. There are half a dozen houses here which carry as fine stocks as are found in many cities twice as large as this one.

A board of trade has recently been organized and has already done much in the interest of the city's business. The officers are A. Moses, president; R.M. Wallace, vice president; and L.S. Carson, secretary and treasurer.

Main Street, Sumter, c. 1890. *South Caroliniana Library.*

In 1887 the Simonds National Bank began business with a capital of $50,000. Last January this was increased to $75,000. Ever since it has been established this bank has paid 4 per cent semi-annual dividends and has now on hand surplus and undivided profits amounting to $10,000. The average amount of deposits is $80,000. The officers are: Andrew Simonds, president; R.M. Wallace, vice president; W. Alston Pringle, Jr., cashier; directors, Andrew Simonds and E.E. Salinas of Charleston; R.M. Wallace, A.J. China, R.D. Lee, Horace Harby, and John Reid of Sumter.

The Bank of Sumter began business last February with a paid in capital of $50,000. It has not yet paid a dividend, but its undivided profits already amount to $4,000. Its deposits average $50,000. The officers are: W.F.B. Haynesworth, president; Marion Moise, vice president; A. White, Jr., cashier; directors, A. Moses, W.F.B. Haynesworth, Marion Moise, T.B. Johnston, A.S. Brown, and C.E. Stubbs.

The Sumter Building and Loan Association began business in June 1885. It has loaned to date, in round numbers, $85,000, at an accrued profit of 70 per cent. This institution has been of incalculable benefit in the improvement of the city and still continues its usefulness actively. The officers are: A.J. China, president; A. Moses, vice president; H. Frank Wilson, secretary and treasurer; directors, M. Moise, W.M. Graham, A.J. China, A. Moses, H. Harby, Neil O'Donnell, John S. Hughson, R.D. Lee, and R.M. Wallace.

The People's Building and Loan Association was organized last February under the following management: R.D. Lee, president; R.O. Purdy, vice president;

Thomas E. Richardson, secretary and treasurer; directors, M. Moise, J.D. Graham, John Reid, E.B. Lowry, A.B. Stuckey, R.D. Lee, and R.G. Purdy.

The following is a classified list of the business houses:

General merchandise—J. Ryttenberg & Sons, Neil O'Donnell, A. Moses, R.P. Monaghan, A.A. Solomons, John Reid, F. Levi, Ducker & Bultman, B.J. Barnett, A.S. & W.A. Brown, Kingman & Co., P. Cosick, J.F. Pate and E.H. Dibble, and Stewart & Smith.

Groceries—W.H. Yates, Moses Green, T.B. Curtis, Croswell & Co., E. Cardarelli, W.J. Andrews, and H.W. Waitis.

Wholesale groceries—Schwerin & Co.

Hardware—R.W. Durant & Son and E.E. Rembert & Co.

Drugs, paints, and oils—A.J. China, J.F.W. DeLorme, and I.A. McKagen.

Clothing and furnishing goods—Brown & Chandler, D.J. Winn, and John Morris.

Dry goods—Schwartz Bros.

Boots and shoes—Bultman Bros.

Furniture—J.D. Craig (also undertaker), Durant & Belitzer, and J.E. Suares.

Buggies, carriages, and wagons—W.M. Graham, E.E. Rembert & Co., Neil O'Donnell, and Horace Harby.

Books and fancy goods—J.A. Schwerin and W.G. Kennedy.

Jewellers—L.W. Folsom and Hoyt Bros.

House-furnishing goods—T.C. Scaffe.

Liquors and tobacco—E.P. Ricker & Co., A.P. Levy & Co., Frank O'Donnell, T.M. Monahan, Morris Bros., and Z.E. Walker.

Millinery—Misses McElhose, Mrs. Waite, Miss Miller, and Misses Loshe & Davis.

Marble dealer—W.P. Smith.

Coal—J.A. Schwerin.

Harness and saddlery—J.J. Muller.

Insurance—A. White & Son, A. Moses, and T.E. Richardson.

Musical instruments and sewing machines—E.E. Bryan.

Merchandise broker—W.A. Bowman.

Cotton buyers—Campbell E. Stubbs; Bentley G. Gibson, representing Knoop, Frerichs & Co.; and Joseph E. Harlee, representing Walker, Fleming & Sloan of Spartanburg.

Fresh meats—W.J. Dorsey, Bradwell & Sessford, and Jacob Bradwell.

Bakeries—M.L. Majewski and J.M. Dicks.

The live stock business of this city is something immense. It is a large industry in itself, and one that grew in advance of others. W.M. Graham has one of the largest sale stables in the State and has probably received more premiums at the State Fair for fine stock than any man in South Carolina. His establishment, exclusive of wagon rooms and buggy and carriage repository, covers at least 20,000 square feet. Horace Harby's stables are another mammoth establishment, which rivals in size those of Mr. Graham. W.E. Epperson has a large and well-appointed livery stable.

We have now seen what commercial advantages this city has to offer. They are many and valuable—sufficient in their way to accomplish much. Yet with them alone for inducements these streets would soon be covered with grass. Material progress will soon change to retrogression unless it is coexistent with mental and social development.

The oldest educational institution of the city is St. Joseph's Academy for young ladies, which was founded in 1863. The Order of the Sisters of Mercy was established in 1829 in Charleston by the illustrious Bishop England, and its members sought this place as a refuge when the city was shelled by the federal fleet. To use the words of their prospectus, the removal to this place "brought forth a generous and hearty welcome."

The Academy was established in a small one-story dwelling house, but as the institution's prosperity increased, each year additions were frequently made, until now the house in which so much of learning and piety is taught is one of the most beautiful structures in the State. There are seven Sisters in charge of St. Joseph's. The curriculum includes ecclesiastical, ancient, and modern history, English and general literature, elocution, botany, drawing, physiology and hygiene, logic, mental philosphy, chemistry, geology, bookkeeping, algebra, astronomy, and French. The art course include drawing and painting in water colors and oils, instrumental and vocal music (specialties), wax and moss work, and plain and ornamental needlework.

In '67 Mrs. L.A. Browne, the widow of a gallant Confederate soldier who laid down his life for the Confederacy on a Virginia battlefield, founded the Sumter Institute. She was assisted by Miss E.E. Cooper. Beginning with scarcely more than a dozen pupils, these two ladies have established one of the finest female colleges in the South. The Institute buildings are one of the sights of the city, and the name of the college is a household word in many parts of the State. The attendance now numbers over one hundred and fifty.

The curriculum is unusually high. The course of mathematics extends through trigonometry. Of the languages, Latin, French, and German are taught. Much care is bestowed on the art department, in which vocal and instrumental music and all kinds of drawing and painting are taught. The Institute has received many premiums for its art exhibits at the State Fair. The alumnae have founded a scholarship which is open to the world.

The personnel of the faculty is as follows: Literary Department—Mrs. L.A. Browne, Miss E.E. Cooper, Miss F.W. Brearley, Miss A.H. Spain, and Miss J.B. Wilson; Department of Music—Miss M.F. Terry and Mrs. D.R. McCollum; Art Department—Mrs. K.D. Jackson; Lectures on Physiology—John S. Hughson, M.D.; Chaplain—the Rev. N.W. Edmunds, D.D.

A graded school was opened this fall with 240 pupils and now has over 275 enrolled. Its curriculum includes a high course in English, Latin, Greek, and

German. The mathematical course extends through geometry. Art and music are the extras. This school is supported by a special tax on the school district, which is the city. The faculty is composed of J.B. Duffie, principal; V.R. Pringle, Miss M.H. Girardeau, Miss J. Florence Hurst, Mrs. L.E. Steinmeyer, Miss E.C. Davis, and Miss Gertrude Waddell, assistants.

There is also a colored graded school supported in the same manner as the white, which is very creditably managed. The teachers are: J.C. Whittaker, principal; James W. Brown, Miss M.A. Savage, and Miss Jennie E. Walker, assistants. There are also several private primary schools for both sexes.

The churches of Sumter are one of its strong points. The Methodists have a very pretty brick church, which was begun by the energetic Mr. Chreitzberg during his pastorate here a few years ago and was finished recently. The Rev. E. Toland Hodges is the incumbent pastor.

The Presbyterians have a plain, but imposing house of worship, which is one of the most comfortable churches in the State. The pastor is the Rev. Dr. Edmunds, who has a wide reputation for his scholarly attainments.

The Baptists have recently renovated their church, a neat and comfortable building. Its pulpit is filled by the Rev. C.C. Brown, one of the most gifted divines of the State.

The Catholics are well represented here, and their church has a large and zealous membership. It is in charge of the Rev. A.J. McNeill.

The Jews have no house of worship but teach the Scriptures to their children in the Masonic Hall.

The press is well represented by the newspaper men of this city.

The *Black River Watchman* was founded in 1850 by A.A. Gilbert and John F. DeLorme. The *True Southron* was established in '66 by Mr. H.L. Darr. Mr. N.G. Osteen soon purchased a half interest in it. After many ups and downs and almost innumerable changes of editors or proprietors, or both, the two papers in '81 were consolidated in the *Watchman and Southron*. Soon after this Mr. Osteen, a self-made man, became sole owner. He began his career here thirty-four years ago as an apprentice. Under his management the *Watchman and Southron* has been very successful and its influence has been steadily extended.

The *Sumter Advance* was founded in '81 by H.L. Darr and P.E. Parmelee. Mr. Parmelee died soon after, and Mr. Darr retained control until his death last year, when the entire management of the paper fell to H.L. Darr, the younger, who has inherited much of the indomitable energy of his father. He enlarged the *Advance* to an "eight-page," every line of which is "set up" in its own office.

The Bar of this place has undoubtedly produced more eminent men since the war than any other in the State—a chief justice, an attorney general, an adjutant and inspector general, and several circuit judges form the main portion of the number of eminent men of the legal fraternity who have recently added to the glory of Sumter. The Bar of today contains a large amount of first-rate talent. The following is a list of its members: Blanding & Wilson, Earle & Purdy, Moise

& Lee, Haynesworth & Cooper, Manning & Ingram, John S. Richardson, John T. Green, T.B. Fraser, Jr., A.B. Stuckey, J.R. Harvin, John R. Keels, and Edwards & Whittaker (colored).

The physicians are: Bossard & Baker, China and China; John S. Hughson, and J.A. Mood; dentists: D.R. Macallum, George W. Dick, J.W. Bookhart, and E.D. Solomons.

The Sumter Light Infantry, formerly the Sumter Rifle Club (which was disbanded during the Chamberlain administration), was organized in '77. It is one of the best drilled companies of the State militia, and numbers about fifty. On its rolls are the names of two ex-Confederates, William Yeadon and W.F. Rhame, who were as punctual when the bugle sounded the charge as they are now when the company meets "in mimicry of war." The officers are: Captain R.A. Brand, First Lieutenant A.C. Phelps, Second Lieutenant F.M. Spann, and Color Sergeant W.F. Rhame.

The secret societies are well represented. There are lodges of the Knights of Honor, I.O.G.T., Knights and Ladies of Honor, A.O.U.W., Knights of Pythias, Legion of Honor, and the Masons, all of which are in a flourishing condition. The Knights of Pythias have only been recently organized, but expect to have uniformed ranks at an early day.

The Electric Light Company began operation on the 1st of the month. Their plant's capacity is 35 arc lights and 500 incandescent lights. The capital stock is about ten thousand dollars and is owned by local capitalists. The arc lights of this company are of 2,000 candle power, which is 800 candle power more than the capacity of the lights in Charleston or Columbia. The mere fact that this is the only city of its size in the State which is lighted by electricity speaks well for its enterprise. The officers of this company are President R.B. Wallace, Vice President A.J. China, and Treasurer and General Manager D.I. Auld.

The Fire Department consists of one steamer, three hand engines, and a hook and ladder company. The supply of water is furnished by wells, but a system of water-works will be established in the near future. Capt. W.R. Delgar is the popular and efficient chief of the Fire Department and he has found an able assistant in W.J. Anderson, Jr.

The municipal government consists of a mayor and four aldermen. Dr. J.A. Mood is mayor, and the board of aldermen is composed of Dr. A.J. China, Mr. D. James Winn, Capt. R.A. Brand, and Mr. Neil O'Donnell.

The Sumter Social Club is a delightful organization which was recently formed by the progressive young men. Its home is neatly and comfortably fitted with all the appointments necessary to furnish a pleasant pastime and amusement to its members and guests. The reading room contains the choicest periodicals and the leading newspapers. Card tables and a pool table have already been put in and soon a billiard table will be added. A gymnasium is spoken of, and when this is established there will be nothing else to desire.

There are several hotels here already which are as good as those generally found in places of this size. They are the Jervey House, whose genial proprietor is among the most popular hotel men in the State, and the Suares and Brunson houses. But the people are not at all satisfied with being "middling" in the matter of facilities for entertaining visitors. Other places no larger than this have fine hotels which are paying well, and the people are determined that Sumter shall have one also. A movement is on foot to build a hotel which will cost at least $50,000. A large portion of this amount has been promised, and with a little more push and encouragement the matter will doubtless be carried through.

It is a general opinion among the most astute real estate men that a fine hotel does a place more good than any other single enterprise. Personal discomfort often blinds the wisest men to the most exceptional advantages. As has already been shown, the climate here is all that a tourist or invalid could desire, and the society is beyond cavil. If there is one characteristic which is stronger than another in the people here, it is hospitality. The population is largely cosmopolitan, and the right hand of fellowship is extended to all who wish to cast their lot with the city and labor for its advancement.

There are fields near here which are veritable paradises for the sportsman. Quail abound in them, with a fair sprinkling of woodcock and snipe. On the streams there is good ducking, and in them fishing that would please the most fastidious anglers. In the remoter swamps some deer and turkey still remain, while in every direction a fox may be unearthed.

Mr. James. R. Randall, the author of "My Maryland," visited this place a few months ago and was charmed by much that he saw. Writing to his paper he says, "Sumter is doing a large business. The streets are choked with bales of cotton. Much is hoped from two railways now pointing in this direction. The street car, however, has not yet come, and gas and electricity are in the vocative." That was only this fall, and here is the electricity already! The street car will be here on time when it is needed.

The Academy of Music, under the able managment of Mr. J.A. Schwerin, has been filled by some of the best companies which come to the South, and throughout the season one may count on Sumter's having its share of theatrical entertainments.

There are many things which may be said to this city's credit which the limits of a newspaper article forbid. In a brief and cursory way the writer has endeavored to call attention to some of the most striking features, and he is confident that upon investigation it will be found that this city possesses much more than has been claimed for it.

News and Courier, November 19, 1889 John I. Green.

Union, the City on the Ridge

Union, a community of 1,609 souls, evidently was a land of very pleasant living in February of 1890. The natural drainage was so perfect that mud never clogged its streets, mineral springs spewed forth waters so beneficial that they often were used as medicine, and food was so plentiful that the town seemed to have more than its share of 300-pound men ... solid evidence of robust health. Union also offered a well-rounded social life where one could choose among the Johnson Rifles, literary clubs, church groups, the Masons, Sons of Temperance, Knights of Honor, and a variety of black benevolent associations such as the Sons and Daughters of Zion and the Sons and Daughters of Mercy. The Farmers' Alliance was active and well organized, and a new graded school was being erected, its costs—despite the efforts of the Sons of Temperance—underwritten by local liquor revenues. Newsman Edward P. McKissick, author of this sketch and several others, was born in Glenn Springs but apparently grew up in Union and knew the area well.

* * *

On a high and picturesque plateau formed by the intersection of the three highest ridges in the county, the lovely town of Union was founded, and its site is so elevated that the mountains are clearly and distinctly visible. Perhaps, however, the best way to indicate the exact topographical position of the town is to say that the water falling in front of the Union Hotel on the east side of the street flows to the Broad River and on the west to the Tyger River. It is a fact worth recording that the town, without a single macadamized street, is entirely free from mud. The streets and sidewalks are always clean and of invariable solidity. The natural drainage is perfect, and there is not an artificial ditch or drain over two feet deep. In a word, the town is a marvel of cleanliness and healthfulness.

In the last half of the 18th century, about 1775, the first settlement of the county was made at what is now known as Pinckney's Ferry by emigrants from Virginia. There was very slow progress in population until the treaty between Governor Glenn and the Cherokee Indians. The centre of government for the country in the northeastern section of the State was at Pinckneyville in Union County on Broad River, the present residence of Col. J.C. Farrar. The present county was formed in the year 1798, when each district was given a name. Union received its name from an old church on Brown's Creek, known as "the Union Church." It was so-called because it was in this church that Christians of all denominations worshipped. In 1823 the present jail and Court House were built of granite, and they have withstood the storms and earthquakes since that time. The old jail still stands at Pinckney and is now occupied by a colored tenant.

A school was taught near Pinckneyville by Dr. William Alexander, which was probably the first school in the upper portion of the State. Two boys, who were in the same spelling class at this school, afterwards met in Washington, one as President of the United States and the other as a Senator: Andrew Jackson and Judge William Smith. From this institution sprang other schools, and now every township in the county has a number of schools.*

Union is rich in historical reminiscences, and a number of spirited engagements occurred here during the Revolutionary War. The Broad, Tyger, and Enoree were scenes of frequent conflict between the patriots and Tories. There are, besides these battlefields, the last vestiges of which are fast fading away forever, other reminders of the war. It was in this county that the notorious "Bloody Bill" Cunningham wreaked his vengeance on the patriotic women during the latter days of the Revolution, and his name is now often recalled by the older citizens who were frightened when children by the old maumas with threats of "bringing old Bloody Bill to ketch you!"

The municipal government is administered by an enterprising town council composed of the following members: Intendant, W.T. Graham; wardens, S.A.E. Parham, J.H. Rodger, R.W. Tinsley, and Dr. Theodore Munro. There is also a board of health, whose duties are many, but whose work amounts to nothing, there being no need for such an organization. The town is always orderly. The only drawback is occasional gambling, which is carried on by the negroes and white men of doubtful character. The chief of police is Mr. George C. May, and his assistant is Mr. John Drayton Smith. Both are capable officers.

The county is represented in the Legislature by Senator Wm. Munro and these Representatives: Col. L.G. McKissick, Dr. A.S. Beatty, and G.B. Fowler. The county officers are: Sheriff, J.G. Long; clerk of court, J.H. McKissick; master, James Munro; school commissioner, William McGowan; auditor, N.B. Morgan; coroner, B.F. Gregory; treasurer, J.B.T. Scott; county commissioners, William Gollman, Jasper Aycock, and J.F. Norman; trial justices at Union, Col. D. Johnson, Sr., and John P. Gage.

The climate has a great deal to do with the excellent health of the people. It is mild, crisp, and invigorating, and today Union presents one of the finest situations for a summer and winter resort in the State. There are several mineral springs in the vicinity and the water from the well at the Union Hotel is very strongly impregnated with limestone—so much so that it has frequently been used as medicine.

Glenn Springs and West Springs are in easy access, and travellers from the south often stop over here before proceeding to these Springs. Union, therefore,

---

*This story, although charming, is apocryphal. Reverend *Joseph* Alexander founded a classical school at Bullock's Creek in nearby York County in the late eighteenth century that some Union County boys attended; however, Jackson and Smith never were among his pupils.

justly claims many advantages as a health resort. People rarely die here, and there are more old citizens in Union than any place of its proportions in the State.

The news is furnished the people every day by the *News and Courier* and once a week by the *Union Times.* Of the latter Mr. Robert Stokes is the versatile editor, and he is assisted by Mr. Samuel S. Stokes as local editor.*

Some time ago a few of the most progressive citizens determined to erect a large graded school building. The matter was brought to the attention of the trustees of the old public schools and the male and female academies and was freely discussed. The result was the appointment of a committee, consisting of Messrs. W.A. Nicholson, H.L. Goss, and R.T. Gee, who were charged with securing plans for a school building to be erected at a cost of about $6,000. This amount will be obtained from the revenue resulting from the liquor licenses. The building will have a capacity of four hundred and will be the best arranged structure of its kind in the upper portion of the State. When the building is ready for occupation teachers of learning and executive ability will be engaged.

The male and female academies have been consolidated into a new system of graded schools under the management of Prof. J.P. Mauzy of Virginia. His assistants are Miss Minnie Gist and Mrs. N.M. Linden of Union, and Miss Kate A. Paxton of Virginia. The music department of the female division of the schools is under the excellent control and management of Miss Sallie Munro. The attendance is very good.

The Clifford Seminary was chartered in 1884 and has proven to be one of the best seminaries of female instruction in the State. It has an unusually full course of study, embracing the regular college branches. To these is added, in each class, a graded course in the fine arts, consisting of drawing in pencil, crayon, and pastel. Instruction is also given, out of school hours, in needlework of various kinds. The success of the institution has been beyond the expectations of the principal. Four times have the buildings been enlarged. Among the pupils are some from New York and Ohio. The faculty of the seminary is as follows: the Rev. B.G. Clifford, principal; Mrs. M.S. Clifford, associate principal; and Mrs. J.G. Oetzel, Miss Susie Scofield, and Miss Lizzie Gregory, assistant professors.

The Howard School is an institution for the colored youth of Union. It has an average attendance of one hundred and sixty pupils and is well managed. C.H. Jones is the superintendent, with Munro Long, an ex-trial justice of the Radical regime, as assistant. Private schools for colored children are also taught in the suburbs.

It is in the busy marts of trade that Union is seen at its best. All the business houses of the place are of a superior character. The following is a complete directory of the merchants of Union.

Foster, Wilkins & Co., dry goods, hardware, and general merchandise; R.T. Gee, dry goods, hardware, and shoes; Rice & McLure, dry goods, groceries, and general merchandise; Farr & Thomson, groceries, cotton, and plantation supplies;

*See the *News and Courier* (February 3, 1890) for a rather extensive biography of English-born Robert Stokes.

Fant Brothers, groceries and plantation supplies; W.H. Sartor, groceries and plantation supplies; H.M. Grimball, dry goods and shoes; Greene Brothers, dry goods, groceries, and general merchandise; John K. Young, dry goods and stationery; W.T. Beaty, dry goods and shoes; McLure & McReace, confectionery and groceries; R.A. Gibbs, drugs, medicines, and cigars; Farr & McIntyre, merchant tailors; D.C. Flynn, dry goods and millinery; Sparks & Graham, dry goods, shoes, clothing, and hats; W.D. Bewley, hardware, guns, and tin shop; Rodgers & Purcell, dry goods and shoes; L.B. Carson, barber shop; G.P. Garrett, books, stationery, and general merchandise; J.B. Porter, groceries and cigars; R.F. Briggs, groceries and dry goods; M.T. Graham, groceries; W.H. Pool, groceries and dry goods; F.G. Trefger, jeweller and watchmaker; H.M. Cohen & Brother, dry goods; J.E. Hunter, broker and commission merchant; L.G. Young, groceries (heavy and fancy), tobacco, and fine candies; Jonas Swink, bar and billiard rooms; W.E. Ray & Co., bar and billiard rooms; John Williard & Co., bar room; N.H. Dunbar, dry goods and groceries; Conway S. Young, dry goods, notions, and confectionery; R.W. Tinsley, jeweller and watchmaker; John Rodger, wagons, buggies, and harness; S.M. Rice, Jr., dry goods and groceries; H.F. Scaife, groceries; T.E. Bailey, furniture, picture frames, and upholstery; Eller & Parham, dry goods and groceries; George Geddes, marble yard; W.A. Nicholson, ware house; T.C. Duncan, groceries, plantation supplies, and cotton; W.D. Arthur, groceries; Roberson & Allen, blacksmith and wagon factory; Thomas Hart, wagons and buggy repair shop; James Hardy, blacksmith; Gallager & Geddes, photographers; Harris & Bros., saw mill and gin; Jacob Rice, saw mill, planing mill, and gin; Posey Brothers, drugs and medicines; D.C. Flynn, furniture; and James Wallace, groceries.

There are three millinery establishments in Union and all are well conducted. They are as follows: Mrs. James Grant, Graham & Sparks, under the management of Miss Estelle Diffendaffer, and Rice & McLure, in charge of Mrs. Mary Vincent.

There is annually about nineteen hundred tons of fertilizer used in Union County. The dealers are: Foster, Wilkins & Co., T.C. Duncan, W.T. Sartor, Farr & Thomson, and W.A. Nicholson.

Fully twelve thousand bales of cotton are shipped from Union each year. The buyers are: Mr. T.S. Fitzsimons, formerly of Charleston, for the Clifton Mills; Farr & Thomson; J.D. Jones, for G.H. McFadden & Bros. of Philadelphia; H.F. McPherson, for the Pacolet Mills; A.C. Lyles, for the Farmers' Alliance; and D.T. McBrayer, for Carroll & Stacy of Gaffney City.

There is scarcely any need for a physician in Union, but the place is such a delightful one to live in that there are several medicine men who, it is said, are in such comfortable circumstances that they spend their time here in the role of gentlemen of elegant leisure. Their names are as follows: Drs. H.S. Beaty, C.T. Murphy, Manning T. Smith, Theodore Munro, and N.W. Culp. The dentists are Drs. Meador & Meador.

There is something suggestive in the fact that there are a very large number of men in Union who weigh nearly three hundred pounds. This has long been the peculiar characteristic of the place, and there is but one way to account for it: good living. Excellent meats of all kinds are furnished by Mr. Warren D. Arthur, who keeps the city market. He is a first-class butcher and has always on hand a good supply of fine meat. Mr. N.P. Dunbar also furnishes people with beef.

There are two livery and sale stables in Union. One is owned by J.C. Hunter & Son, and the other by Graham & Bootles. Mr. W.H. Miller and Mr. C.O. Allen deal in live stock and have their headquarters at these stables.

The Merchants' and Planters' National Bank commenced operations under a charter bearing the date of October 22, 1872. It is a matter of record that in the past sixteen years the bank has not lost a dollar by bad debts and has never resorted to the Courts for the collection of any claim. The capital stock of the bank is $60,000. The officers are: E.R. Wallace, president; George Munro, cashier; and Joseph D. Arthur, bookkeeper. The directors are: F.M. Farr, H.L. Goss, A.H. Foster, Josiah Foster, H.S. Beaty, J.T. Douglas, and W.H. Wallace.

One of the most recent enterprises in Union is the banking house of William A. Nicholson & Son. It has already begun to receive its share of the public patronage, and there is a bountiful supply of brains and money at its back, which insures success. New safes and a large vault have been recently added to the office of the bank, which is adjoining Nicholson's Hall, and the office has been fitted up in a neat and attractive style. The correspondents of this bank are the East River Bank of New York and the Security Savings Bank of Charleston. Mr. William A. Nicholson is president, aided by his son, Mr. Emslie Nicholson, who is cashier. Mr. Nicholson the second is a popular gentleman and a financier of the first water. He is also secretary and treasurer of the Cotton Seed Oil Mill.

The Building and Loan Association is another one of the solid business institutions of Union. The officers are: H.L. Goss, president; J.W. McLure, vice president; W.W. Hughes, secretary and treasurer; William Munro, attorney; directors, H.L. Goss, R. Harris, J.C. Hunter, James Munro, H.M. Grimball, J.W. McLure, W.A. Nicholson, J.A. Fant, and W.H. Sartor.

Whatever other demands for money are made by the county are generally supplied by Messrs. J.C. Hunter, T.C. Duncan, P.M. Cohen, H.L. Goss, and other capitalists. The rate of interest in Union is from 7 to 10 per cent.

Another building and loan association has recently been organized here. It is a branch of the Southern Mutual Building and Loan Association of Atlanta. Its president is Mr. John Rodger, who is ably assisted by a board of competent officers and directors, all of whom are young men.

A Board of Trade has been organized with every business man of any standing in Union as a member. The officers are: F.M. Farr, president; W.A. Nicholson, vice president; B.F. Arthur, secretary and treasurer. The executive committee consists of J.A. Fant, P.M. Cohen, T.C. Duncan, A.H. Foster, and R.T. Gee.

That the Bar of Union is one of the best in the State goes without saying. It is composed of bright, learned, and eloquent lawyers. The members are Col. L.G. McKissick, the Hon. William Munro, Major D.A. Townsend, Capt. C.C. Culp, J.C.

Wallace, W.W. Johnson, T.B. Butler, James M. Gee, C.H. Peake, William McGowan, S.S. Stokes, and John P. Gage. The law offices are all in the immediate vicinity of the Court House and are nicely kept.

The old military spirit still prevails in Union, and she points with pardonable pride to the Johnson Rifles, organized about three years ago. The name honors the Johnson Rifles of the old ante-bellum days, which were so-called as a compliment to Judge David Johnson. The present command is well equipped and has an armory where monthly plume drills take place. The efficiency of the command was tested about a year ago when it was ordered out to defend prisoners in the county jail. The company performed its duty and was thanked by the Adjutant General and the Governor in a special order.

The present officers of the Rifles are as follows: Captain M.W. Culp, First Lieutenant J.E. Hunter, Second Lieutenant W.W. Johnson, Third Lieutenant L.P. Murphy, First Sergeant J.D. Humphries, Second Sergeant W.S. McLure, Third Sergeant Robert Munro, Fourth Sergeant Charles Harmon, Color Bearer J.D. Smith, and Corporals George Trefger, Aug Trefger, Thomas McNally, Charles A. Norman, and Arthur Green. There are about fifty active members of the company, who manifest a deep interest in the welfare and prosperity of the command. The parade ground is near the Cotton Oil Seed Mill.

As a social community Union is unsurpassed. There are several literary organizations in Union, which afford a vast deal of social pleasure. The Young People's Literary Club is one of these. It meets every fortnight and discusses literary subjects. Its officers are: J.E. Hunter, president; Miss Hettie Murphy, vice president; T.B. Butler, critic; Miss Helen Young, treasurer; and W.S. McLure, secretary. The Shakespeare Club is also a popular organization. It meets once every week and the following are its officers: President, Mrs. A.J. Jeter; vice president, Mrs. James Munro. Another organization of pronounced merit is the Chatauqua Circle. Weekly meetings are held. The officers are: Mrs. William Munro, president; Mrs. S.W. Porter, vice president. Besides these there are numerous other social organizations, which bring the young people together and have a tendency to revive the old literary spirit which formerly prevailed in this lovely town.

The secret societies include Union Lodge No. 75, A.F.M., which has lodge rooms over Eller & Parham's store; the Sons of Temperance, whose one hundred and twenty-five members hold weekly meetings, and the Knights of Honor. There are also a number of colored secret societies and orders in Union. It is asserted that the work accomplished by some of these is very benevolent and much good is done to the sick members of the respective orders by their "brothers and sisters." Among them are the Sons and Daughters of Zion, the Sons and Daughters of Mercy, and Palmetto Lodge No. 2276 of the Grand United Order of Odd Fellows.*

*See the *News and Courier* (February 3, 1890) for the names of the officers of many of these groups. This extensive, five-column survey of Union is liberally illustrated with drawings of various unidentified men who may or may not have been local residents.

Union County Courthouse, c. 1900. *South Caroliniana Library.*

In a communication published in the *News and Courier* some time ago the writer of this article showed of what stuff the sterling members of the Alliance in this county are made. It was clearly exhibited that the farmers are in earnest in the great work they have undertaken and that the Alliance in this county is strong and will do some very effective work. The officers are: President, Dr. Robert Little; vice president, Major W.T. Jeter; lecturer, the Rev. M.B. Kelly; assistant lecturer, Mr. W.H. Miller; secretary, Capt. A. Cole Lyle; treasurer, Mr. T.K. Foster; chaplain, Capt. John A. Jefferies; door-keeper, Mr. Gadberry McWhirter; assistant door-keeper,

Mr. James Holder. The County Alliance meets every quarter at the Court House, and the Sub-Alliances meet every fortnight. Mr. A. Cole Lyle is the cotton buyer for the Alliance in Union, and Mr. John Henry Williams is the cotton weigher.

The people of Union are distinctively a church-going and God-fearing people. This is shown by the handsome churches which have been erected here. Each is an ornament to the town and evidences marked architectural taste, with an eye to comfort and elegance. The Methodist Church is a handsome granite building. The pastor is the Rev. Walter I. Herbert. The Baptist Church is the largest in the town, with a steeple symmetrical and beautiful, which can be seen for miles away. The Rev. B.C. Lampley is the pastor of this Church. The Episcopal Church is of granite, and its style is Gothic. Its rector is the Rev. McNeely DuBose, a man of deep learning and piety. The Presbyterian Church was finished about four years ago. It is a commodious building and handsomely finished in the interior. The pastor is the Rev. S.R. Hope.

There are also three colored churches in Union. They are as follows: Baptist Church, the Rev. John Wallace, pastor; A.M.E. Zion Church, the Rev. W. Ingraham, pastor; and the A.M.E. Church, the Rev. J.C. Nichols, pastor.

There is a great abundance of hotels and boarding houses in Union. The Union Hotel, a stately brick building three stories high, is well adapted for the purpose. Mr. W.M. Gibbes, proprietor, keeps a good hotel. The Thomson House is one of the best boarding houses in the State. The Railroad Dinner House, which is also run by Mr. W.M. Gibbes, is one of the most popular to be found anywhere. Mrs. Schoppaul keeps a boarding house. There are besides numerous private boarding houses where one can obtain excellent board at a very reasonable rate.

Prominent among the handsome homes of Union are always noticed those of Judge Wallace, Mr. W.A. Nicholson, Mrs. J.T. Hill, Mr. W.E. Thomson, Mrs. A.H. Jeter, Capt. J.T. Douglass, Mr. R.T. Gee, Capt. A.H. Foster, Mr. James Munro, Mrs. R.J. Gage, the Hon. William Munro, Messrs. H.M. Grimball, John A. Fant, Jr., H.L. Goss, R.M. Stokes, J.H. Rodger, B.F. Arthur, Dr. H.S. Beaty, Messrs. P.B. Cohen, T.C. Duncan, and a number of others. These handsome residences are not confined to any particular locality or fashionable quarter, but whenever a commanding site can be found a good house is built, thus adding materially to the generally attractive appearance of the town.

Whatever may be said of the various resources of Union, there is one which unquestionably will accomplish a great deal of benefit to the town and county—the Union County Seed Oil Manufacturing Company. It has a capital stock of $25,000, all paid in, and is now in operation. It is what is known as a fifteen-ton mill and will consume a greater part of the cotton seed made in the county, at least that which is not gobbled up by the oil trusts. The mill is situated in the immediate vicinity of the Richmond and Danville Railroad depot, and a track has been built to the main line. An electric plant will furnish the lights for the mill, and it is probable that the streets of Union will be lighted shortly with arc lights. The president of the mill is Mr. William A. Nicholson and the secretary is Mr. Emslie Nicholson. The directors are: A.H. Foster, F.M. Farr, William Munro, John A. Fant, Jr., R.T. Gee, P.M. Cohen, and W.A. Nicholson.

Another industry has also been established within the past few months, the Union Brick and Tile Manufacturing Company. Mr. J.H. Rodger is president, and the indications are that it will be a paying investment for those interested in it. The purpose of the company is outlined in its title.

There is a strong probability that a cotton factory will be built here. A movement has been on foot to organize a company for some time past, and the promoters of the idea are much encouraged in work they have undertaken. Over $50,000 has already been subscribed, and it is expected that, with the assistance of outside capital, the amount desired ($10,000) will soon be forthcoming.

It is estimated that the aggregate amount of business annually transacted in Union is about one million dollars. This seems to be a very fair calculation, and the basis for it is contained in the volume of freight hauled to and from Union by the Spartanburg, Union, and Columbia Railroad. At all times of the year the business transacted by this railroad is brisk, and it has been the means of infusing new life into the town. The road was finished to Union in 1858, when the population of the town was about five hundred. Now it is stated on reliable authority that the next census will show that the population of the town is about two thousand. The first president of the road was the Hon. Daniel Wallace, brother of Judge W.H. Wallace, whose influence had a great deal to do with the building of the road. Union has also furnished two other presidents of this road, namely, the late Governor T.B. Jeter and Col. John L. Young, one of the present directors.

Perhaps the oldest employee of the road is Mr. F.H. Counts, the present agent at this place. He has been continuously in the service of the road for the past twenty-nine years, having entered the service of the company when a boy as assistant agent at Alston. Since that time he has served with signal ability in many trusted positions, treasurer, auditor, bookkeeper, and latterly agent at this place.

Recently the management of the road has built a very neat passenger depot and office combined. Mr. T. Matthews is the ticket agent and operator. Mr. S.A.E. Parham is the express agent and is a faithful and competent official. In other words, the business of the Richmond and Danville Railroad at Union is in excellent hands and will increase each succeeding year.

News and Courier, February 3, 1890. E.P. M'K.

Walterboro, Paradise in the Pines

According to Ambrose Gonzales, the magic of the railroad had injected new life into Colleton's county seat. The little community now had a thriving lumber business, an icehouse, a bakery, and numerous other attractions, including some beautiful women. In addition, there was no municipal tax, all such costs being covered by a license fee levied upon the town's lone saloon.

*   *   *

The touch of the steel rails has at last awakened from slumber Colleton's capital, which, bright with new buildings, new paint, and new industries, steps into line with the advancing and progressive towns of South Carolina.

For many years before the war, Walterboro was a summer resort for the Ashepoo and Combahee river planters and was even then famous for a light and pure atmosphere, cool nights, and cold water. In those days lawyers and pretty women were the chief products, and these elements are still prominent in the Walterboro of today.

Until recently Walterboro has been but little known to the outside world, the dreaded hack ride of thirteen miles from Green Pond deterring many commercial travellers and business men from visiting the town. About two years ago, however, the Green Pond, Walterboro, and Branchville Railroad was completed from Green Pond to Walterboro, and now double daily trains are run, making close connection with the trains on the Charleston and Savannah Railway and affording the Walterboro public first-class facilities. With the railroad has come an almost phenomenal increase of business. Formerly the long haul by wagon made cotton culture unprofitable to many planters; and, as very few tons of commercial fertilizers were used, the production was necessarily limited. There has been, however, a remarkable metamorphosis. For the past two seasons hundreds of tons of fertilizers have been shipped here by Charleston firms, and thousands of acres of hitherto unprofitable land have been brought into cultivation and the cotton receipts have quadrupled.

A new and important industry is the lumber business. Two years ago there was only one saw mill in the neighborhood, which is magnificently timbered. Now there are nine and of large capacity. Some of these mills have built tramways to connect with the railroad at Walterboro and their shipments are already very heavy. The abundance and cheapness of lumber has stimulated building, and new stores and dwellings are springing up rapidly.

The town, it will be remembered, was almost totally destroyed by a tornado in April 1879, when one hundred and nine houses and all the churches were

Colleton County Courthouse, Walterboro, site of the state's first nullification meeting in 1828. *Photograph by Carl Julien, reproduced by permission of the University of South Carolina Press from* Sea Islands to Sand Hills. *South Caroliniana Library.*

destroyed. With commendable pluck and energy the people have built up the waste places, and Walterboro is today more prosperous and hopeful than at any period in her existence.

The population is 1,800. The intendant is Mr. B. Stokes, and the wardens are Messrs. M.P. Howell, E.H. Fincken, S.F. Westcoat, S. Hiers, B.G. Hyrne, and B.G. Price, Jr. There is no municipal tax. The revenue of the town is derived from the one bar room, which pays a license of $1,500. From this annual payment the municipality has, in a few years, saved several thousand dollars, which they have just applied to the purchase of a lot and the erection of one of the best school buildings in the State. Mr. Benj. R. Stuart, so well known as an educator in Charleston, has been placed in charge of this academy, with Miss Claudia Stuart and Mrs. A. Klein as assistants.

The following firms operate saw mills in or near Walterboro: Messrs. Wm. Stokes & Son (two mills), Hiers & DuBois, Hiers Bros., Fletcher Mims, Hiers & Dannelly, Pierson & Bros., J.R. Stokes, and W.E. Stokes. A company has recently been organized for the erection of a large rice-pounding and grist mill and canning factory. There are two wagon and buggy factories operated by J.J. Halford and Spartan G. Tant.

The Methodist Church is in charge of the Rev. E.B. Loyless, and the congregation is a large one. The Rev. E.P. Hutson is pastor of the Presbyterian Church, a large and commodious building. The Episcopal congregation, like the Presbyterian, is a large one, and the Rev. E.E. Bellinger is rector.

The hotels are the Colleton Hotel, conducted by E.H. Fincken, and the Wichman House, owned by A. Wichman. S. Hiers and Mrs. Sauls conduct boarding houses.

The *Colleton Press*, owned and edited by Mr. B.G. Price, Jr., is an excellent county newspaper, with an increasing circulation and a liberal advertising patronage. In politics it is staunchly Democratic, and its editorial utterances are clean and conservative.

The post office is conveniently located in a handsome building rented by the Government from Messrs. Terry & Shaffer. Mr. E.M. Jones, the postmaster, is courteous and attentive and deservedly popular.

Dr. B.P. Fishburne is president of the board of health; but, as there is seldom any sickness save on a salesday or during court week, he has nothing at all to do.

No one has contributed more to the building up and industrial development of the new Walterboro than E.H. Fincken, a Charleston boy, who settled there some seven or eight years ago, purchasing at that time the Colleton Hotel. This enterprising citizen has recently built an ice house, established a bakery, and operates in addition a grocery, a fruit store, and a confectionery establishment.

Among the other merchants are: Messrs. Terry & Shaffer, dealers in cotton, guano, and general merchandise; J.W. Burbridge, general merchandise; A. Wichman, general merchandise and cotton buyer; John F. Lucas, general merchandise and cotton; John M. Klein, extensive dealer in drugs and manufacturer of proprietary medicines; G.W.O. Rivers, general merchandise; A.F. Vaughn, fruiterer; W.C.P. Bellinger, general merchandise; Remus Waring, grocery and restaurant; W.L. Lucas, general merchandise; J. Westerberg, jeweller and optician; B.B. Padgett, drugs and general merchandise; J.T. Beach & Bro., general merchandise; A.M. Mercer, general merchandise; D.O. Edwards, fruiterer; A.C. Von Lehe, general merchandise and livery; D.W. Stokes, drugs and groceries; and Warren Bros., general merchandise.

In conclusion it may be hinted that as the climatic conditions of Walterboro seem peculiarly well adapted to the growth and development of the gentler sex, who greatly outnumber their brothers and are unusually attractive, even for South Carolina girls, a pilgrimage to this pineland Mecca is commended to adventurous youths by [A.E.G.].

News and Courier, October 3, 1888. A.E.G.

Winnsboro: Cornwallis Slept Here

In 1889 and again in 1891, Fairfield's county seat was scrutinized by the *News and Courier.* The second report (February 4, 1891) dealt largely with the purchase of the Boylston and Cloud plantations on the Catawba River by an English syndicate. This group allegedly was planning to build a city and two mills on what had once been a U.S. Army garrison. According to this report, "When the question of locating the United States Military Academy was decided, the place came within one vote of being selected, West Point winning by one vote." This tale, intriguing as it may be, appears to be apocryphal. West Point was long an important military base, and in 1794 President Washington authorized an army school there which eight years later developed into the famous academy. The first report on Winnsboro, reproduced here, was more typical of those published in the 1880s—a dollop of history, praise for the present, and predictions for a bright future.

* * *

"There are fair fields, the fairest in this province of Carolina," my Lord Cornwallis is reported to have said as he reined in his horse on the outskirts of what was then the little hamlet of "Wynnsborough" and cast an admiring glance at the pleasing prospect that was spread out before him. In the language of this day and generation, my Lord Cornwallis "knew a good thing when he saw it."

The town of Winnsboro, the county seat of Fairfield County, is supposed to have been named after some members of the "Winn family," as the act of original incorporation makes special mention of John and Richard Winn, who, with their brother Minor, were well-known during the Revolutionary period. The town lies between the Broad and Catawba rivers on the line of the Charlotte, Columbia, and Augusta Railroad, about forty miles north of Columbia. It was a village of note even before the Revolution, and for that reason and also because of its advantages as a depot for supplies, it was selected by Lord Cornwallis as his own headquarters and as an encampment for his army during the period immediately following upon the defeat of Ferguson at King's Mountain. His Lordship remained here about three months (October 1780 to January 1781), and the oak in front of Mount Zion College is pointed out to the curious visitor as the spot near which he pitched his marquée. In 1865 this historic spot was desecrated by having placed upon it the tent of one who resembles Cornwallis, insomuch as they were both commanders of an invading army, but there the points of resemblance cease, for Cornwallis could sometimes be a gentleman—Sherman never could.

In the act of incorporation which was ratified on the 8th of March, 1785, provision is made for markets and fairs for exposing to sale "horses, cattle, grain, hemp, flax, tobacco, indigo, and all sorts of products and merchandise," and no doubt these markets and fairs were well attended and patronized by the Wynns [Winns], Ellisons, Woodwards, Strothers, Youngs, Johnsons, Kirklands, Wellings, Kennedys, Buchanans, Elliotts, McMasters, and others whose names appear in Court records and other documents as among the oldest settlers of the town and this country immediately surrounding it, and no doubt many strangers were also attracted to them; and thus the fame of the place spread abroad, and it became known throughout the land as one of the pleasantest, healthiest, and most flourishing villages in the State.

The town is laid off in squares; the streets, 66 feet from pavement to pavement, are well shaded by willows, elms, and oaks. Congress Street is the main street of the town, and the county Court House, jail, bank, the Winnsboro Hotel, and the principal business houses are here located. Passing by on the railroad Winnsboro does not present an attractive appearance, as unfortunately only the rear of yards and dwellings present themselves to view, but anyone stopping here is at once agreeably surprised and finds it to be a very charming and beautifully situated country town.

Just a pleasant walk from the business part of the town is a twenty-acre park, where under the shade of hickory and oak and within easy reach of "Old Fortune Spring," merry picnic parties are wont to assemble. "The Gordon Rifles" always hold their annual reunions here, and it is a favorite resort. It lacks adornment, however, which is a pity when its picturesque situation is considered.

The county Court House stands near the centre of Congress Street, and the jail, a three-story brick edifice, which is used as a residence for the sheriff as well as a place of confinement for prisoners, stands immediately opposite. The Court House is substantially built of brick on a foundation of native granite and contains, besides the Court room, offices for all of the county officials except the auditor and the school commissioner, who have offices nearby.

The county officers are as follows: B.H. Jennings, clerk of court; H.V. Miller, sheriff; D.S. McDowell, deputy sheriff; Jno. A. Hinnant, judge of probate; J.N. Withers, auditor; James Q. Davis, county treasurer; H.L. Duke, school commissioner; G.S. Hinnant, coroner; county commissioners, Jno. A. Stewart (chairman), Jno. Hollis, and Jno. S. Cathcart; J.J. Neil, clerk of board; school examiners, E.B. Ragsdale, W.H. Witherow, and H.L. Duke; T.M. Cathcart, local trial justice.

The municipal government is composed of the following gentlemen: J.C. Caldwell, intendant; J.M. Beaty, B.J. Quattlebaum, C.A. Douglass, T.W. Lauderdale, wardens; H.N. Obear, attorney; J.N. Withers, clerk; chief of police, W.B. Gilbert; policeman, R.N. McMaster; market keeper, W.R. Garrison; board of health, Dr. J.C. Buchanan, J.N. Hanahan, and J.P. Caldwell.

The levy for town purposes is two and one-half mills, which, with the liquor licenses of $400 for each saloon, affords revenue sufficient for all current expenses and also provides the means with which to pay interest on the bonds issued by the town of Winnsboro in aid of the Mount Zion Collegiate Institute and Graded School. One-fifteenth of the amount of this bonded indebtedness, which was a small one originally, not exceeding seven or eight thousand dollars, is retired annually, and the finances of the town are in a perfectly sound and healthy condition.

The Board of Trade of Winnsboro is composed of all the leading merchants of the town and is entirely engaged in studying out plans for its development. The officers are T.H. Ketchin, president; J.M. Beaty, W.R. Doty, and J.Q. Davis, vice presidents; and R.M. Huey, secretary and treasurer. The trade of the town is estimated at one million dollars per annum, and the cotton shipments at about fifteen thousand bales a year.

The Signal Service is under the charge of Major James Logan, an octogenarian, whose activity puts to the blush some who are many years his senior. The major is an old Confederate veteran and a man of wonderful memory, and by close observation and comparison of season with season, has become almost as good a weather prophet as "old probabilities" himself.

Winnsboro for a town of its size has one of the best fire departments in the Southern States. The chief of the department is R.J. McCarty, assistant chief, W.G. Jordan. The department consists of one steam engine, one hand engine (colored), one hook and ladder truck (colored), and three hose carriages. Siamese couplings are used and 1,500 feet of good rubber hose are on hand always. The value of apparatus and supplies is $5,500, the number of members about 150, the two buildings used by the department are the property of the town, the annual expenses are set down at $600, the water supply for the department is obtained from seven cisterns supplied from roofs of buildings, and the fire alarm is given by the town bell. The town council is now taking steps to erect another engine house, which, with those now in use, will give ample accommodation.

The officers of the Winnsboro Steam Fire Engine Company are: President, J.H. Cummings; vice president, T.K. Elliott; first director, T.W. Lauderdale; second director, T.H. Kitchen; third director, A. Landecker; fourth director, C.F. Cathcart; chief engineer, B.J. Quattlebaum; first assistant engineer, W.A. Beattie; second assistant engineer, H.C. Elliott.

The Gordon Light Infantry was organized in 1876 and named in honor of Governor John B. Gordon of Georgia. It seems scarcely necessary to say that "the Gordons" are a crack military corps, for that fact is known throughout the State. They are a magnificent body of citizen soldiery, and the whole of South Carolina shares the feeling of pride with which Winnsboro justly regards them.

Their armory is a model of its kind; it is not too much to say that it is beyond doubt the finest and most spacious outside of Charleston. It is situated on the second floor of the bank building and is 42 feet in width and 60 in length; the floor is a double one, well oiled or waxed; and, with felt packed between to deaden the sound of drilling, the company exercises can, therefore, be carried on without disturbing in any way the occupants of the stores beneath. There is a neat dressing room at the head of the entrance to the hall, into which light is thrown from the large reflector near the stairway. This dressing room is for the lady friends of the "Gordons" on those festive occasions when the armory is converted into a ball room. The armory is well equipped with gun-racks and the walls adorned with United States flags and with a chart of the Palmetto Regiment, which was presented to the company by Capt. James McFie. Four chandeliers, attached to each of the centre pillars, afford brilliant light on all gala occasions. The closets for uniforms are neatly arranged alongside of the walls; the locks to the closets are no two alike and have duplicate keys, one of which is held by the soldier to whom the uniform in it belongs, and the other by the captain, who is thus enabled to make an inspection whenever he chooses to do so.

The company numbers forty-nine men, rank and file, who are armed with the Springfield improved rifle, with the improved Wingate sight, being about the only corps in the State having this improved weapon. They propose to commence shortly to drill five times a week and will have a library, thus making the hall a pleasant and harmless place of popular resort. Pictures of Gordon, Manigault, Adjt. Gen. Bonham, and other friends of the corps will also shortly be obtained.

Capt. Gordon, one of the first young militia officers of the State, has been in command of this corps since its first organization down to the present time, and by his devotion to its interests has been largely instrumental in bringing it up to its present high standard of excellence. Under his command the company won the first prize in an Inter-State prize drill at Charlotte, N.C., in 1883 and has received the highest compliments from the present adjutant general and his lamented predecessor. The annual picnic of the company takes place every May and is one of the events of Winnsboro.

The commissioned officers of the Gordons are: Capt. W.G. Gordon, First Lieut. J.H. Cummings, and Second Lieut. J.W. Seigler.

Mount Zion Collegiate Institute and Graded School is the pride of Winnsboro and possesses a more than merely local reputation, for it is known to every student of South Carolina history as one of the oldest institutions of learning in the State. It has had continuous existence in some shape or other, saving for the time that Winnsboro was occupied by Cornwallis, ever since it was first established by the Mount Zion Society in 1777. That society was incorporated "for the purpose of founding, endowing, and supporting a public school in the district of Camden" and authority was granted to the corporation "to take and hold any charitable devotion or devises of land or personal estate and to appropriate the same to the endowing and supporting of the said school and to the maintenance and education of such poor and helpless children as they shall judge proper objects of the charity hereby intended."

It would be interesting, if the limits of this sketch permitted, to trace the history of this noble society. Throughout all of the long years of its existence it has steadily maintained the objects of its original organization and has embraced within its membership citizens from various sections of the State, many of them from Charleston, in fact so many that for quite a long period the meetings of the Society were held in that city. Since 1825, however, they have always been held in Winnsboro.

The Institute was changed to a college in 1785, and at that time the buildings were of logs; later on, in 1787, a two-story brick building was erected, and rows of chairs constructed for the accommodation of the student boarders. From 1834 to 1858 the institution was under the management of that famous instructor of youth, J.W. Hudson, and such was the high reputation it acquired that it is said that no other institution of learning in the Southern States stood as high in the estimation of the people, and its graduates held the highest rank in the community.

Under the Hudson administration the building was greatly enlarged; a three-story building was added to the rear, and similar additions made to the north and south. All of these, however, were accidently destroyed by fire in 1867.

Soon afterwards a two-story brick building was erected on the original foundation, and in 1878 a public graded school was established under the management of Prof. R. Means Davis (the gentleman who now so ably fills the chair of history in the South Carolina University) and was continued under his successors to the present time.

The collegiate feature was again revived in 1885, just one hundred years from the granting of the original charter. Bonds were issued by the town to the amount of $7,500, and the additional buildings that were needed were at once erected. The entire structure, as it now stands, whilst not imposing in height, presents a pleasing appearance and is admirably arranged with an eye to the comfort and convenience of the students. The rooms are eight in number, large, well lighted, and well ventilated, and furnished with improved seats, desks, maps, and all necessary apparatus.

The Institute is the happy possessor of one of the most valuable mineral collections in the State. This collection was presented to it by Mrs. Rion, the widow of the lamented Col. James H. Rion, and is of great service to the student of geology and mineralogy.

There is also connected with the Institute an excellent laboratory, which contains all the necessary apparatus for conducting the student through the elementary course in chemistry and in which complete instruction in physics can be given. Among the other scientific instruments in the laboratory I was shown by Prof. Witherow, the courteous and efficient president, a radio-meter, which is said to be the first one ever brought into the State. It would be impossible to enumerate all the features of this portion of the Institution, but it is certainly one of the most complete in point of modern equipment outside of the State University, and as a consequence the students of Mount Zion, when they pass from here to the University, always stand especially high in all scientific branches.

A music room and a drawing room, with the ordinary recitation room, and an office for the president, all connected with each other, are the other main features of the building. The grounds are well arranged; each sex has a separate portion assigned for their use in recess, and to the front of the building there is a ten-acre plot which only needs a little more cultivation and ornamentation to become one of the prettiest and most attractive spots in the whole country.

The Institute is on a gentle eminence and the view from it is a fine one. The monument to Prof. Hudson (by the way, said to be the only public monument in this State to one who was never anything else but a teacher) stands a little in front of the building and under it he lies buried.

Near the left front of the building is the famous oak under which Lord Cornwallis pitched his tent when he occupied Winnsboro. It is an object of tender veneration to these people, and well it might be. It has seen two wars waged for their independence, and under its cool and pleasant shade for more than a century school children have romped and young lovers have breathed out sweet nonsense.

A pretty six-room cottage for the president stands off a slight distance from the school buildings and, judging from its exterior appearance, makes a comfortable home for that gentleman.

The school attendance is excellent and 158 pupils are now enrolled in all of the departments. The corps of instructors are as follows: Prof. W.H. Witherow, president; Prof. D.B. Durr, Dr. John Boyd, Mrs. Emily S. Obear, Miss N.B. Cathcart, and Miss Nannie A. Phinney, assistants. The officers of Mount Zion Society are: H.A. Gaillard, president; A.S. Douglass, senior warden; J.N. Withers, junior warden; and G.H. McMaster, secretary and treasurer. The following are the board of trustees of the Mount Zion Collegiate Institute: J.C. Caldwell, chairman; James A. Brice, J.K. Elliott, J.W. Beaty, J.E. McDonald; and the board of trustees of the school district are: J.C. Caldwell, chairman; Jas. A. Brice, and DuBose Eggleston.

Winnsboro has temples of worship for Presbyterians, Associate Reform Presbyterians, Episcopalians, Baptists, and Methodists, all of which are opened regularly every Sunday for the worship of God. The Episcopal Church is a handsome new brick building but recently finished, the church having been burned in the spring of 1888. The ministers of the respective churches are: Dr. D.E. Jordan, Presbyterian; Rev. J.T. Chalmers, Associate Reform Presbyterian; Rev. J.G. Glass, Episcopal; Rev. A. McA. Pitman, Baptist; and Rev. W.M. Duncan, Methodist. In addition to the above, the colored population has a Presbyterian, a Methodist, a Baptist church, and a Zion Presbyterian church. The white Presbyterian church is one of the longest established in upper Carolina. The Episcopalians have had two churches burned, the first by him whose middle name, "Tecumseh," so aptly typifies his savage nature.

Winnsboro Lodge, A.F.M. No. 11, is, as its number indicates, one of the oldest Masonic bodies in the State, being over one hundred years old. The present officers of the Lodge are: William John J. Neil, S.W.; J.G. McCants, J.W.; J.W. Seigler, treasurer; A.H. Simpson, secretary; C.M. Chandler, S.D.; O.W. Buchanan, J.D.; J.W. Brice, steward; W.H. Williford, A. Landecker, tilers.

The Knights of Honor has 27 members; Dr. R.B. Hanahan, director; H.A.

Gaillard, V.D.; J.S. Connor, register. It was first organized in 1876 and has had only two death losses.

A branch of the Women's Christian Temperance Union was organized by Mrs. Chapin in July of the present year and the members are actively engaged in pressing forward the purposes for which it was formed.

Mindful of those who for the love of liberty and their constitutional rights laid down their lives on their country's altar—our Confederate dead—the ladies of Winnsboro have organized themselves, for the purpose of erecting a suitable monument, into a memorial association and have collected a fund of $800. This will be supplemented from year to year until a sufficient amount be raised to carry out their plans and purposes. Mrs. H.A. Gaillard is president, Mrs. G.H. McMaster and Mrs. F. Greig, vice presidents, and Mrs. J.Q. Davis, secretary and treasurer.

Winnsboro, like all wide-awake towns, has a land and improvement company. This company was chartered in May 1889 and organized by the election of W.H. Kerr, president, C.A. Douglas, vice president; H.N. Obear, secretary and treasurer; McDonald & Douglass solicitors. Directors: W.H. Kerr, C.A. Douglass, H.W. Obear, T.H. Ketchin, J.E. McDonald, and Jas. Q. Davis. The purpose of the company is to buy and sell real estate.

The Fairfield Savings and Loan Association was organized in February 1888, 812 shares at the par value of $100 each having been subscribed, which represents a capital stock of $81,200. The shares are paid on the instalment plan, one dollar a share a month. At the annual meeting of stockholders in February 1889, the president's report showed a profit of forty-eight cents per share. So promptly were the payments made that the penalties for the year for non-payment of monthly instalments amounted to only $7.45, and the penalty account for this year will not be much. There are over a hundred stockholders, composed of all classes of citizens. The officers are: James Q. Davis, president; T.W. Lauderdale, vice president; W.G. Jordan, secretary and treasurer; McDonald & Douglass, solicitors; directors, James Q. Davis, T.W. Lauderdale, W.R. Doty, U.G. Desportes, J.M. Beaty, I.N. Withers, T.H. Ketchin, W.C. Beaty, B.J. Quattlebaum; J.M. Stewart, A.F. Ruff, J.R. Craig, J.E. McDonald, and C.A. Douglass.

The Winnsboro National Bank is one of the best managed banks in the State. A semi-annual dividend of 5 per cent is regularly paid, and a few years ago the dividends for the year amounted to 15 per cent. The capital stock is $75,000, with a reserve fund of $25,000. Its business is conducted in the handsome three-story building belonging to the bank and situated in the centre of the town. G.H. McMaster is president, A.S. Douglass, vice president, T.K. Elliott, cashier, W.G. Jordan, teller, and A.S. Douglass, attorney. The directors are G.H. McMaster, A.S. Douglass, J.G. McCants, James A. Brice, T.W. Lauderdale, Wm. Johnson, and T.D. Feaster.

The Elliott Gin Manufacturing Company was organized in 1888, the company purchasing the name, good will, and shops of Mr. J. McKinney Elliott. Mr. Elliott continued to superintend the manufacture of the gins, a business in which he had spent the last years of his life. The Elliott gin enjoys an Inter-State reputation, and the guarantee of the company is that each machine sold shall give entire satisfaction. The shops are situated in the northern part of the town in Congress Street, where these gins have been built for many years. The officers are: T.H. Ketchin, president; Thos. W. Woodward, vice president; T.K. Elliott, secretary and treasurer; directors—T.H. Ketchin, T.W. Woodward, T.K. Elliott, J.M. Elliott, J.M. Beaty, and Jas. Q. Davis.

The Winnsboro Oil and Fertilizer Company is erecting a twenty-five ton mill and will soon be ready for manufacturing. The officers of the company are: Ulysses G. Desportes, president; J.K. Elliott, vice president; R.G. McMaster, secretary and treasurer; E.B. Ragsdale, solicitor; directors—T.H. Ketchin, W.R. Doty, W.B. McCreight, E.B. Ragsdale, G.H. McMaster, J.M. Beaty, J.M. Stuart, C.G. Desportes, and J.K. Elliott. Mr. H.O. Hipp is the superintendent.

The buildings of the company are situated on the corner of Vanderhorst and Calhoun streets and consist of the mill proper, the ginnery, the fertilizer building, and the scale room and offices. The oil mill building is of Winnsboro brick, two stories high, 40 by 50 feet. The ginnery buildings are frame structures and consist of engine and boiler rooms, gin house, lint room, and seed room. The motive power is a twenty-five horse power boiler, and it runs two sixty-saw Elliott gins and condensers. Twenty bales a day can be ginned by this machinery. The seed cotton room is divided into stalls from which the seed is conducted to the gins through a Taylor cotton elevator, and after the lint has been separated the seed is taken by a Caldwell screw conveyor to the seed house, where it is kept until ready to go to the oil mill.

The entire cost of the plant is about $17,000. The capital stock of the company is $16,000, paid in. The milling machinery was purchased of the Cardwell Machinery Company. The engines and boilers, the first fifty-horse power and the latter sixty-horse power, were purchased of the Ivans Sons Company of New Decatur, Ala., and the work of construction has been supervised by President Desportes, who has planned all of the leading features. A Taylor & Cox fire extinguisher is connected with the ginnery, and by means of it the lint room can be filled with steam and hot water in a few seconds, and every particle of lint completely saturated, so that there seems to be no danger of a fire occurring in this model establishment.

The Winnsboro Wagon Company, conducted by Messrs. Mathews & Cummings, are engaged in the manufacture of one-horse wagons and buggies and are also agents for some of other make. They carry on extensive repair work and a large jobbing trade along the line of the Charlotte, Columbia, and Augusta Railroad, and have, in the two years of their existence here, established a high reputation for the excellent quality of the vehicles they place on the market. The shops employ about ten hands.

The Winnsboro Cotton Mill is not yet built, but the contract for it is about to be let out, and in a few weeks, perhaps in a few days, the work will be under way.

Winnsboro general store, c. 1900. *South Caroliniana Library.*

The design of the company is to manufacture hosiery at first, but in time they will put out other goods. The capital stock at present is $50,000, payable in monthly instalments, but the amount will be increased whenever it becomes necessary. The officers of the company are: J.M. Stuart, president; Jas. R. Davis, vice president; J.Q. Davis, secretary and treasurer; directors—J.M. Stuart, J.Q. Davis, T.K. Elliott, G.H. McMaster, J.M. Beaty, J.H. Ketchin, W.C. Beaty, Samuel Cathcart, and James K. Davis.

The county Alliance has established a business agency here next door to the bank, with Mr. J.B. Crosby in charge. The agency buys Alliance cotton by the order of that organization.

The other cotton buyers located at this place are Turner & Coan, representing Carroll & Stacey; C.A. Withers, representing Saunders & Orr; T.J. Cuetos, representing Heath, Springs & Co.; D.J. Macauly; R.J. McCarley & Co.; and E. Prioleau, representing S.M. Inman & Co. Winnsboro purchasers claim to be ahead of other interior towns and within a small fraction of exporting ports, and they have in consequence brought to this market hundreds of bales which have heretofore gone elsewhere.

The *Winnsboro News and Herald*, owned and edited by Messrs. J.Q. Davis and W.D. Douglass, is one of the staunchest and most progressive of up-country journals. It is Democratic to the core, wide-awake to the business interests of Winnsboro, and doing everything in its power to promote those interests. It is now a tri-weekly, and it is a pleasure to learn that it is in a prosperous condition.

Winnsboro has two hotels. One, the Winnsboro Hotel, is in the large, four-story McMaster Building; the other, known as the Hotel Durand, conducted by Mrs. Durand, has been only recently rebuilt and is opposite the railroad depot. Both houses are well patronized.

The postoffice is under the charge of Mr. DuBose Eggleston as postmaster, with Mr. Madden, assistant. Mr. J.H. Skinner is telegraph operator, express and ticket agent; Max Sengenheimer, assistant. Mr. W.B. McCreight is railroad agent and cotton weigher.

The Bar Association is composed of all the attorneys in Winnsboro and is organized as follows: A.S. Douglass, president; James G. McCants, E.B. Ragsdale, G.W. Ragsdale, J.E. McDonald (solicitor, 8th Circuit), Charles A. Douglass, H.N. Obear, W.D. Douglass, Osmond W. Buchanan, J.W. Hanahan, Thomas M. Cathcart, Henry A. Gaillard, and John J. Neil.

The practicing physicians of Winnsboro are Drs. R.B. Hanahan, Sr., R.B. Hanahan, Jr., J.C. Buchanan, and J.R. McMaster, Jr.

There are about fifty business houses in all in Winnsboro. The following are the names of the merchants and tradesmen who represent the business of the place: Fire and life insurance—J.N. Withers, J.F. McMaster, J.C. Caldwell, and W.H. Kerr; J.O. Boag, dry goods, millinery, sewing machines, etc.; Macauly & Turner, dry goods; W.R. Doty & Co., plantation supplies; A.M. Sims, groceries; John Russell (colored), groceries; L. Landdecker, wines, liquors, etc.; A. Williford, sale stables; Q.D. Williford & Co., dry goods, clothing, etc.; J.M. Beaty & Co., dry goods, clothing, groceries; etc.; J.F. McMaster, plantation supplies; H.M. Huey, groceries; W.W. Ketchin, stores, hardware, etc.; Caldwell & Ruff, dry goods, notions, etc.; S.S. Gibson, family groceries; Sand Simpson, groceries; R.P. Lumpkin, liquors, groceries; W.C. Beaty, plantation supplies; J.J. Gerig & Co., furniture; C.G. Desportes, plantation supplies, etc.; A.B. Cathcart, groceries; W.G. Roache, tailor; Winnsboro Wagon Company shops; J.P. Matthews, plantation supplies; Dr. J.R. McMaster, drugs; J.D. McCarley & Co., groceries; —— McCarley, family groceries; Mrs. A.L. McCarley, millinery; J.C. Smith, wines, liquors, etc.; McMaster, Brice & Ketchin, drugs, millinery, dry goods, etc.; Probst & Co., family groceries; G.W. Crawford & Son, sale stables; Chas. Muller, watches, jewelry, etc.; F.W. Habernicht, wines, liquors, oysters, etc.; Gerig & Seigler, hardware, harness, etc.; Center & Clarke, dry goods, notions, etc.; Connor & Chandler, watches, clocks, jewelry, etc.; G.A. White, confectioner and baker; T.T. Lumpkin, liquor, wines, etc.; W.H. Stirke, family groceries; S.C. McDowell, groceries and confections; H. Landecker, New York Racket Store; D.A. Hendrix, Big Racket Store; J.J. Neil, ginnery; S.S. Wolfe, family groceries; D. Lauderdale, plantation supplies, dry goods, and millinery; R.W. Phillips, furniture and confectionery; Dr. B.J. Quattlebaum, dentist; A.M. Creighton, marble and granite yards; H.S. Gilison, blacksmith; and Simon McIntosh, blacksmith. The beards and hair of the town are cared for at Skinner's tonsorial parlor.

What Winnsboro now needs as much as anything is more railroad development. She possesses a population of about 2,000, is blessed with a fine healthy climate, good soil, pure water, fine agricultural support, and inexhaustible granite quarries right at her door. She has fine educational facilities; her sons are brave, thrifty, and industrious; her daughters as fair and virtuous as can be found anywhere under the sun; and all that she needs to become as prosperous as any of her neighbors is more means of communication with the outside world. The best lands of Fairfield County lie twenty miles off the line of any railroad, and this is, and always will be, until remedied, a great drawback to her future prosperity.

A project is now on foot to bring Winnsboro into connection with the Robertson system of roads by running a line from Catawba Falls to this point and thence over its own rails to Columbia. It is said that this would be a shorter route to Columbia than by the Charlotte, Columbia, and Augusta Railroad. It is thirty miles from here to Catawba Junction and sixty miles from that point to Columbia, Winnsboro being just half way between. If Fairfield grades the road to the county line, the other work, it is said, will be done, and Winnsboro will then be a competitive point and thus share the advantages of other favored localities, for she can then trade north of her via the Three C's and the Robertson system, or south of her via the Richmond and Danville or the Three C's extension from Catawba Falls, just as circumstances dictate. May she obtain every advantage she desires and deserves!

News and Courier, November 4, 1889. C.M.D.

Yorkville, "Queen City of the Hills"

In the late summer of 1888 the tracks of the ill-fated "Three C's" railroad—the Charleston, Cincinnati, and Chicago—were moving rapidly across York County toward North Carolina. The immediate result was a series of banquets, speeches, and balls to mark the line's progress. In August, Rock Hill was the scene of revelry, and a few weeks later it was Yorkville's turn. Shortly after the celebration at the county seat, this sketch by Edward P. McKissick appeared in the *News and Courier.*

* * *

What Yorkville will be may best be learned from what it was under former conditions and circumstances. What it is includes all its inactive and latent resources, all of which will be herein so presented that one may take in the situation at a glance, and he who does will not be slow to predict that Yorkville, at the close of the next decade, will have so far outstripped the town of the present that it will well merit its peculiarly descriptive title, "The Queen City of the Hills."

The government of Yorkville is administered by the intendant, Capt. G.W.S. Hart, and the following wardens: W.B. Moore, J.E. Jeffers, S.L. Miller, and J.J. Hunter. All of these, it should be noted, are young men of sterling worth and ability and are representative citizens of the State. The police department is composed of Chief R.E. O'Farrell and two assistants, Ellie Montgomery and J.W. Neeley, and is quite sufficient to preserve order in this growing and prosperous municipality.

The fire department is made up of a hook and ladder company and a hand fire engine company. The former is composed of white citizens, while the latter is made up entirely of colored men. This department is thoroughly organized and is as efficient as it can be with the facilities that are afforded in these machines. The street department is under the direct supervision and control of the town council and is efficient in every scope. This is testified to by the excellent condition of the streets and pavements throughout the town. There is also a health department in connection with the municipal government, which, however, is hardly necessary, inasmuch as Yorkville is noted far and wide for its healthfulness and immunity from infectious maladies.

The climate is mild and invigorating, and Yorkville presents one of the finest situations for a delightful summer and winter resort that can be found in the South. It is seldom too cold nor too hot here, and consequently the weather is generally delightful. Coupled with this pleasant climate is the natural drainage in Yorkville, which precludes the possibility of any material disorders that sometimes assail other towns. The town is situated on several hills, and it is related that when the rain falls from the county Court House, one stream flows down to the Catawba

River, while the one flowing from the opposite side of the building runs into the Broad River.

In passing it might be well to state that the government of Yorkville is managed in a wise and judicious manner, and hence it is one of the model municipalities of the State. The sale of whiskey is forbidden in the town of Yorkville.

The following are the present officers of York County: Sheriff, R.H. Glenn; Clerk of the Court, Joseph F. Wallace; Judge of Probate, J.W. Williams; Coroner, John M. Caldwell; School Commissioner, Lewis A. Johnston; Treasurer, H.D.A. Neeley; Auditor, W.B. Williams; County Commissioners, J.B. Allison, R.W. Whitesides, and E.R. Mills; Senator, John G. Black; Representatives, W.B. Wilson, W.M. Walker, John D. Hamilton, and W.H. Stewart. The manner in which the county affairs are managed and controlled is a tribute to the good judgment and wise policy of these officials. The expenses of the county amount to about $28,500 per year.

It is a remarkable fact that five different lines of railroads now traverse portions of York County. The Charleston, Cincinnati, and Chicago will, when finished, run through the entire length of York County. This road will develop other towns in the county, and it will be the means whereby Yorkville will reap a rich harvest in the near future. Then there is the Chester and Lenoir Railroad, which connects Yorkville with Chester on the Charlotte, Columbia, and Augusta Railroad and with Gastonia on the Atlanta and Richmond Air Line Railroad. Then the Charlotte, Columbia, and Augusta Railroad runs through York County and adds to the wealth of the county in no small manner. Yorkville is now connected with this great thoroughfare by the Three C's Railroad at Rock Hill. In the southern portion of the county the Georgia, Carolina, and Northern Railroad also passes through and will be the means of developing that portion of the county. Through the northern portion of the county runs the Atlanta and Richmond Air Line Railroad. So it will be readily observed that Yorkville will vie with any town in the State in regards to railroads and rail facilities. The contract for building a magnificent depot here for the Three C's Railroad has been given out, and W.B. Moore & Co. will furnish the lumber. A large covered platform will be erected, and a tool house and section master's house in the immediate vicinity of the depot will be put up as soon as possible.

The business houses of Yorkville are of a very superior character and are as imposing as many in more pretentious cities where much more business is done. They are all of a substantial structure and built mainly of brick. The following is a list of the merchants in this thriving town: W.W. Jenkins, general merchandise; J.H. Riddle, groceries and cotton; Henderson Brothers, general merchandise; G.F. Schorb, stoves and tinware; G.L. McNeil & Son, dry goods; G.H. Oleary, furniture and saddles; J.W. Dobson, groceries; W.B. Moore & Co., general merchandise; Lowery & Starr, drugs; J.C. Kuykendall, drugs; A.Y. Cartwright & Co., dry goods; Kennedy Brothers & Barron, dry goods; Parish & Kennedy, groceries; Mrs. F.M. Dobson, millinery; M. & H.C. Strauss, dry goods; Withers Adickes, groceries;

H.F. Adickes, dry goods; Latta Brothers, groceries and cotton; Hunter & Oakes, dry goods; Mrs. J. Bolton Smith, millinery; A. Rose, general merchandise; May & May, drugs; M.C. Willis, buggies and carriages; R.B. Lowery, general merchandise; J.R. Ashe, general merchandise and cotton; W.C. Lattimer, general merchandise; T.B. McClain, general merchandise; Hope, Peagram & Co., groceries and cotton; and Frank Hopperfield, groceries and marble yard.

The following is a list of cotton buyers: J.A. Latta buys about 2,500 bales per year; J.H. Riddle, 3,000; J.R. Ashe, 2,000; Hope, Peagram & Co., 3,500. The dealers in fertilizer are: W.H. Herndon, J.H. Riddle, J.C. Kuykendall, Withers Adickes, Latta Brothers, F. Hopperfield, J.R. Ashe, W.C. Latimer, and Hope, Peagram & Co. These buyers import to Yorkville about eighteen hundred tons of fertilizers annually and purchase direct from the markets of Charleston and Baltimore.

The dealers in live stock are: S.A. McElwain, T.M. Whittaker, John A. Dorrison, and W.D. Glenn.

It is estimated that over three-quarters of a million dollars of business is done annually in Yorkville. It is said that at least ten thousand bales of cotton are shipped annually from Yorkville to Charleston and elsewhere.

The Yorkville Exchange Bank has a capital stock of $30,000 and does a large business all the year around. The officers are: President, T.S. Jeffreys; vice president, Jos. F. Wallace; cashier, Frank A. Gilbert. This institution does a general banking business and is in a strong and prosperous condition. There is also a building and loan association, which is in a good financial condition.

Educationally Yorkville is somewhat behind the times, for there is no well-established institution of learning within her limits. Whatever schools there are here are of a private character, and this is a cause of great regret. In former times Yorkville was an educational centre. Here was situated the famous King's Mountain Military School, founded in 1855 by Col. Asbury Coward and the lamented Col. Micah Jenkins. Until a few years ago this institution was still maintained. The building where the school was established is an imposing structure, built very much on the plan of the Citadel Academy in Charleston. It is still owned by Col. Coward, and the hope is that, with the influx of inhabitants to Yorkville that will be brought about by the completion of the Three C's Road, the famous old institution will be reopened.

Another institution of learning which has been closed by force of circumstances is the Yorkville Female College. The building is one of the handsomest in Yorkville, and when the College was in its palmy days, it is said, over two hundred young ladies attended it. The building is now owned by several gentlemen in Yorkville, and there is every reason to hope that the College will be reopened.

The churches here are the Episcopal, of which the Rev. Theo. D. Bratton is pastor; the Methodist, with the Rev. W.W. Daniel as pastor; the Baptist, whose pastor is the Rev. R.G. Patrick; the Associate Reformed Presbyterian, of which the Rev. J.C. Galloway is pastor; and the Presbyterian, with the Rev. T.R. English as pastor. Besides these churches there are two colored churches in Yorkville.

Belle of old Yorkville, 1883. *John Schorb Collection, Archives and Special Collections Department, Dacus Library, Winthrop College.*

The hotels in Yorkville are the Parish House and the Yorkville Hotel. Of the former Mr. C.G. Parish is proprietor, while the latter is owned and run by Mr. Henry Smith. Both hotels are well regulated and are complete in all their appointments and are about equal in their popularity.

The prominent residences that this correspondent noted were the handsome and elegant homes of Judge I.D. Witherspoon, Dr. R.A. Bratton, John R. Ashe, W.B. Moore, Mrs. Metts, Col. James F. Hart, Mr. C.F. Spencer, Prof. Herndon, Col. W.B. Wilson, Mr. W.C. Willis, and others. The fine residences of Yorkville are not confined to any one street or locality, but are scattered all about the town, and hence the Queen City of the Hills is a pretty place from one end to the other.

Yorkville, besides being in direct communication with the world by railroad and telegraph, is connected with Rock Hill by a telephone line, and this latter facility is a great benefit to both cities.

The news is furnished to the people here by the *News and Courier* and the *Yorkville Enquirer.* The latter paper is an old established weekly journal, of which Mr. L.M. Grist is editor and proprietor. It is a first-class weekly paper and is in a very prosperous condition.

The Jenkins Rifles, named in honor of the heroic Col. Jenkins and organized in 1876 by Col. A. Coward, is a fine organization. The esprit de corps is excellent, and it is in good condition. Its commander is Capt. Withers Adickes.

The mineral deposits of York County are numerous and rich. The list of mineral deposits found in the county includes gold, iron, copper, tin, baryta, manganese, limestone, and other minerals usually found in this section.

It is a matter of fact, as well as history, that an iron mine in York County was developed before the Revolutionary War and worked for many years. It was discontinued, however, as there were then no facilities for exporting the iron or importing charcoal to smelt the ore. All the wood within a radius of ten miles was burnt during the operations in the mines and consequently the expense was too great to continue the operations. In later days the King's Mountain Iron Works in this county has been worked with great profit, and is now a valuable property. The ore found in York County is very superior in quality and compares favorably with the famous Cranberry ore. There are four or five gold mines that never have been developed in this county, and it is said that the gold ore found is of the richest quality. It is diffused all over the county in large quantities. Then, too, there is a very valuable copper mine in York County. It is known as the Mary Mine, and needs only development to make it one of the most paying mines in the South. It is now offered for sale. An excellent and exhaustless mine of baryta, a sulfate of barium, has been worked to some extent in this county and is a valuable property. It is used in the adulteration of flour, sugar, and other white substances. It is also used in making white paint and appears akin to kaolin. This mine is valuable and will doubtless now be worked to its fullest extent. The tin mines scattered over this section of the county are said to be numerous and produce a good quality of this ore. Manganese is found in large quantities in this county and is reported to be of a fine and valuable quality. If all these mines were only worked by competent companies and the mines could be developed as they should be, it is not difficult to foretell how rich the county would become.

All that is now lacking to develop these resources are several companies of capitalists, and now that York County offers so many facilities for mining operations there is some reason to hope for any early organization of such a company as is here needed.

The field products of this famous old county are too well known to be mentioned in this correspondence.

The three things that are now most needed in Yorkville are a well-established institution of learning, a cotton factory, and a big hotel. When these are established, and with the good prospect now before the people here, nothing other than prosperity can come. All these must inevitably be established in the near future, for the people of Yorkville are now alive to the needs of the hour.

The Queen City of the Hills, it will be seen, is a very hard place to leave. In departing, however, it is impossible, with a full knowledge of what material and progressiveness it contains, to be free from the assuring conviction that Yorkville has now received an impulse that will result in the achievement of greater and better things. Her people are wide awake to the needs of the hour; the field is rich enough and broad enough to be assured of the verification of the golden promises of a prosperous future that are now made on all sides.

News and Courier, September 25, 1888. E.P. McK.

Appendix 1

Population: Counties, Cities, Towns, and Villages, 1880–1890[1]

	1880	1890
Abbeville County	40,815	46,854
Abbeville	1,543	1,696
Cokesbury	365	355
Donalds		216
Due West	449	644
Greenwood	745	1,326
Hodges	271	255
Lowndesville	116	268
Ninety Six	468	445
Troy		311
Verdery		86
Aiken County	28,112	31,822
Aiken	1,817	2,362
Ellenton	94	138
Graniteville	1,669	1,791
Hamburg	485	484
Langley	800	671
Perry		69
Sallys		252
Sievern		87
Vaucluse	657	580
Windsor		51
Anderson County	33,612	43,696
Anderson	1,850	3,018
Belton	314	494
Honea Path	228	365
Pelzer		1,878
Pendleton	672	476
Piedmont[2]		1,242
Williamston		935
Barnwell County	39,857	44,613
Appleton		358
Bamberg	648	696
Barnwell	648	937
Blackville	684	962

[1]Adapted from the 1890 Census, volume 15, pp. 306–10. Only communities reported separately from rural population are cited.
[2]Part of, see Greenville County.

	1880	1890
Elko	149	100
Graham	403	366
Williston	426	503
Beaufort County	30,176	34,119
Beaufort	2,549	3,587
Bluffton	170	421
Grahamville	274	293
Hardeeville	252	649
Port Royal	387	524
Berkeley County[3]		55,428
Eutawville		224
Holly Hill		814
Lincolnville	350	388
Marysville		421
Monks Corner		113
Mount Pleasant	783	1,138
Pecks		69
St. Stephen	79	230
Summerville[4]	636	1,288
Charleston County[5]	102,800	59,903
Charleston	49,984	54,955
Chester County	24,153	26,660
Blackstock[6]	56	108
Chester	1,899	2,703
Lownesville		283
Richburg	121	186
Chesterfield County	16,345	18,468
Cheraw	918	976
Clarendon County[7]	19,190	23,233
Foreston		282
Manning		1,069
Colleton County	36,386	40,293
Hendersonville	263	286

[3]Formed from Charleston County in 1882.
[4]Part of, see Colleton County.
[5]Part of now in Berkeley County, formed in 1882.
[6]Part of, see Fairfield County.
[7]Part of now in Florence County, formed in 1888.

	1880	1890
Jacksonboro	50	58
Reevesville		109
Ridgeville	250	212
St. George	279	629
Summerville[8]	735	931
Walterboro	691	1,171
Darlington County[9]	34,485	29,134
Darlington	940	2,389
Hartsville		342
Edgefield County	45,844	49,259
Clintonward		161
Edgefield	808	1,168
Johnston	463	827
Modoc		102
Parksville		145
Ridge Spring	328	390
Trenton		302
Fairfield County	27,765	28,599
Blackstock[10]		30
Blythewood		98
Ridgeway		249
Winnsboro	1,500	1,738
Woodward		396
Florence County[11]		25,027
Cartersville		314
Florence	1,914	3,395
Timmonsville	557	516
Georgetown County	19,613	20,857
Georgetown	2,557	2,895
Greenville County	37,496	44,310
Fountain Inn		212
Greenville	6,160	8,607
Greer	97	320
Piedmont[12]	565	1,194

[8]Part of, see Berkeley County.
[9]Part of now in Florence County, formed in 1888.
[10]Part of, see Chester County.
[11]Formed in 1888 from Clarendon, Darlington, Marion, and Williamsburg counties.
[12]Part of, see Anderson County.

	1880	1890
Hampton County	18,741	20,544
Brunson	167	470
Hampton	169	318
Varnville		553
Horry County	15,574	19,256
Conway	575	677
Little River	50	82
Kershaw County	21,538	22,361
Camden	1,780	3,533
Lancaster County	16,903	20,761
Haile Gold Mine		209
Kershaw[13]		165
Lancaster	681	1,094
Laurens County	29,444	31,610
Clinton	459	1,021
Cross Hill	149	216
Goldville		204
Laurens	752	2,245
Princeton		195
Waterloo		291
Lexington County	18,654	22,181
Batesburg	286	528
Leesville	177	229
Lewiedale	141	115
Lexington	262	342
Peak	62	143
Marion County[14]	34,107	29,976
Dillon		82
Marion	824	1,640
Mullins		242
Nichols	122	57
Marlboro County	20,598	23,500
Bennettsville	343	978
Blenheim		95

[13]Part of, portion in Kershaw County not reported separately.
[14]Part of now in Florence County, formed in 1888.

	1880	1890
Newberry County	26,497	26,434
Helena		481
Newberry	2,342	3,020
Prosperity	357	565
Oconee County	16,256	18,687
Walhalla	789	820
West Union	192	235
Westminster	162	532
Orangeburg County	41,395	49,393
Branchville	517	732
Elloree		311
Fort Motte	107	279
Orangeburg	2,140	2,964
Rowesville	125	174
St. Matthews	271	524
Springfield		221
Pickens County	14,389	16,389
Central	184	396
Easley	327	421
Liberty	149	211
Pickens	212	283
Richland County	28,573	36,821
Columbia	10,036	15,353
Spartanburg County	40,409	55,385
Campobello	99	137
Clifton		2,639
Cowpens	112	349
Gaffney	400	1,631
Glendale		468
Glenn Springs	219	138
Inman		134
Landrum		155
Pacolet Mills		1,125
Reidville	156	266
Spartanburg	3,253	5,544
Whitney Mills		336
Woodruff	254	380

	1880	1890
Sumter County	37,037	43,605
Bishopville	144	422
Magnolia	151	484
Mayesville	396	706
Sumter	2,011	3,865
Union County	24,080	25,363
Jonesville	206	286
Union	1,267	1,609
Williamsburg County[15]	24,110	27,777
Kingstree	384	539
York County	30,713	38,831
Blacksburg	145	1,245
Clover	73	287
Fort Mill	290	689
Hickory Grove		134
Rock Hill	809	2,744
Yorkville	1,330	1,553

[15]Part of now in Florence County, formed in 1888.

Appendix 2

J.E. Norment's Major Articles and Community Sketches in the *News and Courier,* 1895–1897.

1895

January 26	Darlington Tobacco Growers
February 23	Anderson
April 23	Spartanburg and Glenn Springs
May 30	Greenwood
July 22	Ridge Spring (Edgefield County)
July 24	Williamsburg County
August 15	Marlboro County
September 12	Darlington
October 17	Florence
December 9	McColl
December 20	Sumter

1896

February 1	Tobacco Land in Carolina
February 25	Puddin' Swamp (Sumter, Clarendon, and Williamsburg counties)
March 26	Williamsburg County
April 16	Rock Hill
May 25	Cheraw
June 14	Gold Mines in Carolina
August 15	Marion
October 8	Dillon
November 15	Darlington Guards
December 24	Laurens

1897

March 1	Clinton
May 1	Bamberg
July 8	Newberry
July 24	Greenwood
August 11	Chester
September 17	Anderson
September 29	Orangeburg
October 12	Abbeville
November 27	Winnsboro
November 29	The Cheraw Fair
December 25	Christmas in Darlington

In 1898, Norment became a local correspondent, reporting general news from the Darlington area; however, he did produce several small feature articles during that year.

January 3	Greenwood
February 4	Sumter
February 9	Darlington Tobacco
February 14	Farming in South Carolina
October 3	Mullins
October 27	Greenwood

Index

Books edited and written by John Hammond Moore

South Carolina Newspapers

The South Carolina Highway Department, 1917-1987

Wiley: One Hundred and Seventy-five Years of Publishing

Over-Sexed, Over-Paid, and Over Here: Americans in Australia, 1941-1945

The Faustball Tunnel: German POWs in America and Their Great Escape

Australians in America, 1876-1976

Albemarle: Jefferson's County, 1727-1976

The Young Errol: Flynn Before Hollywood

The Juhl Letters to the *"The Charleston Courier"*: A View of the South, 1865-1871

The American Alliance: Australia, New Zealand, and the United States, 1940-1970

Research Materials in South Carolina: A Guide

Before and After; or, The Relations of the Races at the South

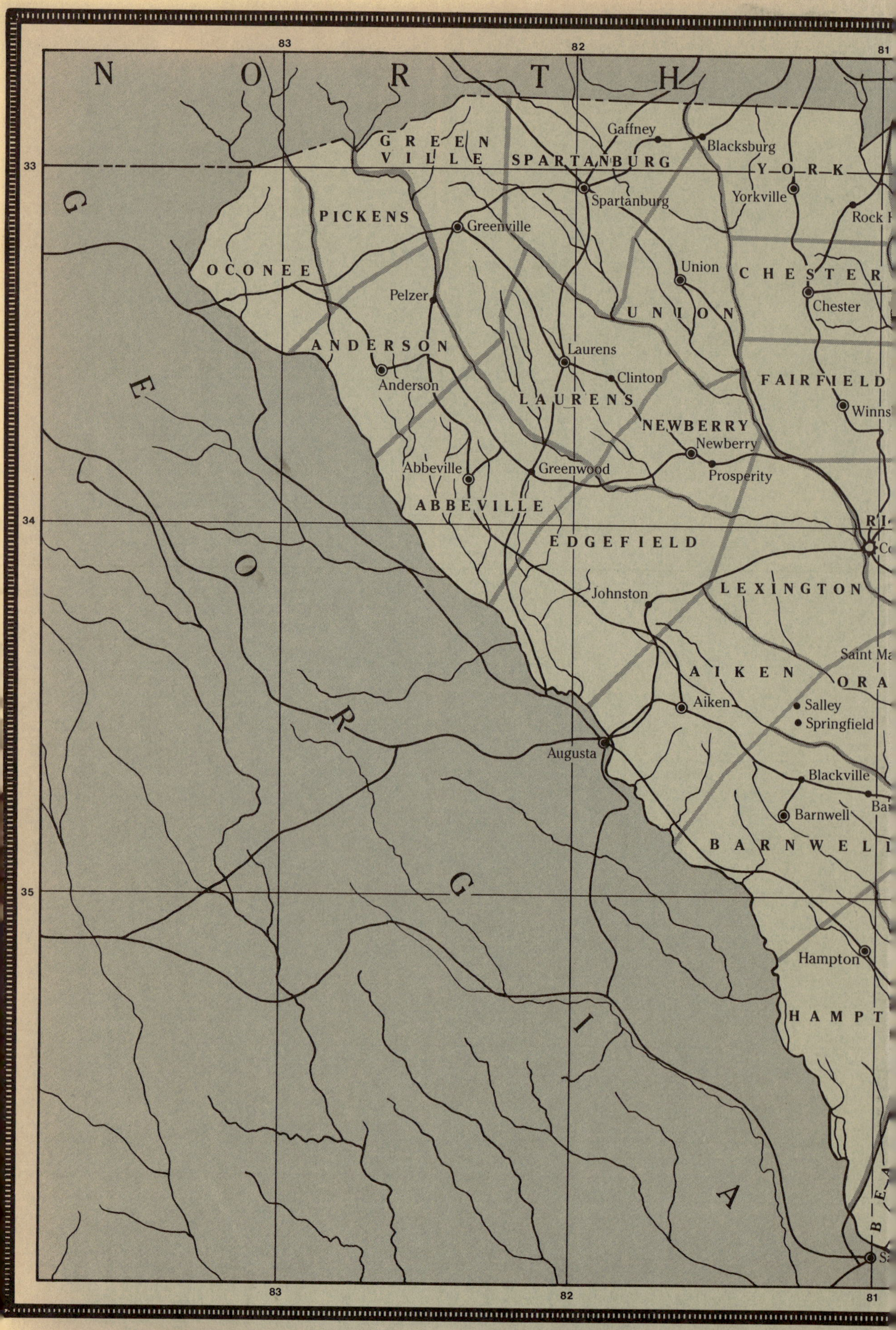

83
82
81
N O R T H
G E O R G I A
GREEN VILLE
SPARTANBURG
Gaffney
Blacksburg
YORK
Yorkville
Rock H
Spartanburg
PICKENS
Greenville
OCONEE
Union
CHESTER
Chester
Pelzer
UNION
ANDERSON
Laurens
Clinton
Anderson
FAIRFIELD
Winns
LAURENS
NEWBERRY
Newberry
Prosperity
Abbeville
Greenwood
ABBEVILLE
EDGEFIELD
Johnston
LEXINGTON
Saint Ma
AIKEN
ORA
Aiken
Salley
Springfield
Augusta
Blackville
Barnwell
BARNWELL
Hampton
HAMPT
BEA
33
34
35